Shojo Beat

D0896436

kimi ni todoke
From Me to You

Vol. 21
Story & Art by
Karuho Shiina

Volume 21

Contents

Story Thus Far

Sawako Kuronuma has always been a loner. Though not by choice, this optimistic 16-year-old girl can't seem to make any friends. Stuck with the unfortunate nickname "Sadako" after the haunting movie character, rumors about her summoning spirits have been greatly exaggerated. With her shy personality and scary looks, most of her classmates will barely talk to her, much less look into her eyes for more than three seconds lest they be cursed. Thanks to Kazehaya, who always treats her nicely, Sawako makes her first friends at school, Ayane and Chizu. Eventually, Sawako finds the courage to date Kazehaya.

The time has come for Sawako and her friends to think about their futures after high school. Sawako wants to find a job in town, but Pin challenges her to pursue her dream of teaching. Meanwhile, Kazehaya's plans for the future run into a father-shaped roadblock. After Kazehaya talks to Sawako about his complicated relationship with his father, his future plans begin to change.

Valentine's Day arrives. For the second year in a row, Sawako isn't able to give chocolate to Kazehaya at school. However, unlike the year before, she musters up the courage to deliver the chocolate to him at home! And thus passes their second Valentine's Day together.

Kimi ni todoke

From Me to You

Episode 84: White Day

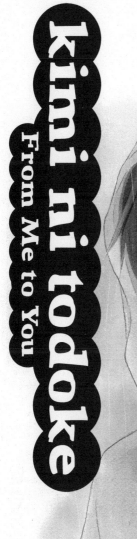

Karuho Shiina

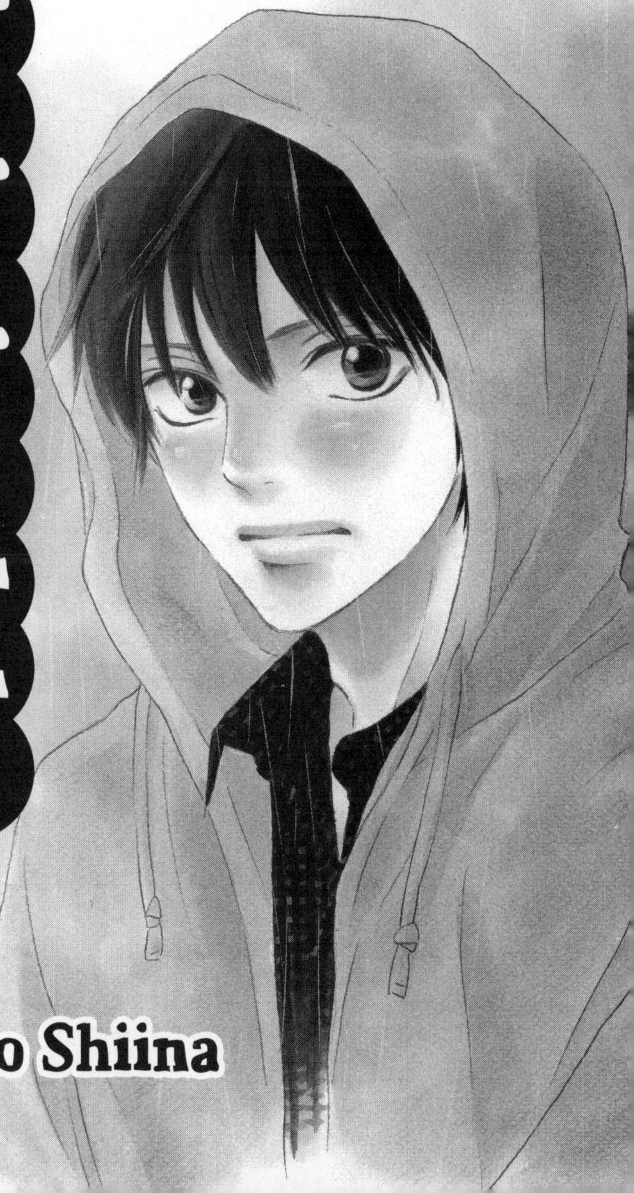

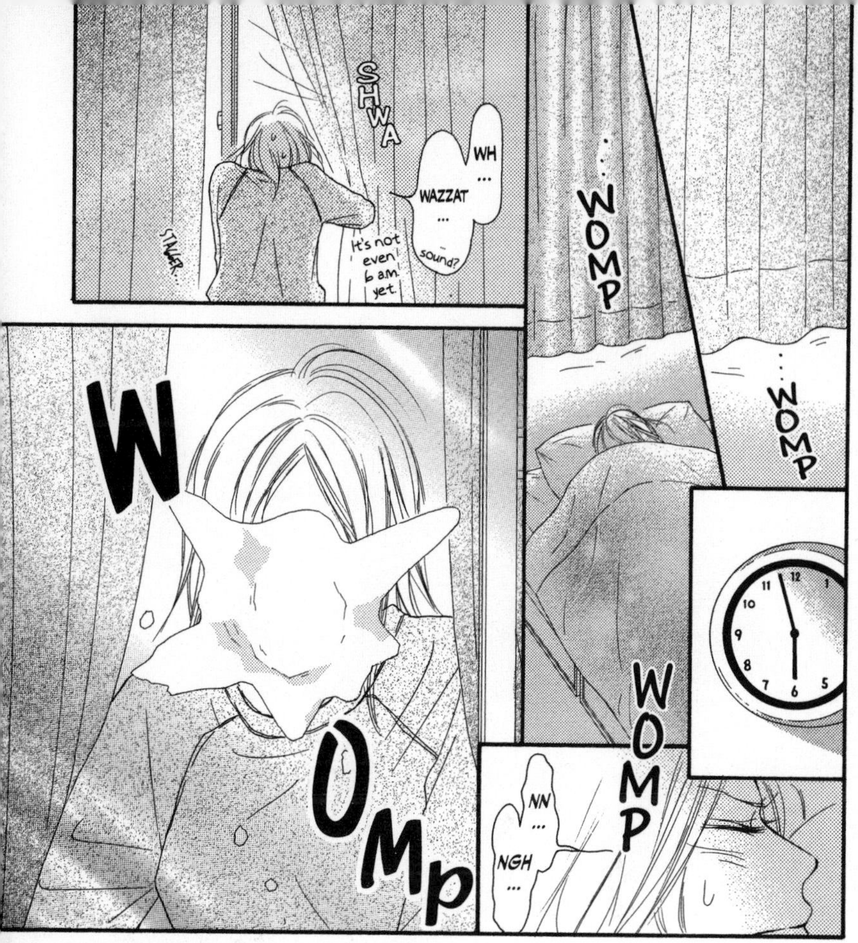
...WOMP
...WOMP
SHWA
WH... WAZZAT... sound?
It's not even 6 a.m. yet.
STAGGER...
WOMP
NN... NGH...
WOMP

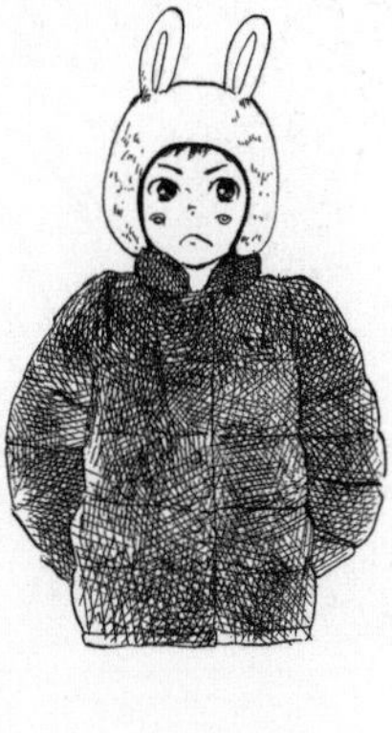

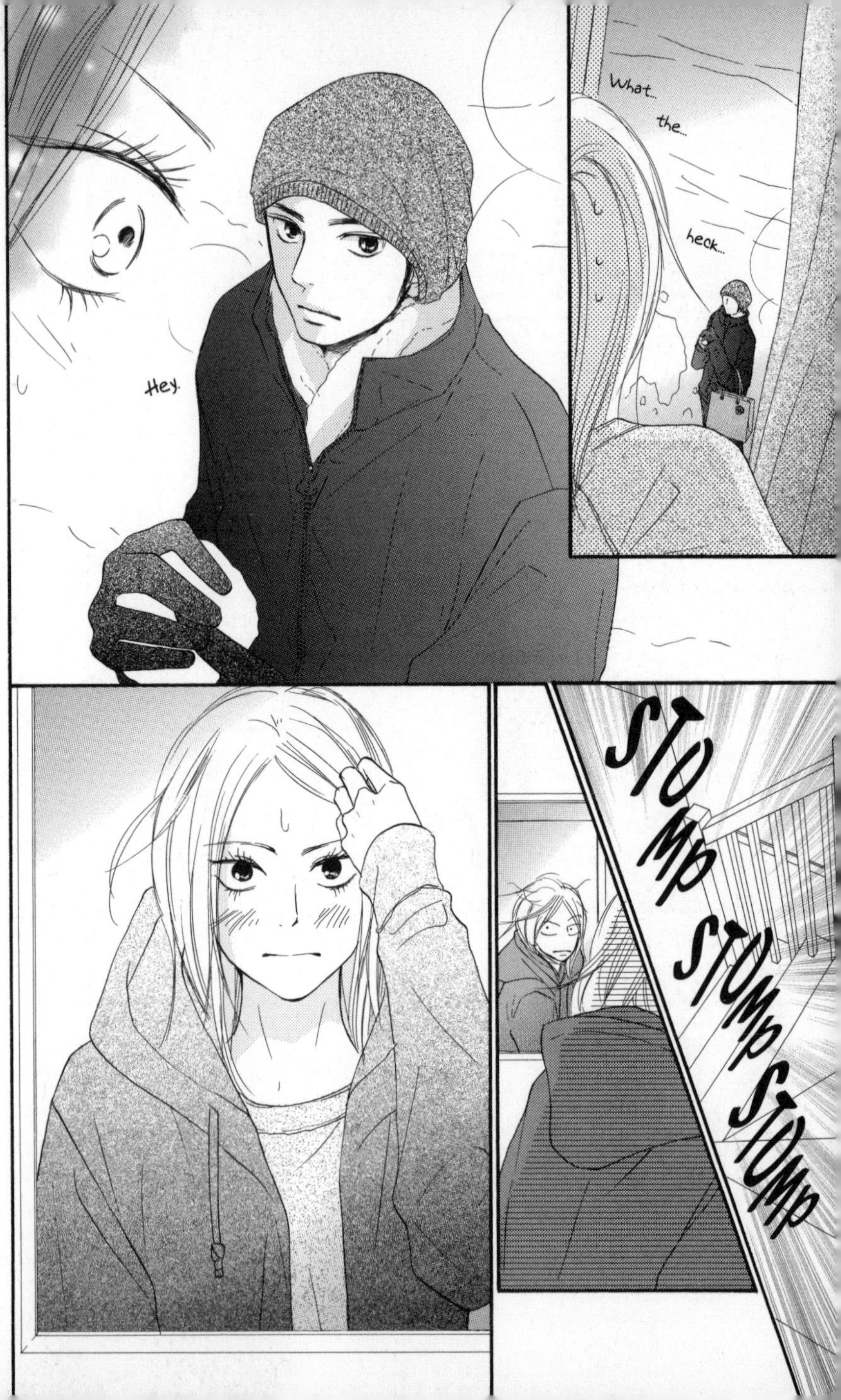
What...
the...
heck...
Hey.
STOMP STOMP STOMP STOMP

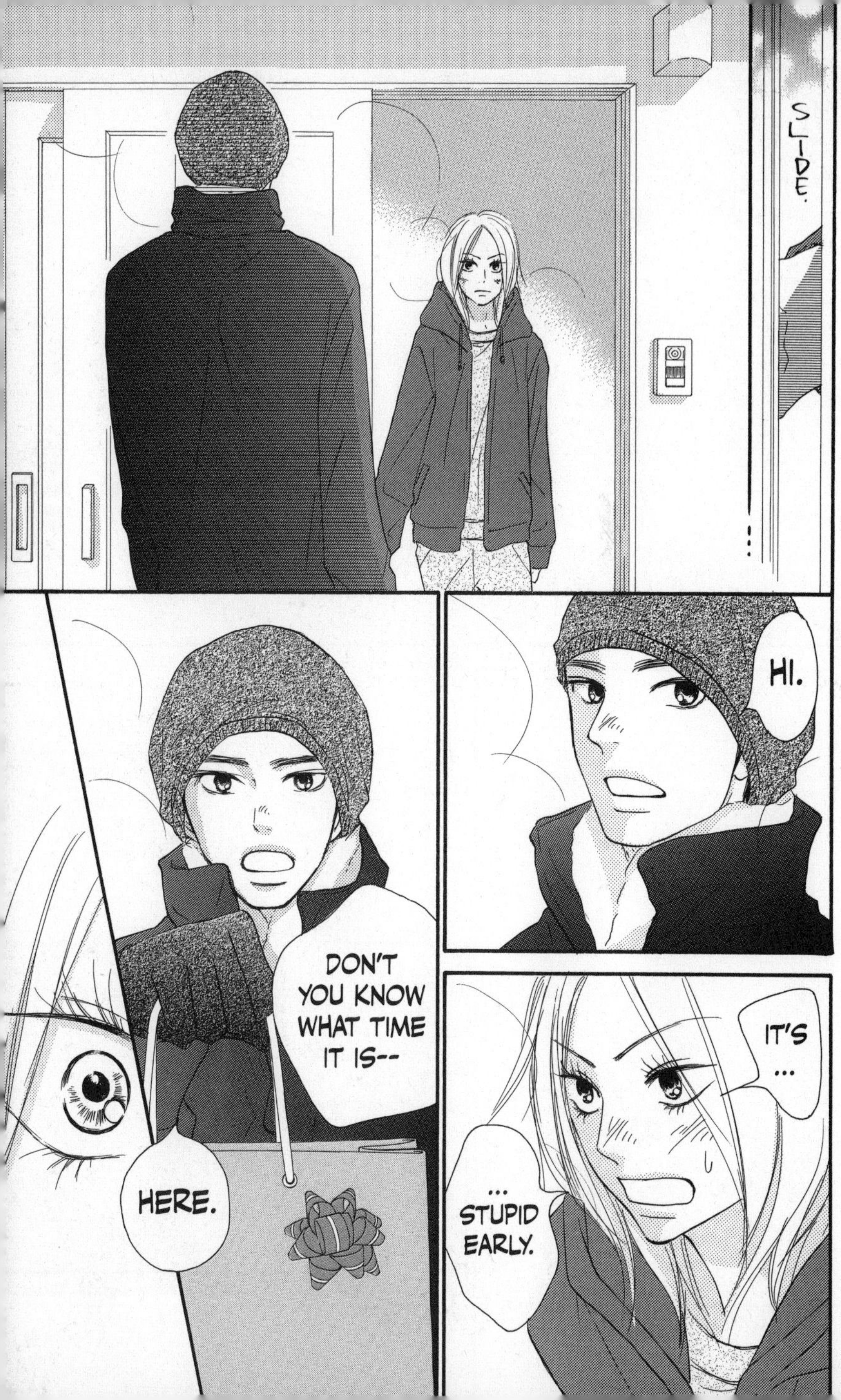
SLIDE.
...
HI.
IT'S ...
... STUPID EARLY.
DON'T YOU KNOW WHAT TIME IT IS--
HERE.

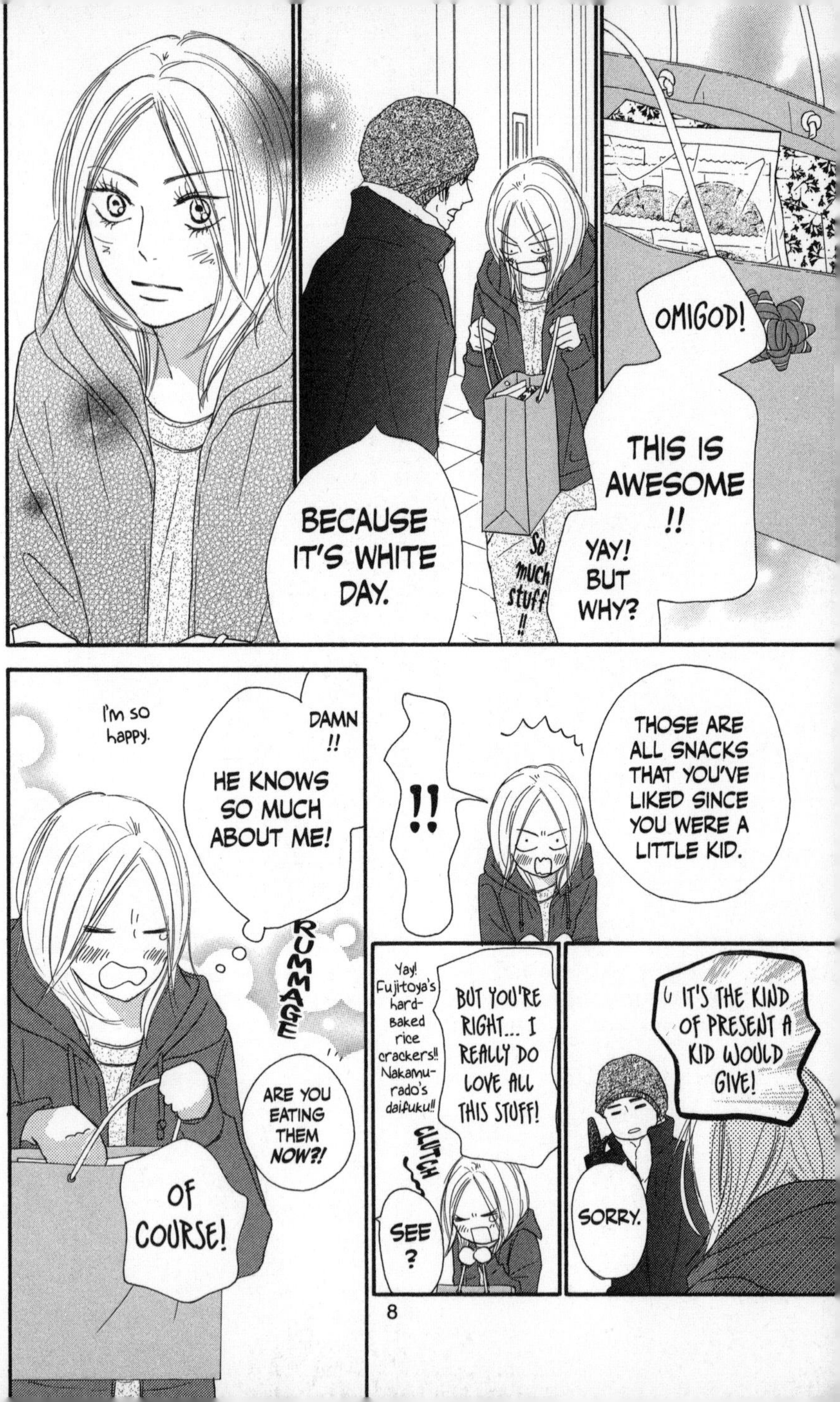
OMIGOD!
THIS IS AWESOME !!
YAY! BUT WHY?
So much stuff!!
BECAUSE IT'S WHITE DAY.
THOSE ARE ALL SNACKS THAT YOU'VE LIKED SINCE YOU WERE A LITTLE KID.
!!
IT'S THE KIND OF PRESENT A KID WOULD GIVE!
SORRY.
BUT YOU'RE RIGHT... I REALLY DO LOVE ALL THIS STUFF!
Yay! Fujitoya's hard-baked rice crackers!! Nakamura-do's daifuku!!
CLUTCH
SEE?
DAMN !!
HE KNOWS SO MUCH ABOUT ME!
I'm so happy.
RUMMAGE
ARE YOU EATING THEM NOW?!
OF COURSE!

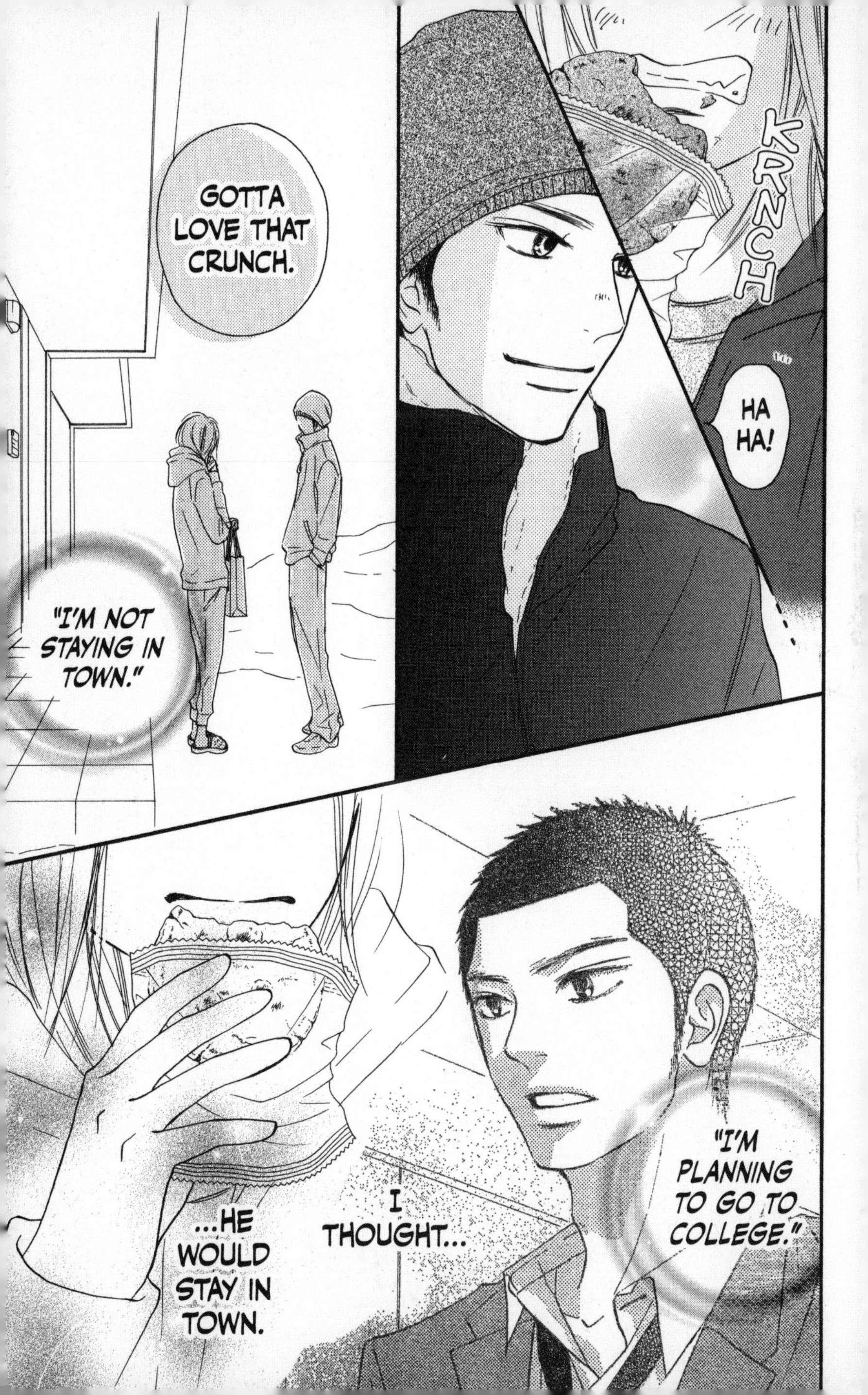
KRNCH
HA HA!
GOTTA LOVE THAT CRUNCH.
"I'M NOT STAYING IN TOWN."
"I'M PLANNING TO GO TO COLLEGE."
I THOUGHT...
...HE WOULD STAY IN TOWN.

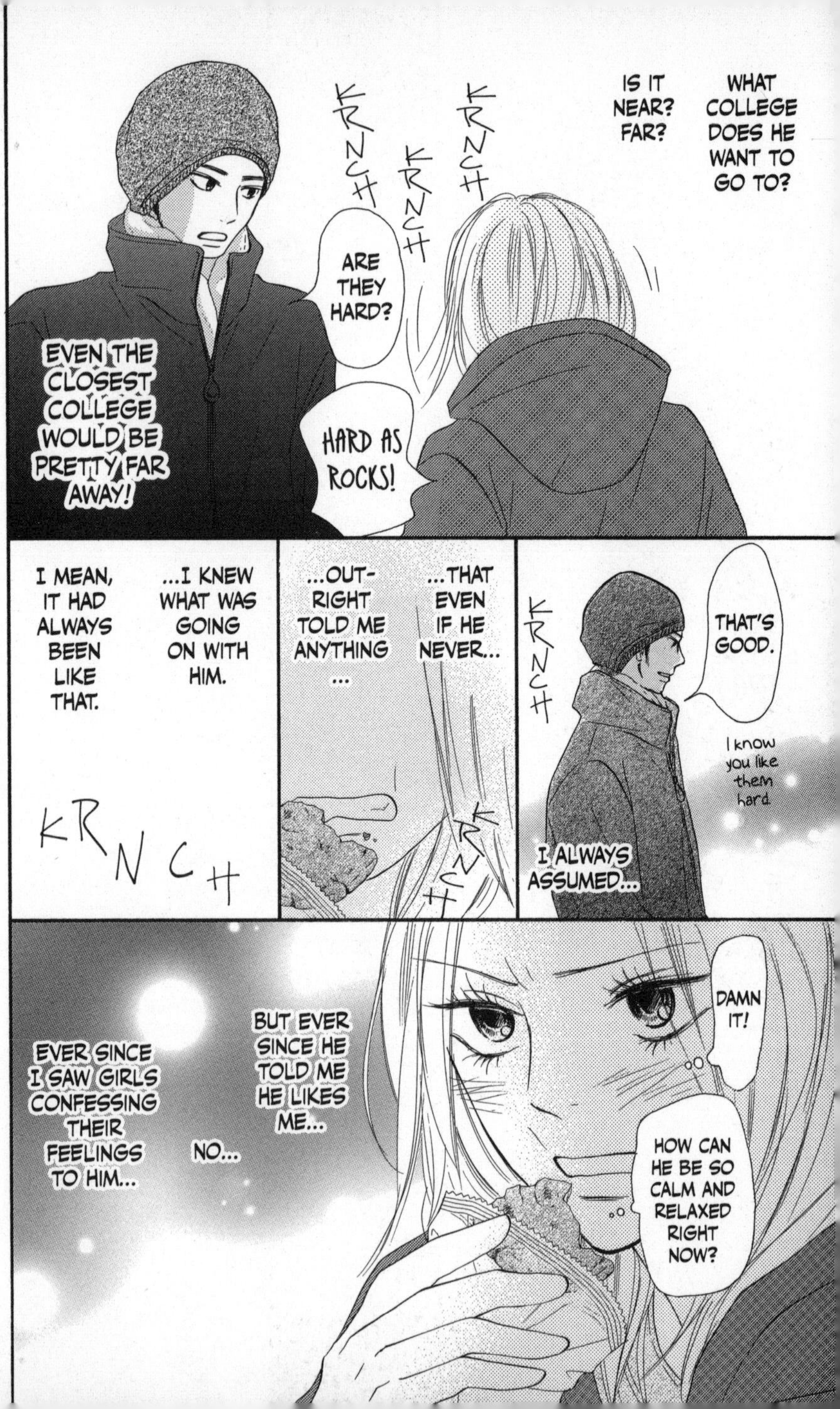
WHAT COLLEGE DOES HE WANT TO GO TO?
IS IT NEAR? FAR?
KRNCH
KRNCH
KRNCH
ARE THEY HARD?
HARD AS ROCKS!
EVEN THE CLOSEST COLLEGE WOULD BE PRETTY FAR AWAY!
THAT'S GOOD.
KRNCH
I know you like them hard
I ALWAYS ASSUMED...
...THAT EVEN IF HE NEVER...
...OUT-RIGHT TOLD ME ANYTHING ...
KRNCH
...I KNEW WHAT WAS GOING ON WITH HIM.
I MEAN, IT HAD ALWAYS BEEN LIKE THAT.
KRNCH
DAMN IT!
HOW CAN HE BE SO CALM AND RELAXED RIGHT NOW?
BUT EVER SINCE HE TOLD ME HE LIKES ME...
NO...
EVER SINCE I SAW GIRLS CONFESSING THEIR FEELINGS TO HIM...

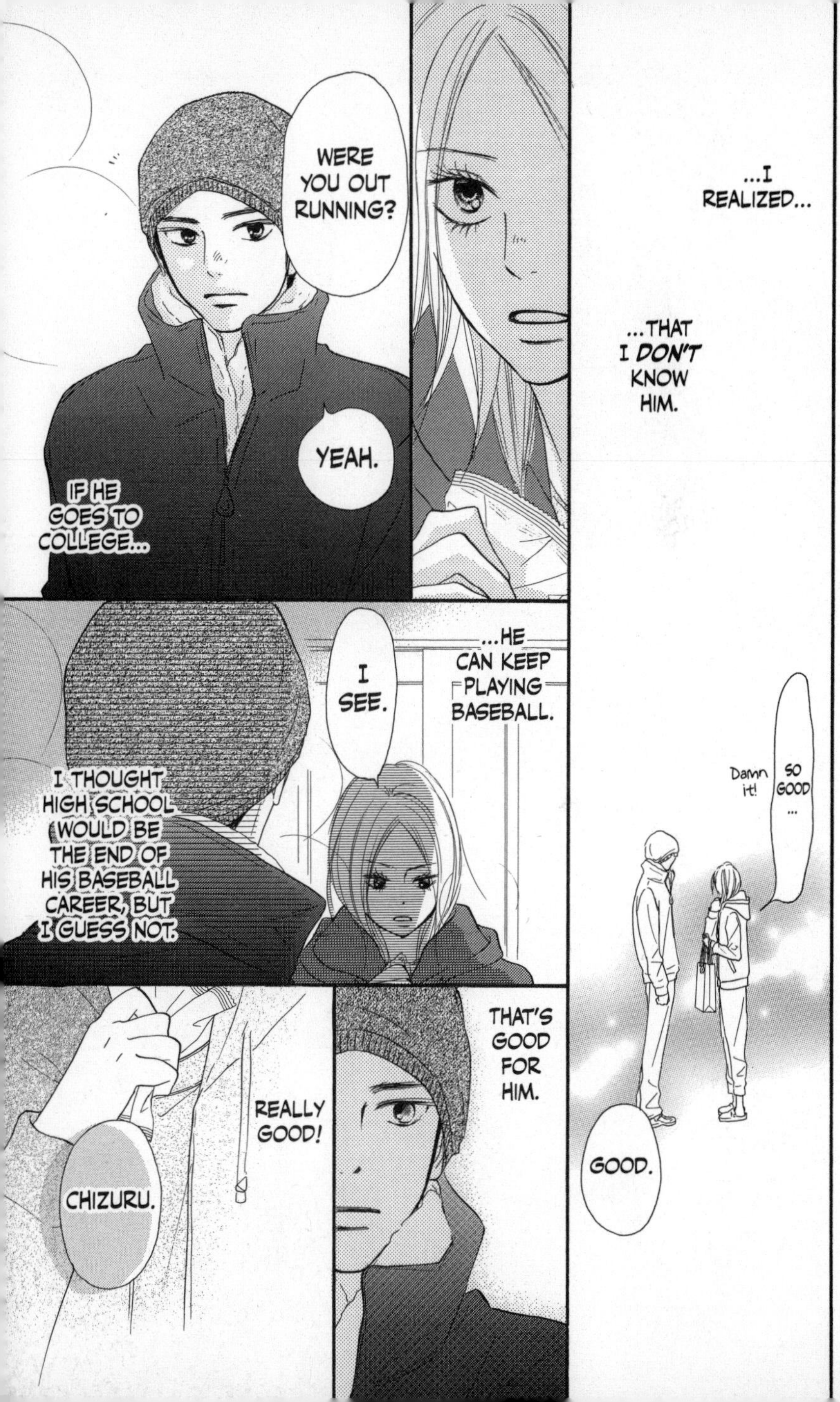
...I REALIZED...
...THAT I DON'T KNOW HIM.
SO GOOD...
Damn it!
GOOD.
WERE YOU OUT RUNNING?
YEAH.
IF HE GOES TO COLLEGE...
...HE CAN KEEP PLAYING BASEBALL.
I SEE.
I THOUGHT HIGH SCHOOL WOULD BE THE END OF HIS BASEBALL CAREER, BUT I GUESS NOT.
THAT'S GOOD FOR HIM.
REALLY GOOD!
CHIZURU.

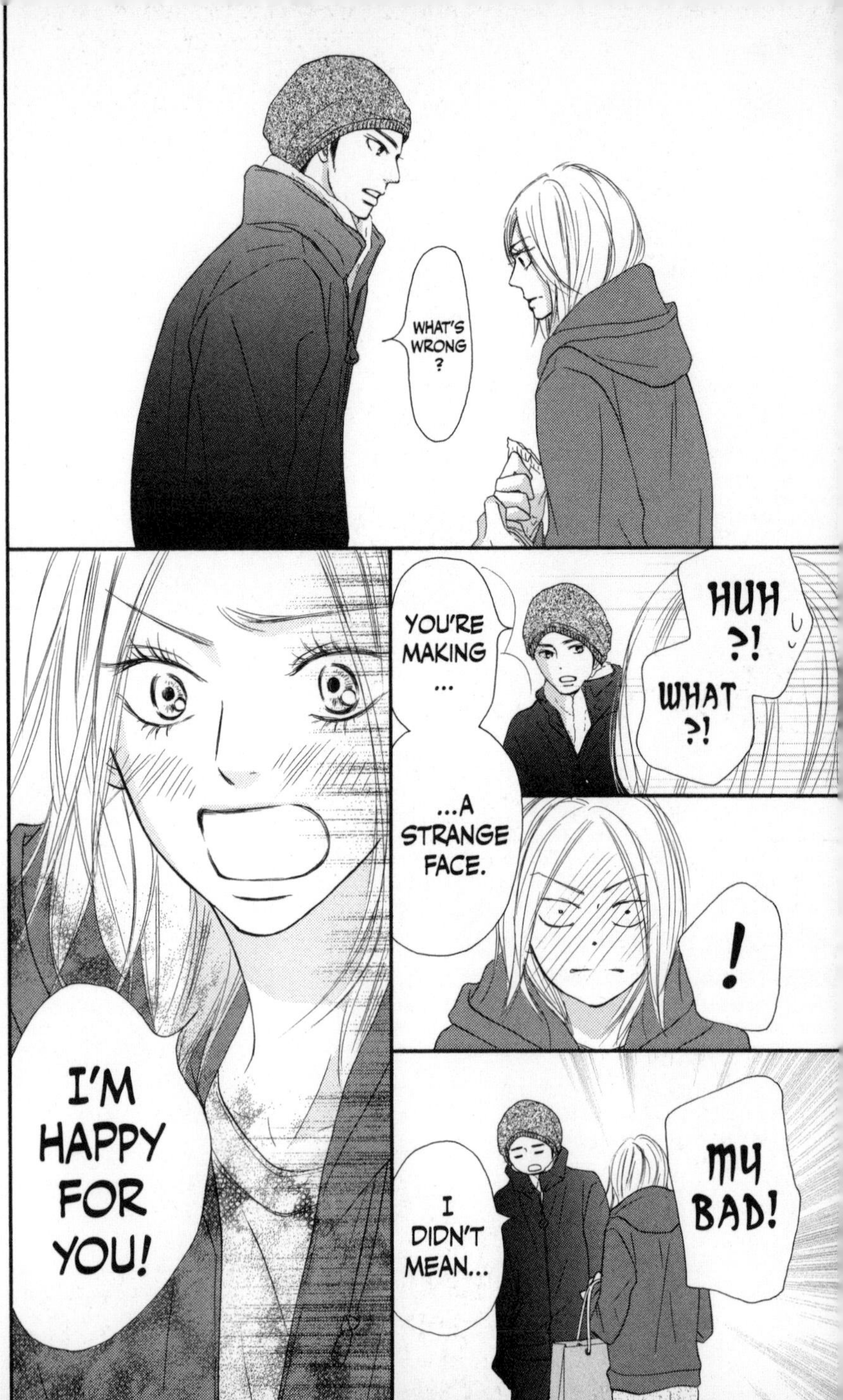
WHAT'S WRONG ?
HUH ?! WHAT ?!
YOU'RE MAKING ...
...A STRANGE FACE.
!
MY BAD!
I DIDN'T MEAN...
I'M HAPPY FOR YOU!

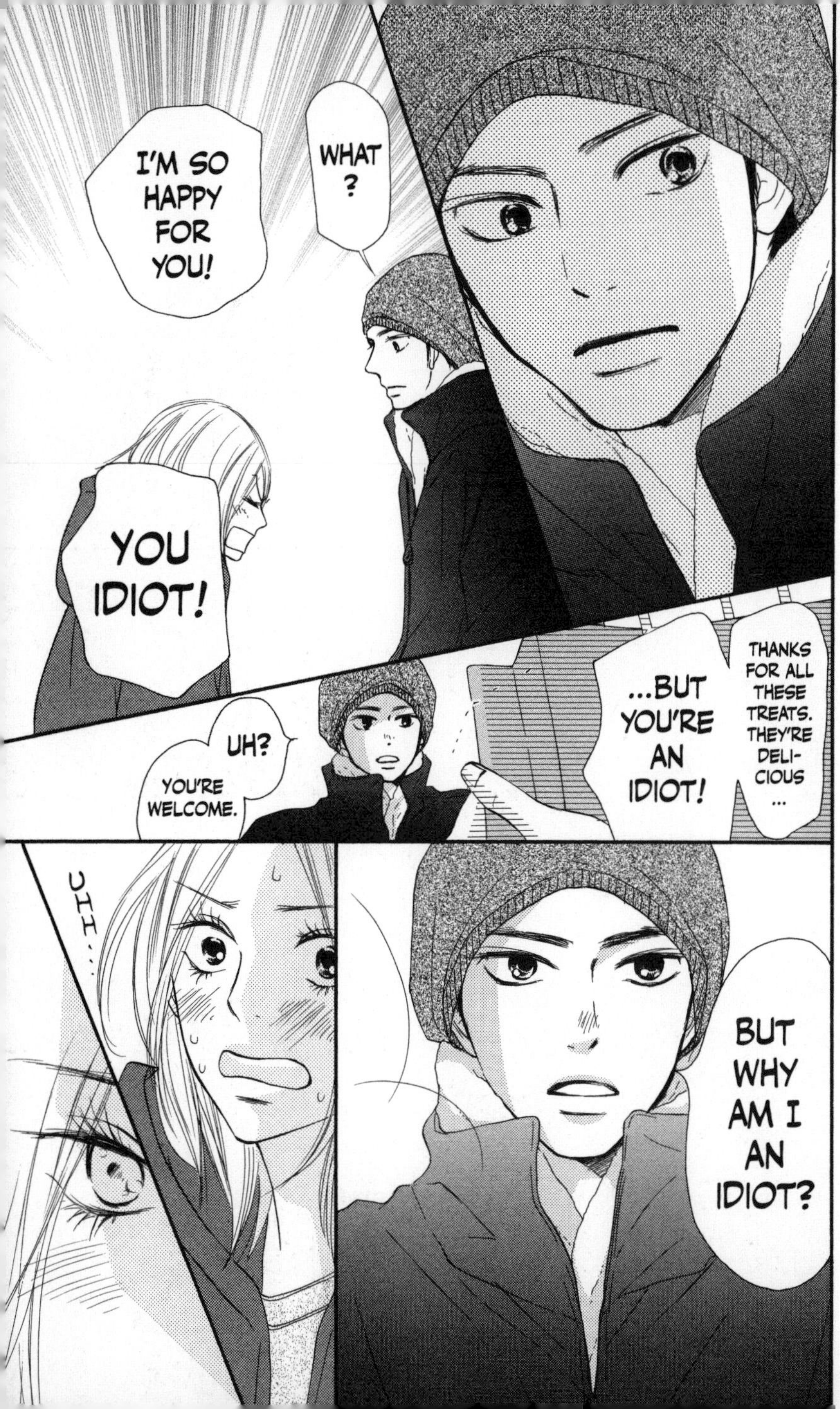
WHAT?
I'M SO HAPPY FOR YOU!
YOU IDIOT!
THANKS FOR ALL THESE TREATS. THEY'RE DELICIOUS...
...BUT YOU'RE AN IDIOT!
UH?
YOU'RE WELCOME.
BUT WHY AM I AN IDIOT?
UHH...

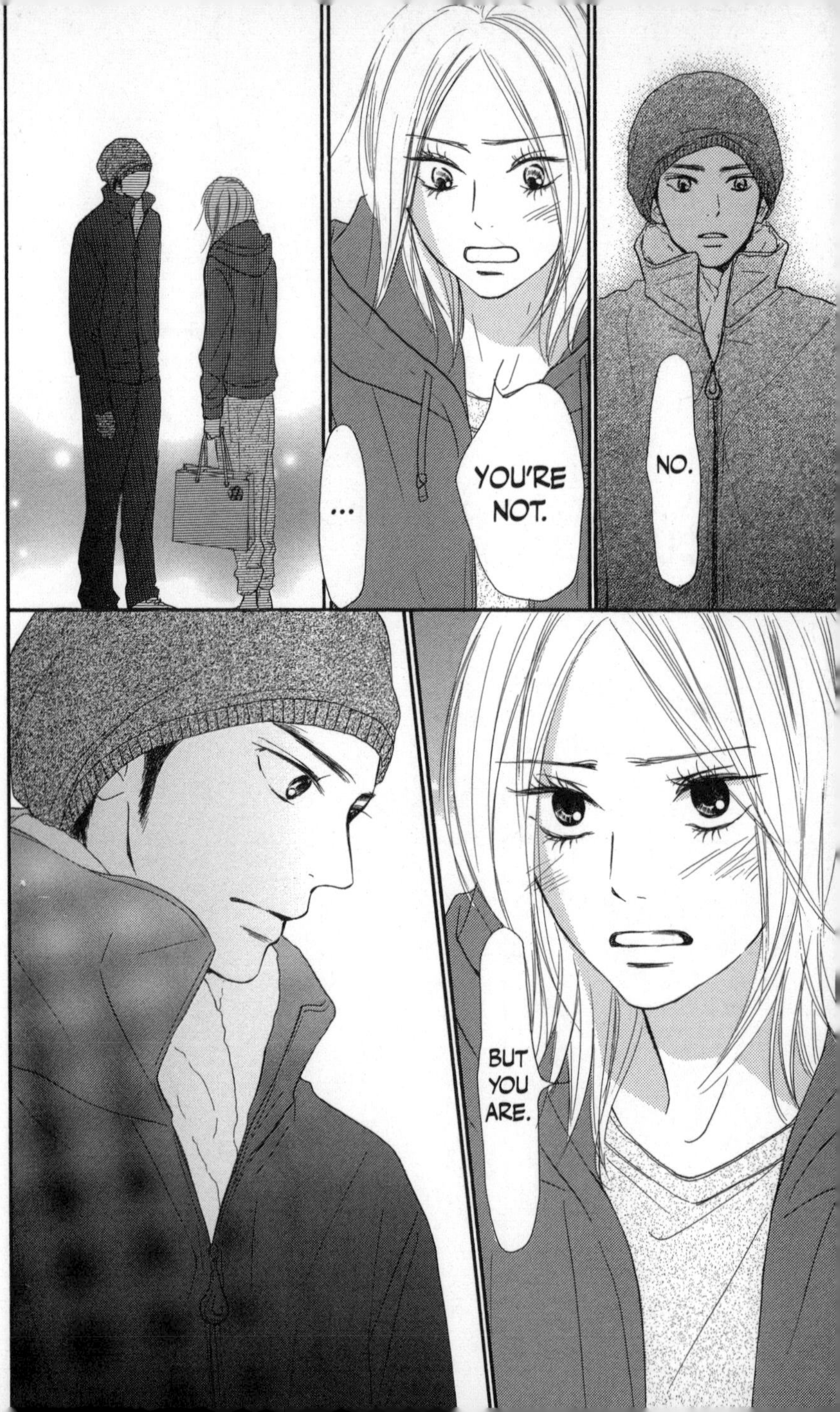
NO.
YOU'RE NOT.
...
BUT YOU ARE.

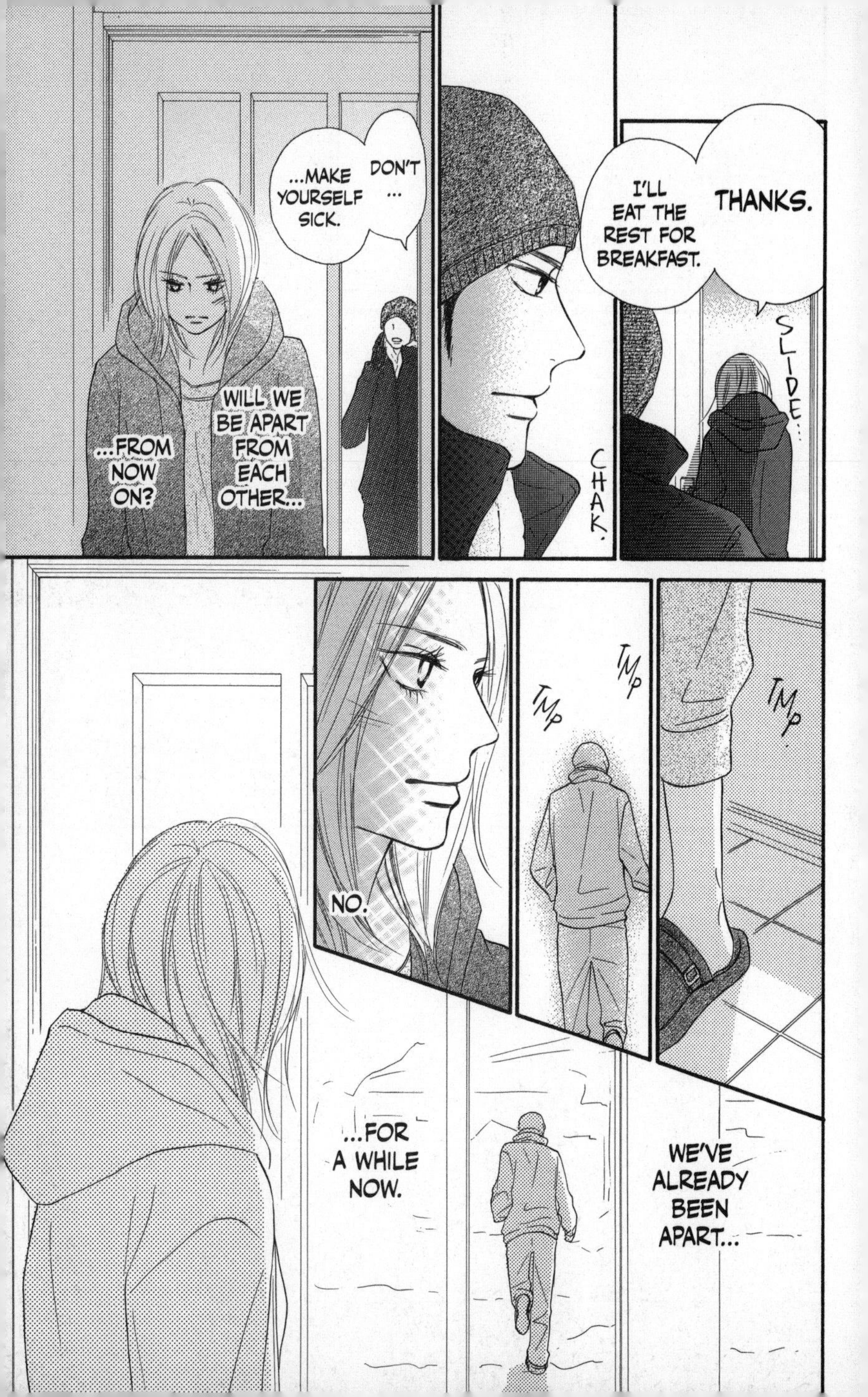

THANKS.
I'LL EAT THE REST FOR BREAKFAST.
SLIDE...
CHAK.
DON'T ...
...MAKE YOURSELF SICK.
WILL WE BE APART FROM EACH OTHER...
...FROM NOW ON?
TMP
TMP
TMP
NO.
WE'VE ALREADY BEEN APART...
...FOR A WHILE NOW.

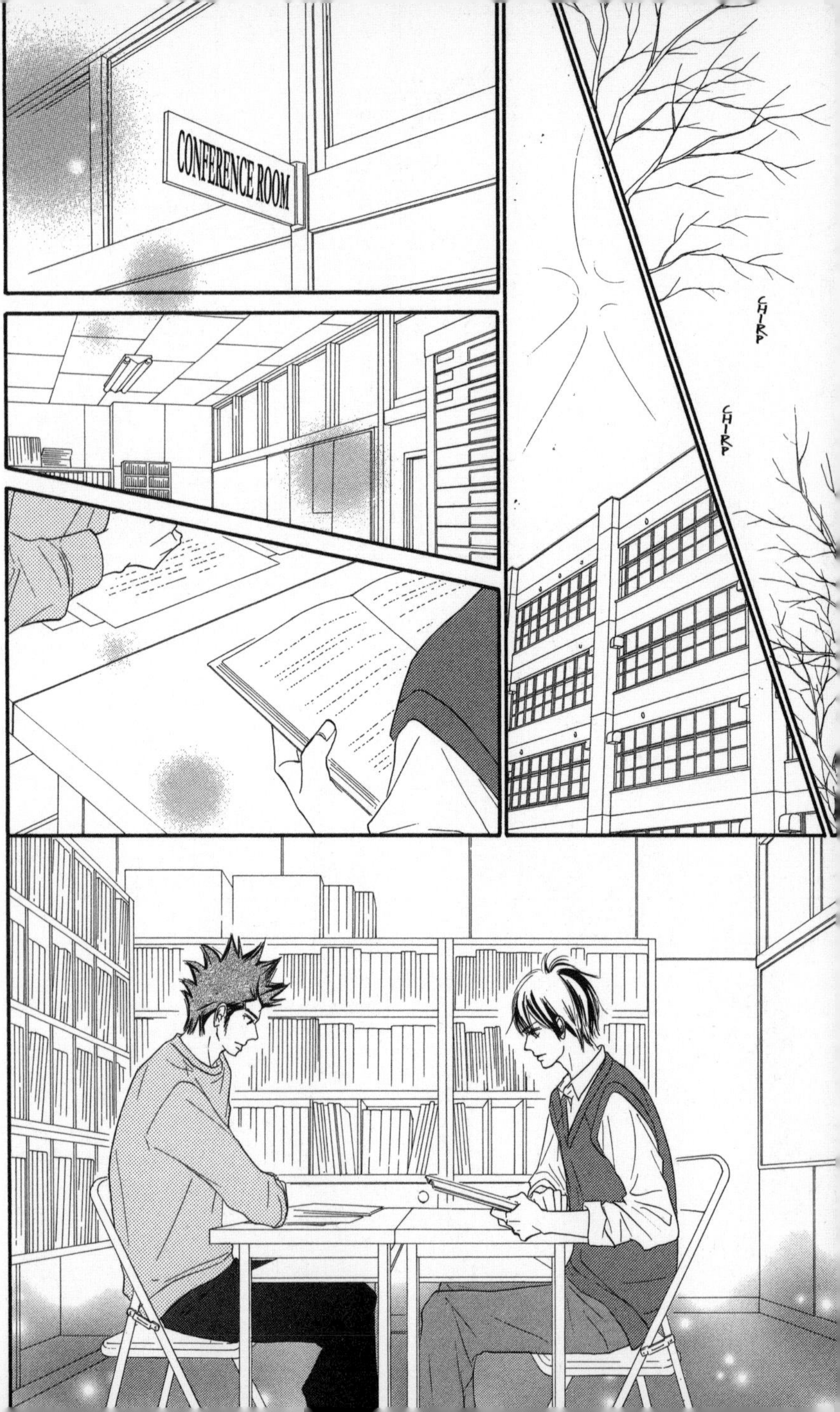
CHIRP
CHIRP
CONFERENCE ROOM

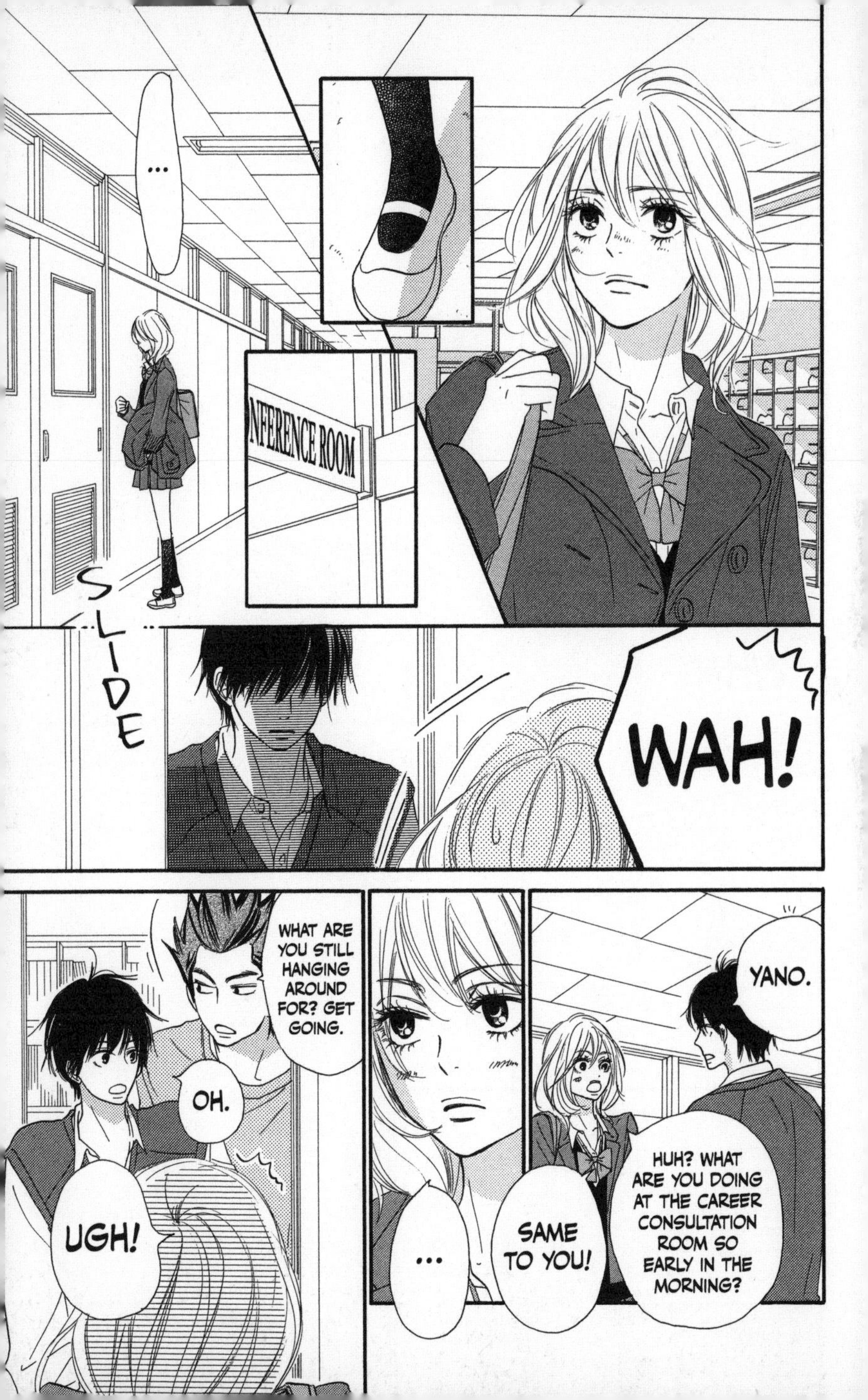
NFERENCE ROOM
...
SLIDE
WAH!
YANO.
HUH? WHAT ARE YOU DOING AT THE CAREER CONSULTATION ROOM SO EARLY IN THE MORNING?
SAME TO YOU!
...
WHAT ARE YOU STILL HANGING AROUND FOR? GET GOING.
OH.
UGH!

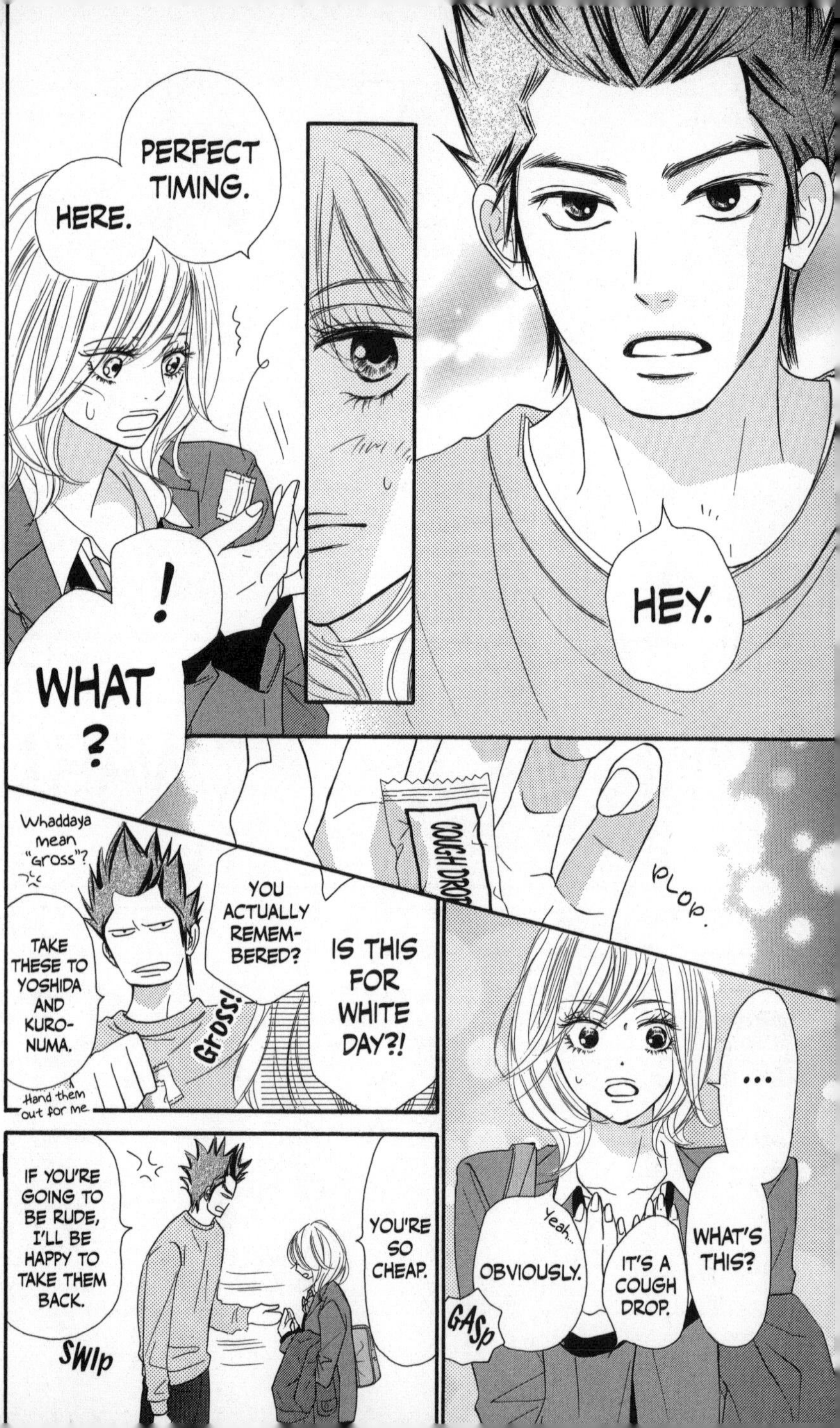
HEY.
PERFECT TIMING.
HERE.
!
WHAT ?
plop.
COUGH DROP
...
WHAT'S THIS?
IT'S A COUGH DROP.
Yeah...
OBVIOUSLY.
GASp
IS THIS FOR WHITE DAY?!
YOU ACTUALLY REMEM-BERED?
Gross!
Whaddaya mean "gross"?
TAKE THESE TO YOSHIDA AND KURO-NUMA.
Hand them out for me.
YOU'RE SO CHEAP.
IF YOU'RE GOING TO BE RUDE, I'LL BE HAPPY TO TAKE THEM BACK.
SWIp

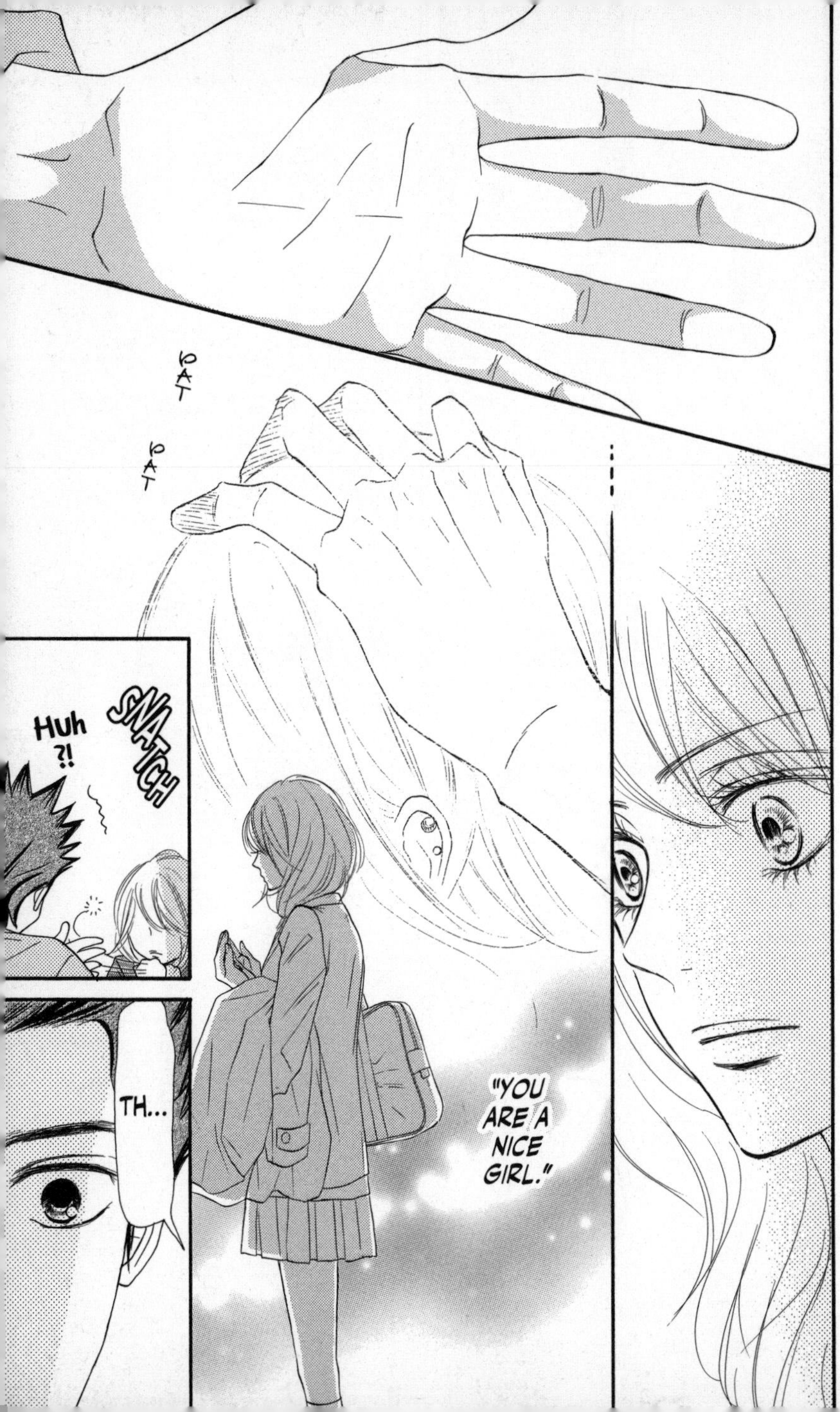
PAT
PAT
"YOU ARE A NICE GIRL."
SNATCH
Huh ?!
TH...

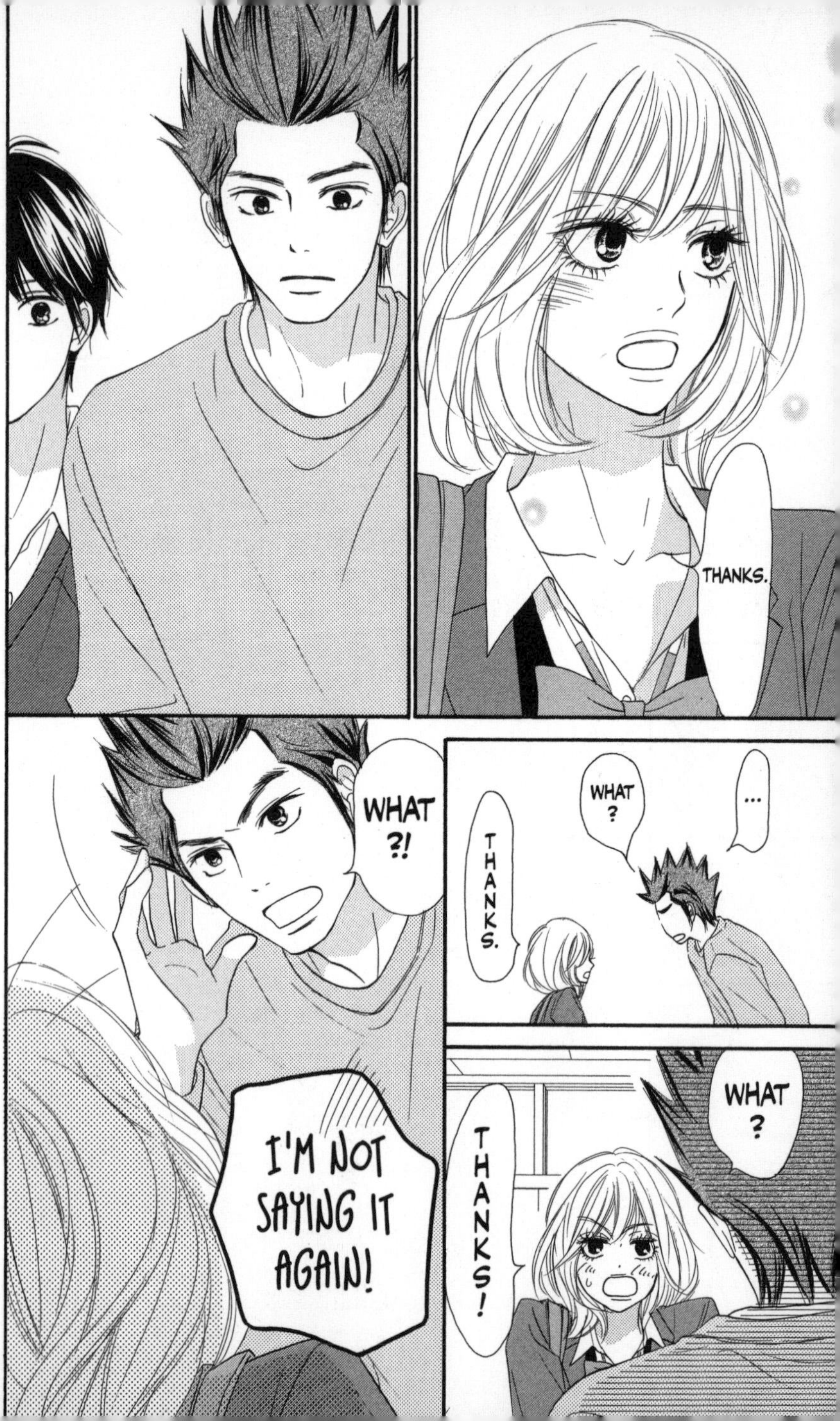
THANKS.
...
WHAT ?
THANKS.
WHAT ?
THANKS!
WHAT ?!
I'M NOT SAYING IT AGAIN!

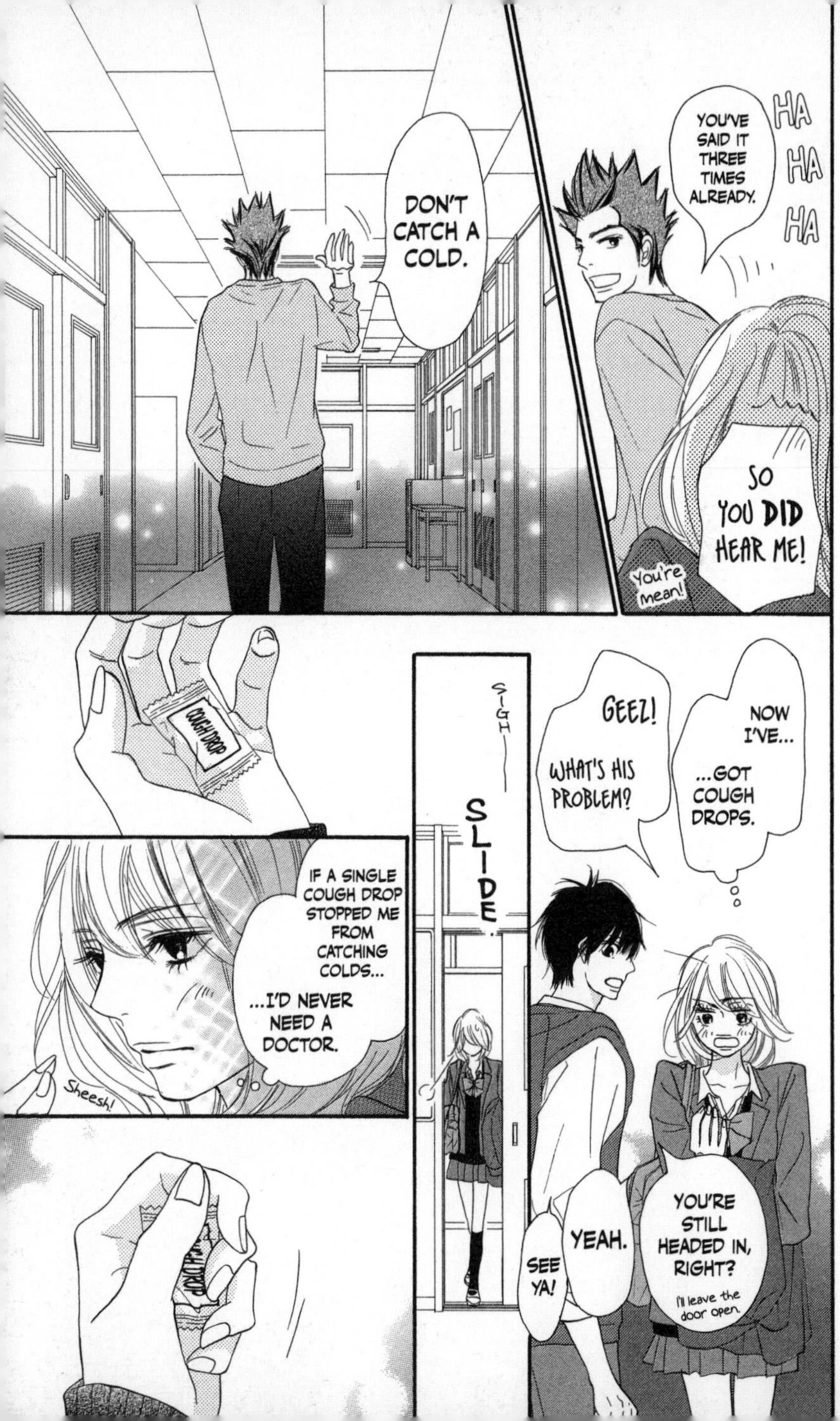
HA
HA
HA
YOU'VE SAID IT THREE TIMES ALREADY.
SO YOU **DID** HEAR ME!
You're mean!
DON'T CATCH A COLD.
NOW I'VE...
...GOT COUGH DROPS.
GEEZ!
WHAT'S HIS PROBLEM?
SIGH
SLIDE
YOU'RE STILL HEADED IN, RIGHT?
I'll leave the door open.
YEAH.
SEE YA!
COUGH DROP
IF A SINGLE COUGH DROP STOPPED ME FROM CATCHING COLDS...
...I'D NEVER NEED A DOCTOR.
Sheesh!

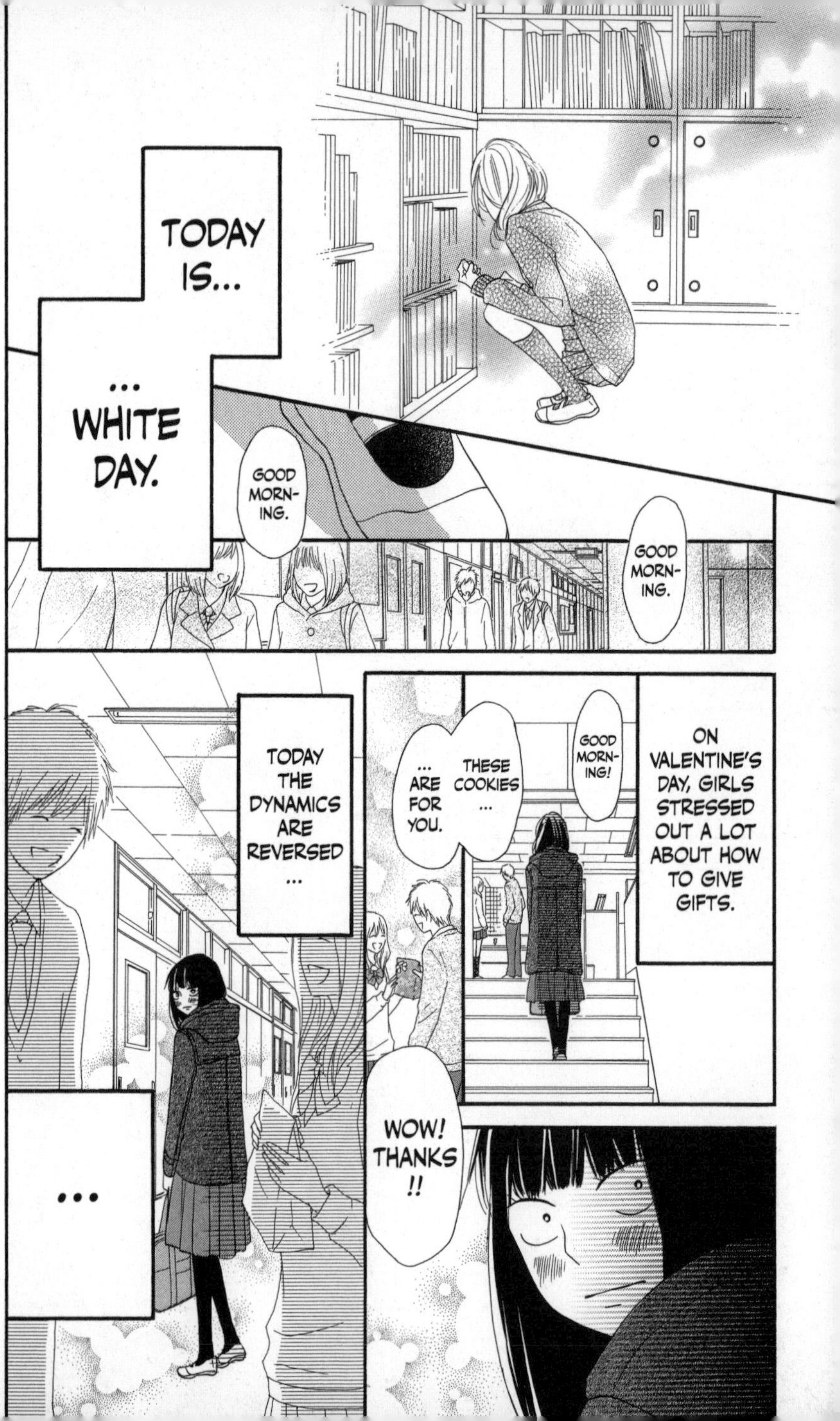

TODAY IS...
...WHITE DAY.
GOOD MORNING.
GOOD MORNING.
ON VALENTINE'S DAY, GIRLS STRESSED OUT A LOT ABOUT HOW TO GIVE GIFTS.
GOOD MORNING!
THESE COOKIES...
...ARE FOR YOU.
TODAY THE DYNAMICS ARE REVERSED...
WOW! THANKS!!
...

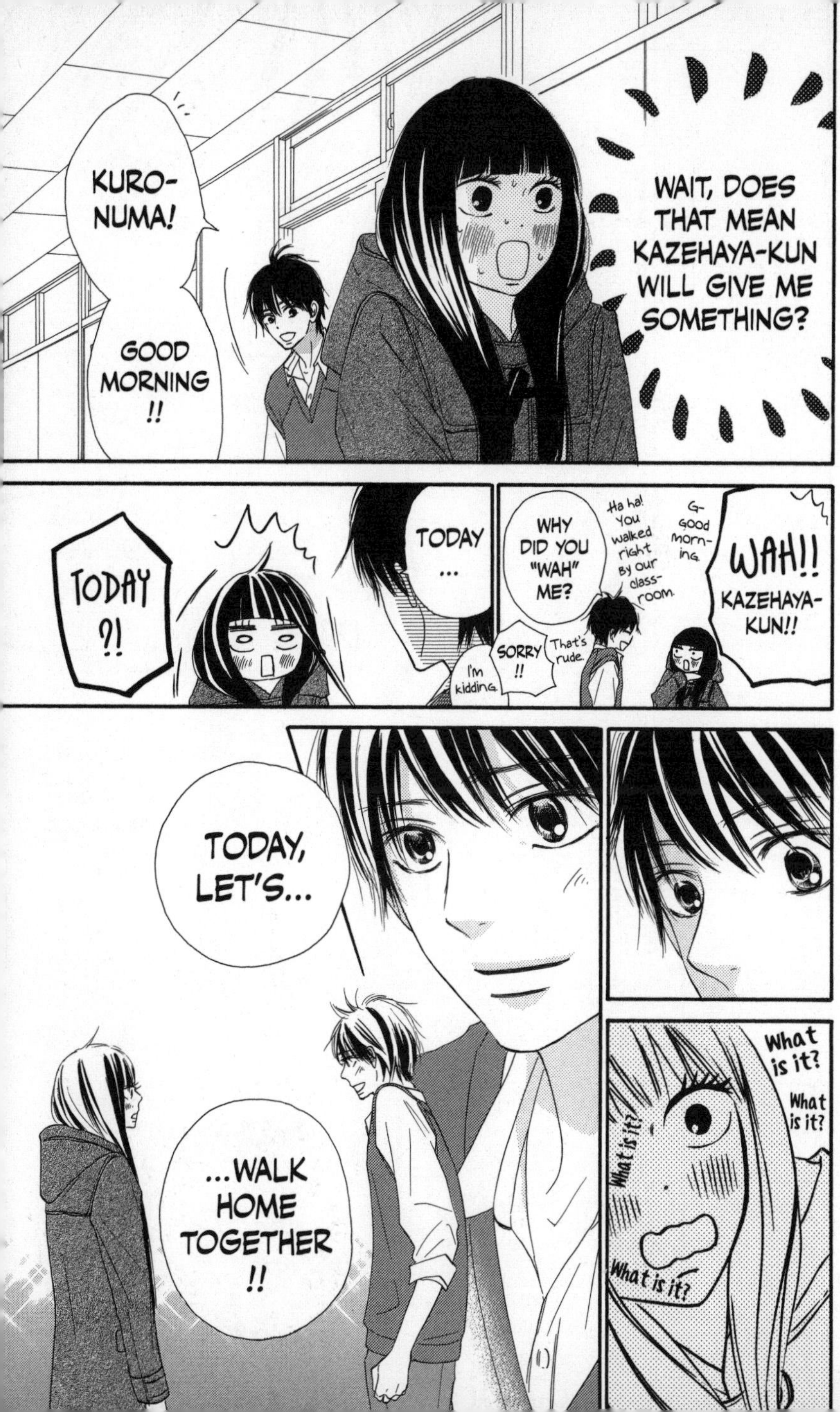
WAIT, DOES THAT MEAN KAZEHAYA-KUN WILL GIVE ME SOMETHING?
KURO-NUMA!
GOOD MORNING!!
WAH!! KAZEHAYA-KUN!!
G-Good morn-ing.
Ha ha! You walked right by our class-room.
WHY DID YOU "WAH" ME?
That's rude.
SORRY!!
I'm kidding.
TODAY...
TODAY?!
What is it?
What is it?
What is it?
What is it?
TODAY, LET'S...
...WALK HOME TOGETHER!!

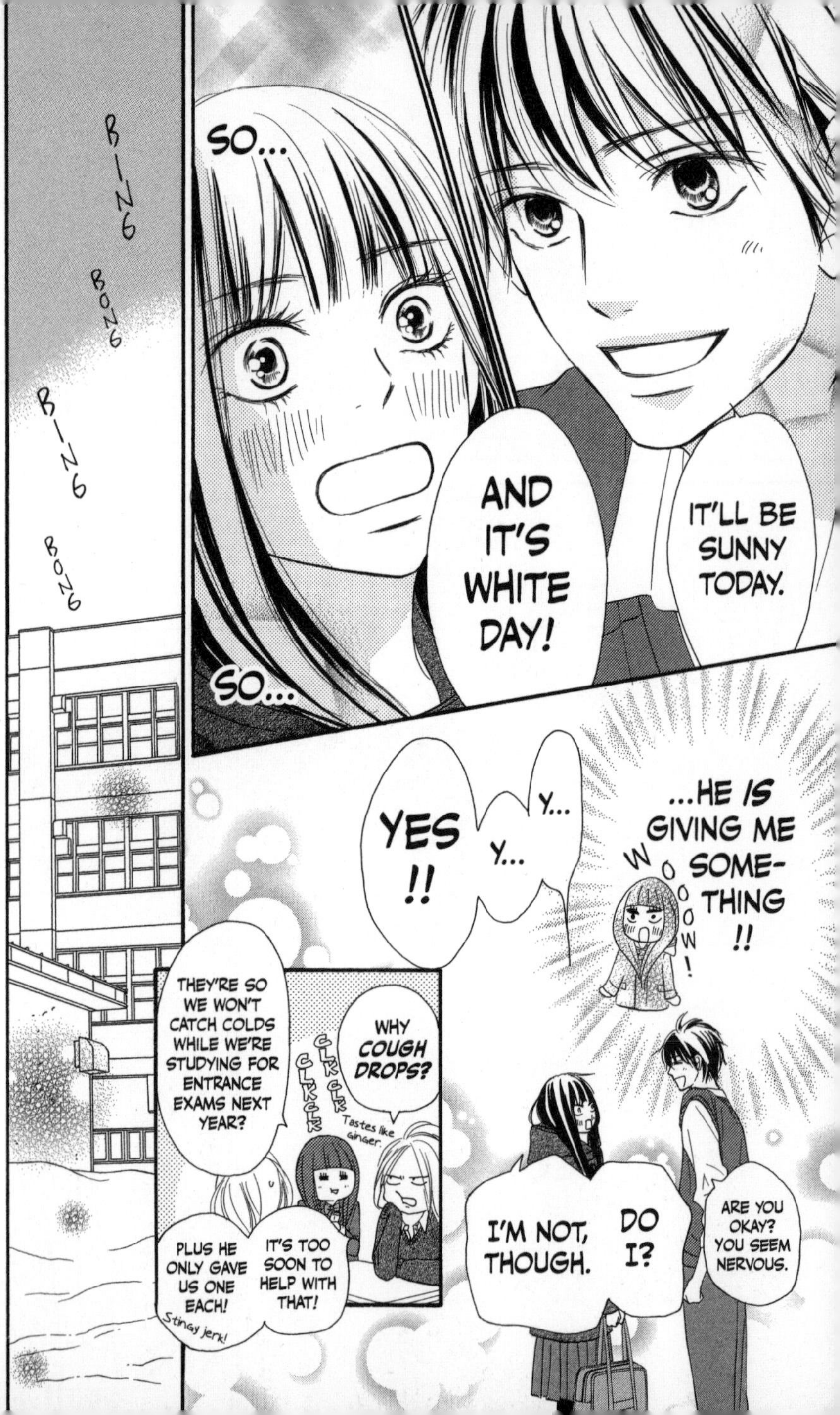
IT'LL BE SUNNY TODAY.
AND IT'S WHITE DAY!
SO...
SO...
...HE *IS* GIVING ME SOME-THING!!
WOOOOW!
Y... Y...
YES!!
ARE YOU OKAY? YOU SEEM NERVOUS.
DO I?
I'M NOT, THOUGH.
WHY *COUGH DROPS?*
CLK CLK CLK CLK
Tastes like ginger.
THEY'RE SO WE WON'T CATCH COLDS WHILE WE'RE STUDYING FOR ENTRANCE EXAMS NEXT YEAR?
IT'S TOO SOON TO HELP WITH THAT!
PLUS HE ONLY GAVE US ONE EACH!
Stingy jerk!
BING BONG
BING BONG

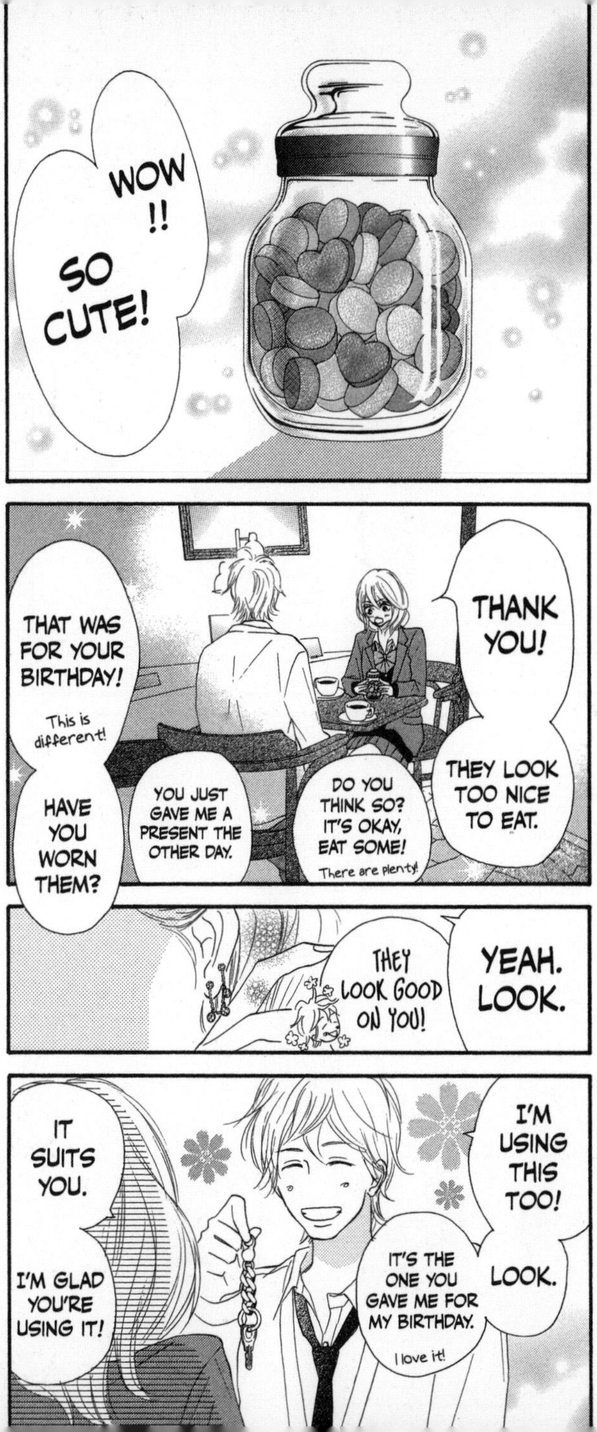
WOW!!
SO CUTE!
THANK YOU!
THEY LOOK TOO NICE TO EAT.
DO YOU THINK SO? IT'S OKAY, EAT SOME!
There are plenty!
YOU JUST GAVE ME A PRESENT THE OTHER DAY.
THAT WAS FOR YOUR BIRTHDAY!
This is different!
HAVE YOU WORN THEM?
YEAH. LOOK.
THEY LOOK GOOD ON YOU!
I'M USING THIS TOO!
LOOK.
IT'S THE ONE YOU GAVE ME FOR MY BIRTHDAY.
I love it!
IT SUITS YOU.
I'M GLAD YOU'RE USING IT!

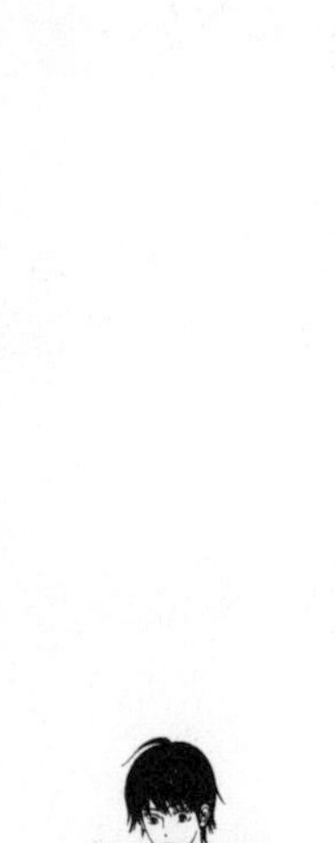

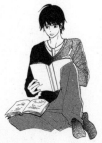

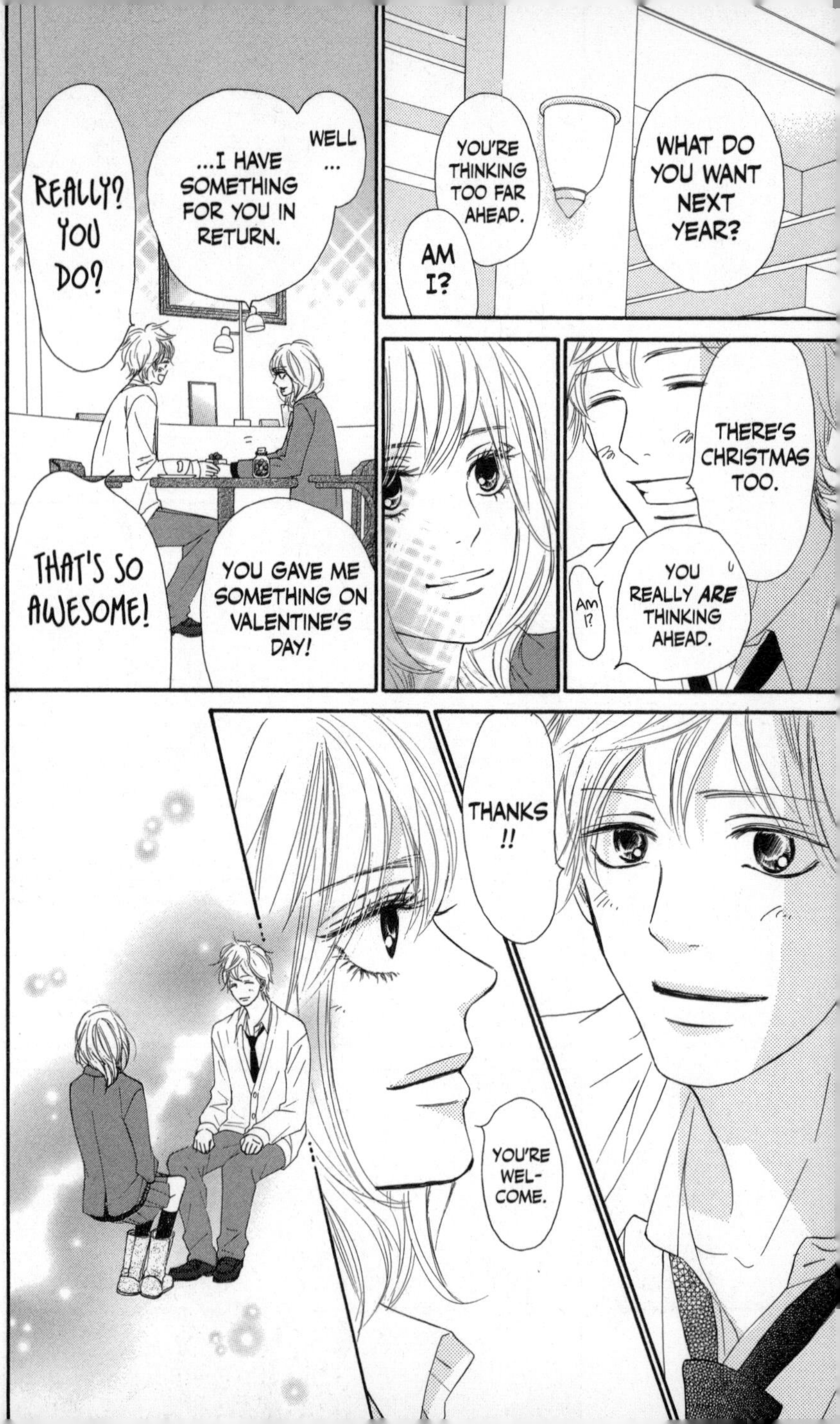
WHAT DO YOU WANT NEXT YEAR?
YOU'RE THINKING TOO FAR AHEAD.
AM I?
THERE'S CHRISTMAS TOO.
YOU REALLY ARE THINKING AHEAD.
AM I?
WELL ...
...I HAVE SOMETHING FOR YOU IN RETURN.
REALLY? YOU DO?
YOU GAVE ME SOMETHING ON VALENTINE'S DAY!
THAT'S SO AWESOME!
THANKS !!
YOU'RE WEL- COME.

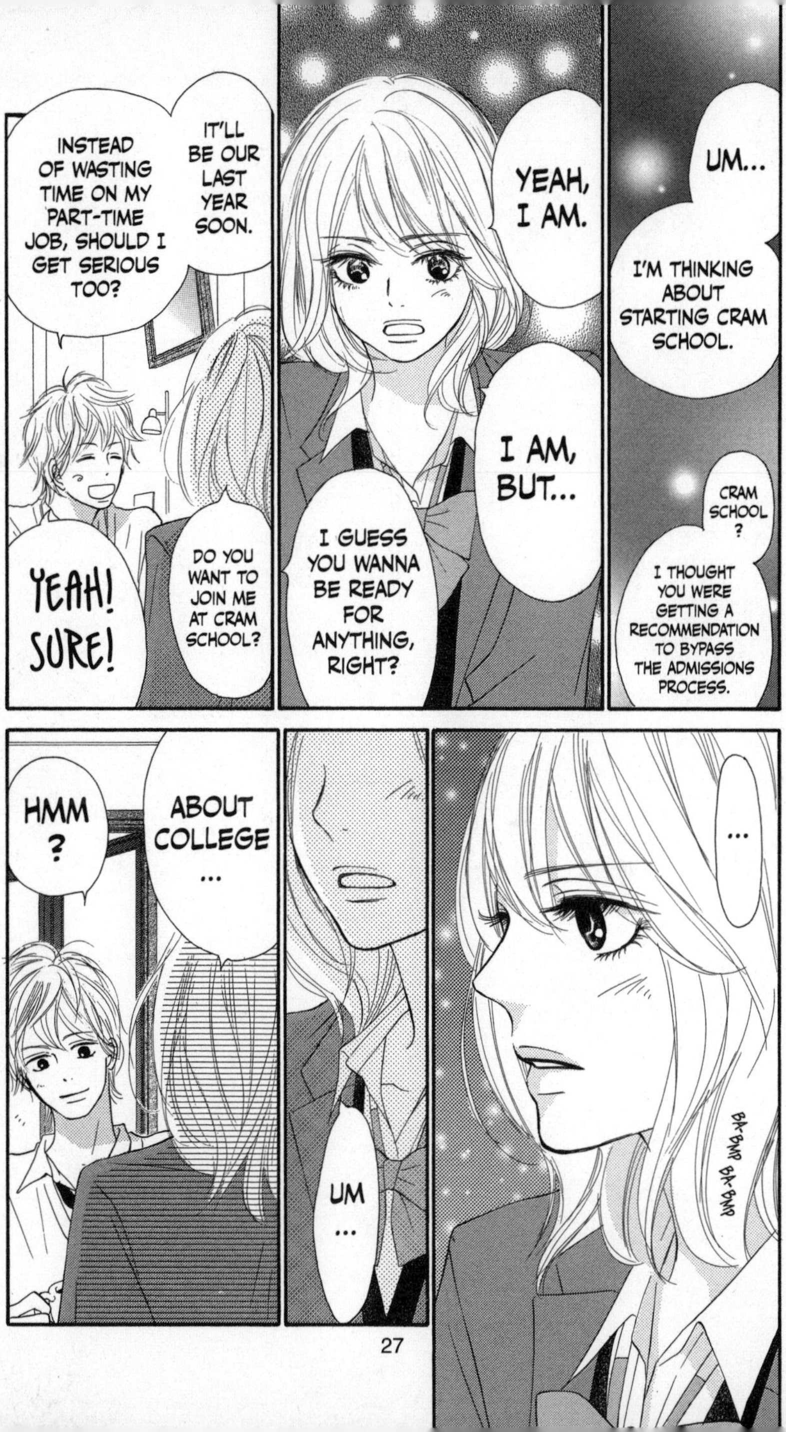
UM...
I'M THINKING ABOUT STARTING CRAM SCHOOL.
CRAM SCHOOL?
I THOUGHT YOU WERE GETTING A RECOMMENDATION TO BYPASS THE ADMISSIONS PROCESS.
YEAH, I AM.
I AM, BUT...
I GUESS YOU WANNA BE READY FOR ANYTHING, RIGHT?
IT'LL BE OUR LAST YEAR SOON.
INSTEAD OF WASTING TIME ON MY PART-TIME JOB, SHOULD I GET SERIOUS TOO?
DO YOU WANT TO JOIN ME AT CRAM SCHOOL?
YEAH! SURE!
...
BA-BMP BA-BMP
UM...
ABOUT COLLEGE...
HMM?

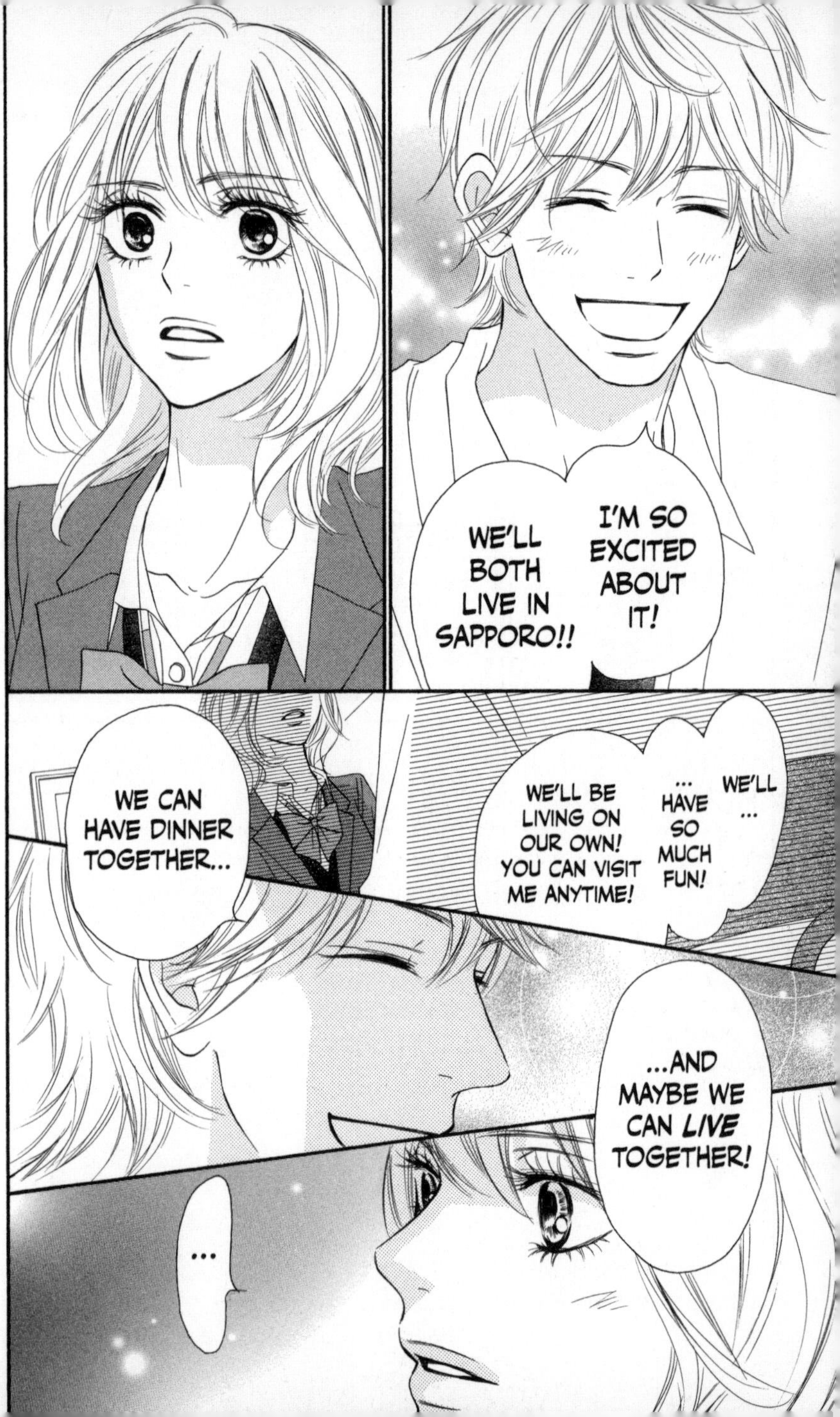
I'M SO EXCITED ABOUT IT!
WE'LL BOTH LIVE IN SAPPORO!!
WE'LL...
...HAVE SO MUCH FUN!
WE'LL BE LIVING ON OUR OWN! YOU CAN VISIT ME ANYTIME!
WE CAN HAVE DINNER TOGETHER...
...AND MAYBE WE CAN *LIVE* TOGETHER!
...

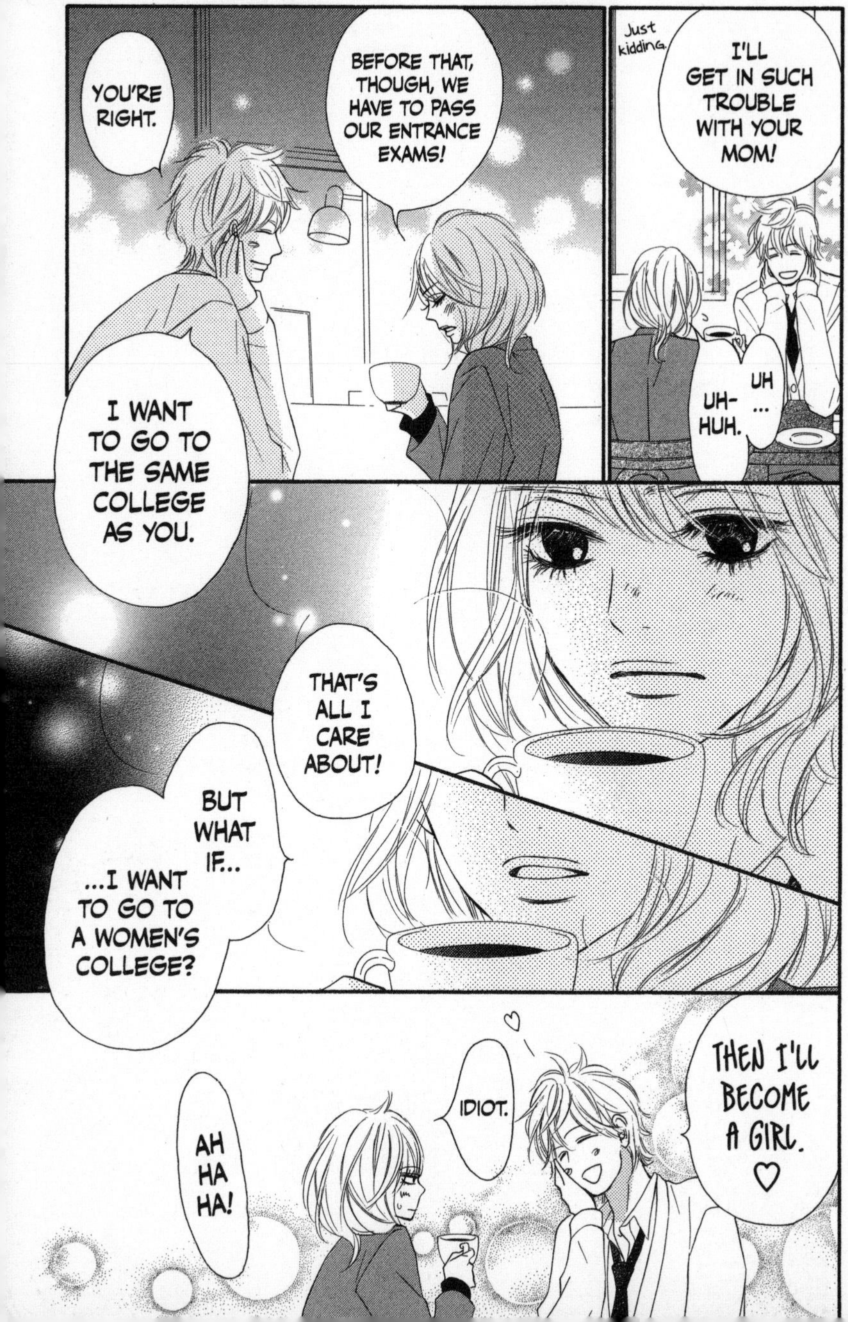
I'LL GET IN SUCH TROUBLE WITH YOUR MOM!
Just kidding.
UH ...
UH-HUH.
BEFORE THAT, THOUGH, WE HAVE TO PASS OUR ENTRANCE EXAMS!
YOU'RE RIGHT.
I WANT TO GO TO THE SAME COLLEGE AS YOU.
THAT'S ALL I CARE ABOUT!
BUT WHAT IF...
...I WANT TO GO TO A WOMEN'S COLLEGE?
THEN I'LL BECOME A GIRL. ♡
IDIOT.
AH HA HA!

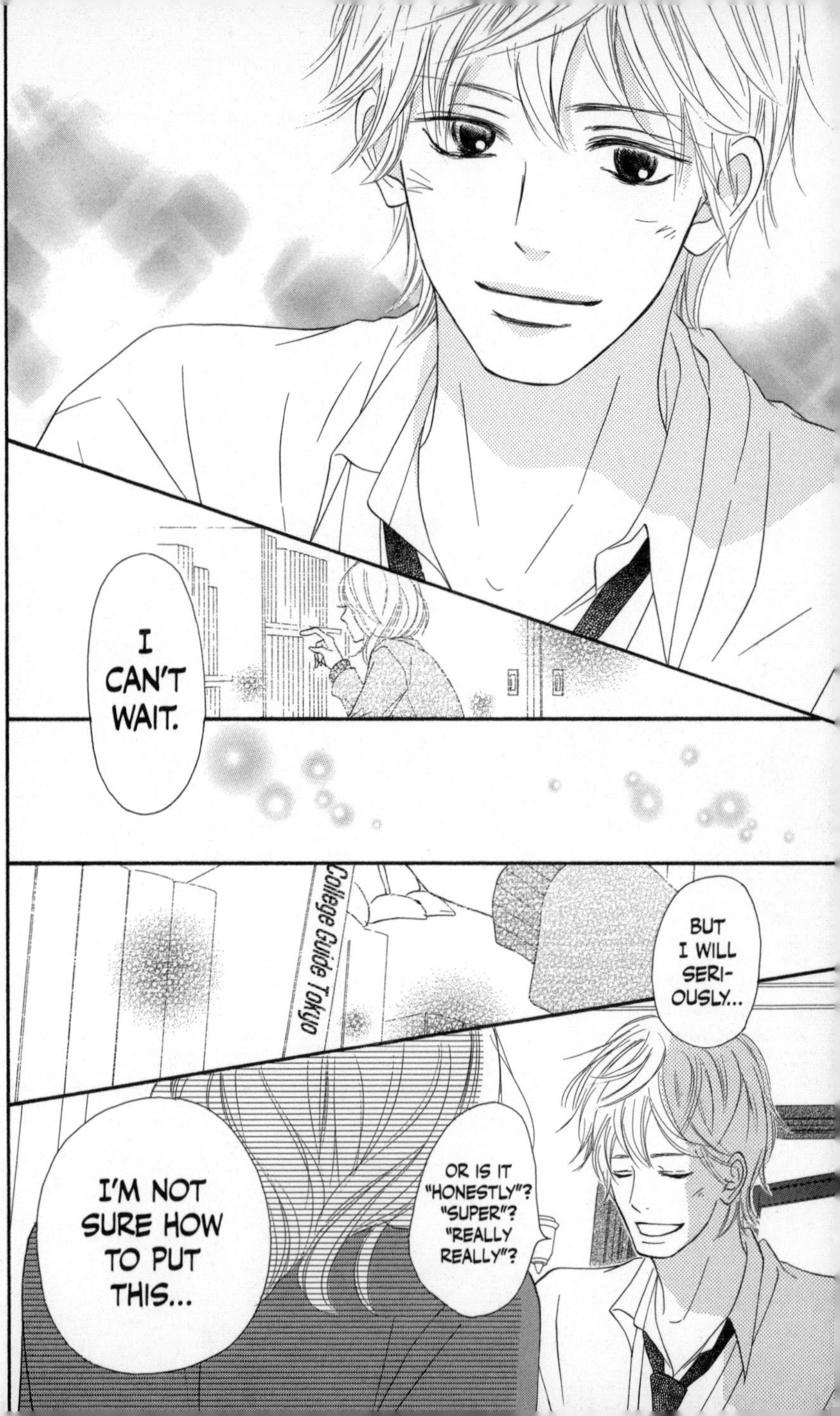
I CAN'T WAIT.
BUT I WILL SERI-OUSLY...
College Guide Tokyo
OR IS IT "HONESTLY"? "SUPER"? "REALLY REALLY"?
I'M NOT SURE HOW TO PUT THIS...

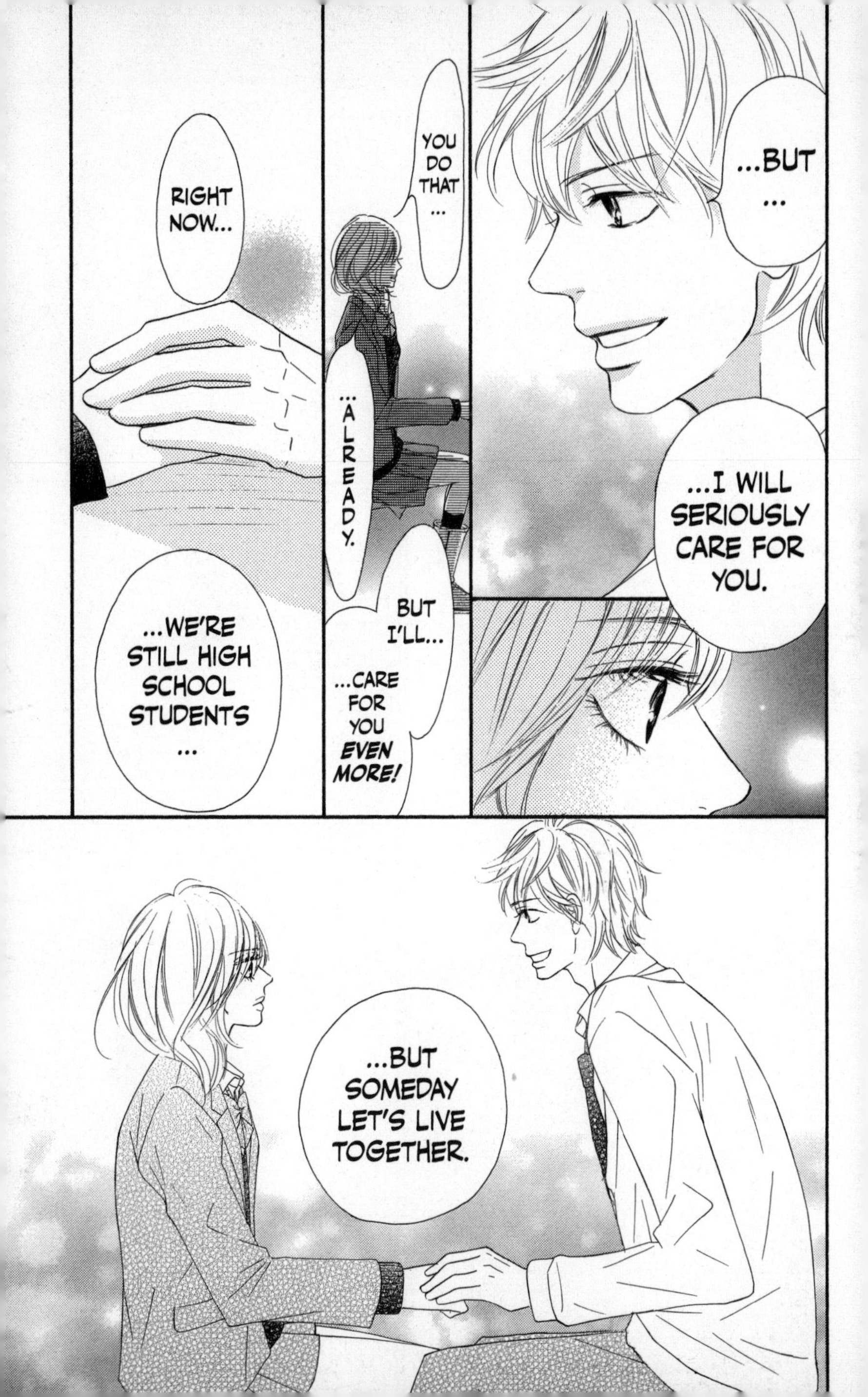
...BUT ...
...I WILL SERIOUSLY CARE FOR YOU.
YOU DO THAT ...
...ALREADY.
BUT I'LL...
...CARE FOR YOU *EVEN MORE!*
RIGHT NOW...
...WE'RE STILL HIGH SCHOOL STUDENTS ...
...BUT SOMEDAY LET'S LIVE TOGETHER.

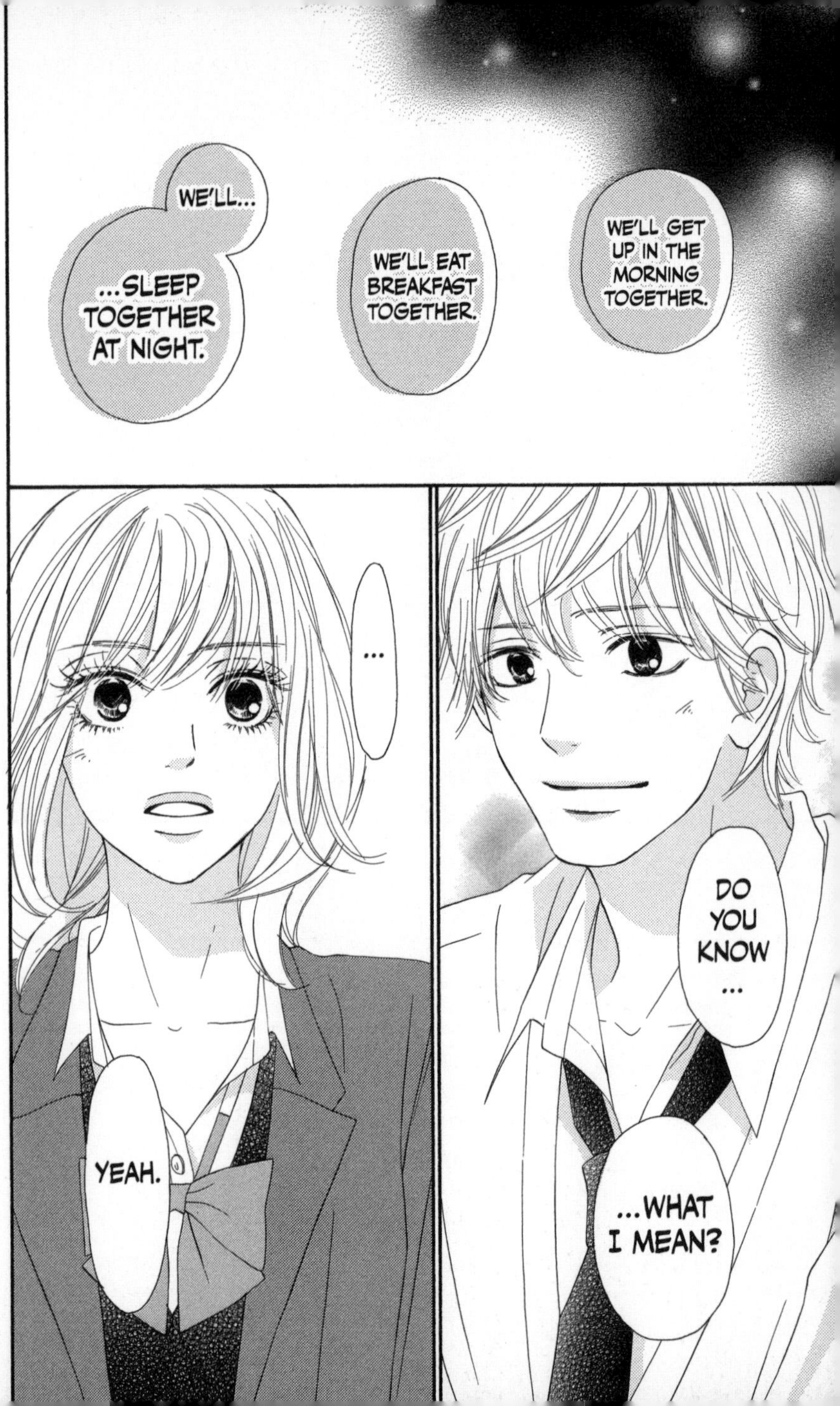
WE'LL GET UP IN THE MORNING TOGETHER.
WE'LL EAT BREAKFAST TOGETHER.
WE'LL...
...SLEEP TOGETHER AT NIGHT.
DO YOU KNOW ...
...WHAT I MEAN?
...
YEAH.

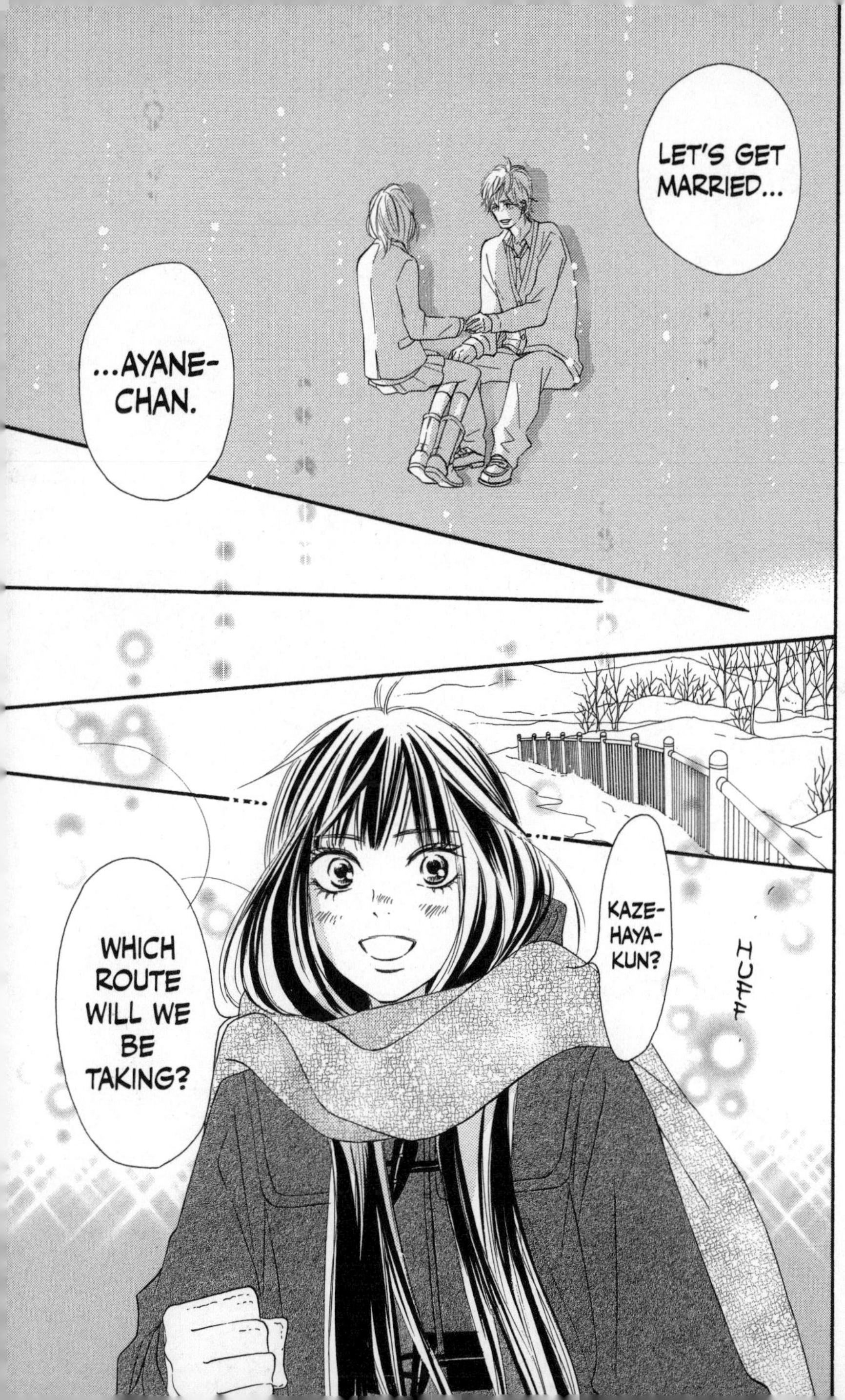
LET'S GET MARRIED...
...AYANE-CHAN.
HUFF
KAZE-HAYA-KUN?
WHICH ROUTE WILL WE BE TAKING?

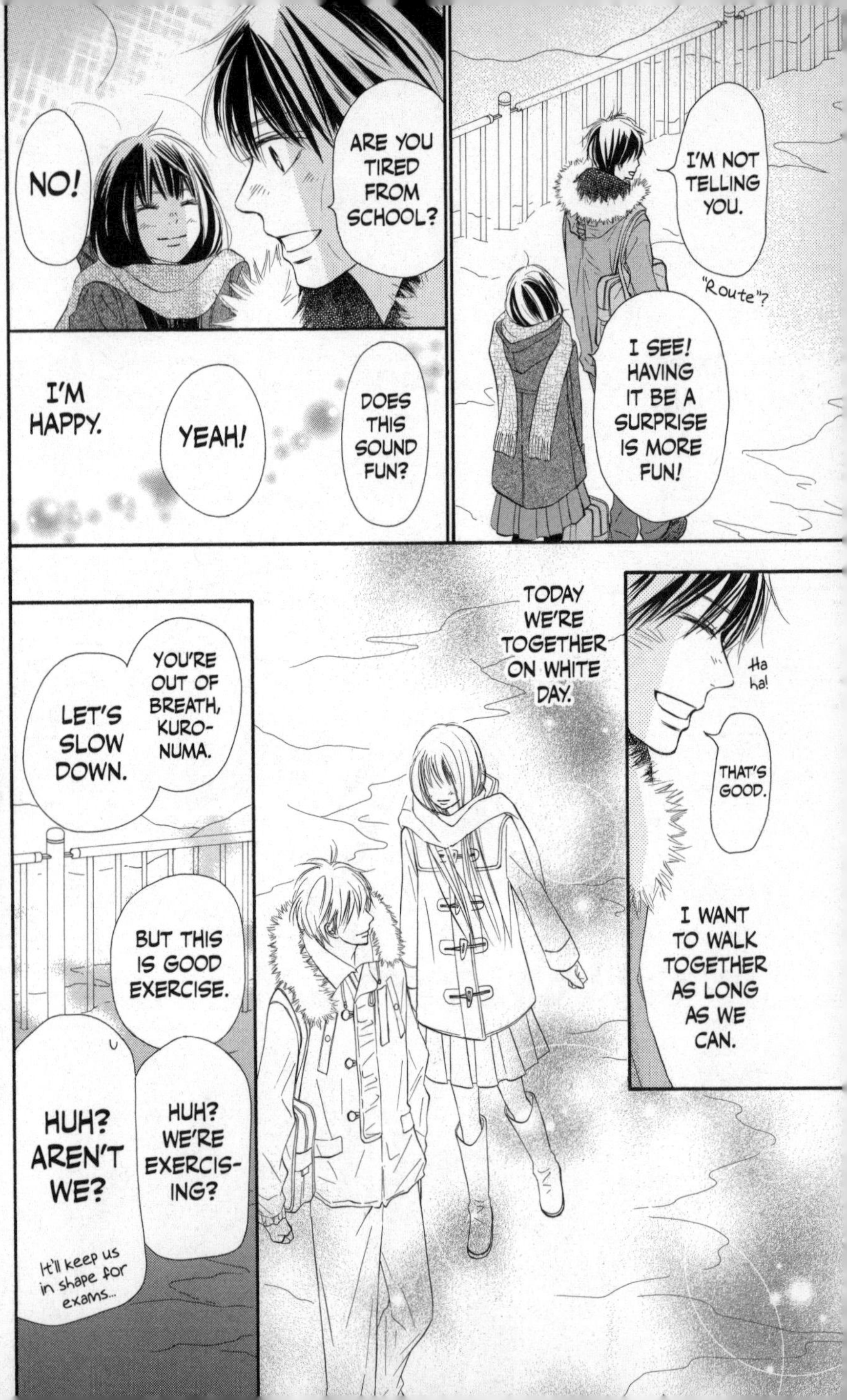
I'M NOT TELLING YOU.
"Route"?
I SEE! HAVING IT BE A SURPRISE IS MORE FUN!
ARE YOU TIRED FROM SCHOOL?
NO!
DOES THIS SOUND FUN?
YEAH!
I'M HAPPY.
Ha ha!
THAT'S GOOD.
I WANT TO WALK TOGETHER AS LONG AS WE CAN.
TODAY WE'RE TOGETHER ON WHITE DAY.
YOU'RE OUT OF BREATH, KURO-NUMA.
LET'S SLOW DOWN.
BUT THIS IS GOOD EXERCISE.
HUH? WE'RE EXERCIS-ING?
HUH? AREN'T WE?
It'll keep us in shape for exams...

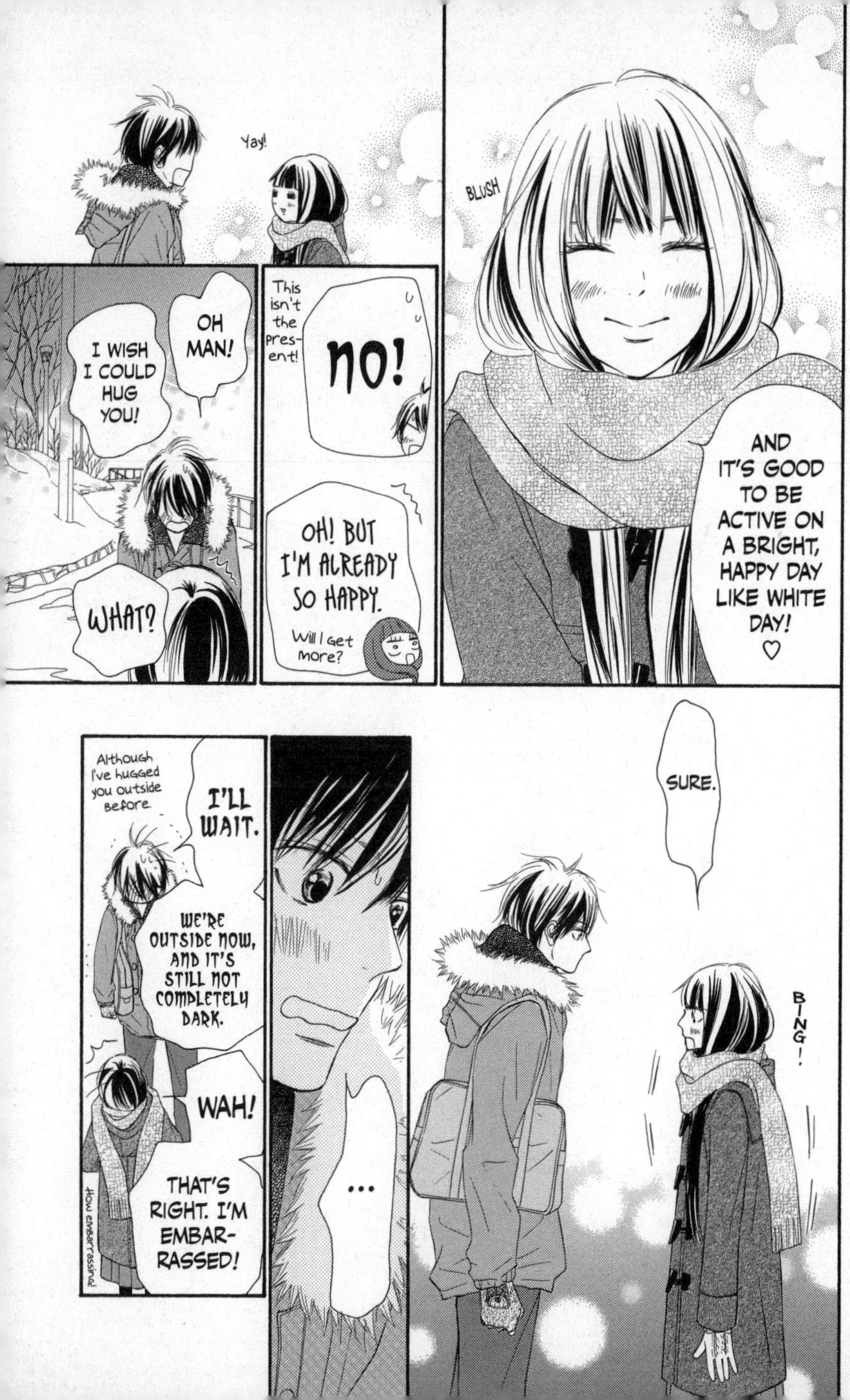
BLUSH
AND IT'S GOOD TO BE ACTIVE ON A BRIGHT, HAPPY DAY LIKE WHITE DAY! ♡
Yay!
This isn't the pres-ent!
no!
OH! BUT I'M ALREADY SO HAPPY.
Will I get more?
OH MAN!
I WISH I COULD HUG YOU!
WHAT?
SURE.
BING!
...
I'LL WAIT.
Although I've hugged you outside before.
WE'RE OUTSIDE NOW, AND IT'S STILL NOT COMPLETELY DARK.
WAH!
THAT'S RIGHT. I'M EMBAR-RASSED!
How embarrassing!

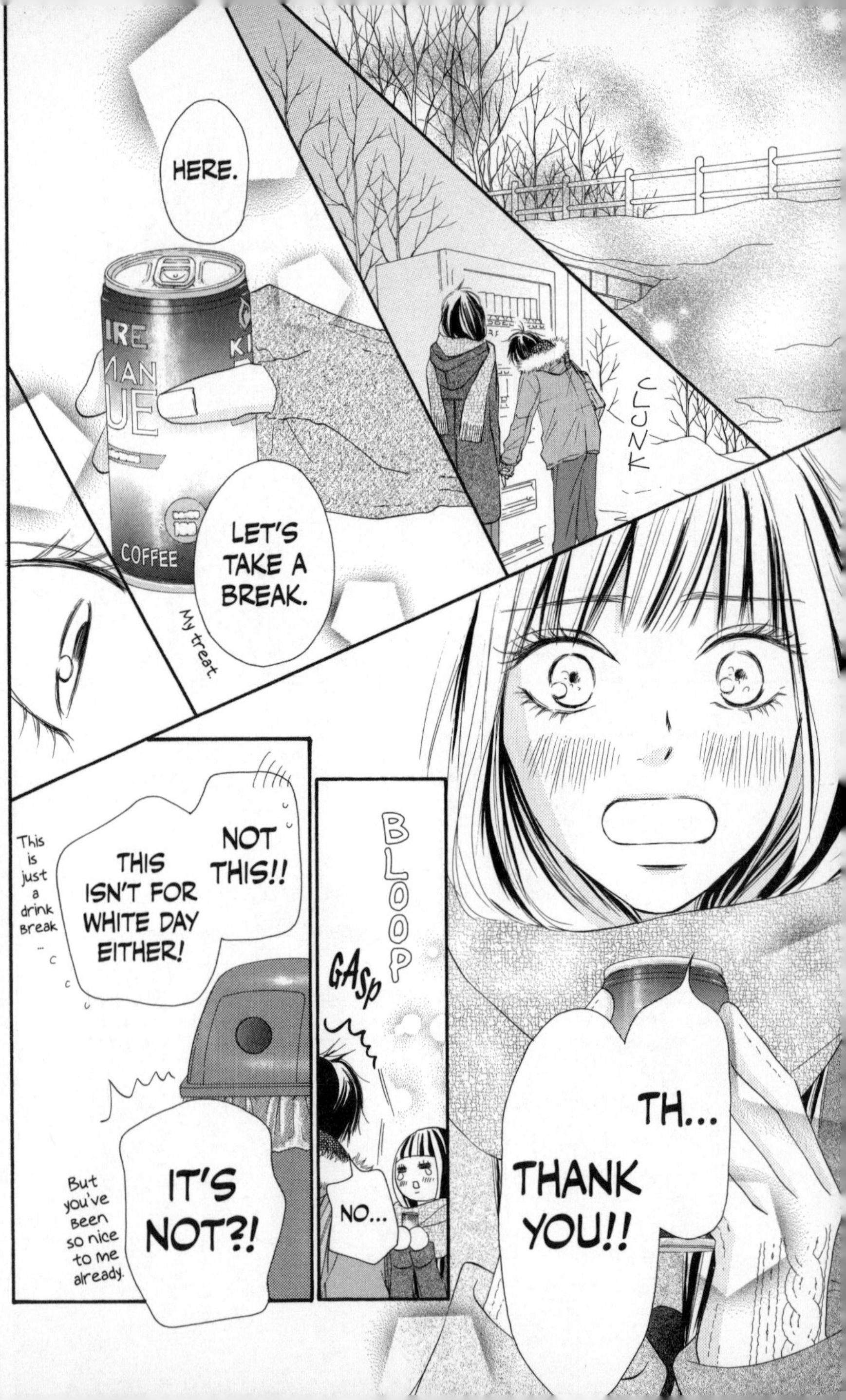
CLUNK
HERE.
COFFEE
LET'S TAKE A BREAK.
My treat.
TH...
THANK YOU!!
BLOOP
GASp
NO...
NOT THIS!!
THIS ISN'T FOR WHITE DAY EITHER!
This is just a drink break...
IT'S NOT?!
But you've been so nice to me already.

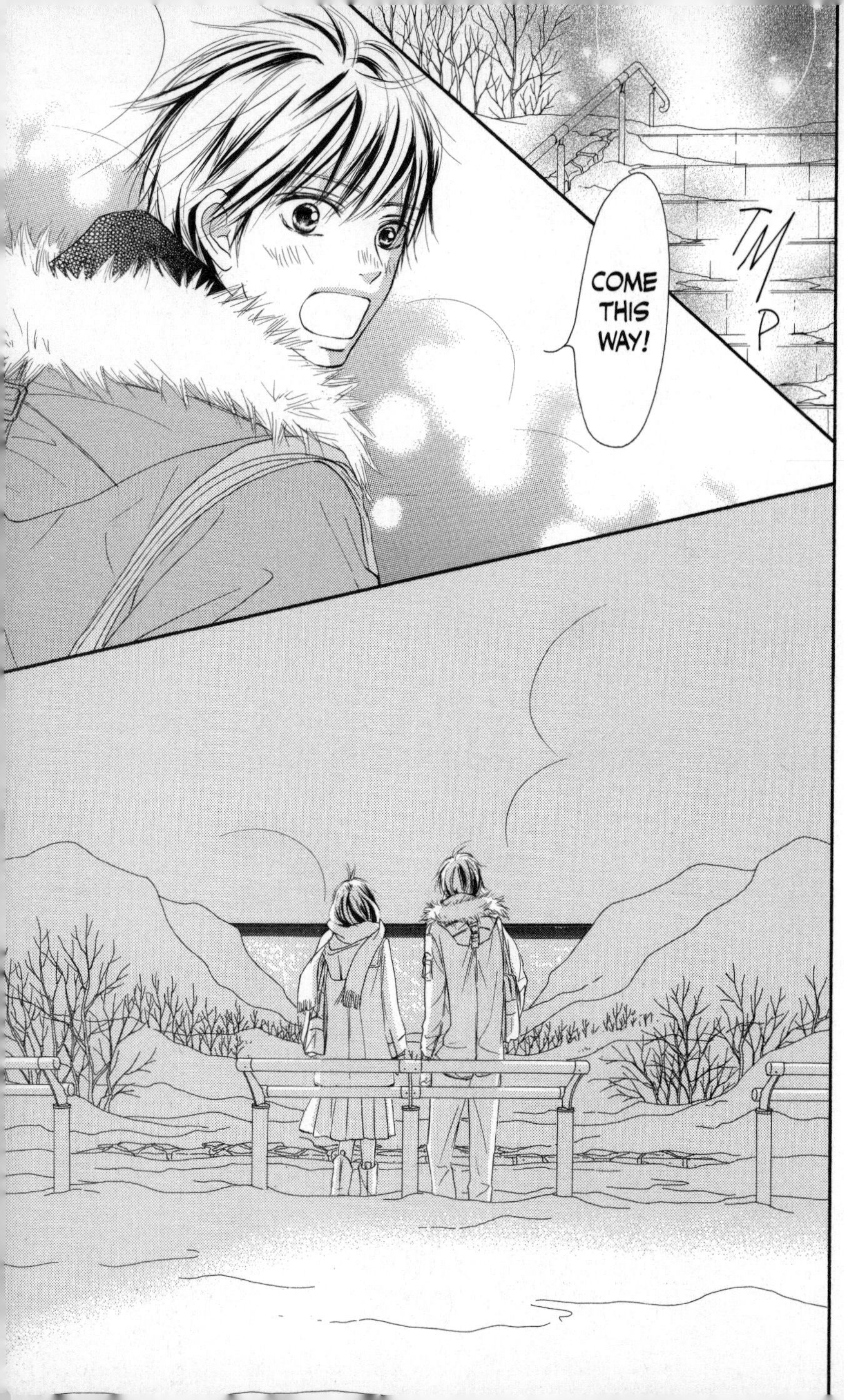
TMP
COME THIS WAY!

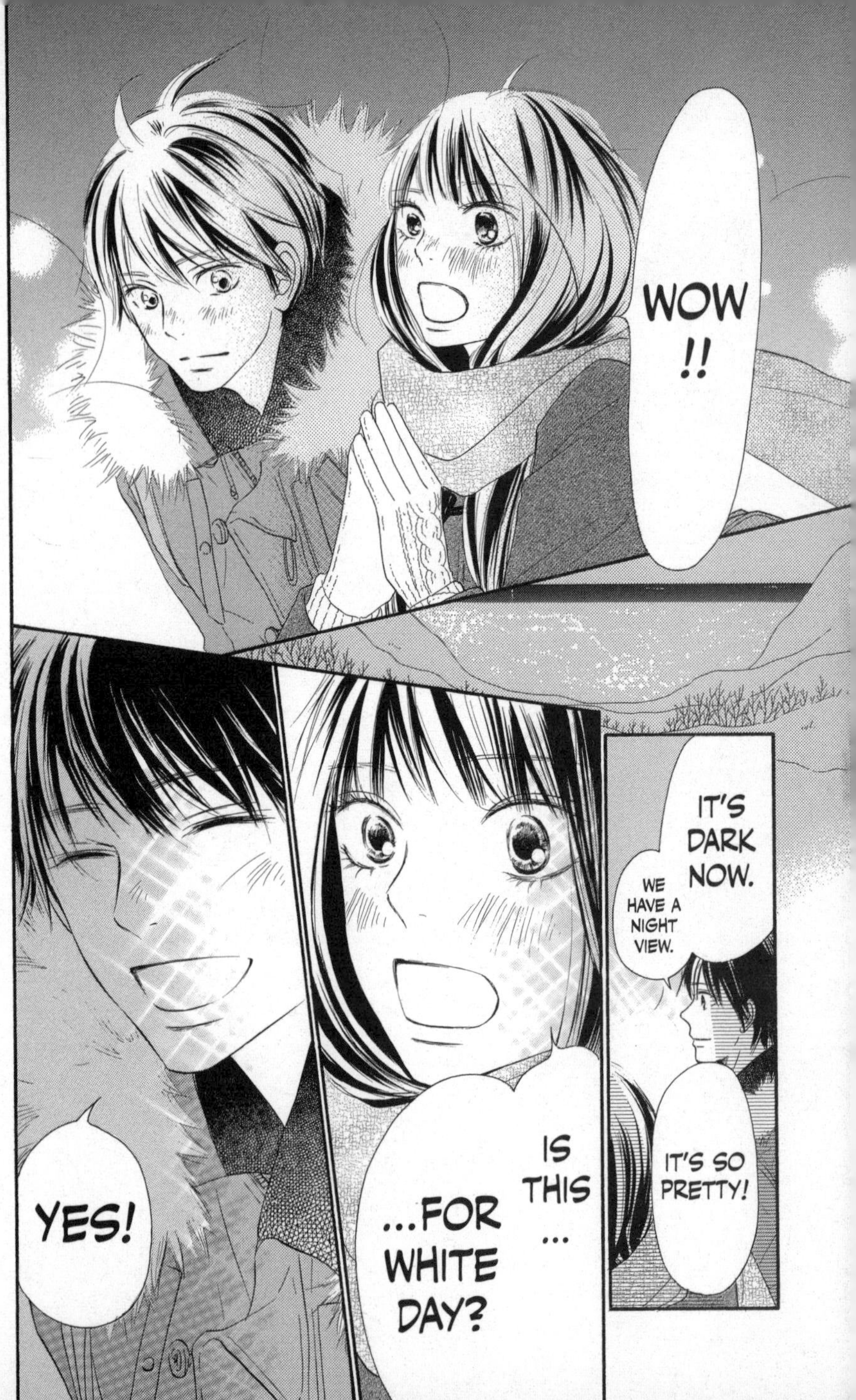
WOW!!
IT'S DARK NOW.
WE HAVE A NIGHT VIEW.
IT'S SO PRETTY!
IS THIS...
...FOR WHITE DAY?
YES!

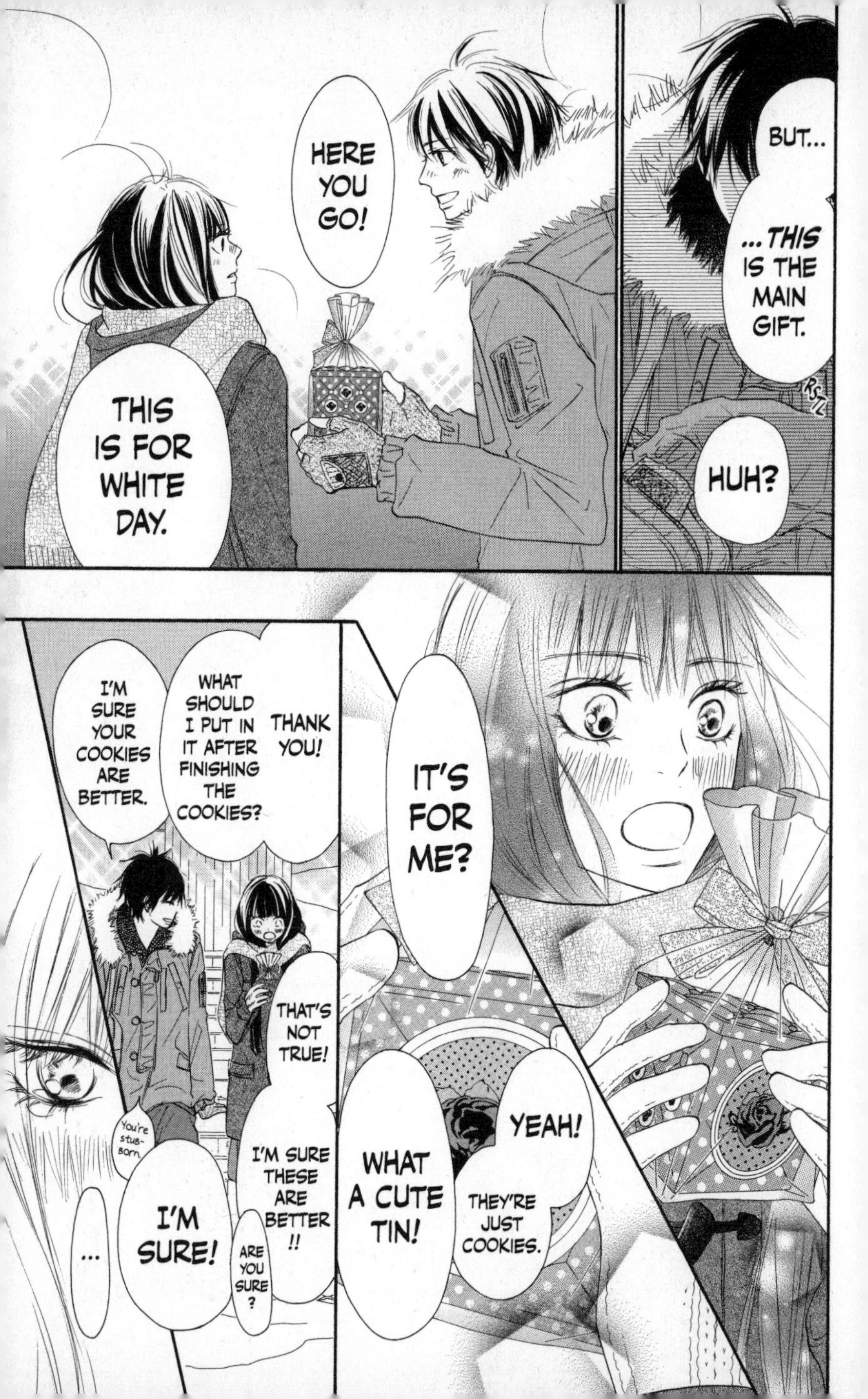
BUT...
...THIS IS THE MAIN GIFT.
RSTL
HUH?
HERE YOU GO!
THIS IS FOR WHITE DAY.
IT'S FOR ME?
YEAH!
WHAT A CUTE TIN!
THEY'RE JUST COOKIES.
THANK YOU!
WHAT SHOULD I PUT IN IT AFTER FINISHING THE COOKIES?
I'M SURE YOUR COOKIES ARE BETTER.
THAT'S NOT TRUE!
I'M SURE THESE ARE BETTER!!
You're stub-born.
ARE YOU SURE?
I'M SURE!
...

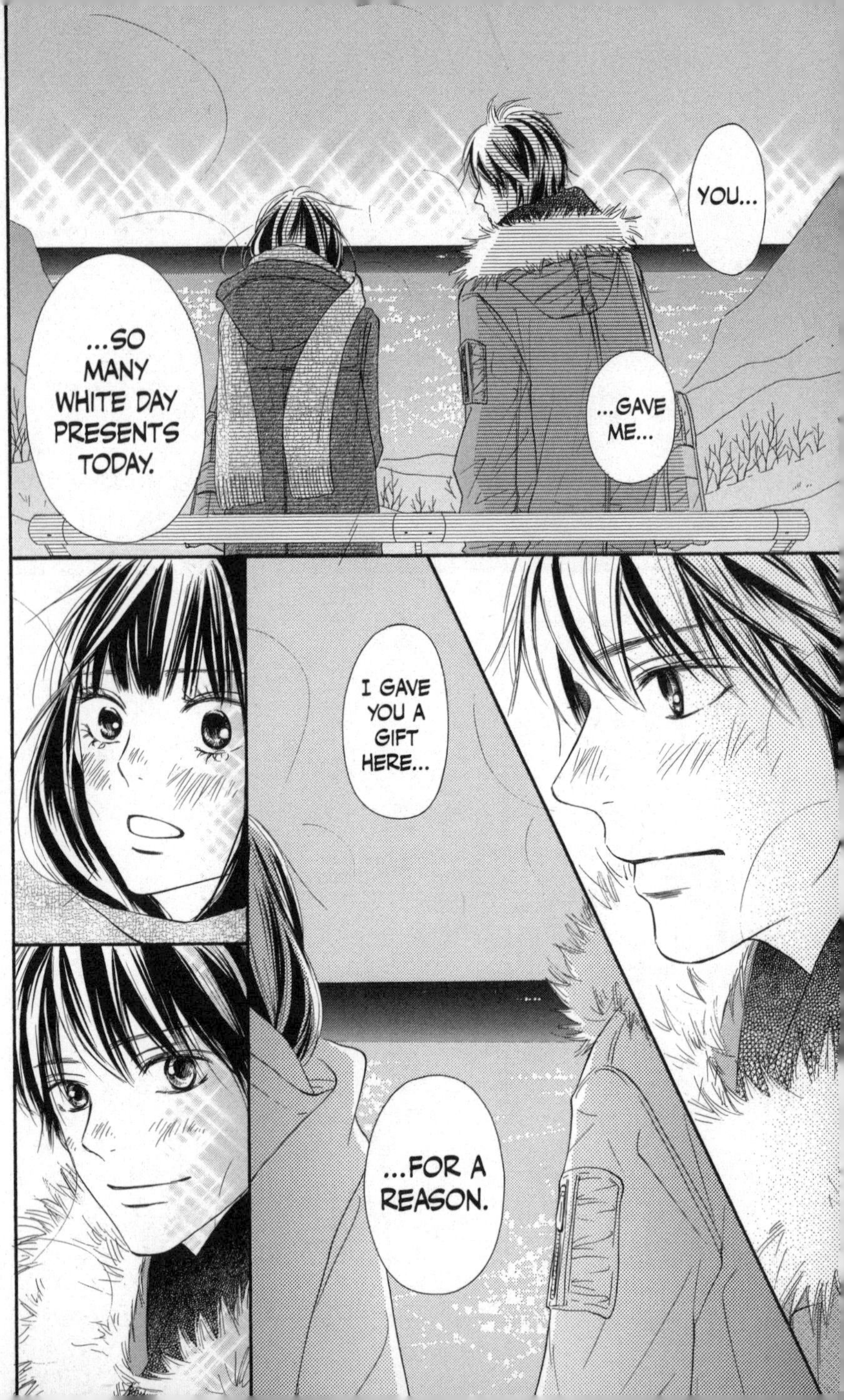
YOU...
...GAVE ME...
...SO MANY WHITE DAY PRESENTS TODAY.
I GAVE YOU A GIFT HERE...
...FOR A REASON.

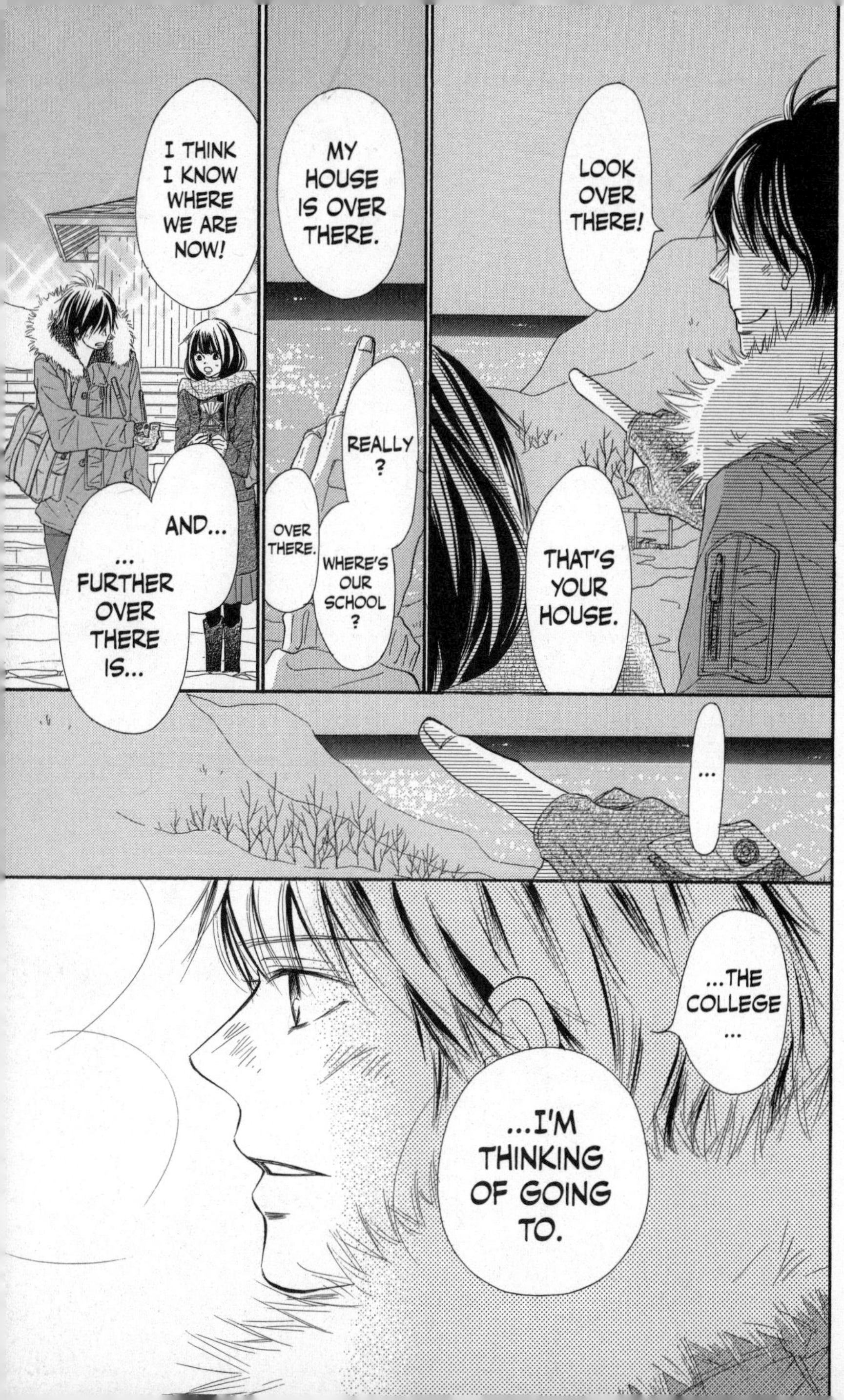
LOOK OVER THERE!
THAT'S YOUR HOUSE.
MY HOUSE IS OVER THERE.
REALLY?
WHERE'S OUR SCHOOL?
OVER THERE.
I THINK I KNOW WHERE WE ARE NOW!
AND...
... FURTHER OVER THERE IS...
...
...THE COLLEGE...
...I'M THINKING OF GOING TO.

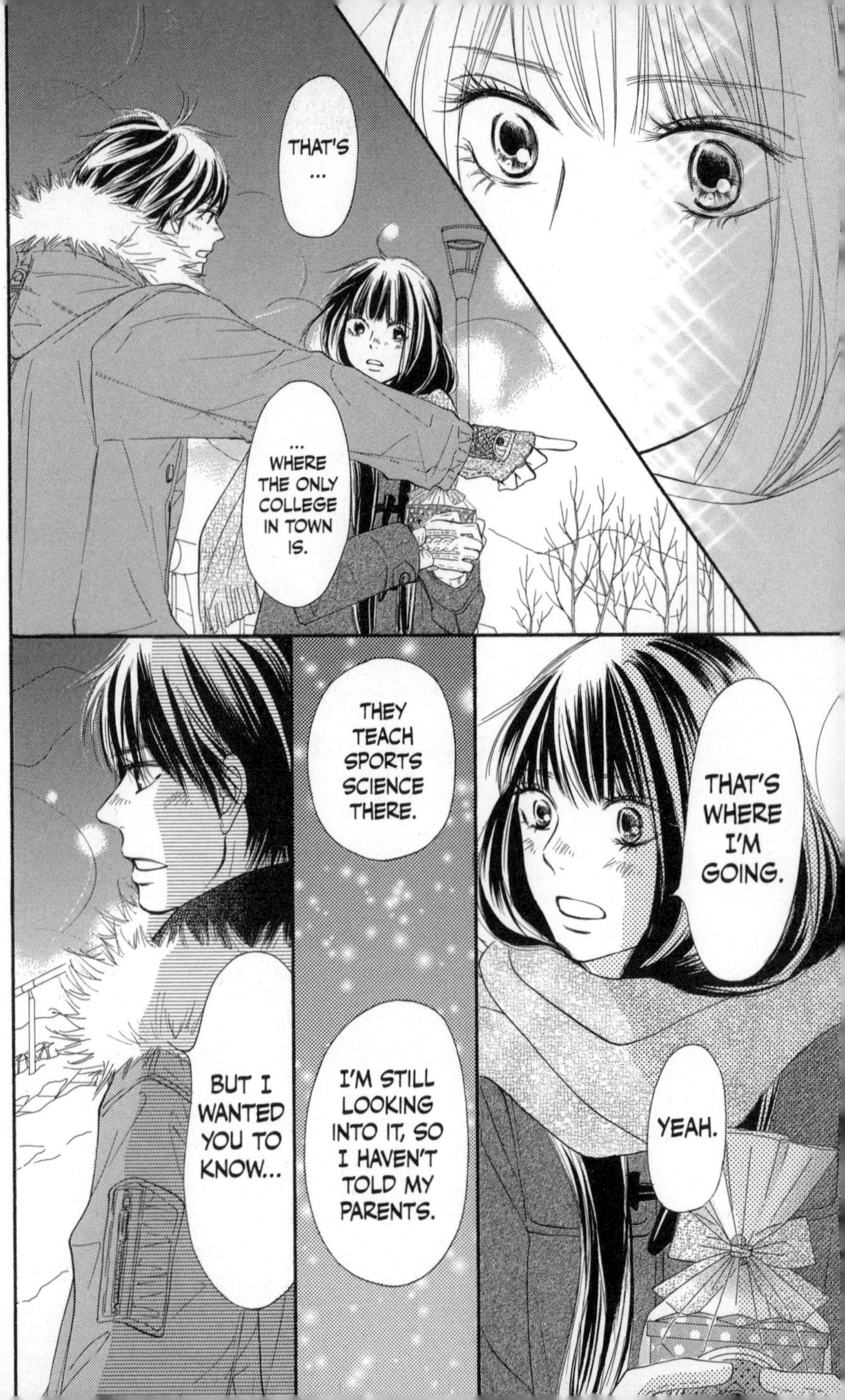
THAT'S ...
... WHERE THE ONLY COLLEGE IN TOWN IS.
THAT'S WHERE I'M GOING.
YEAH.
THEY TEACH SPORTS SCIENCE THERE.
I'M STILL LOOKING INTO IT, SO I HAVEN'T TOLD MY PARENTS.
BUT I WANTED YOU TO KNOW...

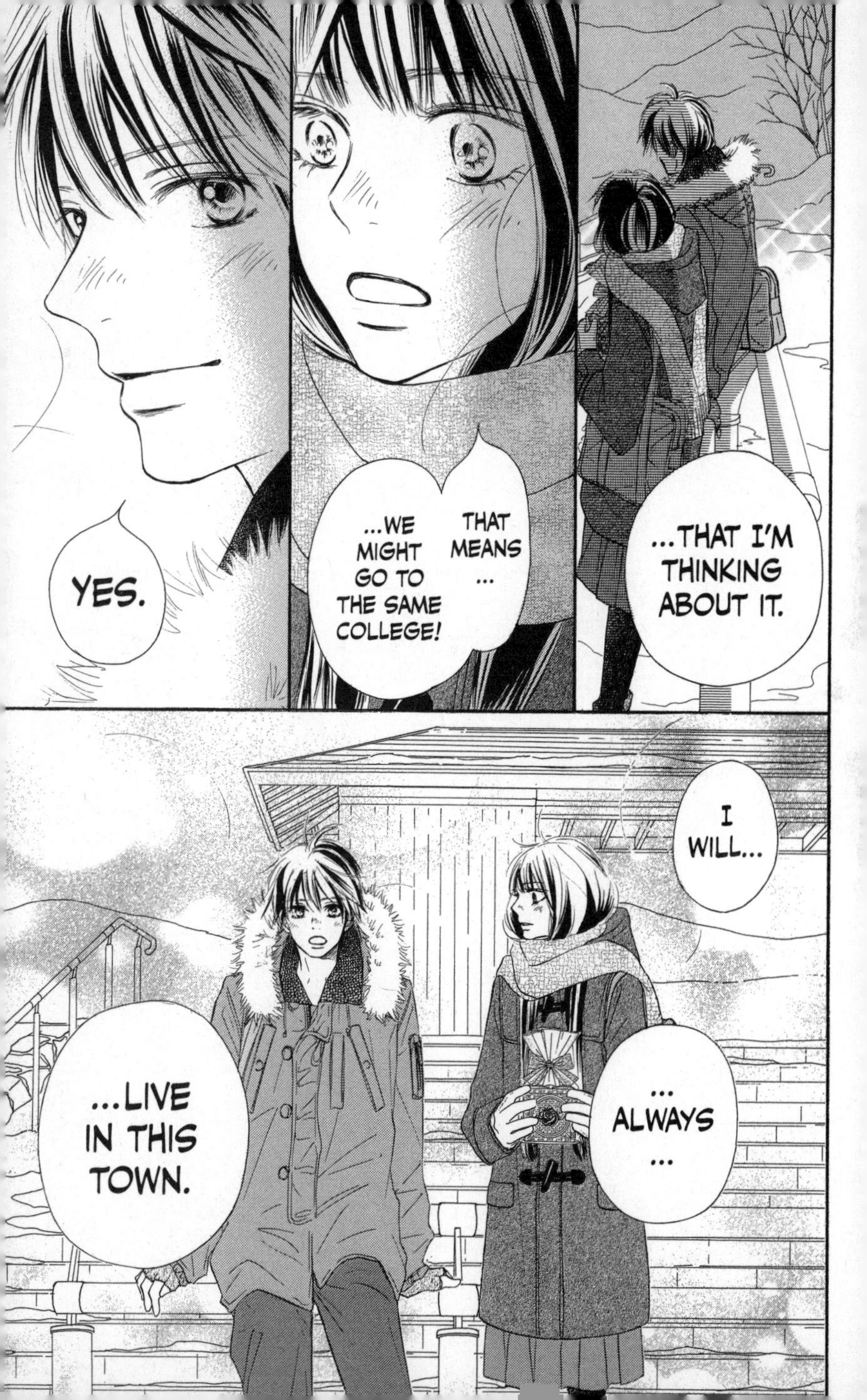
...THAT I'M THINKING ABOUT IT.
THAT MEANS ...
...WE MIGHT GO TO THE SAME COLLEGE!
YES.
I WILL...
... ALWAYS ...
...LIVE IN THIS TOWN.

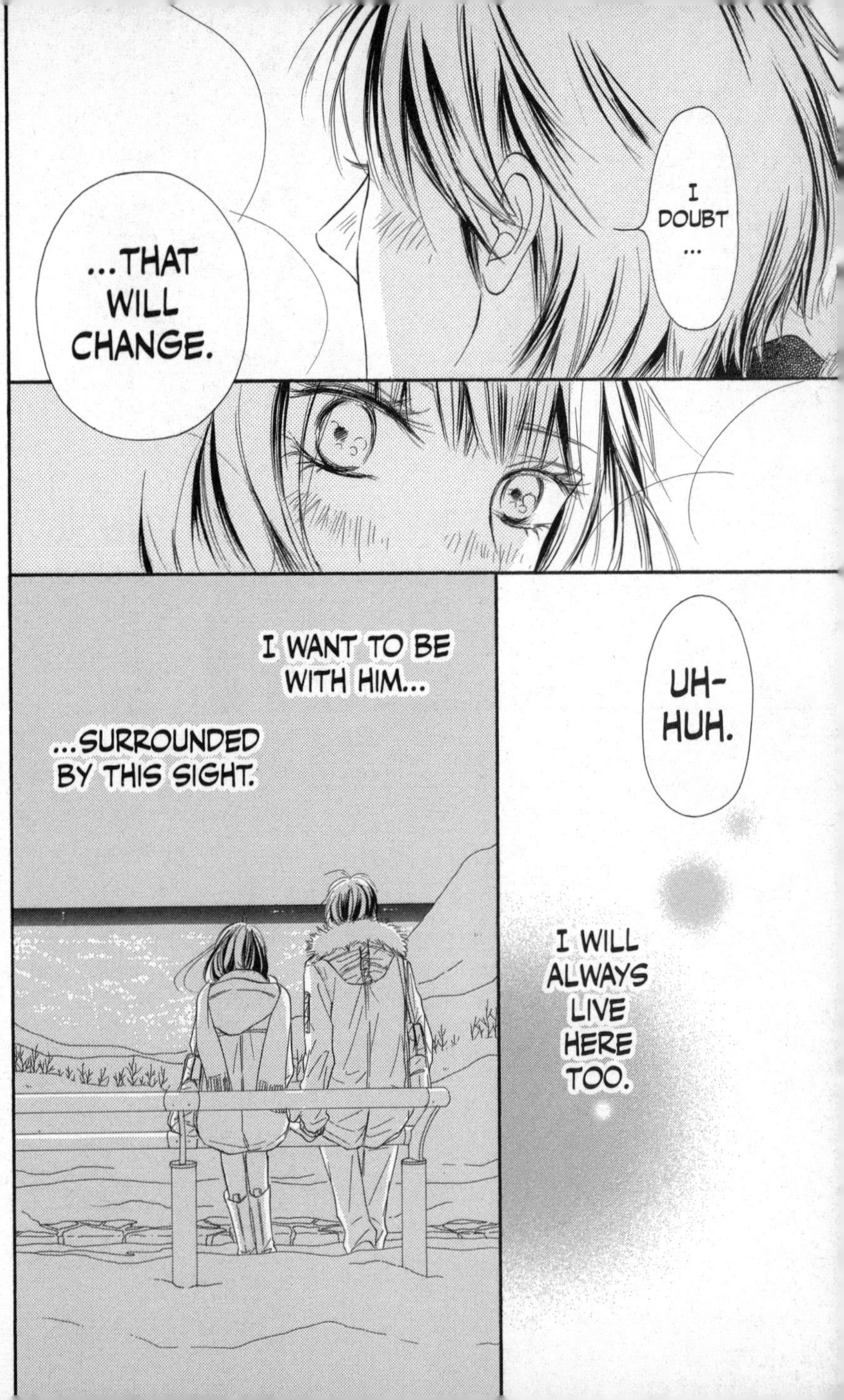
I DOUBT...
...THAT WILL CHANGE.
UH-HUH.
I WILL ALWAYS LIVE HERE TOO.
I WANT TO BE WITH HIM...
...SURROUNDED BY THIS SIGHT.

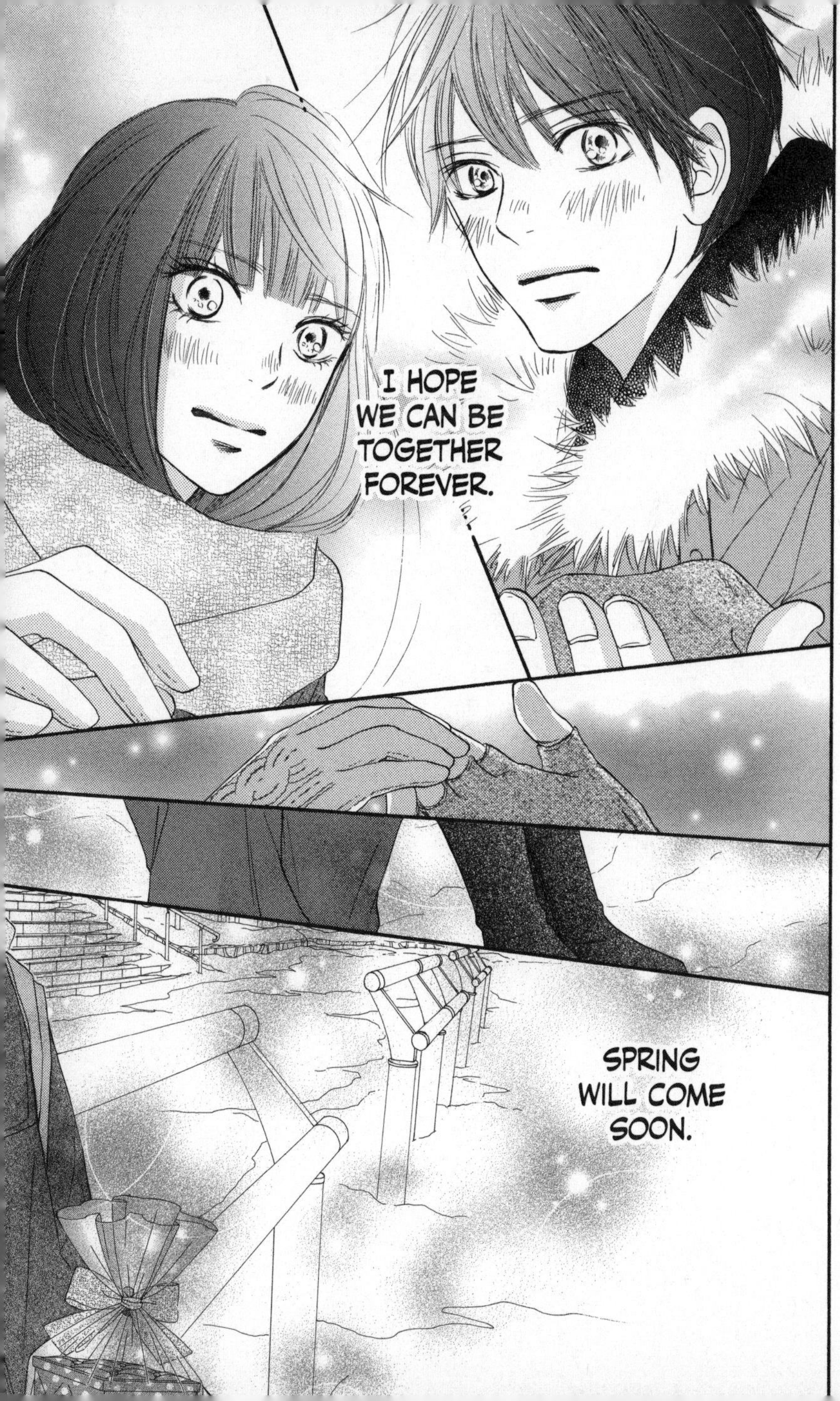
I HOPE WE CAN BE TOGETHER FOREVER.
SPRING WILL COME SOON.

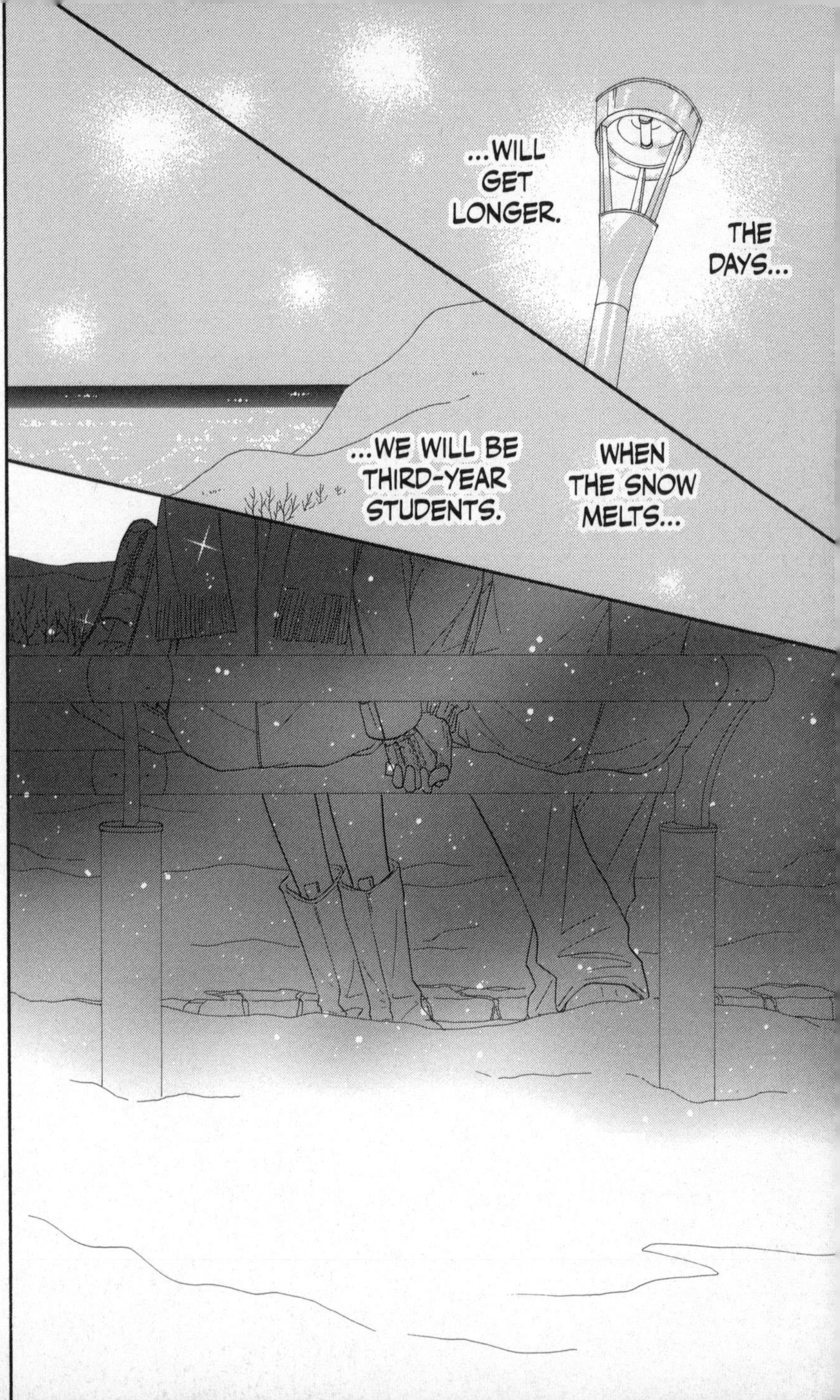
THE DAYS...
...WILL GET LONGER.
WHEN THE SNOW MELTS...
...WE WILL BE THIRD-YEAR STUDENTS.

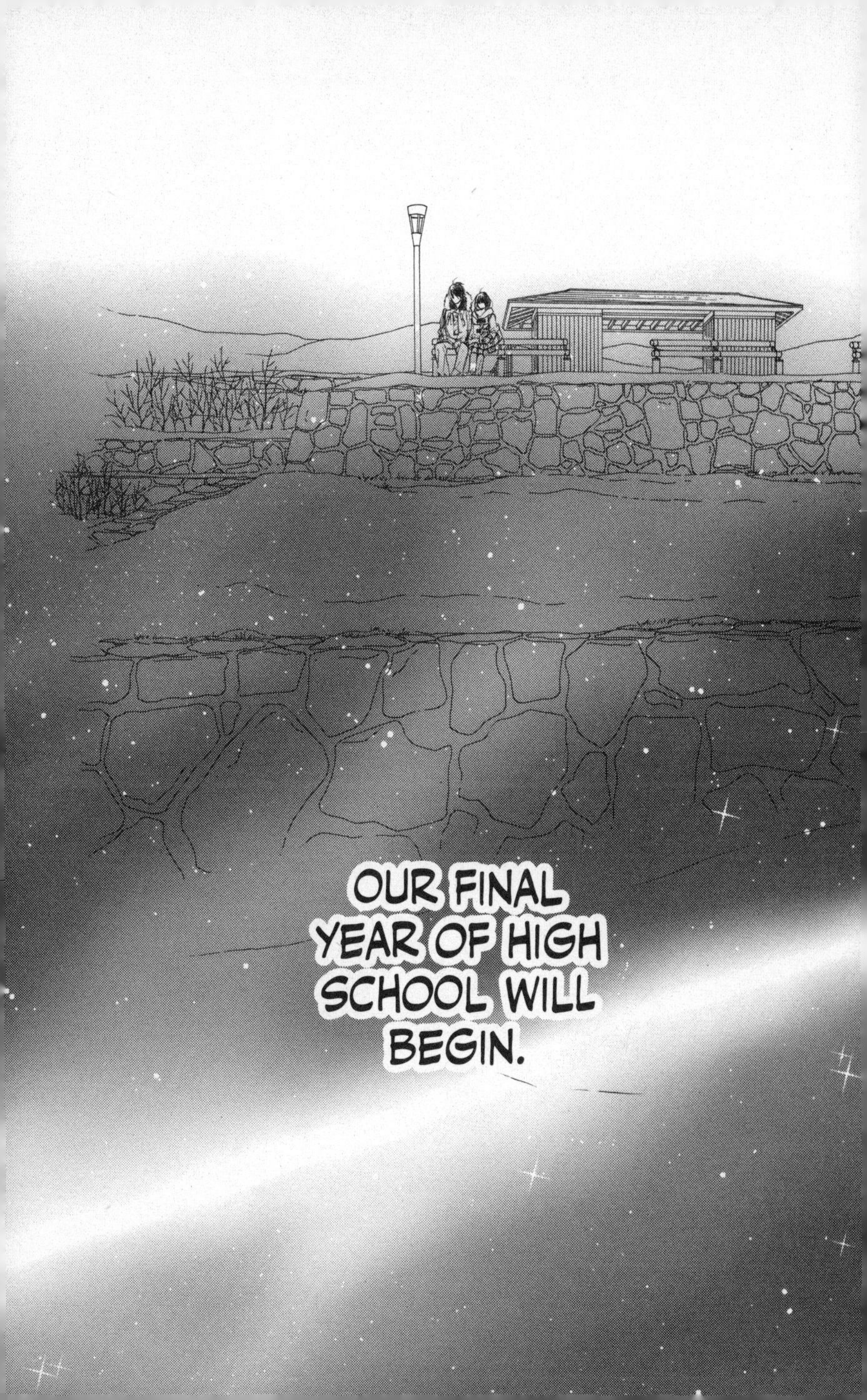
OUR FINAL YEAR OF HIGH SCHOOL WILL BEGIN.

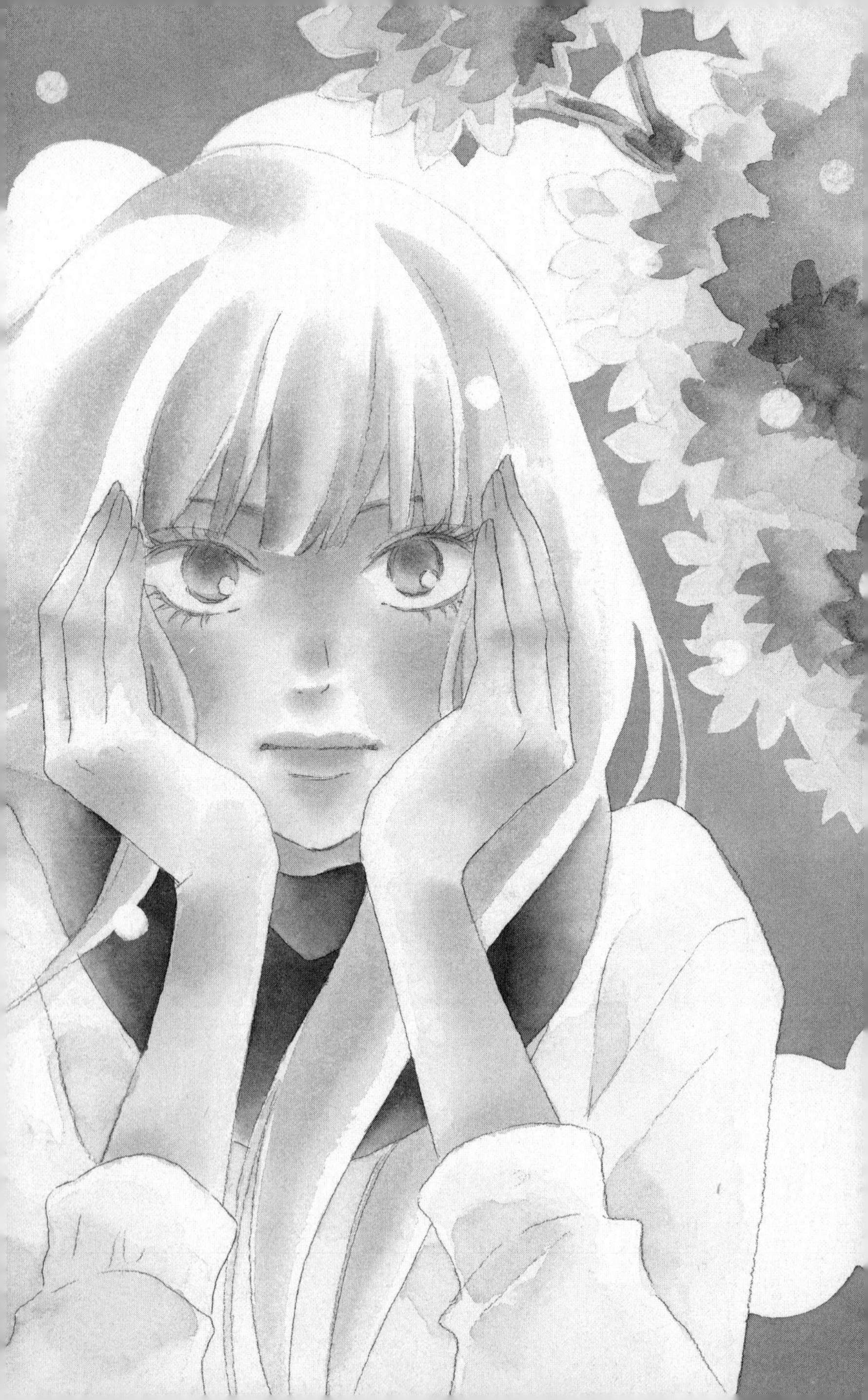

Episode 85: Final Year

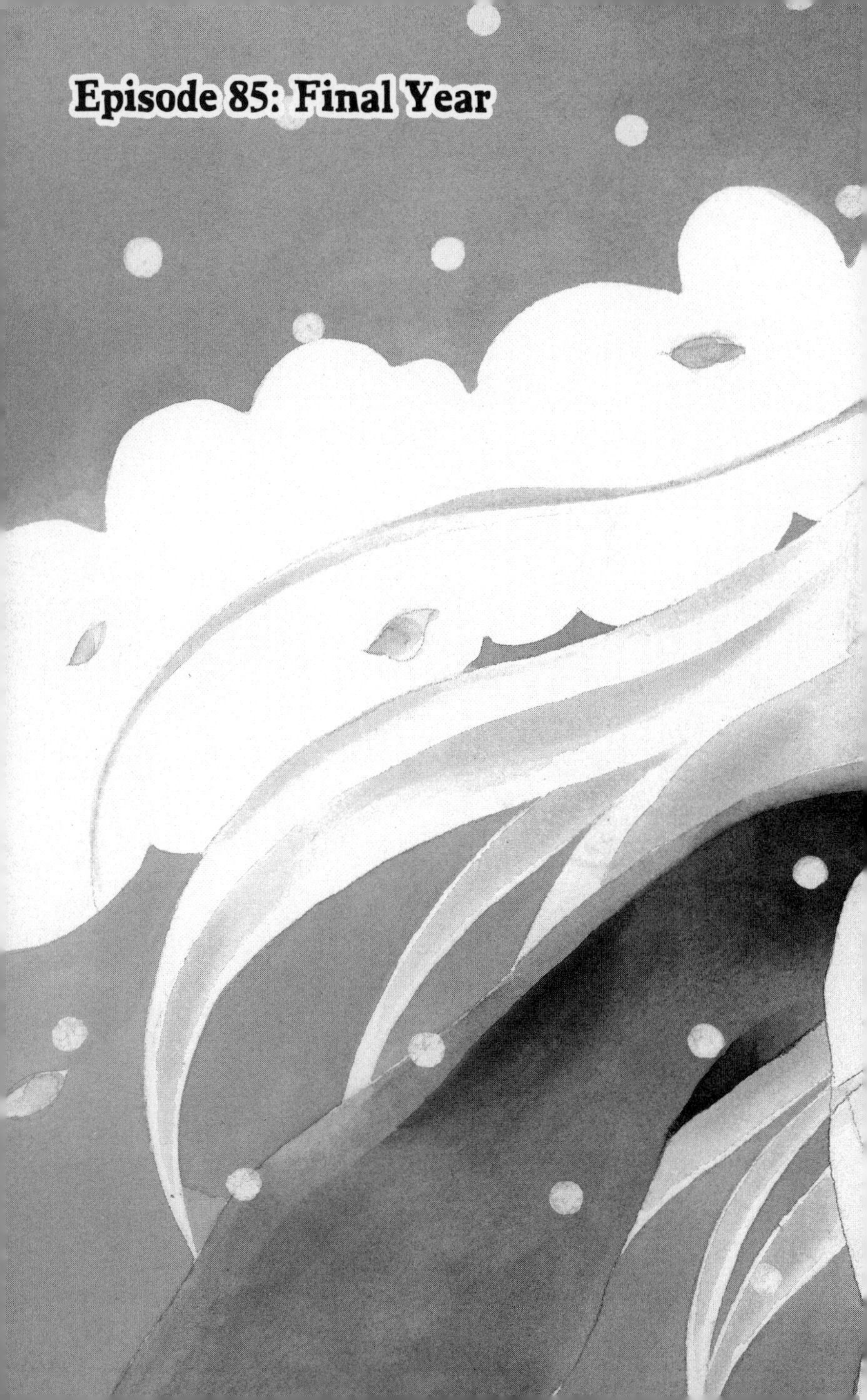

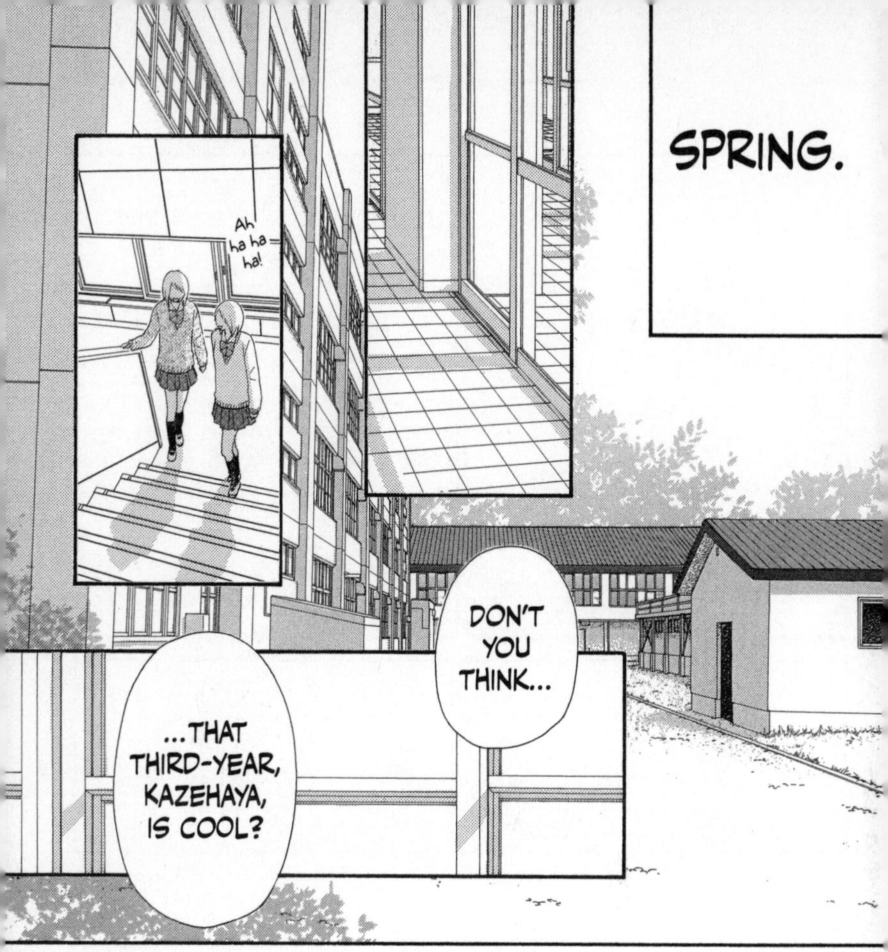
SPRING.
Ah ha ha ha!
DON'T YOU THINK...
...THAT THIRD-YEAR, KAZEHAYA, IS COOL?

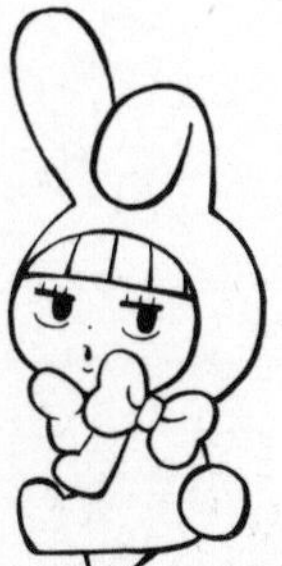

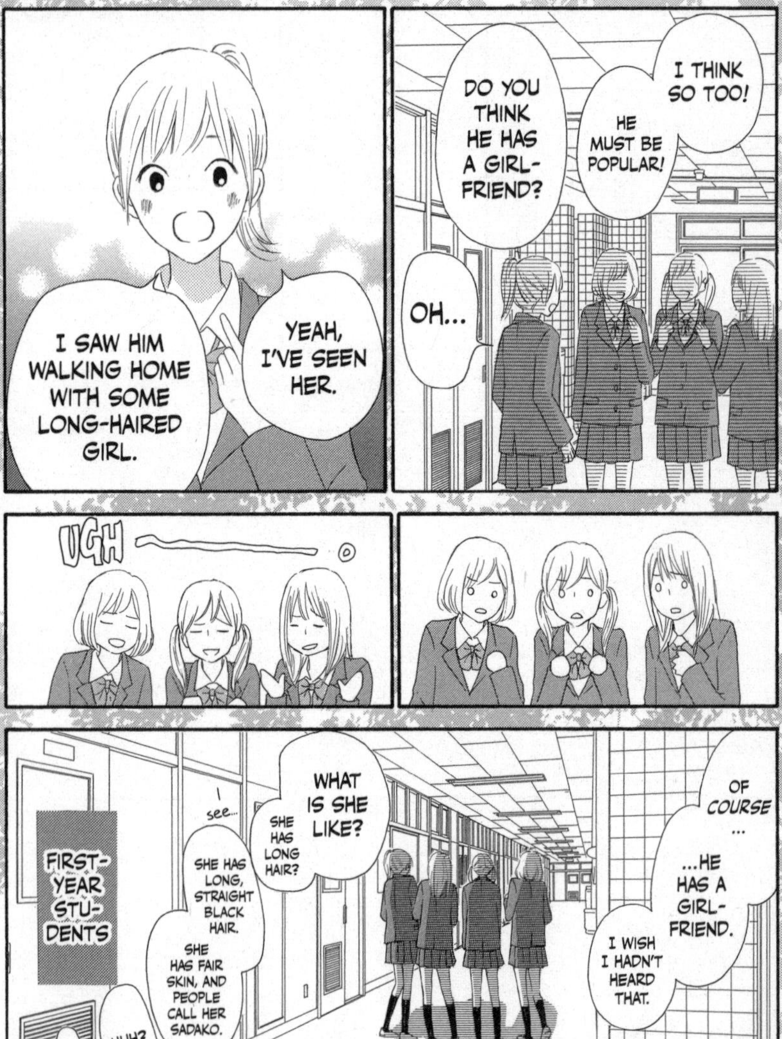
I THINK SO TOO!
HE MUST BE POPULAR!
DO YOU THINK HE HAS A GIRL-FRIEND?
OH...
YEAH, I'VE SEEN HER.
I SAW HIM WALKING HOME WITH SOME LONG-HAIRED GIRL.
UGH
OF COURSE...
...HE HAS A GIRL-FRIEND.
I WISH I HADN'T HEARD THAT.
WHAT IS SHE LIKE?
SHE HAS LONG HAIR?
I see...
FIRST-YEAR STU-DENTS
SHE HAS LONG, STRAIGHT BLACK HAIR.
SHE HAS FAIR SKIN, AND PEOPLE CALL HER SADAKO.
HUH? SADAKO?!
IS SHE PRETTY?

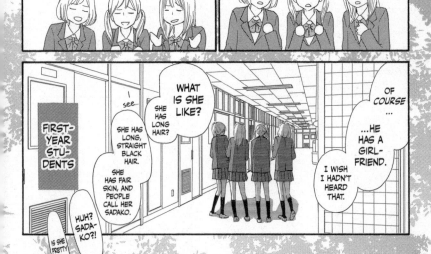

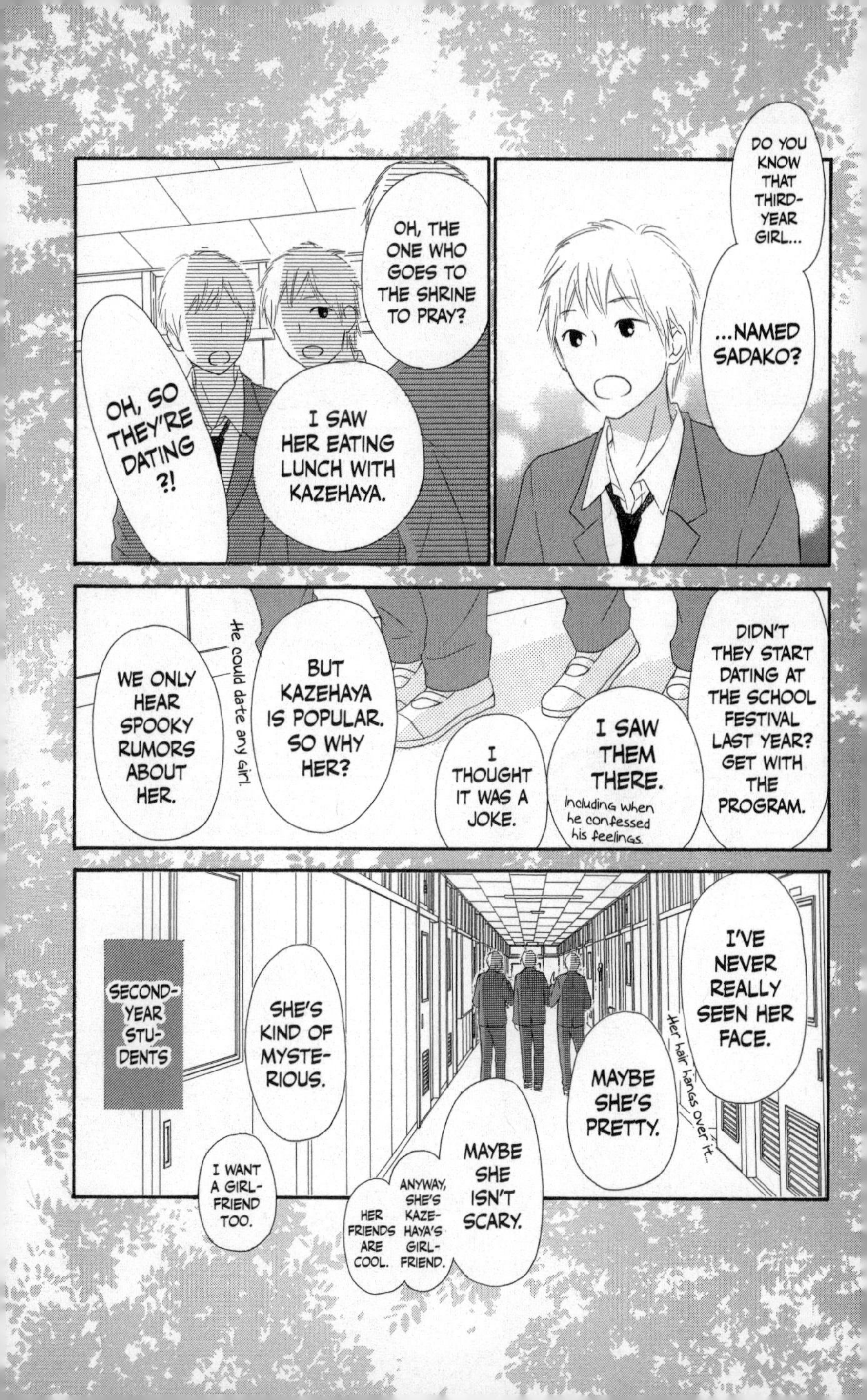
DO YOU KNOW THAT THIRD-YEAR GIRL...
...NAMED SADAKO?
OH, THE ONE WHO GOES TO THE SHRINE TO PRAY?
I SAW HER EATING LUNCH WITH KAZEHAYA.
OH, SO THEY'RE DATING?!
DIDN'T THEY START DATING AT THE SCHOOL FESTIVAL LAST YEAR? GET WITH THE PROGRAM.
I SAW THEM THERE.
Including when he confessed his feelings.
I THOUGHT IT WAS A JOKE.
BUT KAZEHAYA IS POPULAR. SO WHY HER?
He could date any girl.
WE ONLY HEAR SPOOKY RUMORS ABOUT HER.
I'VE NEVER REALLY SEEN HER FACE.
Her hair hangs over it...
MAYBE SHE'S PRETTY.
MAYBE SHE ISN'T SCARY.
ANYWAY, SHE'S KAZE-HAYA'S GIRL-FRIEND.
HER FRIENDS ARE COOL.
SHE'S KIND OF MYSTE-RIOUS.
I WANT A GIRL-FRIEND TOO.
SECOND-YEAR STU-DENTS

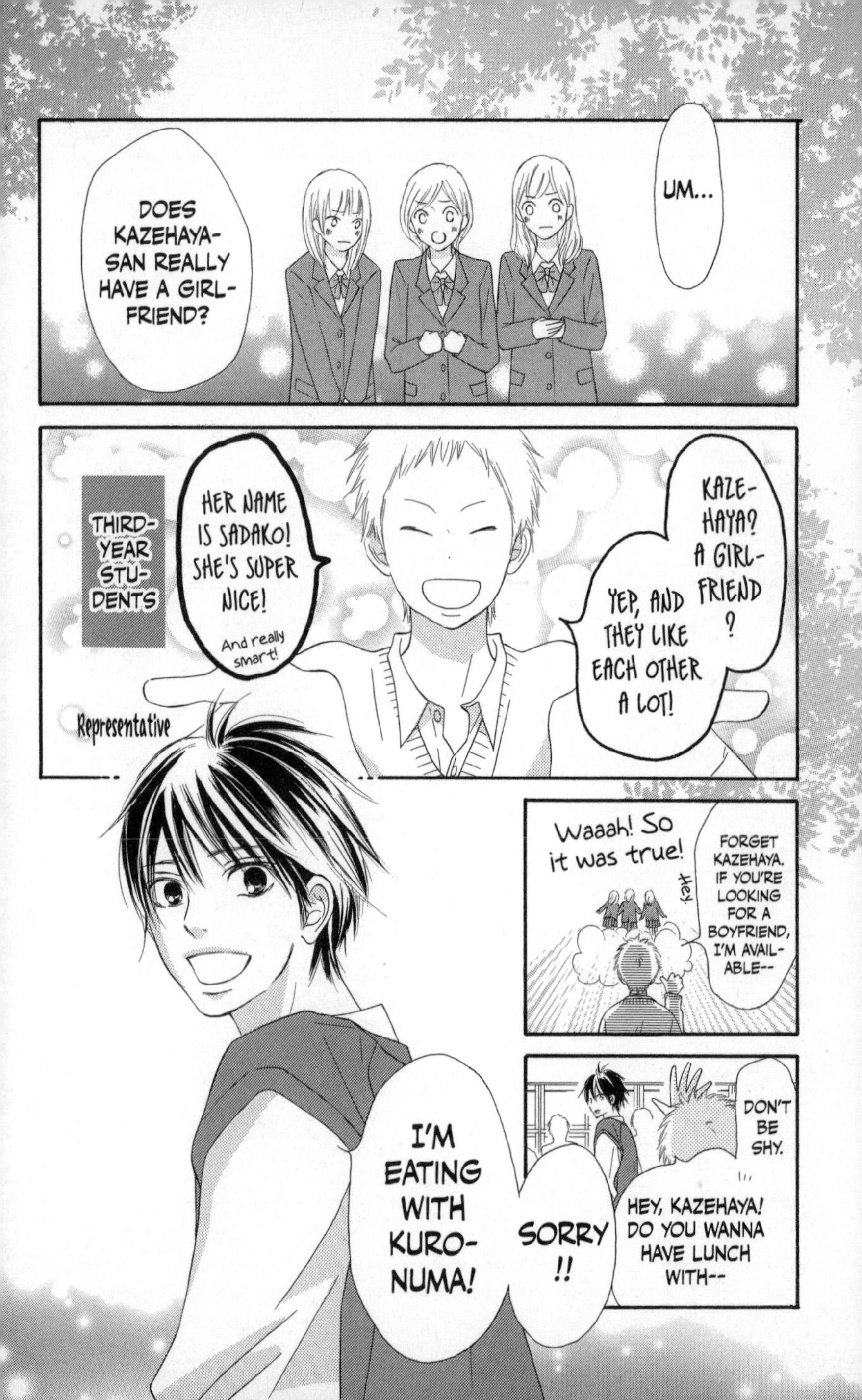
UM...
DOES KAZEHAYA-SAN REALLY HAVE A GIRLFRIEND?
KAZEHAYA? A GIRLFRIEND?
YEP, AND THEY LIKE EACH OTHER A LOT!
HER NAME IS SADAKO! SHE'S SUPER NICE!
And really smart!
THIRD-YEAR STUDENTS
Representative
FORGET KAZEHAYA. IF YOU'RE LOOKING FOR A BOYFRIEND, I'M AVAILABLE--
Hey.
Waaah! So it was true!
DON'T BE SHY.
HEY, KAZEHAYA! DO YOU WANNA HAVE LUNCH WITH--
SORRY!!
I'M EATING WITH KURONUMA!

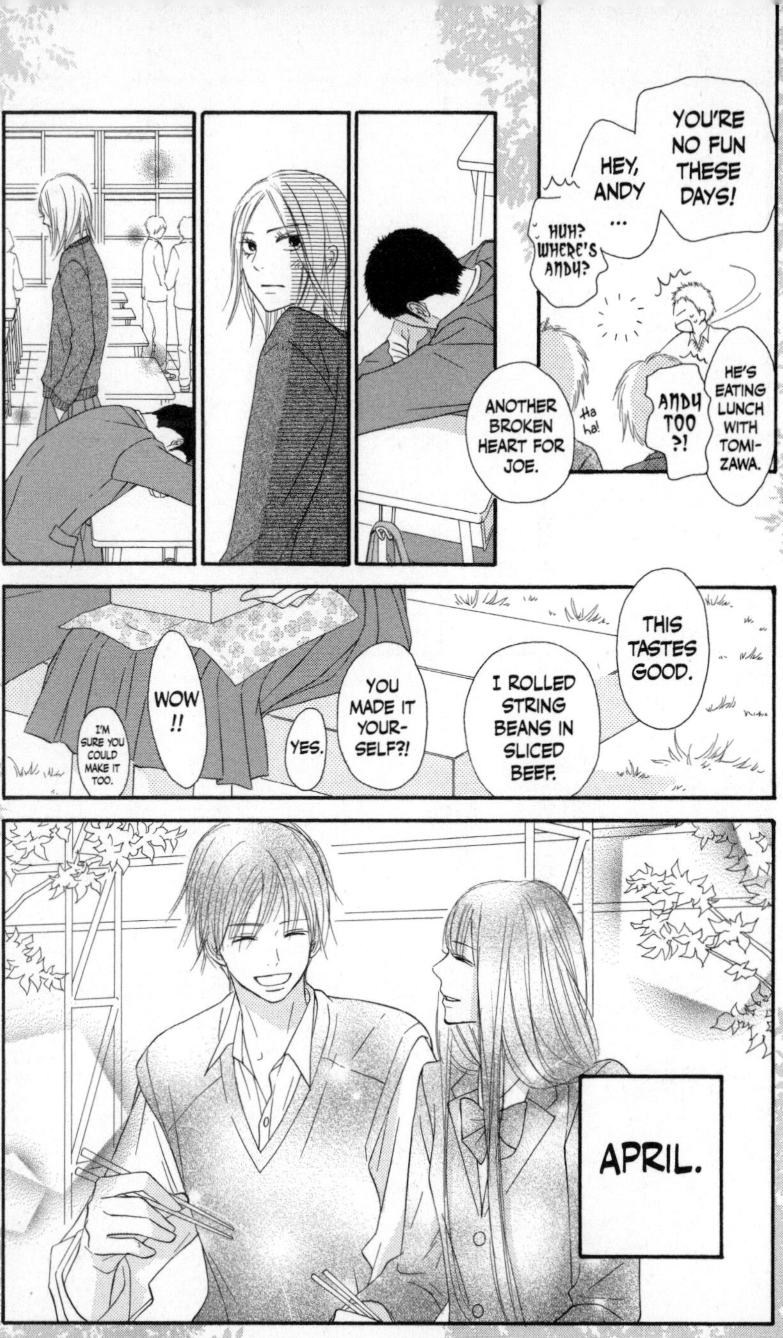
YOU'RE NO FUN THESE DAYS!
HEY, ANDY ...
HUH? WHERE'S ANDY?
HE'S EATING LUNCH WITH TOMI-ZAWA.
ANDY TOO ?!
Ha ha!
ANOTHER BROKEN HEART FOR JOE.
THIS TASTES GOOD.
I ROLLED STRING BEANS IN SLICED BEEF.
YOU MADE IT YOUR-SELF?!
YES.
WOW !!
I'M SURE YOU COULD MAKE IT TOO.
APRIL.

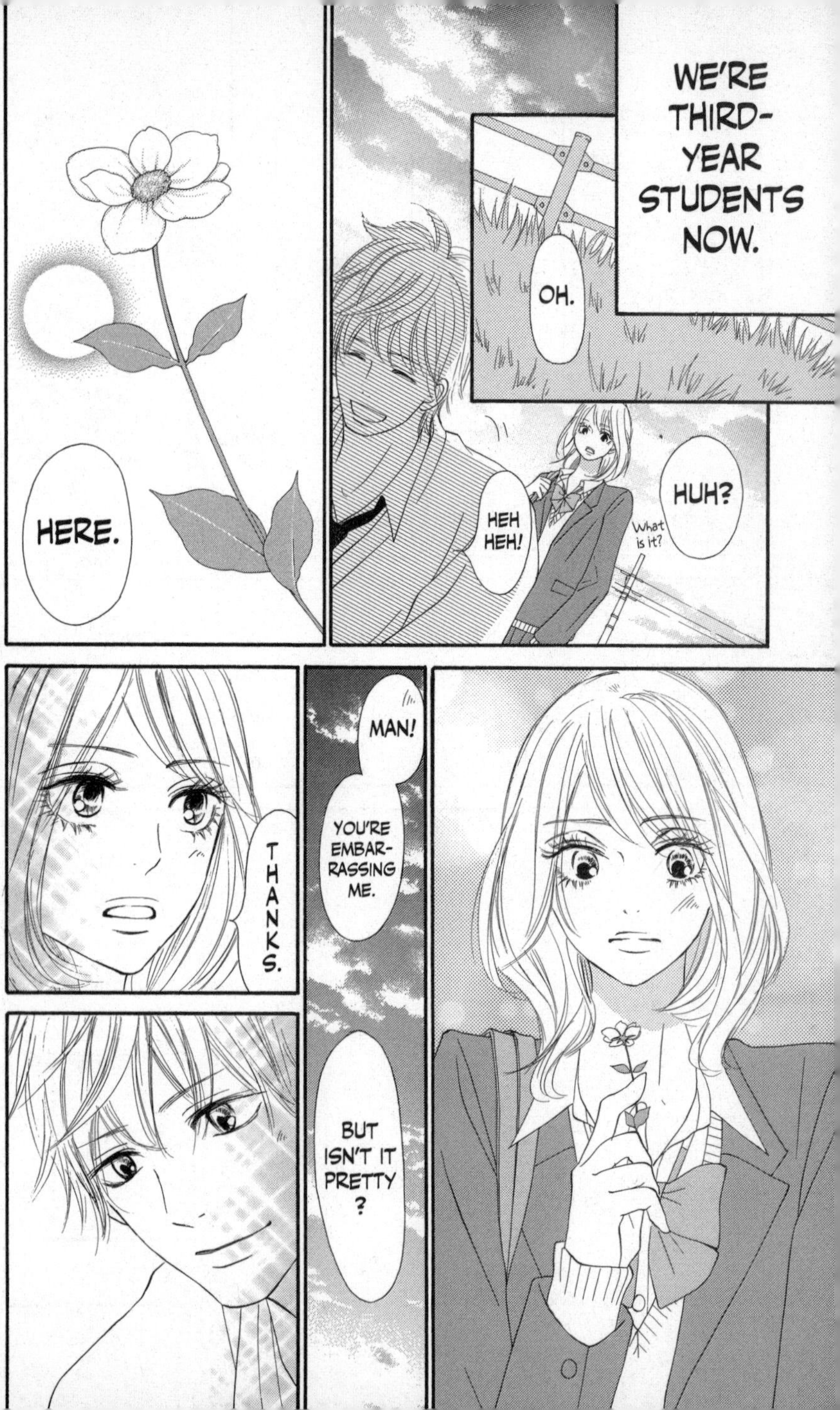
WE'RE THIRD-YEAR STUDENTS NOW.
OH.
HUH?
What is it?
HEH HEH!
HERE.
MAN!
YOU'RE EMBARRASSING ME.
BUT ISN'T IT PRETTY?
THANKS.

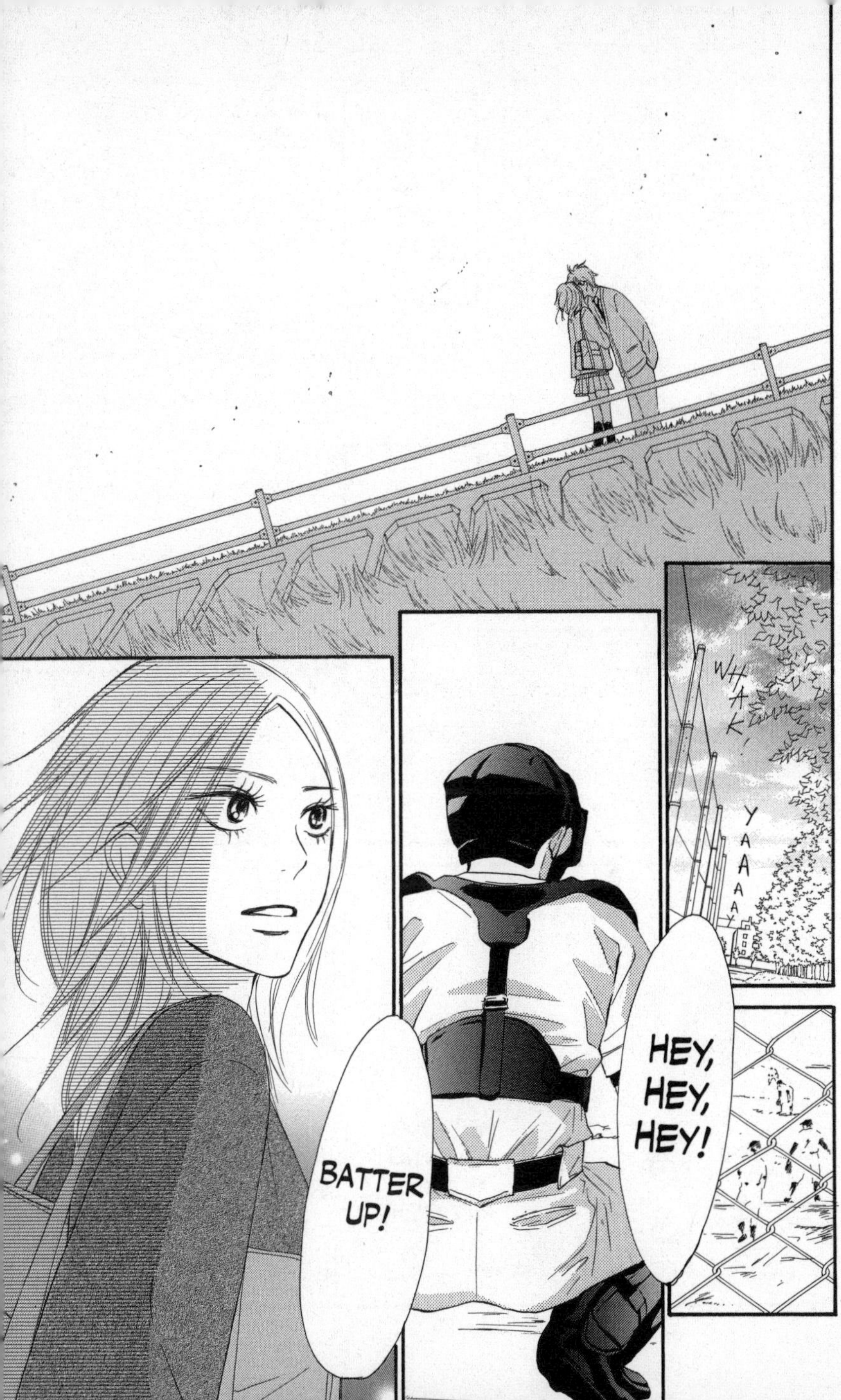
WHAK
YAAAAAY
HEY, HEY, HEY!
BATTER UP!

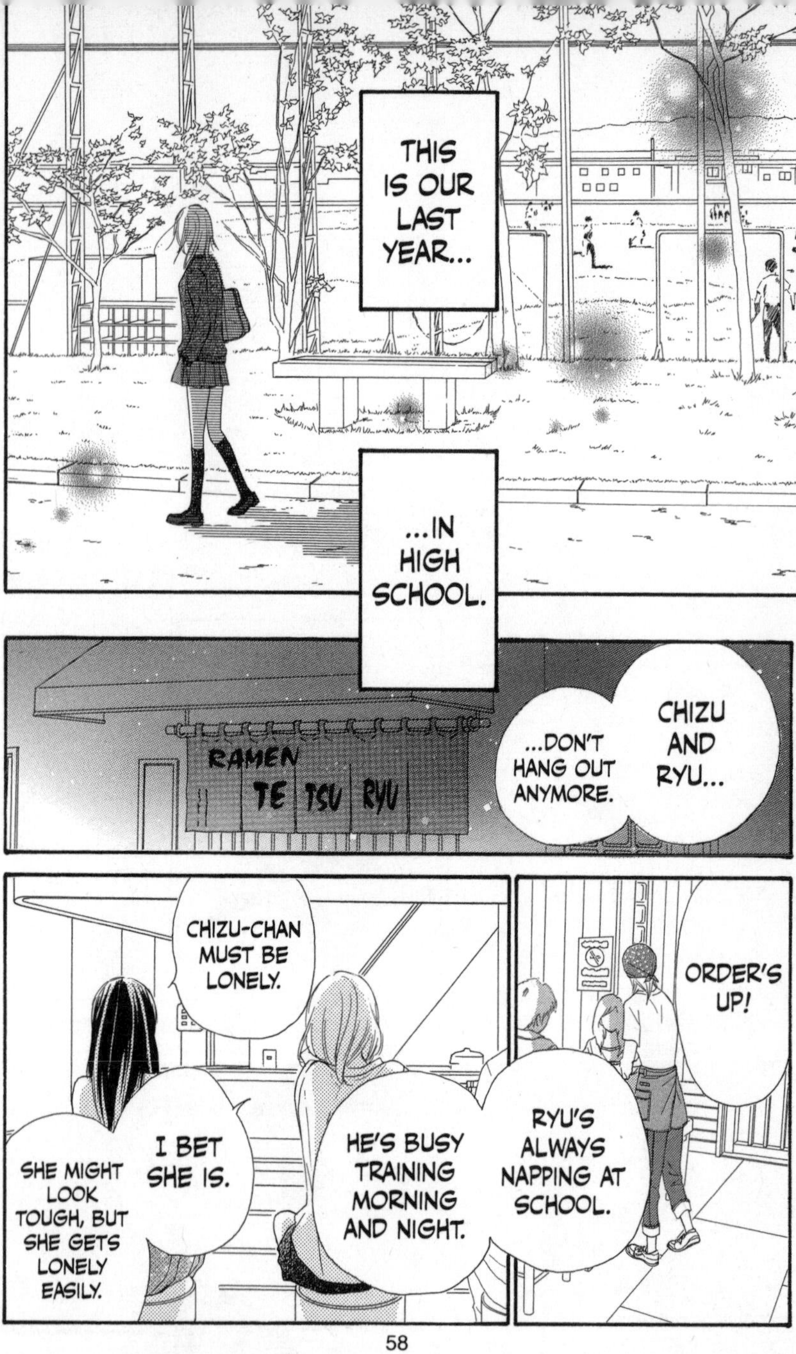

THIS IS OUR LAST YEAR...
...IN HIGH SCHOOL.
CHIZU AND RYU...
...DON'T HANG OUT ANYMORE.
RAMEN TE TSU RYU
ORDER'S UP!
RYU'S ALWAYS NAPPING AT SCHOOL.
CHIZU-CHAN MUST BE LONELY.
HE'S BUSY TRAINING MORNING AND NIGHT.
I BET SHE IS.
SHE MIGHT LOOK TOUGH, BUT SHE GETS LONELY EASILY.

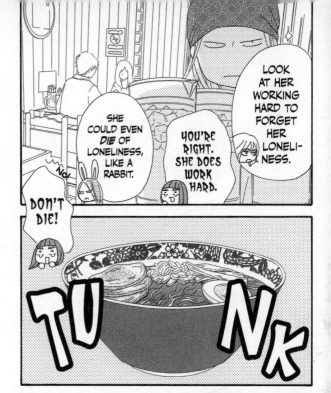

LOOK AT HER WORKING HARD TO FORGET HER LONELINESS.
YOU'RE RIGHT. SHE DOES WORK HARD.
SHE COULD EVEN *DIE* OF LONELINESS, LIKE A RABBIT.
No!
DON'T DIE!
TUNK
COULD YOU STOP TALKING ABOUT ME WHEN I'M RIGHT HERE, PLEASE?!
OH, THANKS!!
WHAT TIME DO YOU GET OFF TONIGHT?
NINE!!
I can hear you!
I'M NOT DYING!
I'M NOT LONELY!
WE'LL WAIT FOR YOU THEN.
Thanks for the meal!

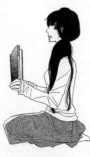

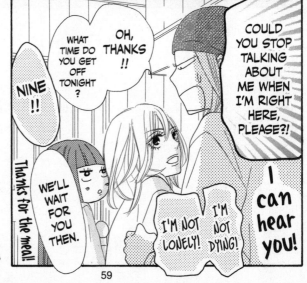

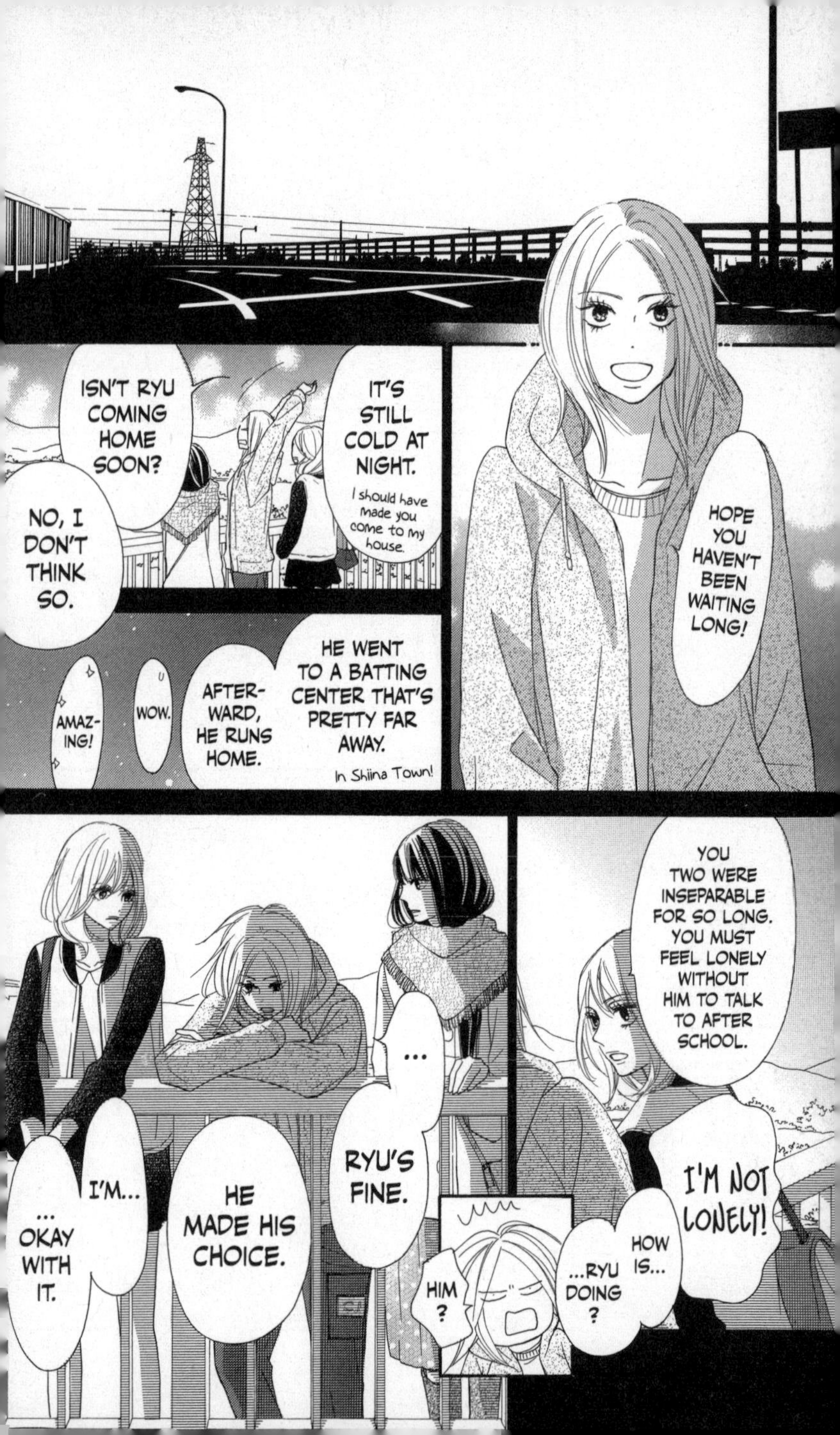
HOPE YOU HAVEN'T BEEN WAITING LONG!
IT'S STILL COLD AT NIGHT.
I should have made you come to my house.
ISN'T RYU COMING HOME SOON?
NO, I DON'T THINK SO.
HE WENT TO A BATTING CENTER THAT'S PRETTY FAR AWAY.
In Shiina Town!
AFTER-WARD, HE RUNS HOME.
WOW.
AMAZ-ING!
YOU TWO WERE INSEPARABLE FOR SO LONG. YOU MUST FEEL LONELY WITHOUT HIM TO TALK TO AFTER SCHOOL.
I'M NOT LONELY!
HOW IS...
...RYU DOING?
HIM?
...
RYU'S FINE.
HE MADE HIS CHOICE.
I'M...
...OKAY WITH IT.

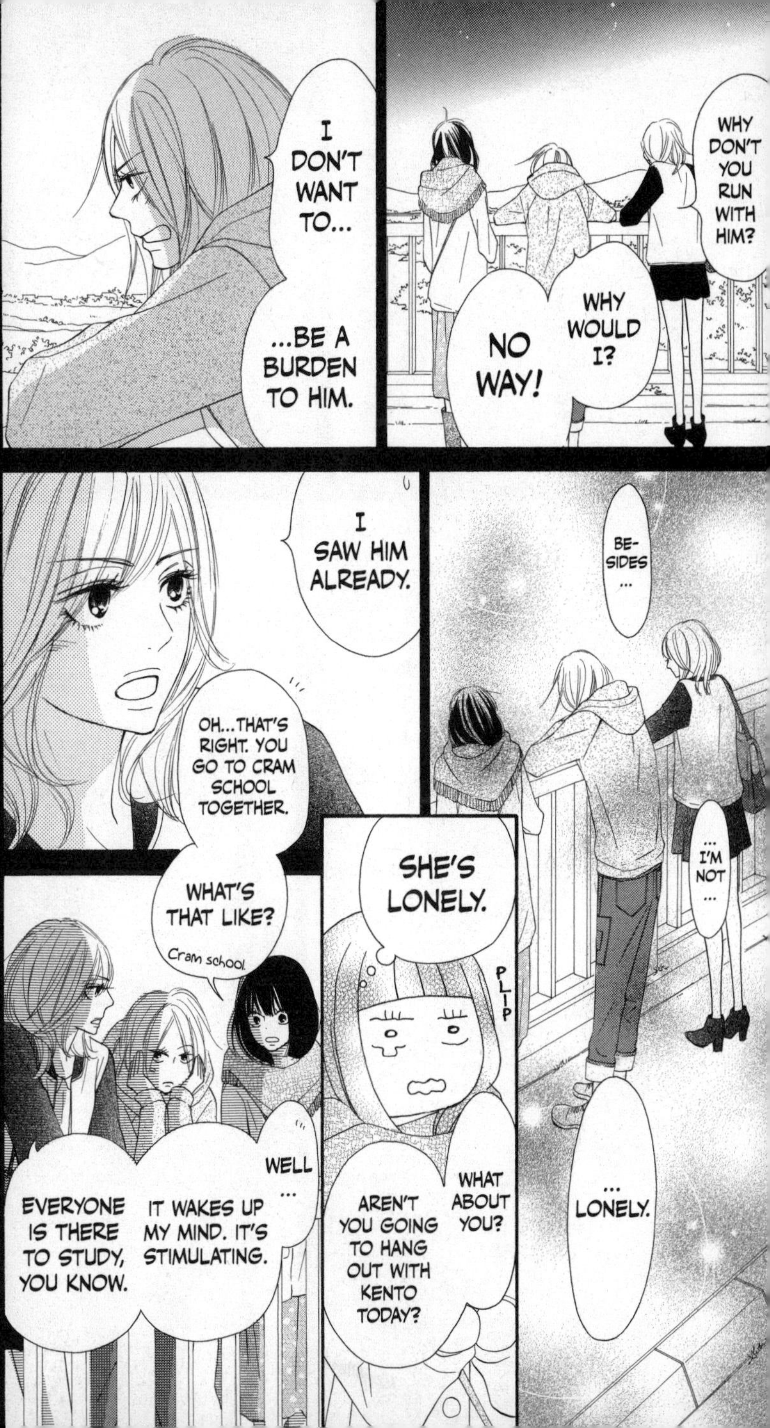
WHY DON'T YOU RUN WITH HIM?
WHY WOULD I?
NO WAY!
I DON'T WANT TO...
...BE A BURDEN TO HIM.
BESIDES...
...I'M NOT...
...LONELY.
I SAW HIM ALREADY.
OH...THAT'S RIGHT. YOU GO TO CRAM SCHOOL TOGETHER.
WHAT'S THAT LIKE?
Cram school.
SHE'S LONELY.
PLIP
WHAT ABOUT YOU?
AREN'T YOU GOING TO HANG OUT WITH KENTO TODAY?
WELL...
IT WAKES UP MY MIND. IT'S STIMULATING.
EVERYONE IS THERE TO STUDY, YOU KNOW.

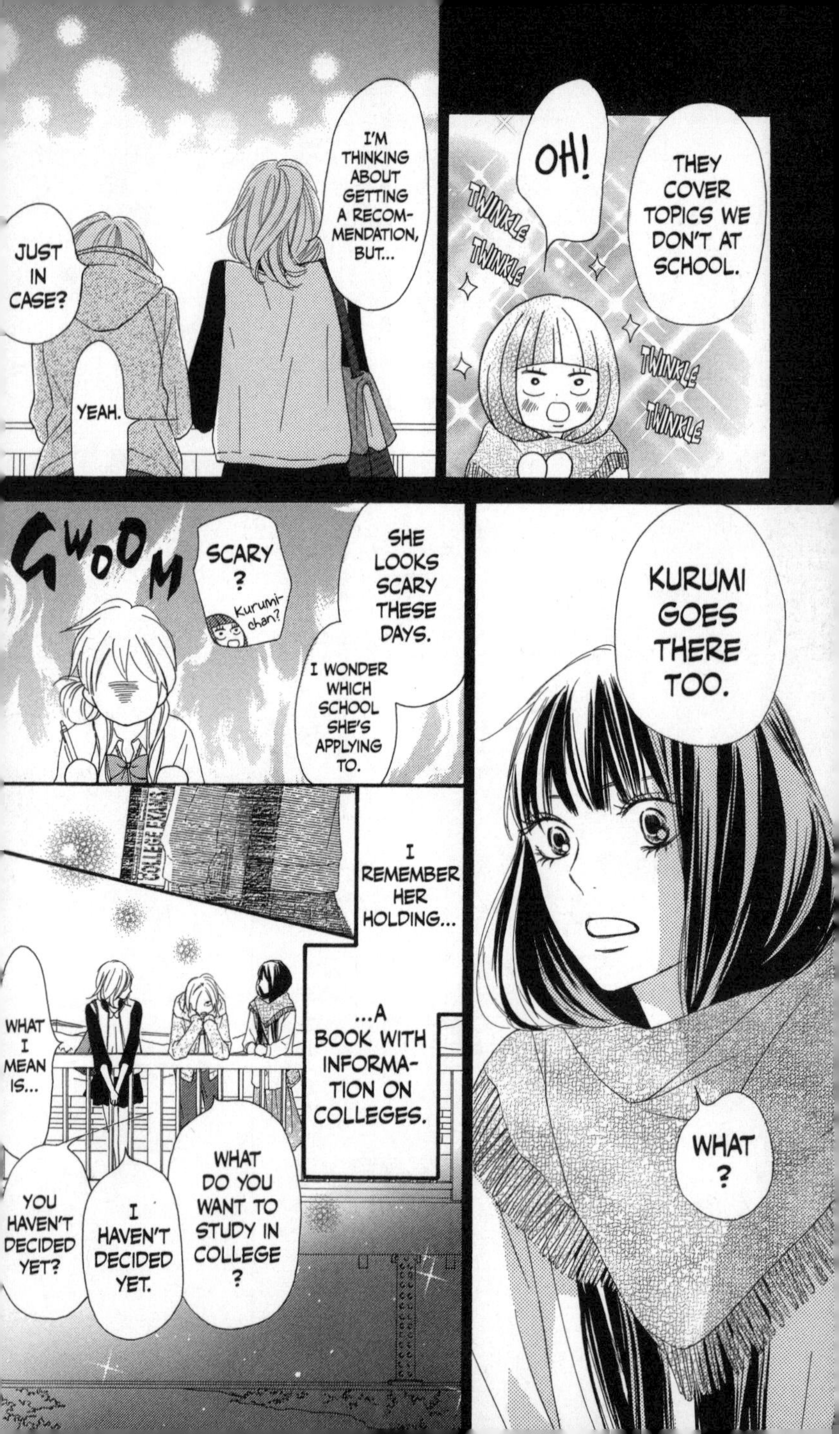
THEY COVER TOPICS WE DON'T AT SCHOOL.
OH!
TWINKLE TWINKLE
TWINKLE TWINKLE
I'M THINKING ABOUT GETTING A RECOM-MENDATION, BUT...
JUST IN CASE?
YEAH.
KURUMI GOES THERE TOO.
WHAT?
SHE LOOKS SCARY THESE DAYS.
I WONDER WHICH SCHOOL SHE'S APPLYING TO.
SCARY?
Kurumi-chan?
GWOOM
I REMEMBER HER HOLDING...
COLLEGE EXAMS
...A BOOK WITH INFORMA-TION ON COLLEGES.
WHAT DO YOU WANT TO STUDY IN COLLEGE?
I HAVEN'T DECIDED YET.
YOU HAVEN'T DECIDED YET?
WHAT I MEAN IS...

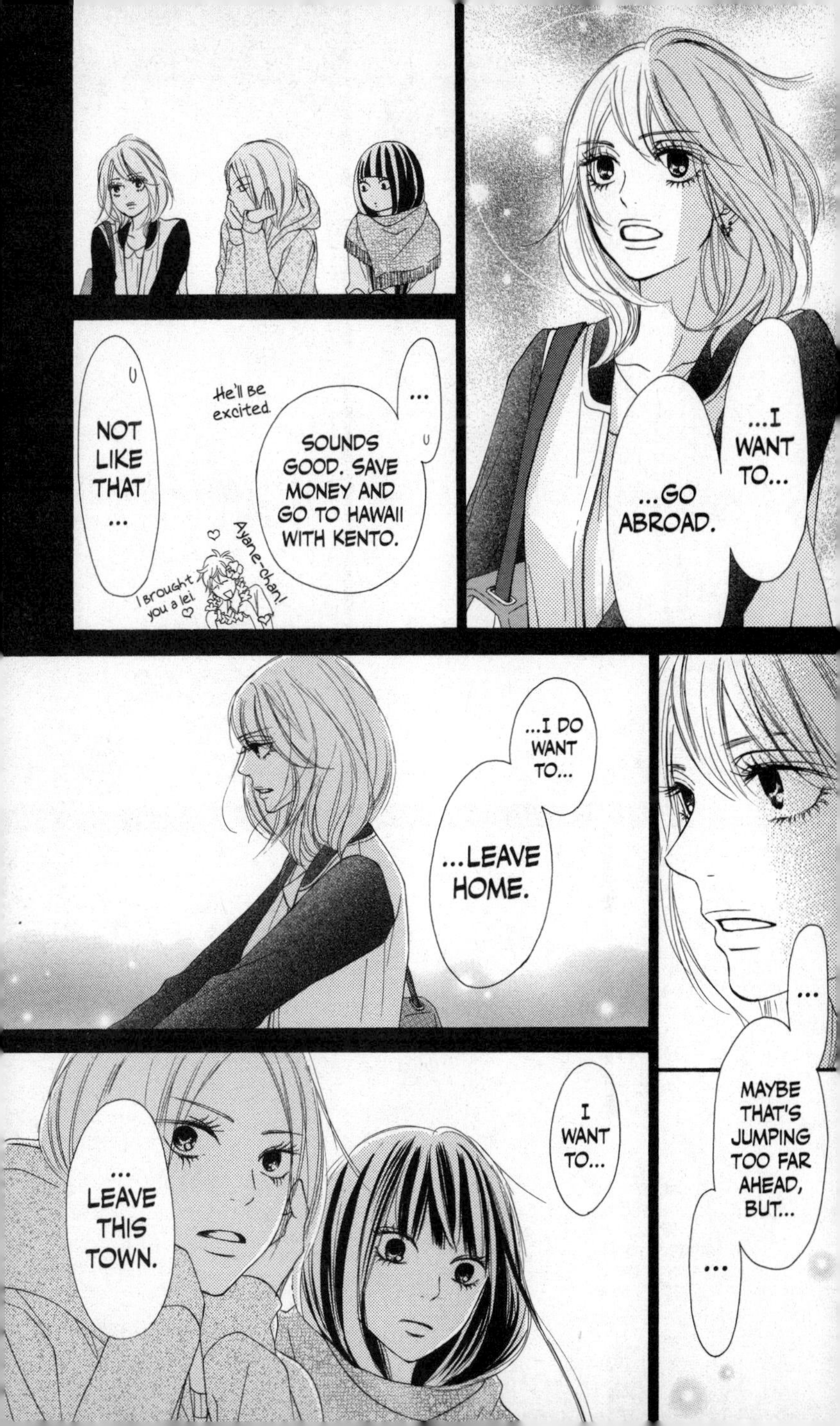
...I WANT TO...
...GO ABROAD.
...
SOUNDS GOOD. SAVE MONEY AND GO TO HAWAII WITH KENTO.
He'll be excited.
Ayane-chan!
I brought you a lei.
NOT LIKE THAT...
...
MAYBE THAT'S JUMPING TOO FAR AHEAD, BUT...
...
...I DO WANT TO...
...LEAVE HOME.
I WANT TO...
...LEAVE THIS TOWN.

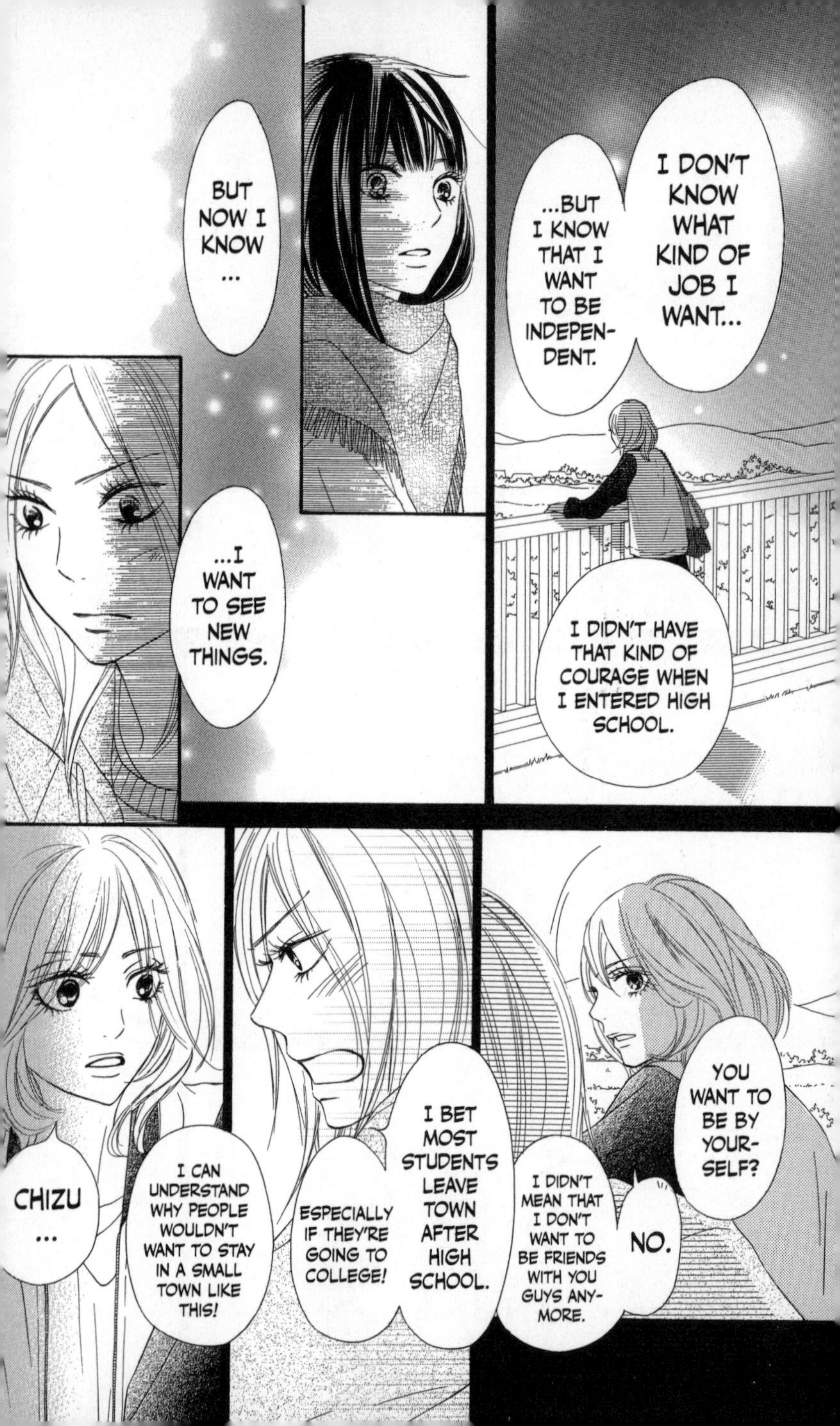
I DON'T KNOW WHAT KIND OF JOB I WANT...
...BUT I KNOW THAT I WANT TO BE INDEPENDENT.
I DIDN'T HAVE THAT KIND OF COURAGE WHEN I ENTERED HIGH SCHOOL.
BUT NOW I KNOW ...
...I WANT TO SEE NEW THINGS.
YOU WANT TO BE BY YOURSELF?
NO.
I DIDN'T MEAN THAT I DON'T WANT TO BE FRIENDS WITH YOU GUYS ANYMORE.
I BET MOST STUDENTS LEAVE TOWN AFTER HIGH SCHOOL.
ESPECIALLY IF THEY'RE GOING TO COLLEGE!
I CAN UNDERSTAND WHY PEOPLE WOULDN'T WANT TO STAY IN A SMALL TOWN LIKE THIS!
CHIZU ...

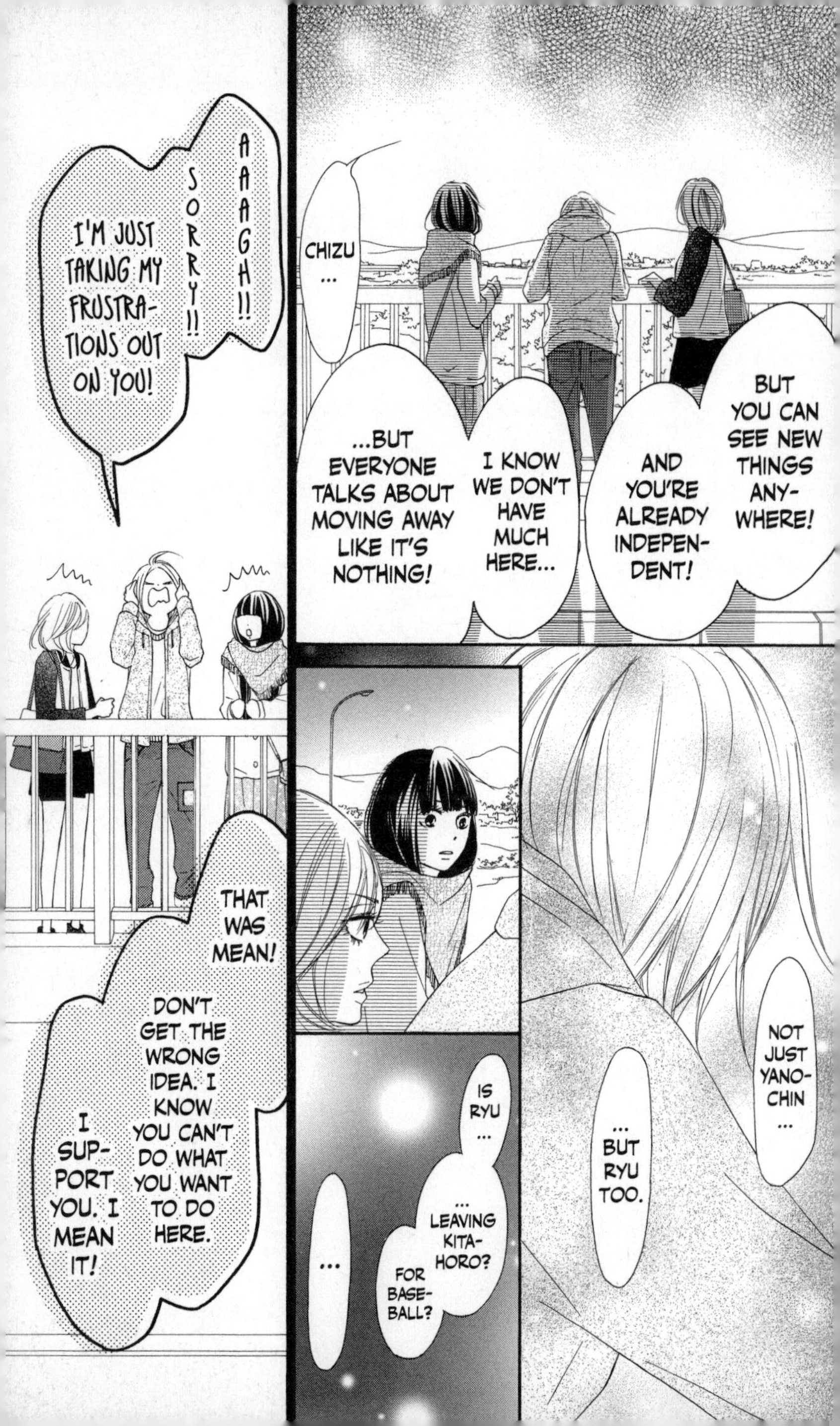
BUT YOU CAN SEE NEW THINGS ANY-WHERE!
AND YOU'RE ALREADY INDEPEN-DENT!
I KNOW WE DON'T HAVE MUCH HERE...
...BUT EVERYONE TALKS ABOUT MOVING AWAY LIKE IT'S NOTHING!
CHIZU ...
NOT JUST YANO-CHIN ...
... BUT RYU TOO.
IS RYU ...
... LEAVING KITA-HORO?
FOR BASE-BALL?
...
AAAAGH!!
SORRY!!
I'M JUST TAKING MY FRUSTRA-TIONS OUT ON YOU!
THAT WAS MEAN!
DON'T GET THE WRONG IDEA. I KNOW YOU CAN'T DO WHAT YOU WANT TO DO HERE.
I SUP-PORT YOU. I MEAN IT!

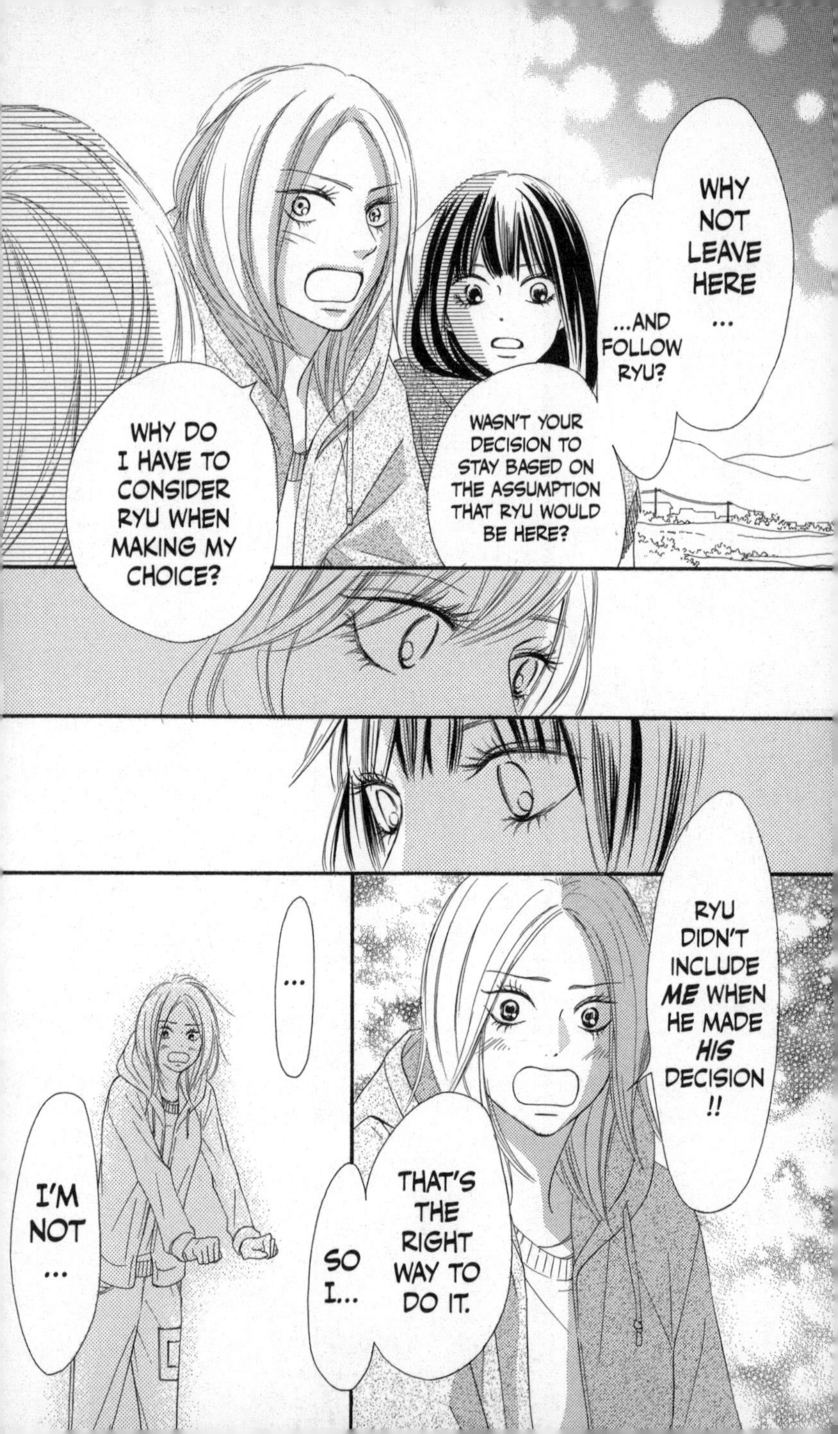
WHY NOT LEAVE HERE ...
...AND FOLLOW RYU?
WASN'T YOUR DECISION TO STAY BASED ON THE ASSUMPTION THAT RYU WOULD BE HERE?
WHY DO I HAVE TO CONSIDER RYU WHEN MAKING MY CHOICE?
RYU DIDN'T INCLUDE *ME* WHEN HE MADE *HIS* DECISION !!
THAT'S THE RIGHT WAY TO DO IT.
SO I...
...
I'M NOT ...

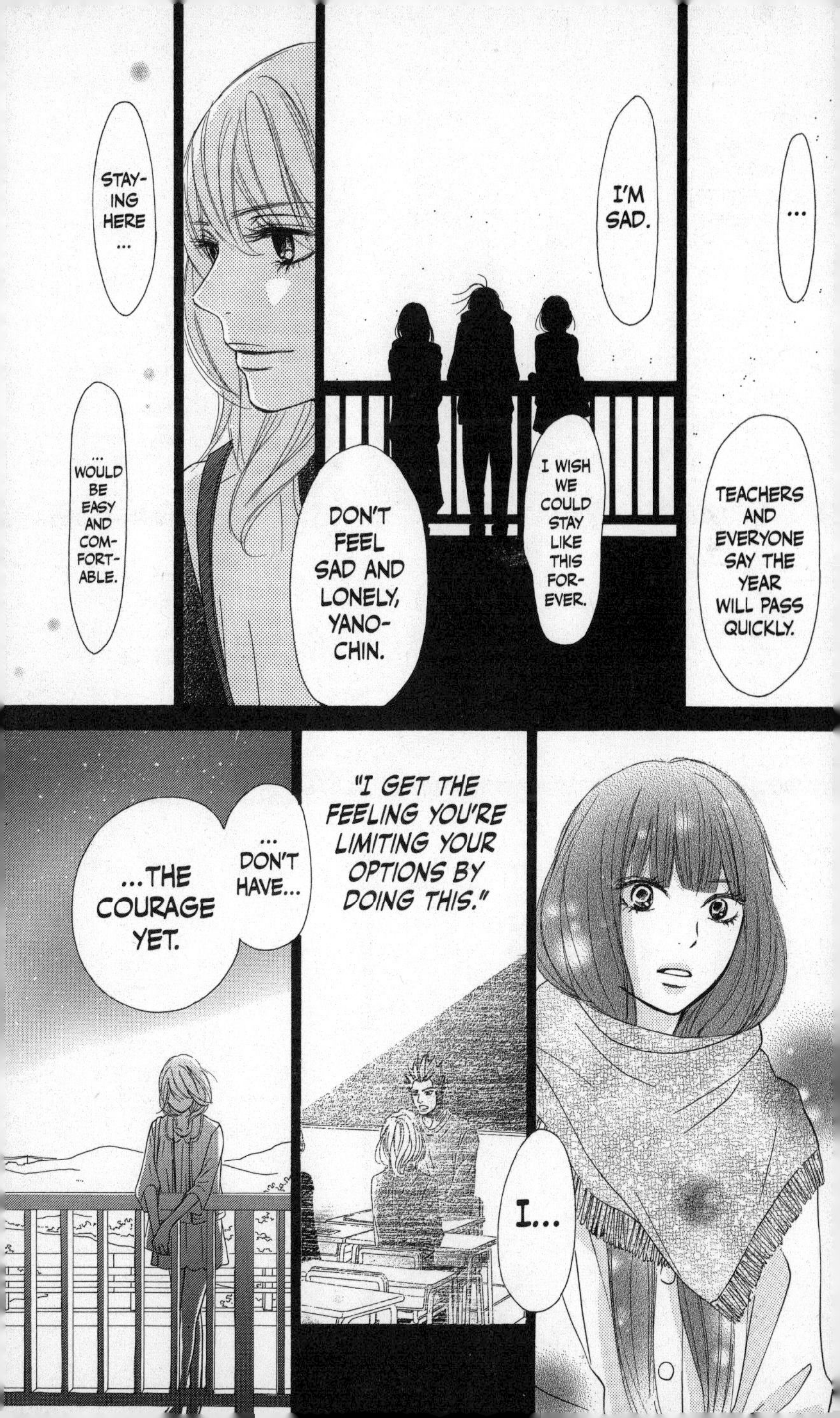
...
TEACHERS AND EVERYONE SAY THE YEAR WILL PASS QUICKLY.
I'M SAD.
I WISH WE COULD STAY LIKE THIS FOREVER.
DON'T FEEL SAD AND LONELY, YANO-CHIN.
STAYING HERE...
...WOULD BE EASY AND COMFORTABLE.
I...
"I GET THE FEELING YOU'RE LIMITING YOUR OPTIONS BY DOING THIS."
...DON'T HAVE...
...THE COURAGE YET.

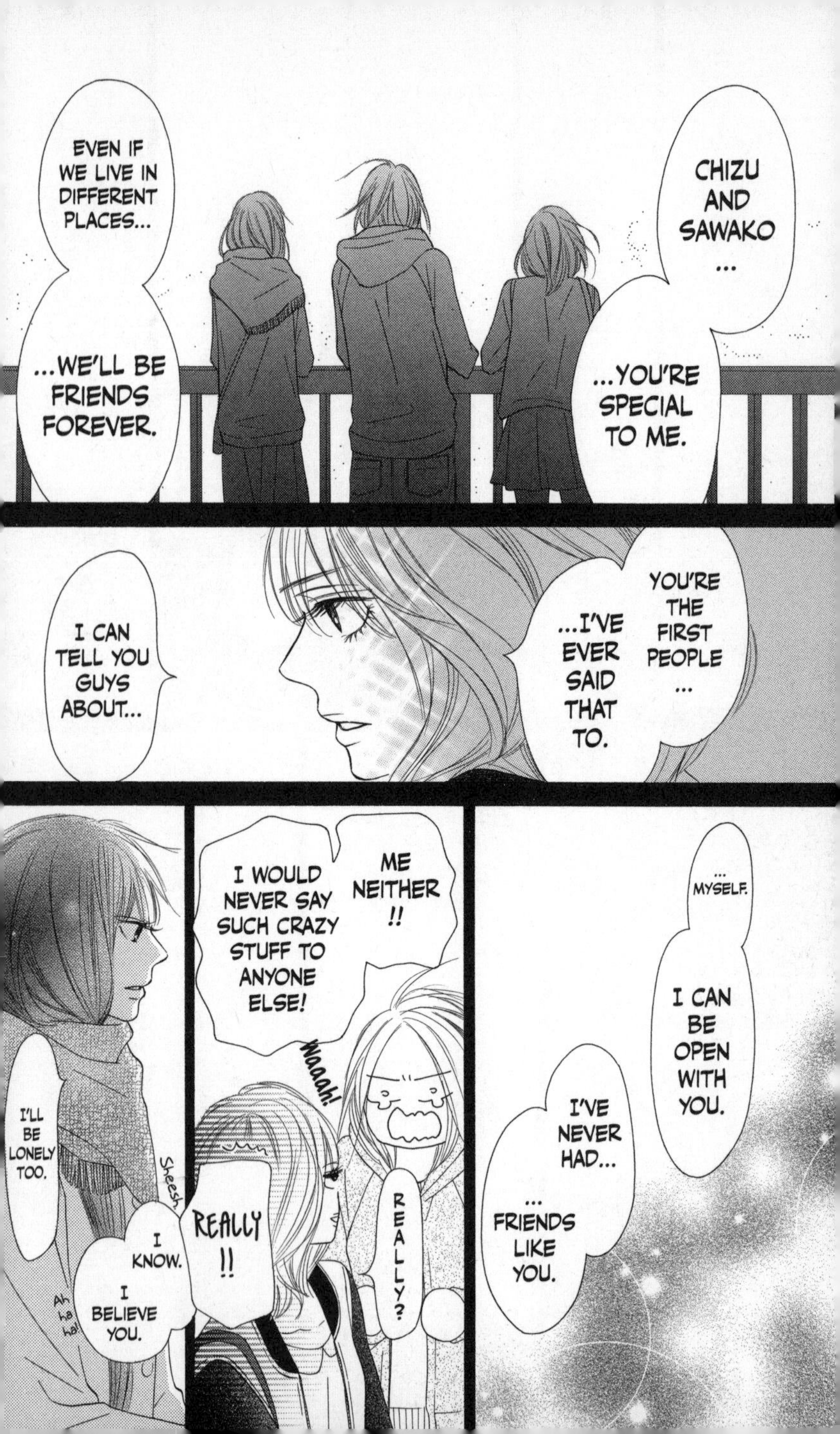
CHIZU AND SAWAKO ...
...YOU'RE SPECIAL TO ME.
EVEN IF WE LIVE IN DIFFERENT PLACES...
...WE'LL BE FRIENDS FOREVER.
YOU'RE THE FIRST PEOPLE ...
...I'VE EVER SAID THAT TO.
I CAN TELL YOU GUYS ABOUT...
... MYSELF.
I CAN BE OPEN WITH YOU.
I'VE NEVER HAD...
... FRIENDS LIKE YOU.
ME NEITHER !!
I WOULD NEVER SAY SUCH CRAZY STUFF TO ANYONE ELSE!
Waaah!
REALLY?
REALLY !!
I'LL BE LONELY TOO.
Sheesh
I KNOW.
I BELIEVE YOU.
Ah ha ha!

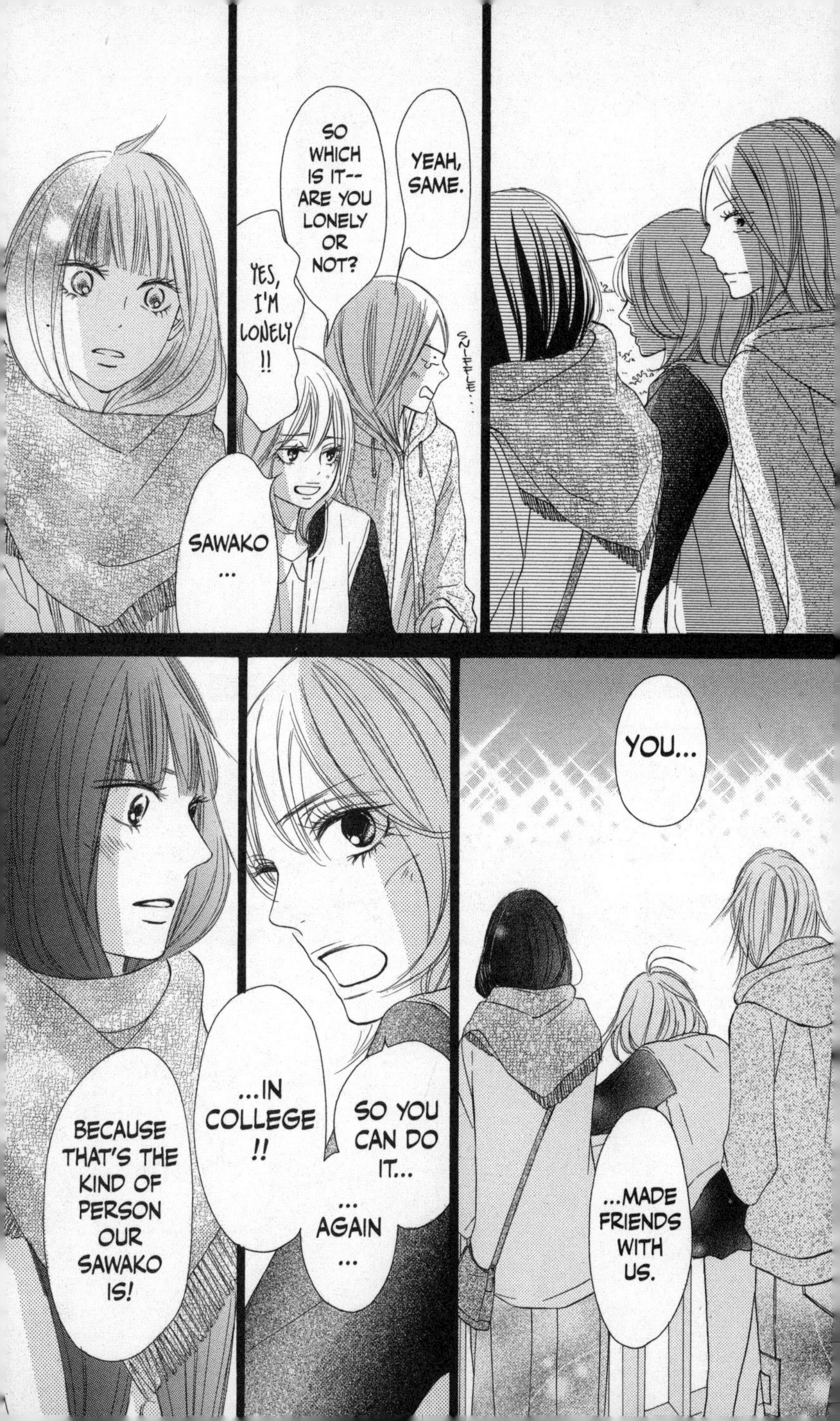
YEAH, SAME.
SO WHICH IS IT-- ARE YOU LONELY OR NOT?
SNIFFLE...
YES, I'M LONELY !!
SAWAKO ...
YOU...
...MADE FRIENDS WITH US.
SO YOU CAN DO IT...
... AGAIN ...
...IN COLLEGE !!
BECAUSE THAT'S THE KIND OF PERSON OUR SAWAKO IS!

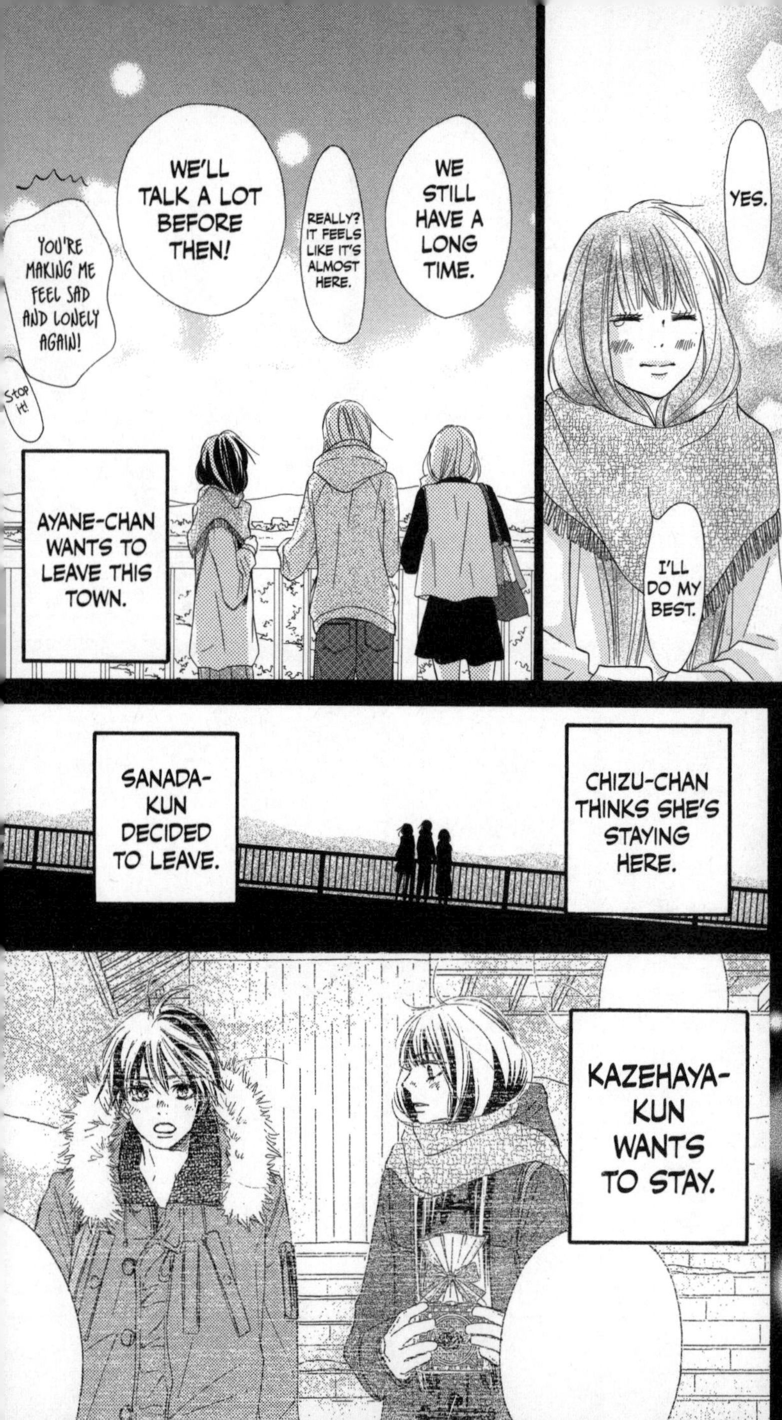
YES.
I'LL DO MY BEST.
WE STILL HAVE A LONG TIME.
REALLY? IT FEELS LIKE IT'S ALMOST HERE.
WE'LL TALK A LOT BEFORE THEN!
YOU'RE MAKING ME FEEL SAD AND LONELY AGAIN!
Stop it!
AYANE-CHAN WANTS TO LEAVE THIS TOWN.
CHIZU-CHAN THINKS SHE'S STAYING HERE.
SANADA-KUN DECIDED TO LEAVE.
KAZEHAYA-KUN WANTS TO STAY.

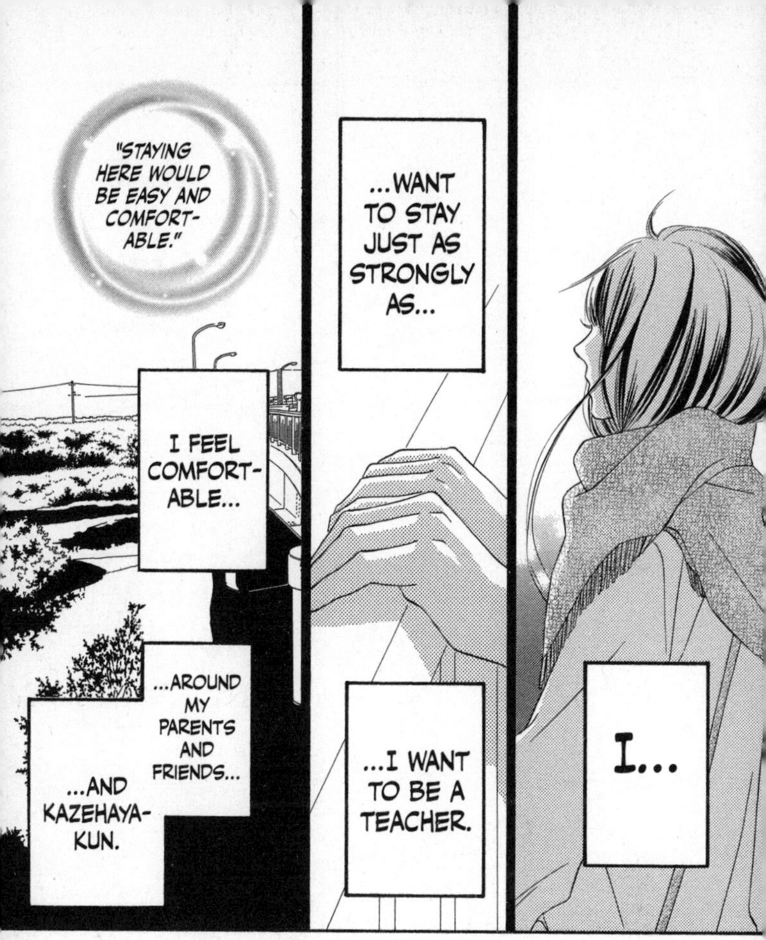
I...
...WANT TO STAY JUST AS STRONGLY AS...
...I WANT TO BE A TEACHER.
"STAYING HERE WOULD BE EASY AND COMFORT-ABLE."
I FEEL COMFORT-ABLE...
...AROUND MY PARENTS AND FRIENDS...
...AND KAZEHAYA-KUN.

I THOUGHT WE WOULD BE TOGETHER FOREVER.

BUT WE ALL HAVE DIFFERENT PATHS AND FUTURES AHEAD OF US.

THAT'S THE WAY IT GOES.

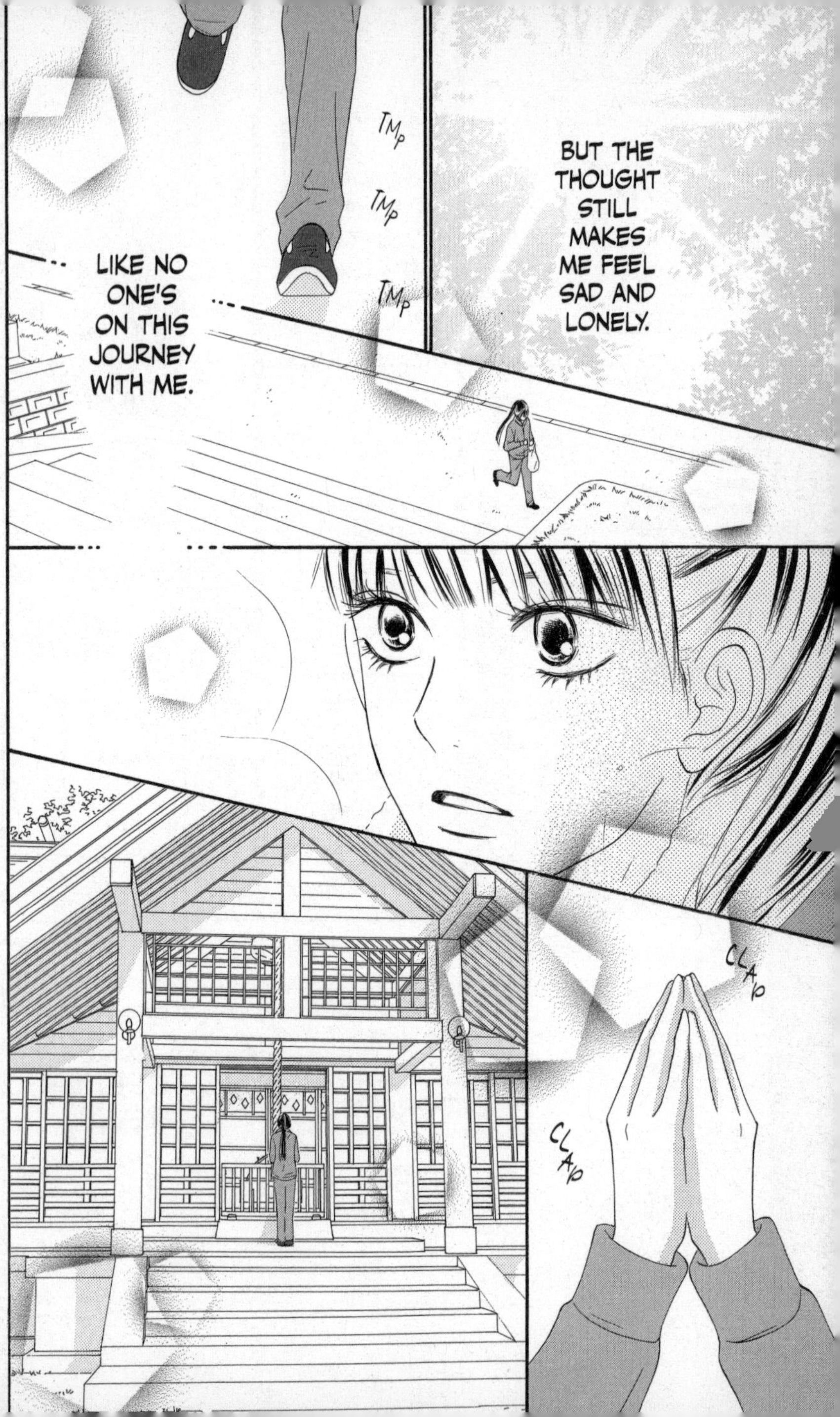
BUT THE THOUGHT STILL MAKES ME FEEL SAD AND LONELY.
TMP
TMP
TMP
LIKE NO ONE'S ON THIS JOURNEY WITH ME.
CLAP
CLAP

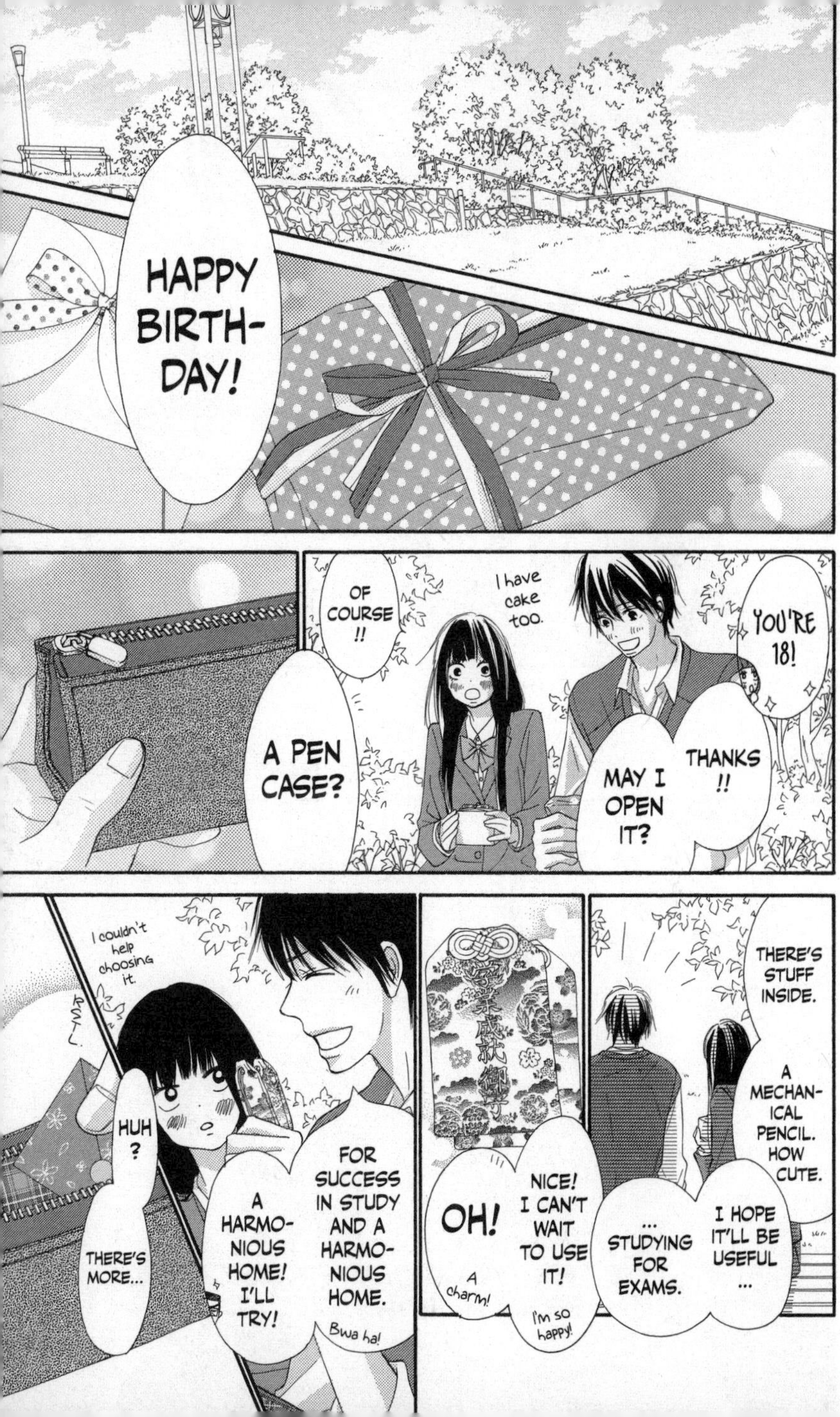
HAPPY BIRTH-DAY!
YOU'RE 18!
THANKS!!
MAY I OPEN IT?
I have cake too.
OF COURSE!!
A PEN CASE?
THERE'S STUFF INSIDE.
A MECHANICAL PENCIL. HOW CUTE.
I HOPE IT'LL BE USEFUL...
...STUDYING FOR EXAMS.
NICE! I CAN'T WAIT TO USE IT!
I'm so happy!
OH!
A charm!
学業成就御守
FOR SUCCESS IN STUDY AND A HARMONIOUS HOME.
Bwa ha!
A HARMONIOUS HOME! I'LL TRY!
I couldn't help choosing it.
HUH?
THERE'S MORE...

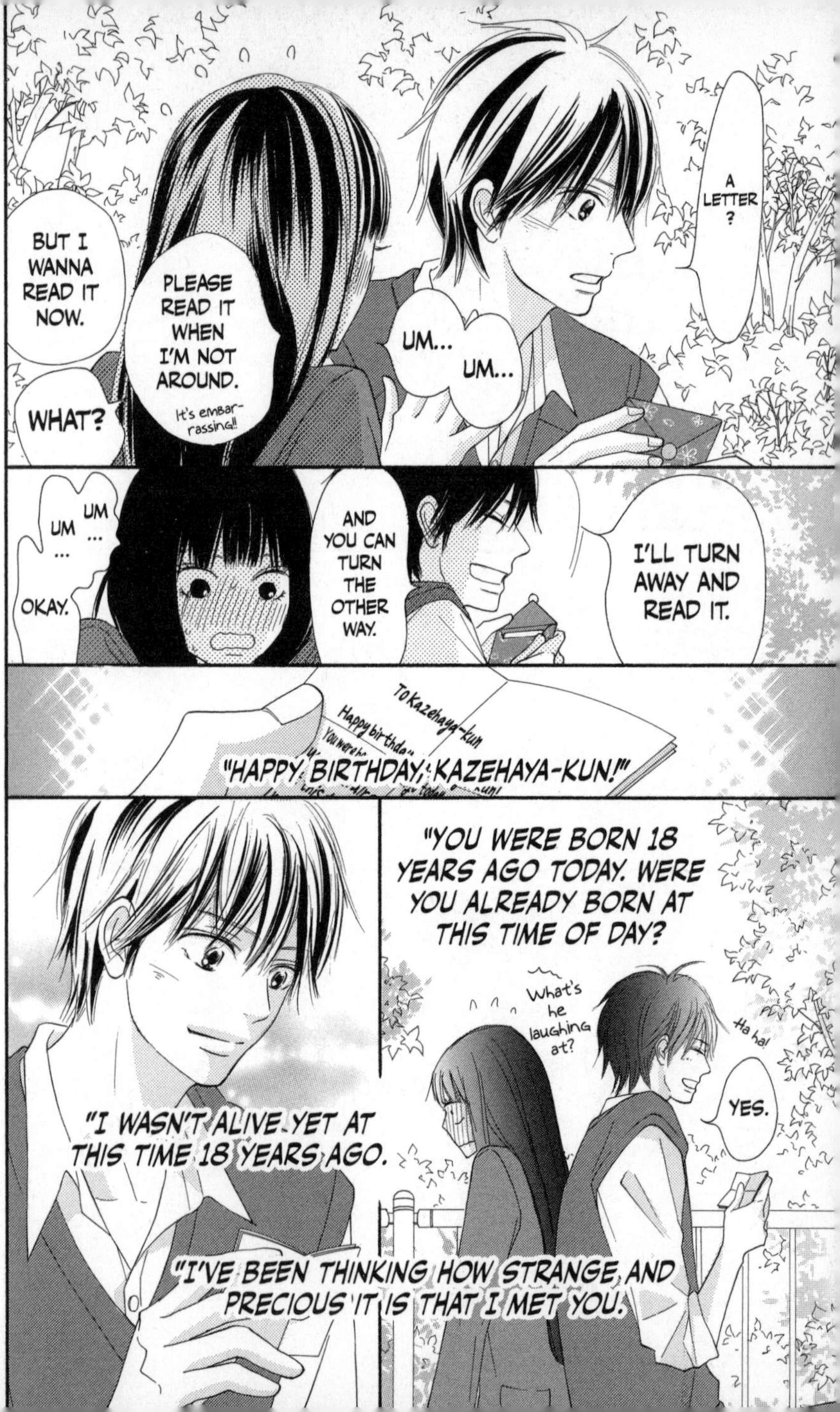
A LETTER?
UM... UM...
PLEASE READ IT WHEN I'M NOT AROUND.
It's embarrassing!!
BUT I WANNA READ IT NOW.
WHAT?
I'LL TURN AWAY AND READ IT.
AND YOU CAN TURN THE OTHER WAY.
UM ... UM ...
OKAY.
To Kazehaya-kun
Happy birthday
"HAPPY BIRTHDAY, KAZEHAYA-KUN!"
"YOU WERE BORN 18 YEARS AGO TODAY. WERE YOU ALREADY BORN AT THIS TIME OF DAY?
Ha ha!
YES.
What's he laughing at?
"I WASN'T ALIVE YET AT THIS TIME 18 YEARS AGO.
"I'VE BEEN THINKING HOW STRANGE AND PRECIOUS IT IS THAT I MET YOU.

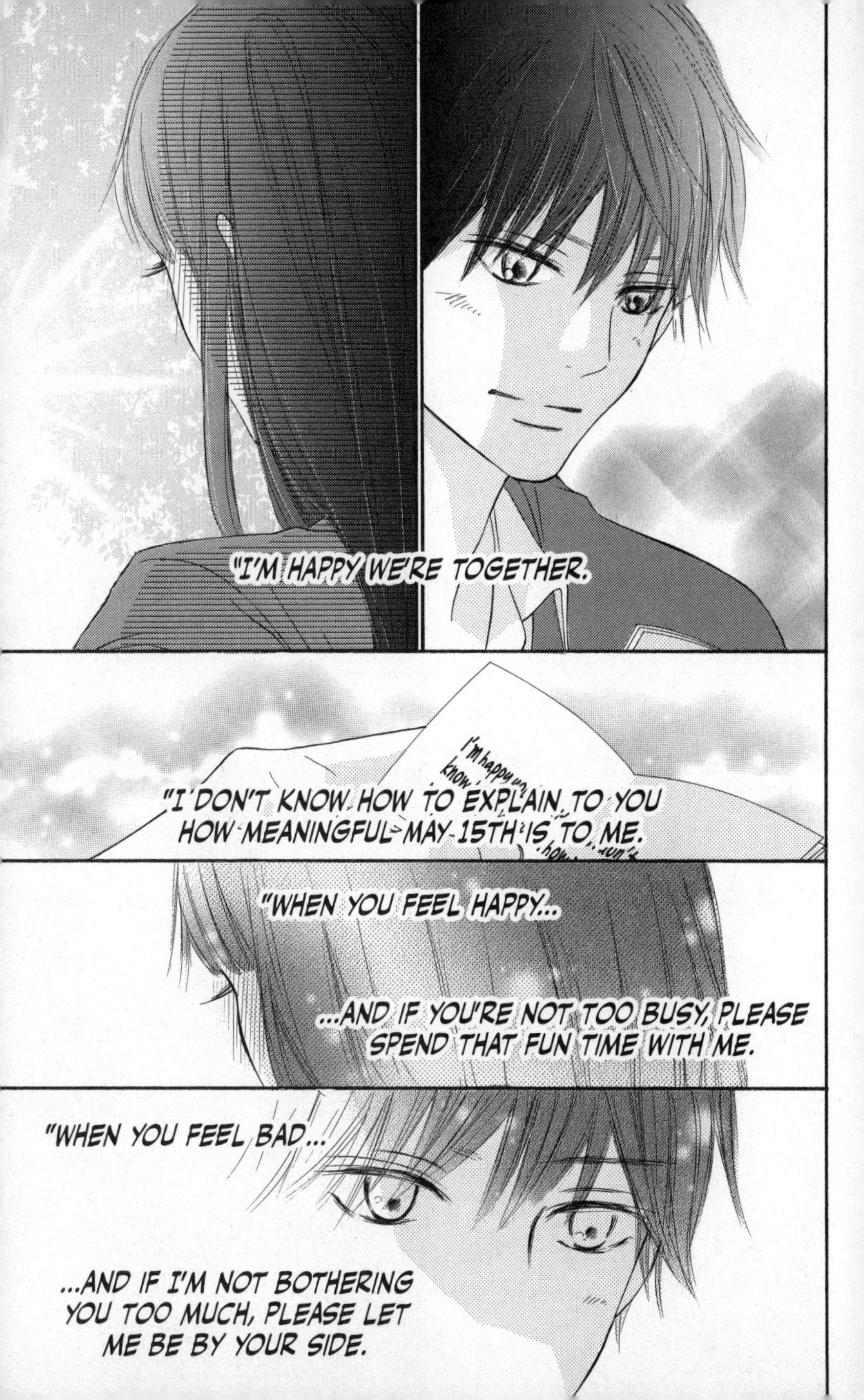
"I'M HAPPY WE'RE TOGETHER.
"I DON'T KNOW HOW TO EXPLAIN TO YOU HOW MEANINGFUL MAY 15TH IS TO ME.
"WHEN YOU FEEL HAPPY...
...AND IF YOU'RE NOT TOO BUSY, PLEASE SPEND THAT FUN TIME WITH ME.
"WHEN YOU FEEL BAD...
...AND IF I'M NOT BOTHERING YOU TOO MUCH, PLEASE LET ME BE BY YOUR SIDE.

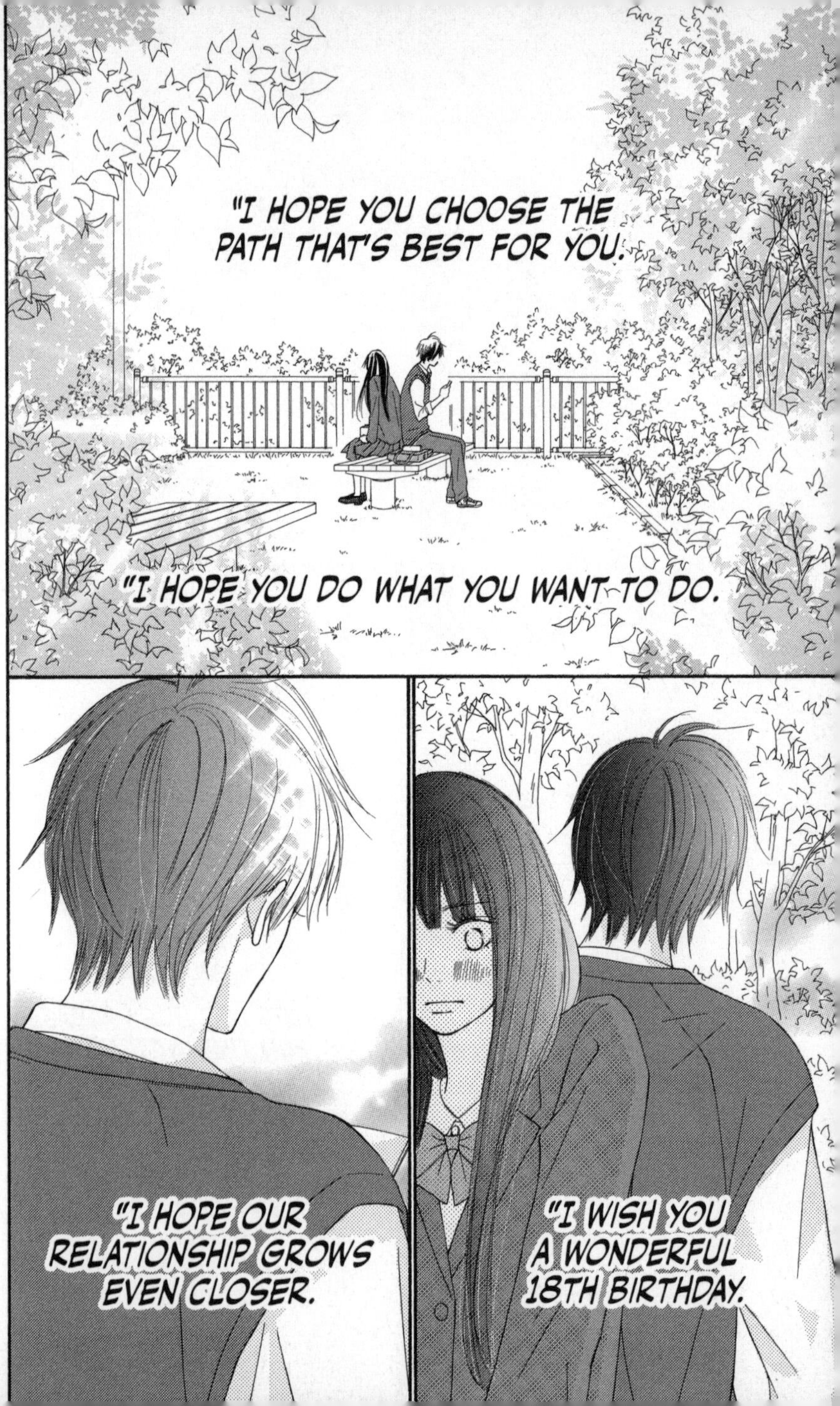
"I HOPE YOU CHOOSE THE PATH THAT'S BEST FOR YOU.
"I HOPE YOU DO WHAT YOU WANT TO DO.
"I WISH YOU A WONDERFUL 18TH BIRTHDAY.
"I HOPE OUR RELATIONSHIP GROWS EVEN CLOSER.

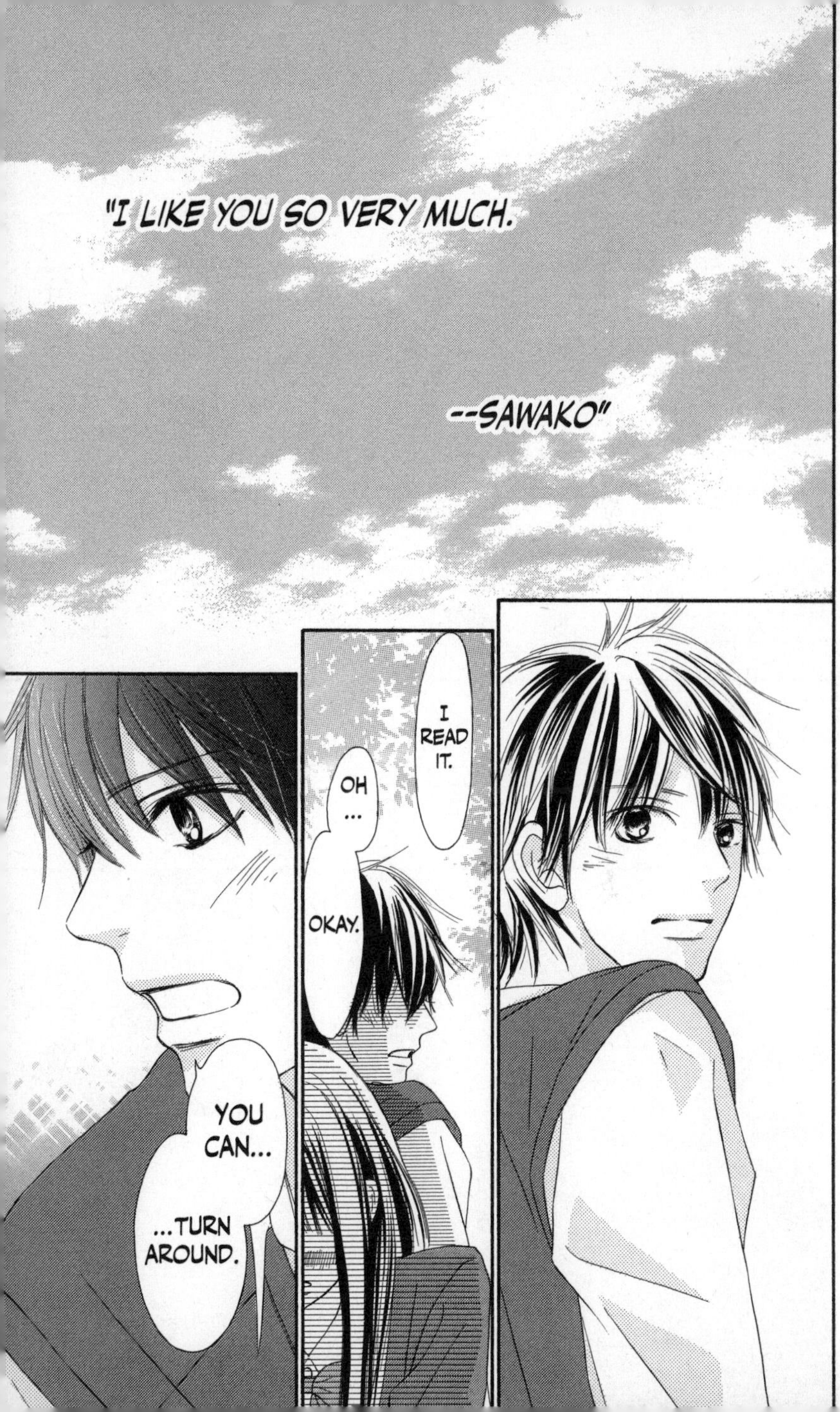
"I LIKE YOU SO VERY MUCH.
--SAWAKO"
I READ IT.
OH ...
OKAY.
YOU CAN...
...TURN AROUND.

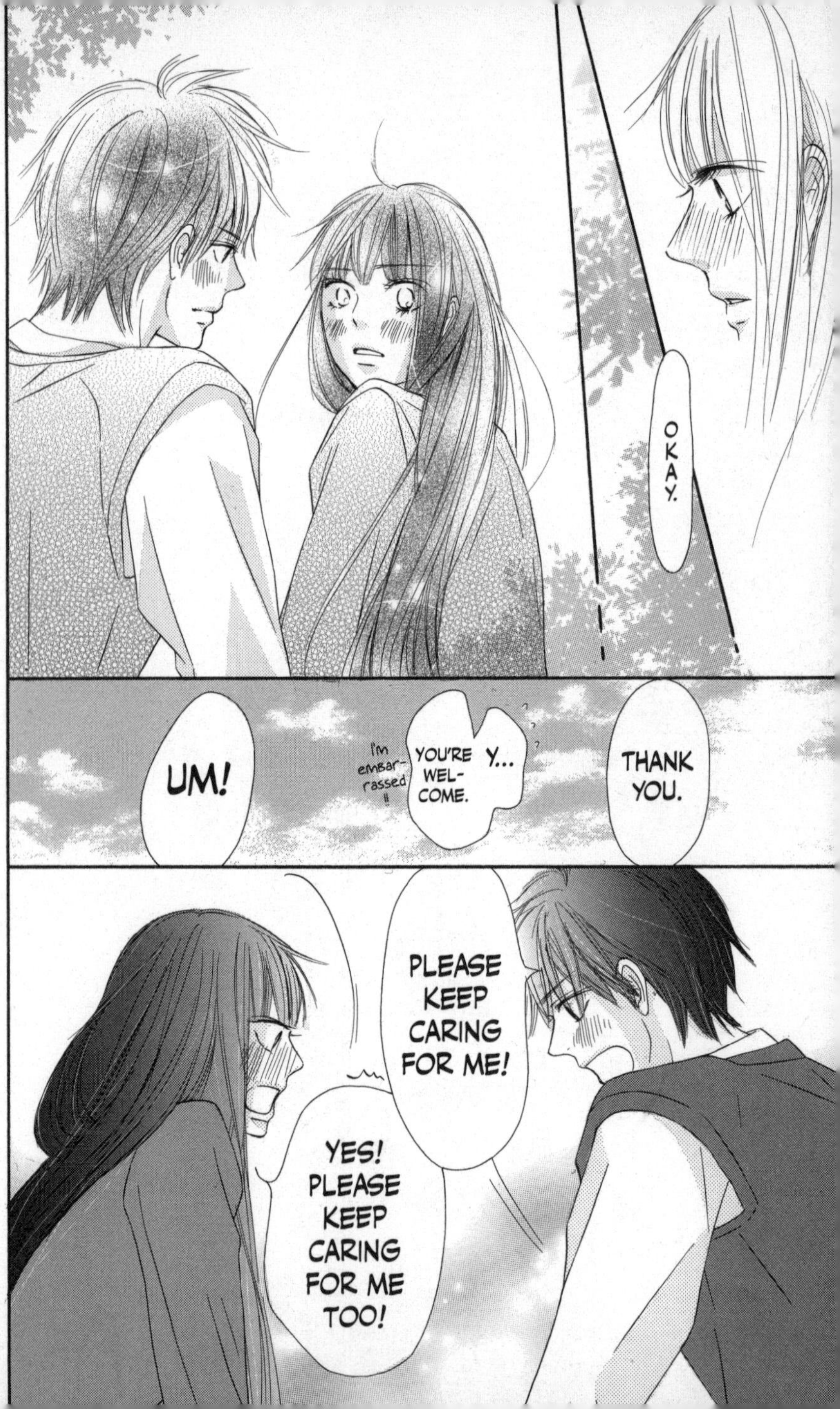
OKAY.
THANK YOU.
Y...
YOU'RE WEL-COME.
I'm embar-rassed!!
UM!
PLEASE KEEP CARING FOR ME!
YES! PLEASE KEEP CARING FOR ME TOO!

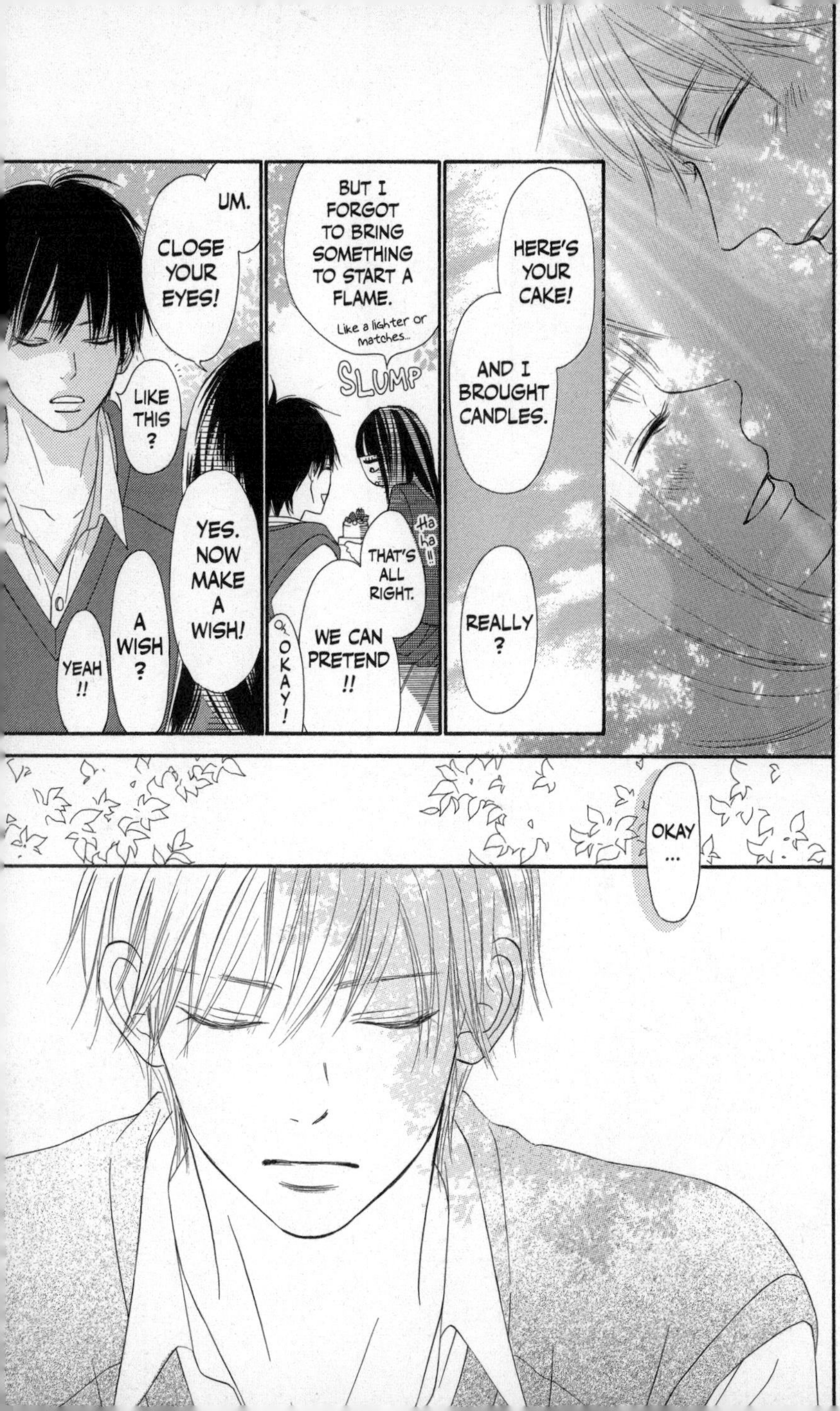
HERE'S YOUR CAKE!
AND I BROUGHT CANDLES.
REALLY?
BUT I FORGOT TO BRING SOMETHING TO START A FLAME.
Like a lighter or matches...
SLUMP
Ha ha!!
THAT'S ALL RIGHT.
WE CAN PRETEND!!
OKAY!
UM.
CLOSE YOUR EYES!
LIKE THIS?
YES. NOW MAKE A WISH!
A WISH?
YEAH!!
OKAY...

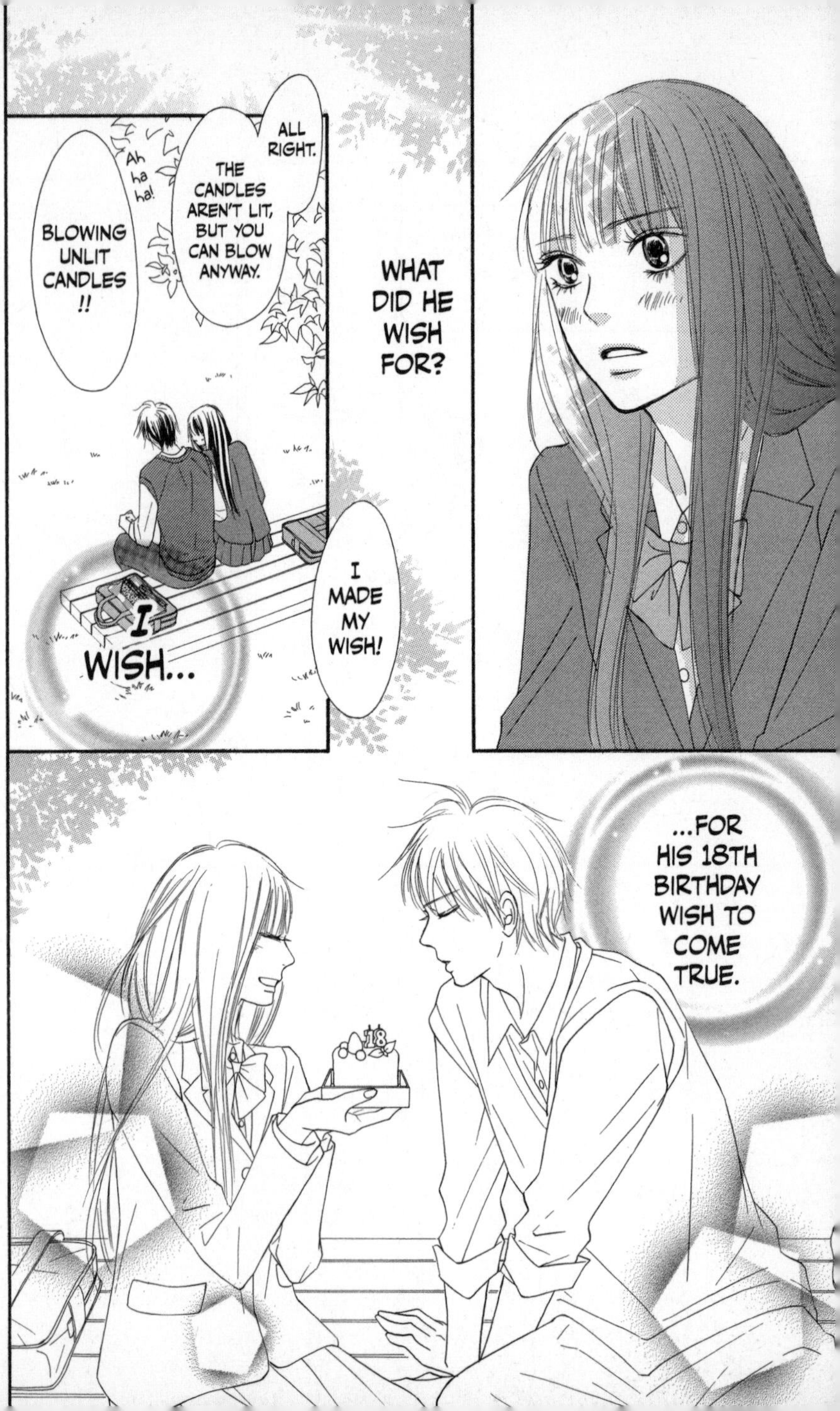
WHAT DID HE WISH FOR?
ALL RIGHT. THE CANDLES AREN'T LIT, BUT YOU CAN BLOW ANYWAY.
Ah ha ha!
BLOWING UNLIT CANDLES !!
I MADE MY WISH!
I WISH...
...FOR HIS 18TH BIRTHDAY WISH TO COME TRUE.

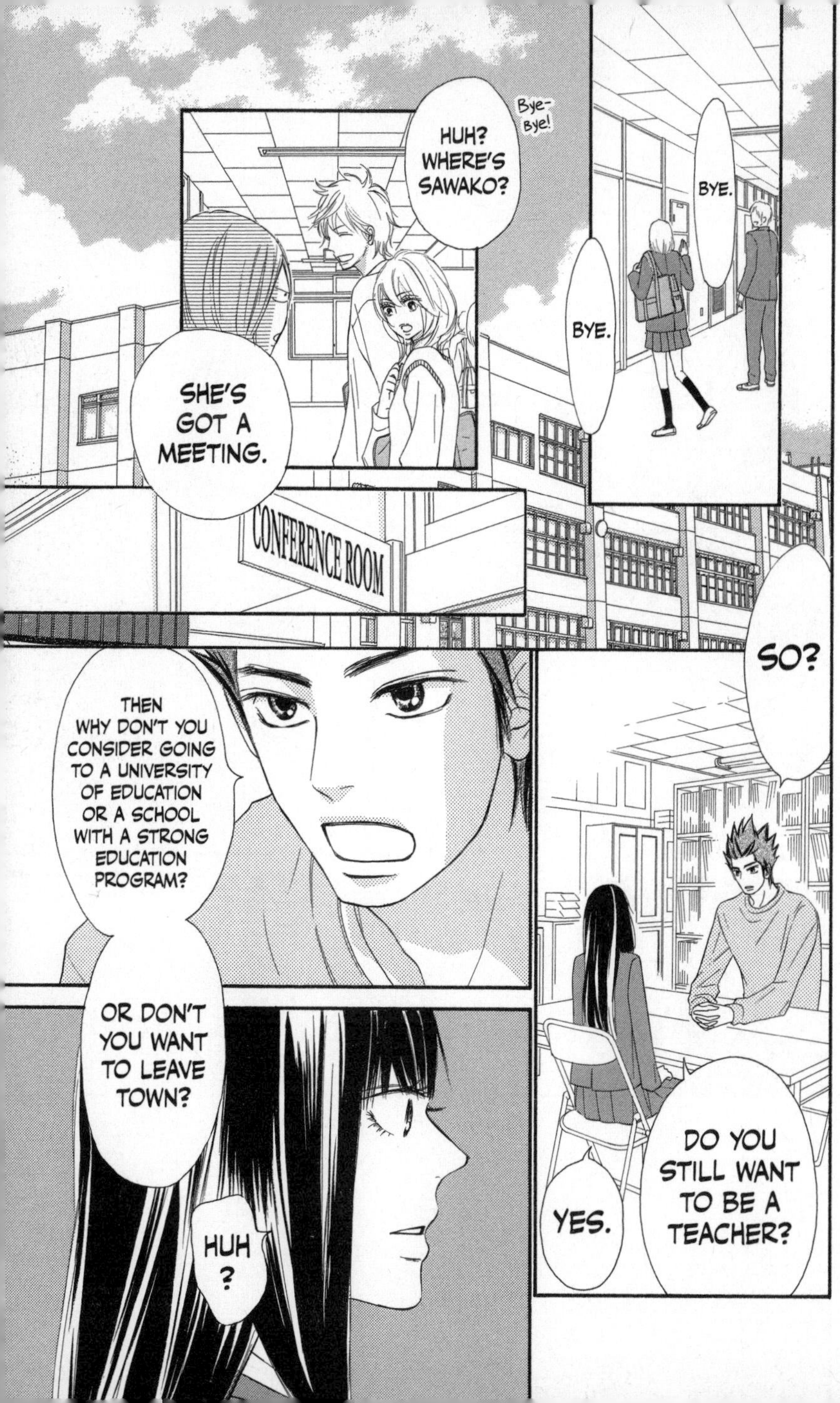
BYE.
BYE.
Bye-Bye!
HUH? WHERE'S SAWAKO?
SHE'S GOT A MEETING.
CONFERENCE ROOM
SO?
DO YOU STILL WANT TO BE A TEACHER?
YES.
THEN WHY DON'T YOU CONSIDER GOING TO A UNIVERSITY OF EDUCATION OR A SCHOOL WITH A STRONG EDUCATION PROGRAM?
OR DON'T YOU WANT TO LEAVE TOWN?
HUH?

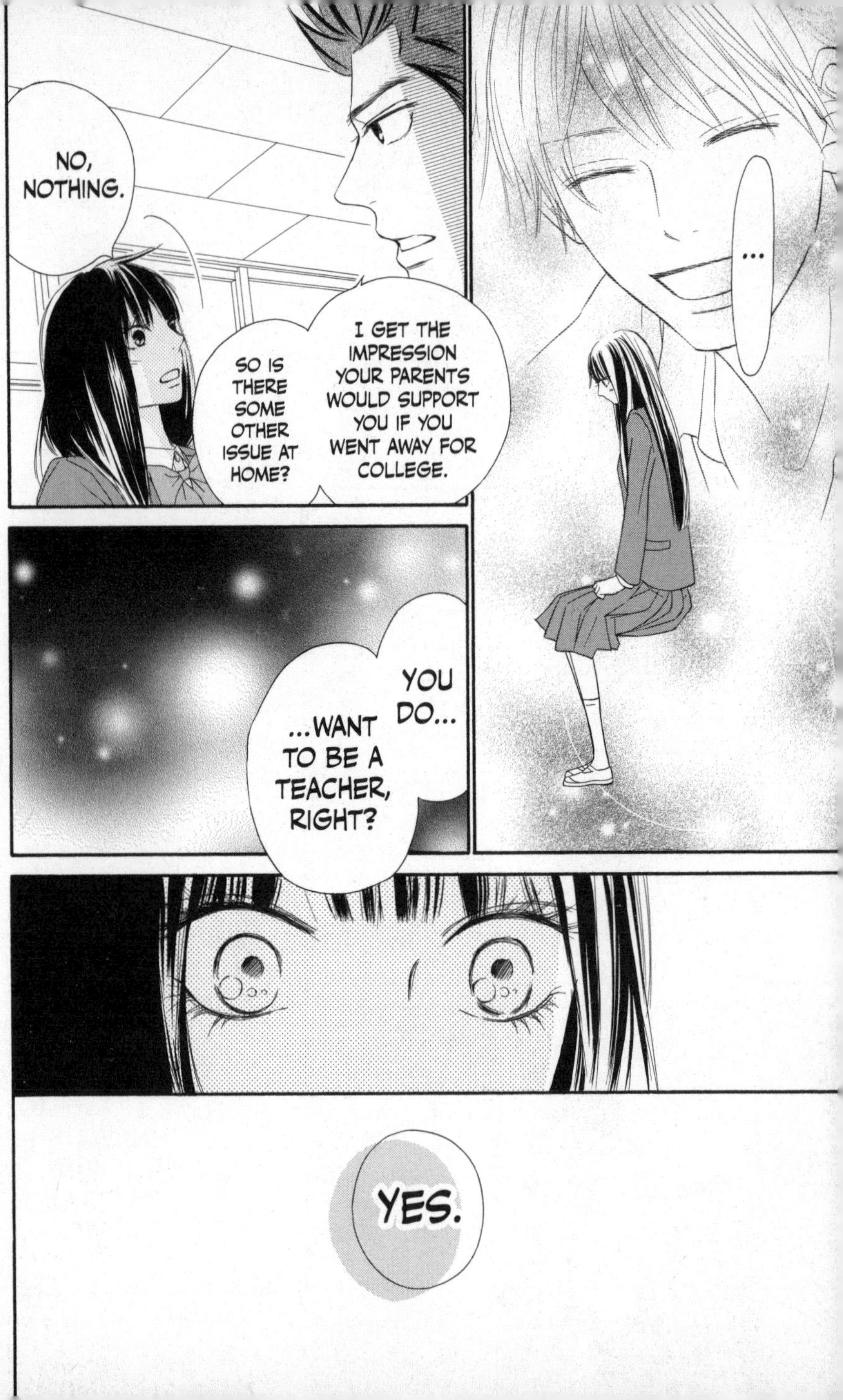
...
I GET THE IMPRESSION YOUR PARENTS WOULD SUPPORT YOU IF YOU WENT AWAY FOR COLLEGE.
SO IS THERE SOME OTHER ISSUE AT HOME?
NO, NOTHING.
YOU DO...
...WANT TO BE A TEACHER, RIGHT?
YES.

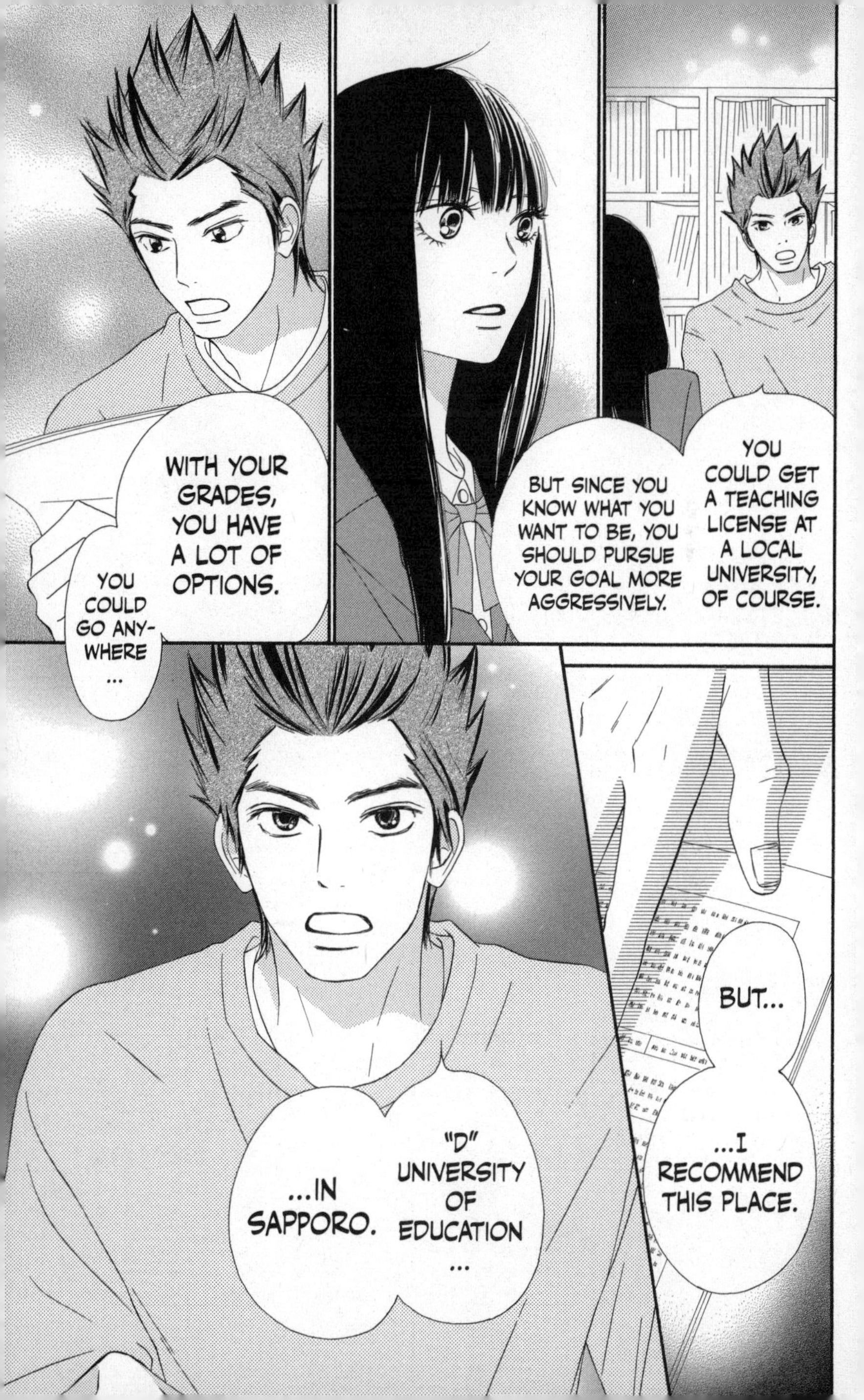
YOU COULD GET A TEACHING LICENSE AT A LOCAL UNIVERSITY, OF COURSE.
BUT SINCE YOU KNOW WHAT YOU WANT TO BE, YOU SHOULD PURSUE YOUR GOAL MORE AGGRESSIVELY.
WITH YOUR GRADES, YOU HAVE A LOT OF OPTIONS.
YOU COULD GO ANY-WHERE...
BUT...
...I RECOMMEND THIS PLACE.
"D" UNIVERSITY OF EDUCATION...
...IN SAPPORO.

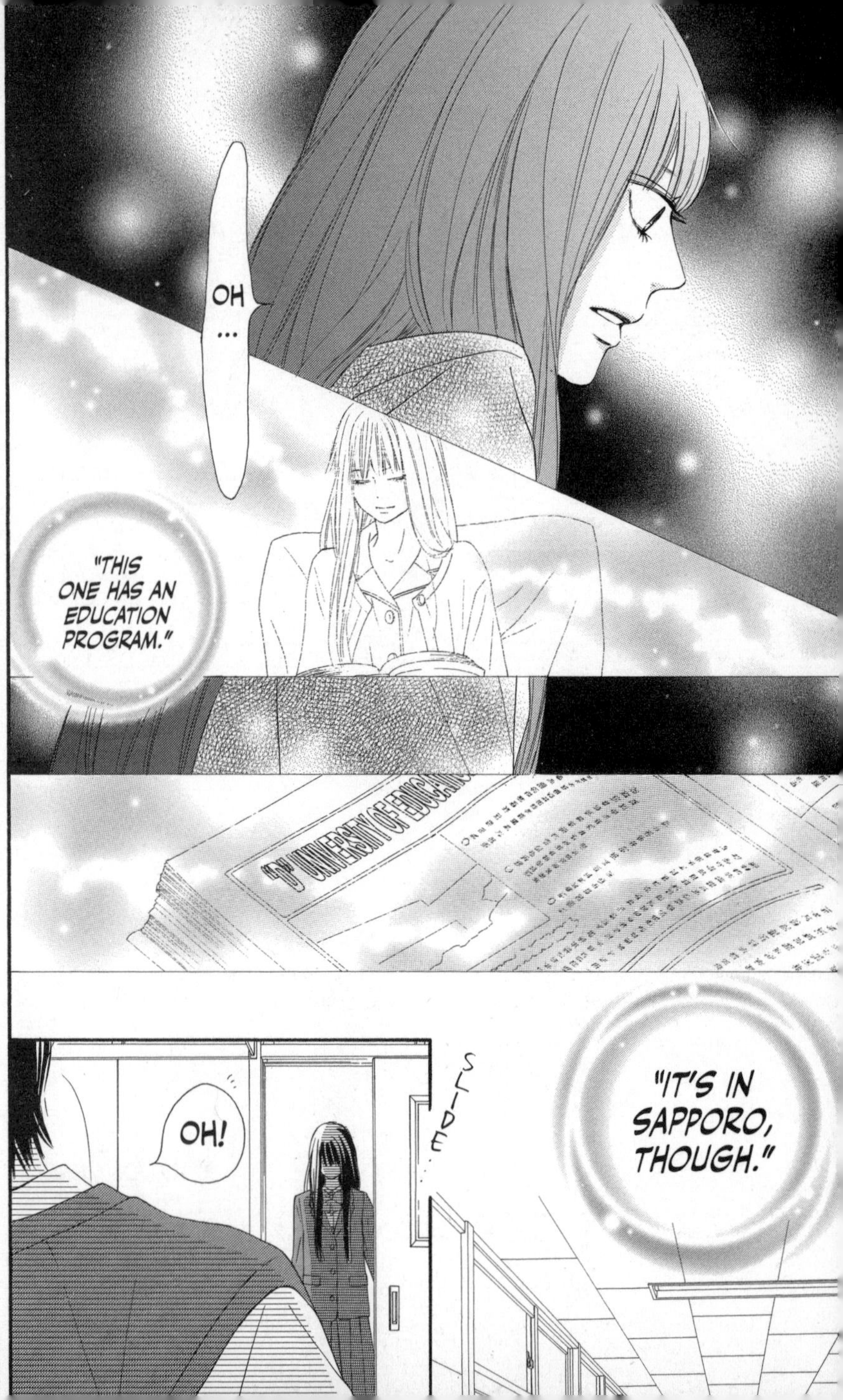
OH ...
"THIS ONE HAS AN EDUCATION PROGRAM."
"IT'S IN SAPPORO, THOUGH."
SLIDE...
OH!

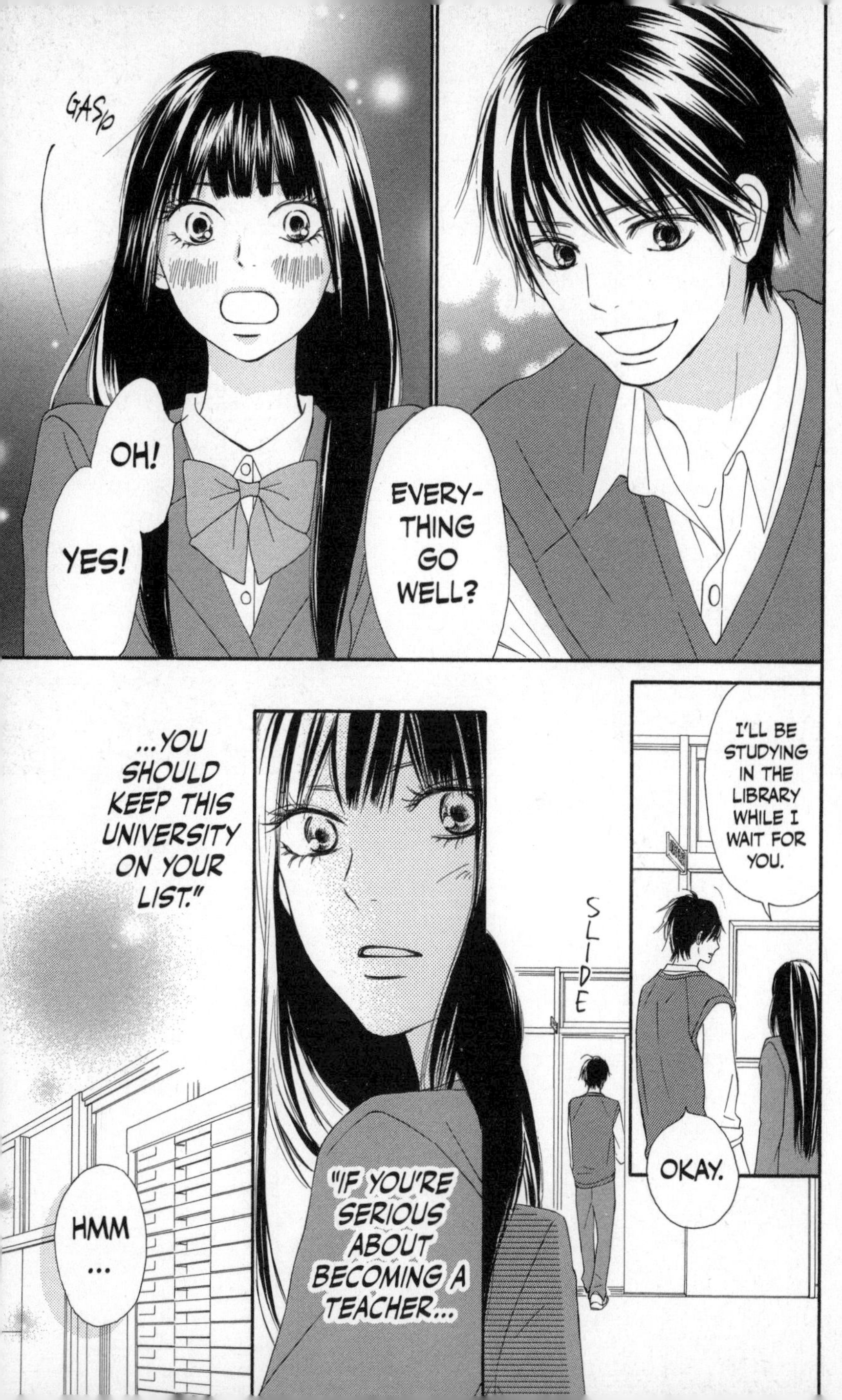
EVERY-THING GO WELL?
GASP
OH!
YES!
I'LL BE STUDYING IN THE LIBRARY WHILE I WAIT FOR YOU.
SLIDE
OKAY.
"IF YOU'RE SERIOUS ABOUT BECOMING A TEACHER...
...YOU SHOULD KEEP THIS UNIVERSITY ON YOUR LIST."
HMM ...

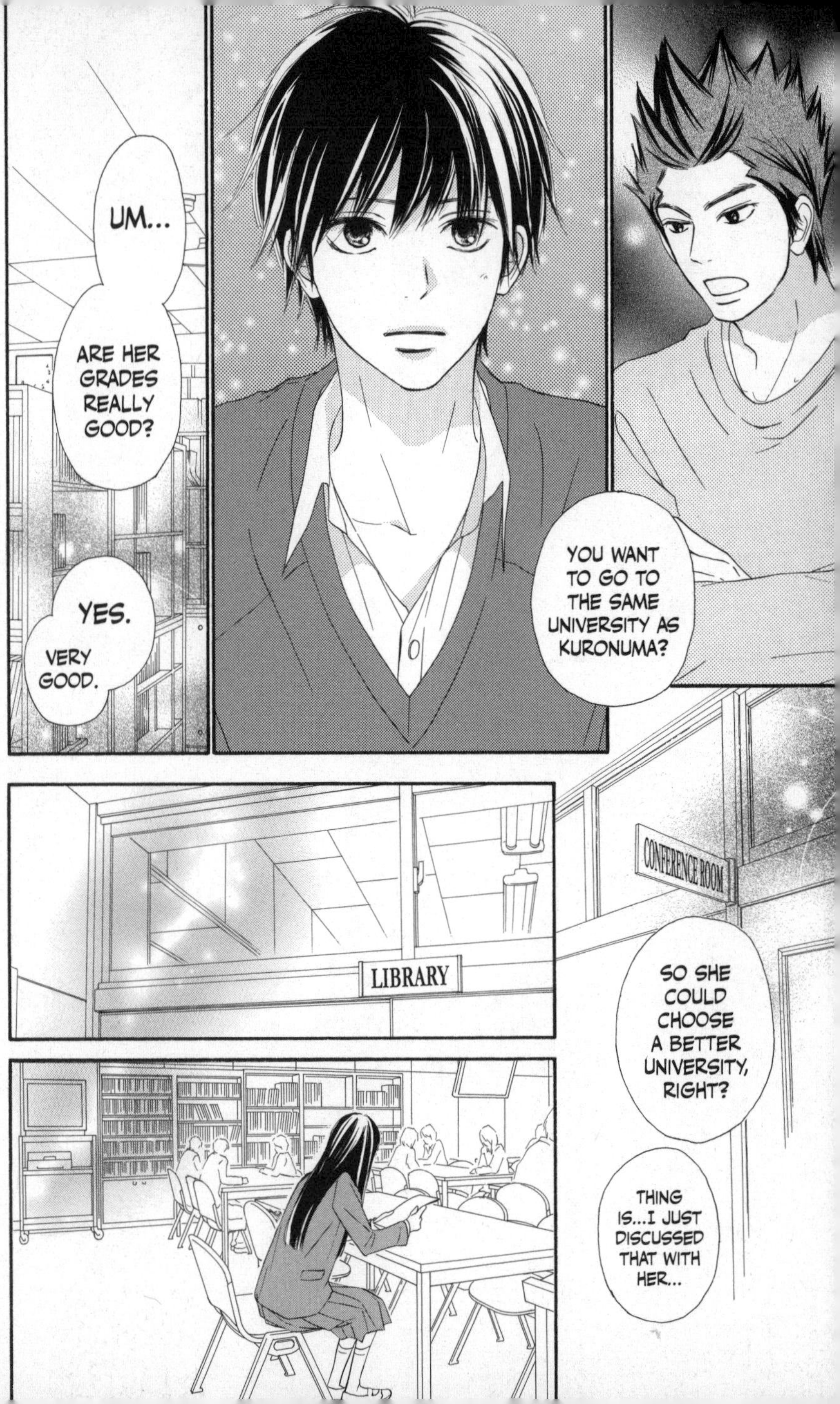
YOU WANT TO GO TO THE SAME UNIVERSITY AS KURONUMA?
UM...
ARE HER GRADES REALLY GOOD?
YES.
VERY GOOD.
CONFERENCE ROOM
SO SHE COULD CHOOSE A BETTER UNIVERSITY, RIGHT?
THING IS...I JUST DISCUSSED THAT WITH HER...
LIBRARY

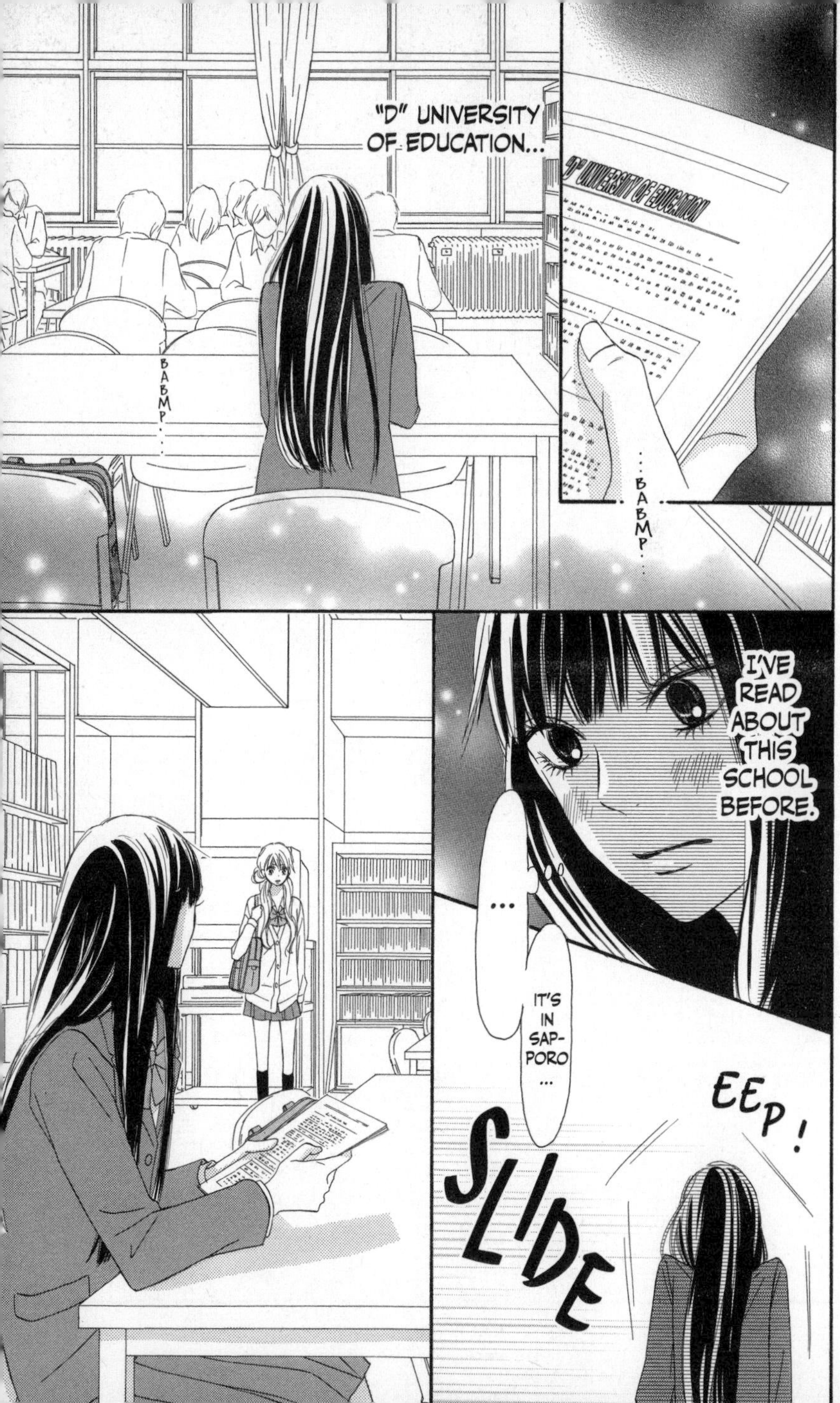
"D" UNIVERSITY OF EDUCATION
...BABMP...
"D" UNIVERSITY OF EDUCATION...
BABMP...
I'VE READ ABOUT THIS SCHOOL BEFORE.
...
IT'S IN SAPPORO...
EEP!
SLIDE

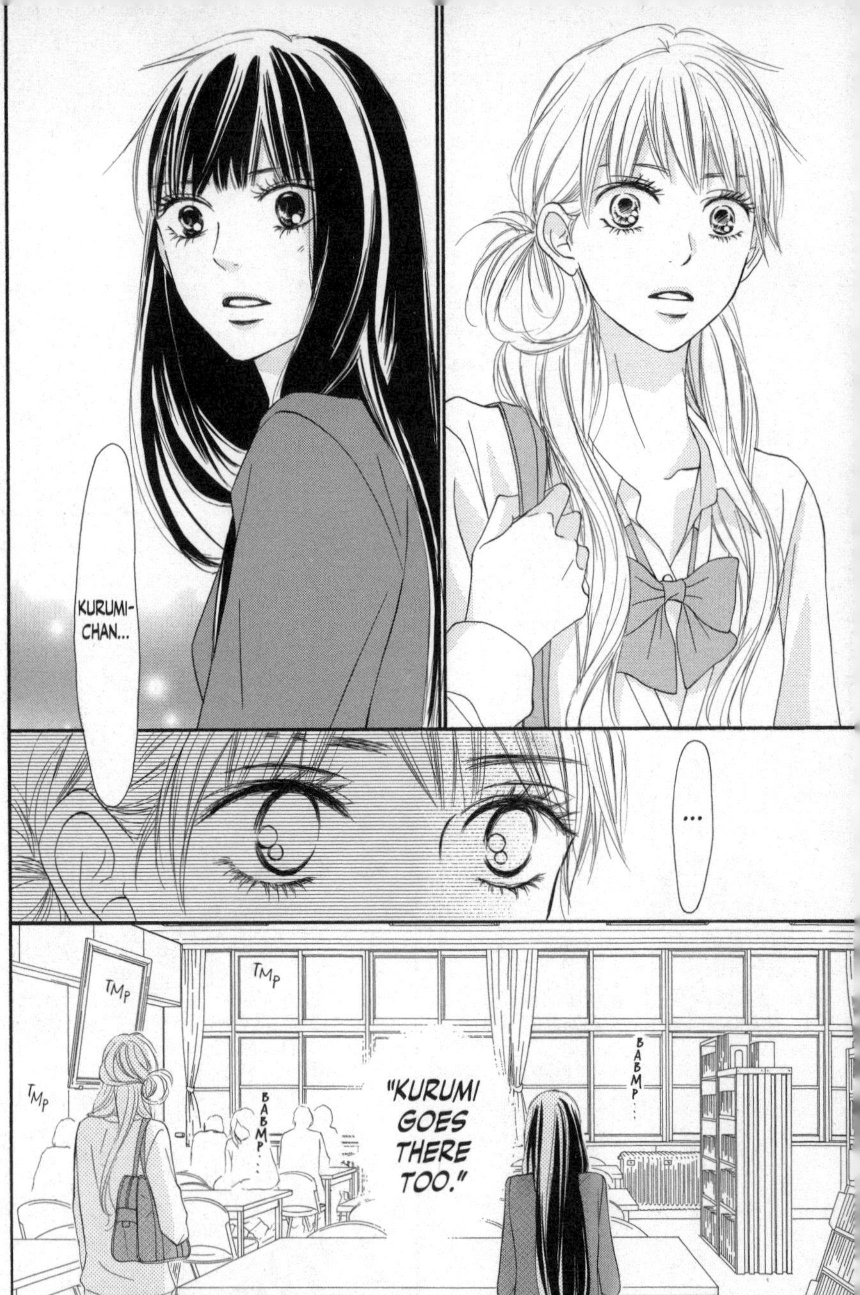
KURUMI-CHAN...
...
BABMP...
"KURUMI GOES THERE TOO."
BABMP...
TMP
TMP
TMP

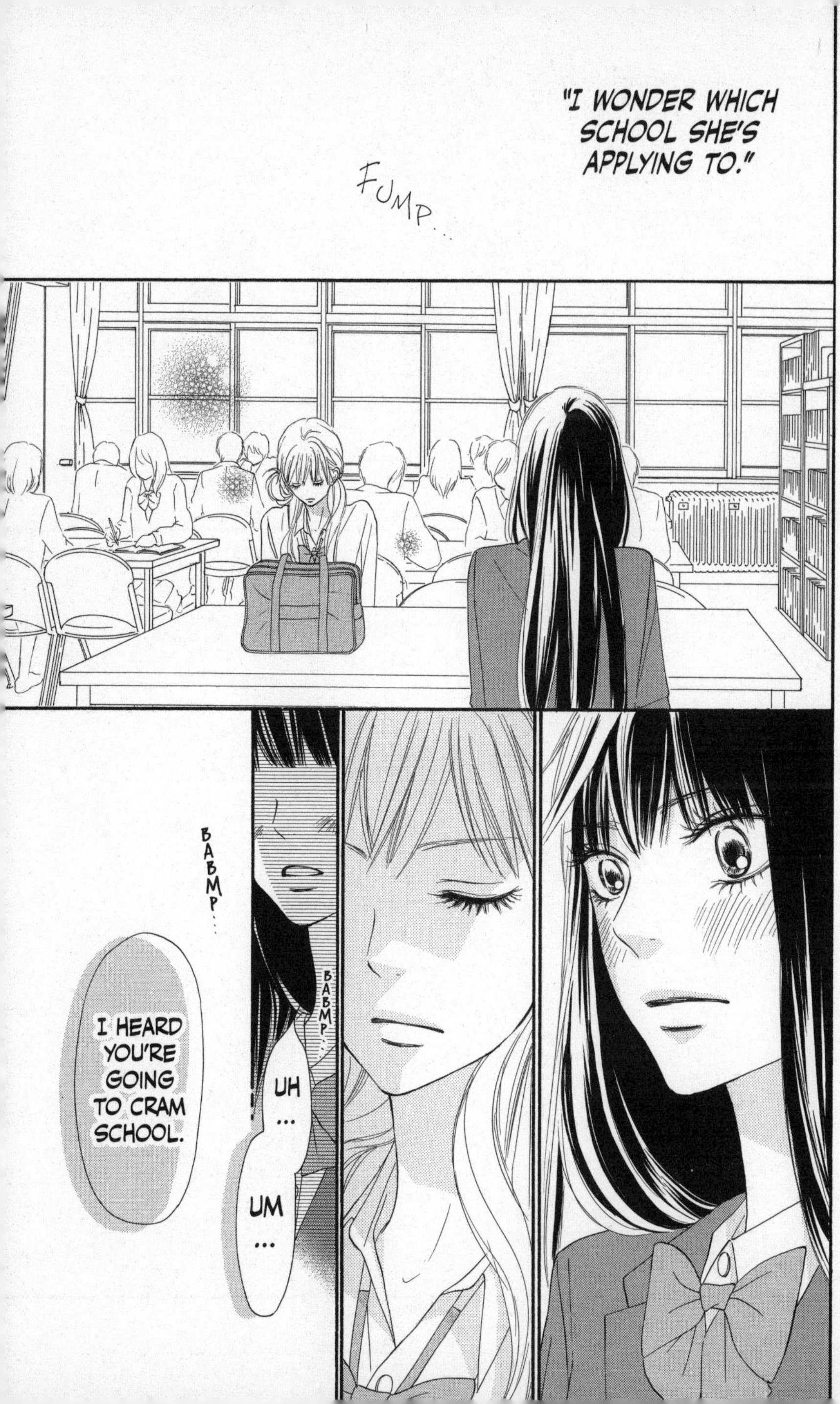
"I WONDER WHICH SCHOOL SHE'S APPLYING TO."
FUMP...
BABMP...
BABMP...
I HEARD YOU'RE GOING TO CRAM SCHOOL.
UH...
UM...

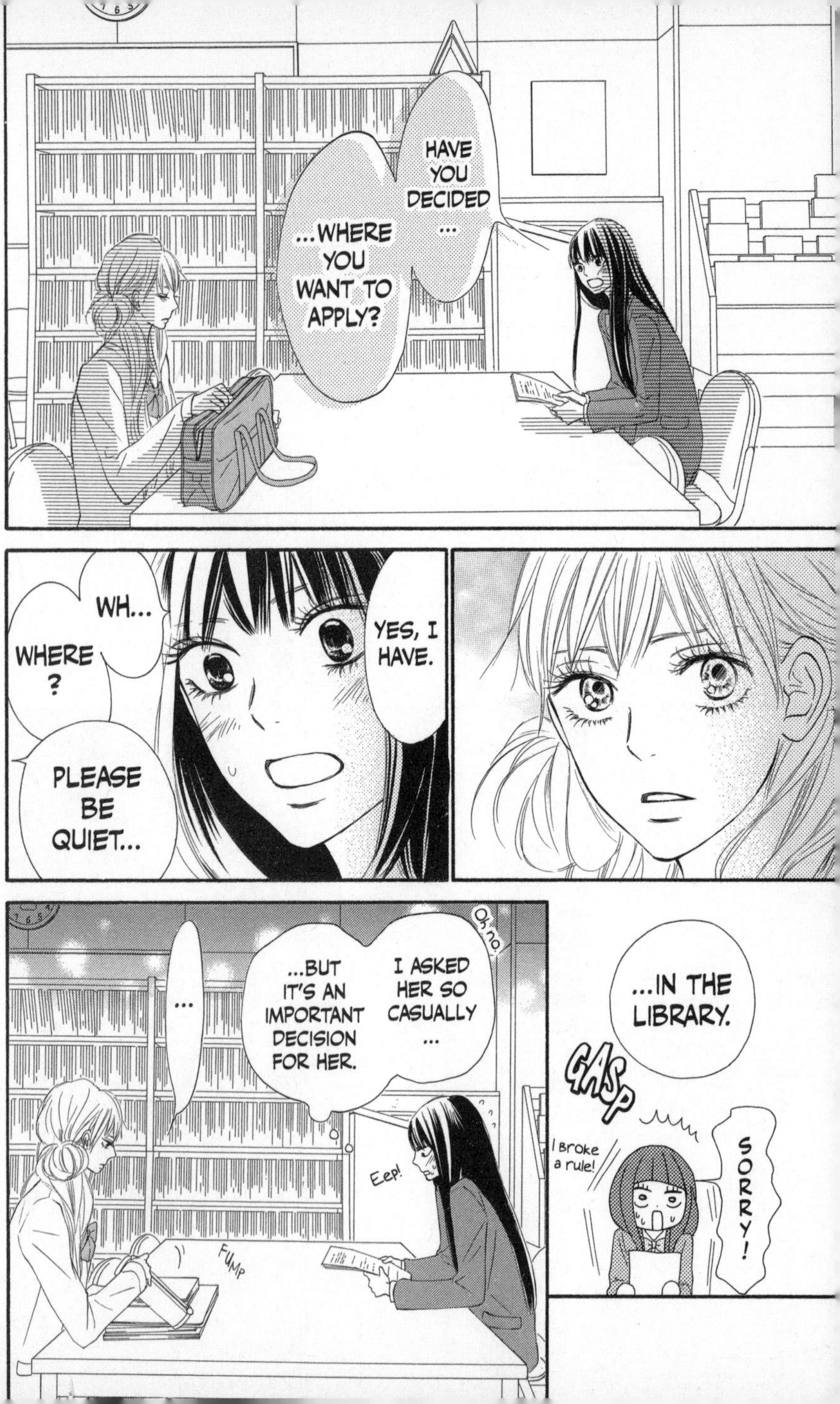
HAVE YOU DECIDED...
...WHERE YOU WANT TO APPLY?
YES, I HAVE.
WH... WHERE?
PLEASE BE QUIET...
...IN THE LIBRARY.
GASP
SORRY!
I broke a rule!
Oh no.
I ASKED HER SO CASUALLY...
...BUT IT'S AN IMPORTANT DECISION FOR HER.
Eep!
...
FUMP

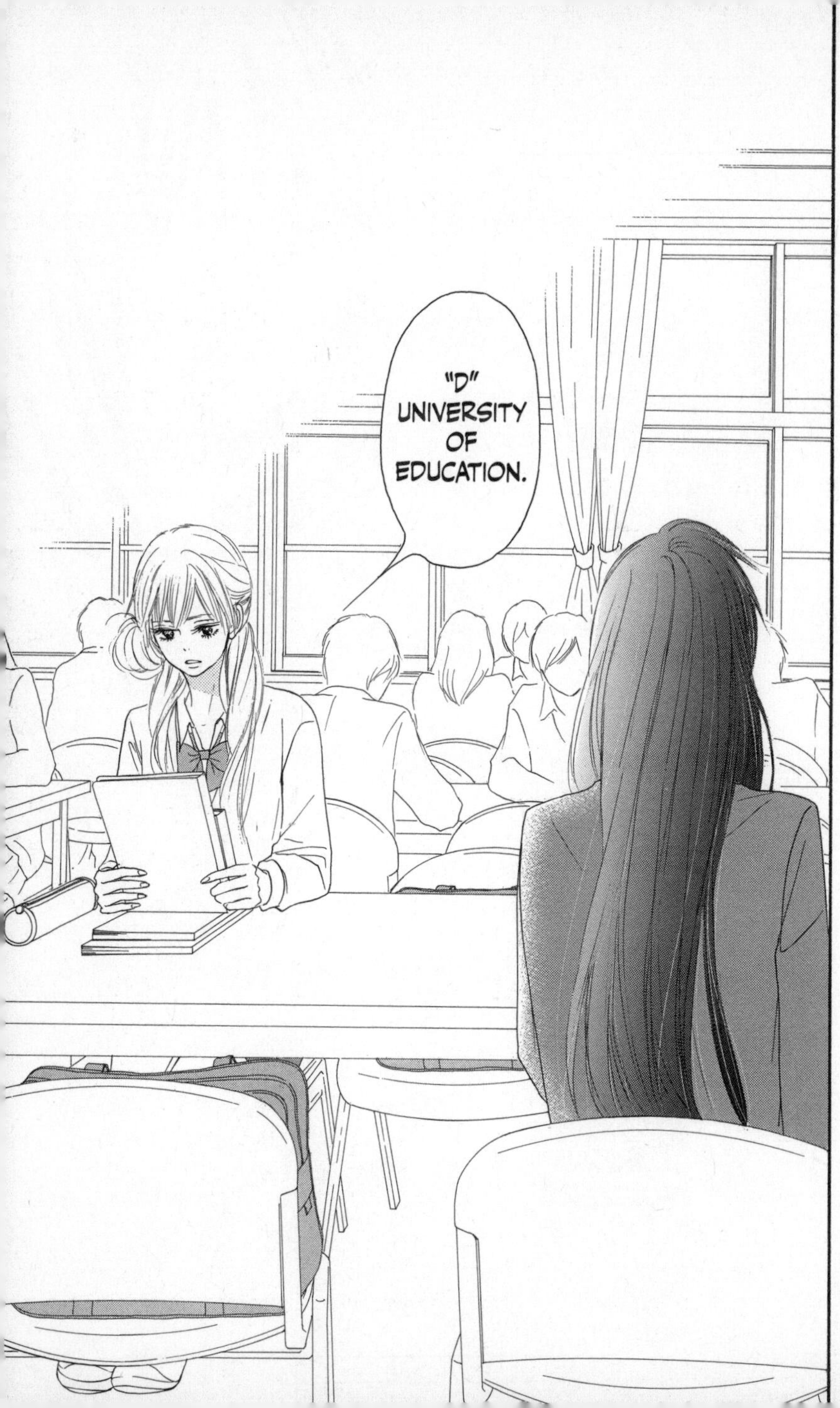
"D" UNIVERSITY OF EDUCATION.

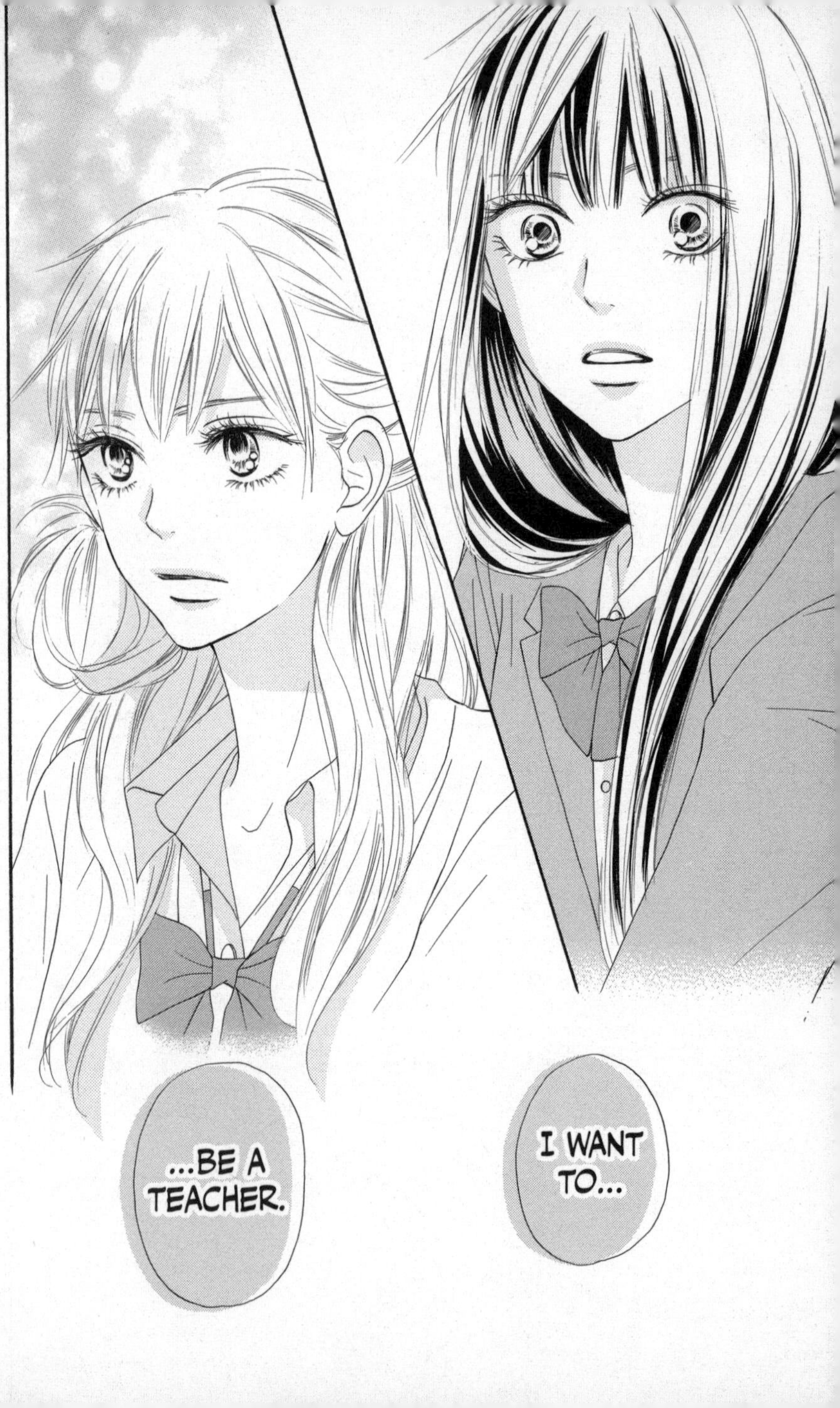
I WANT TO...
...BE A TEACHER.

Episode 86: Exam Preparation

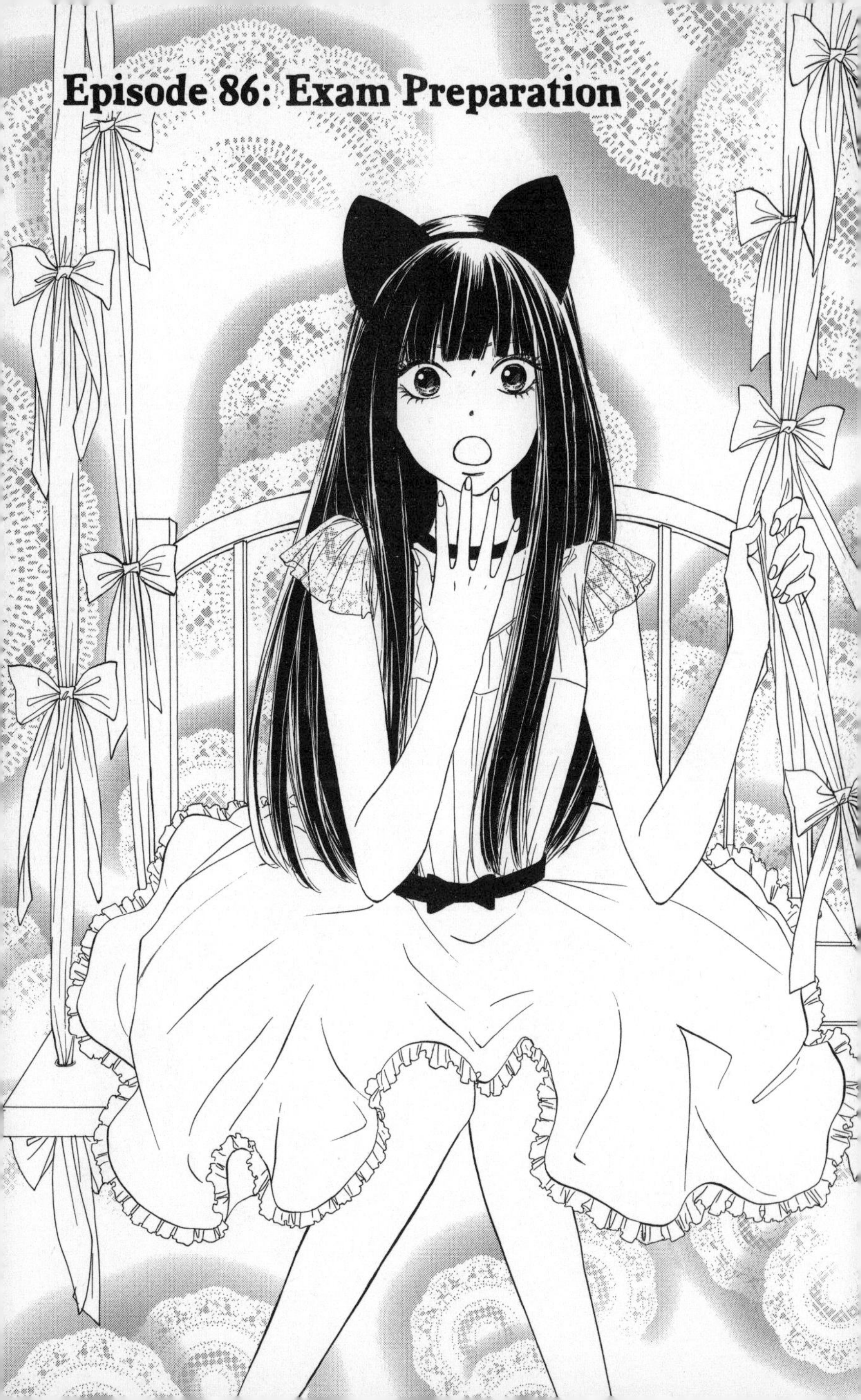

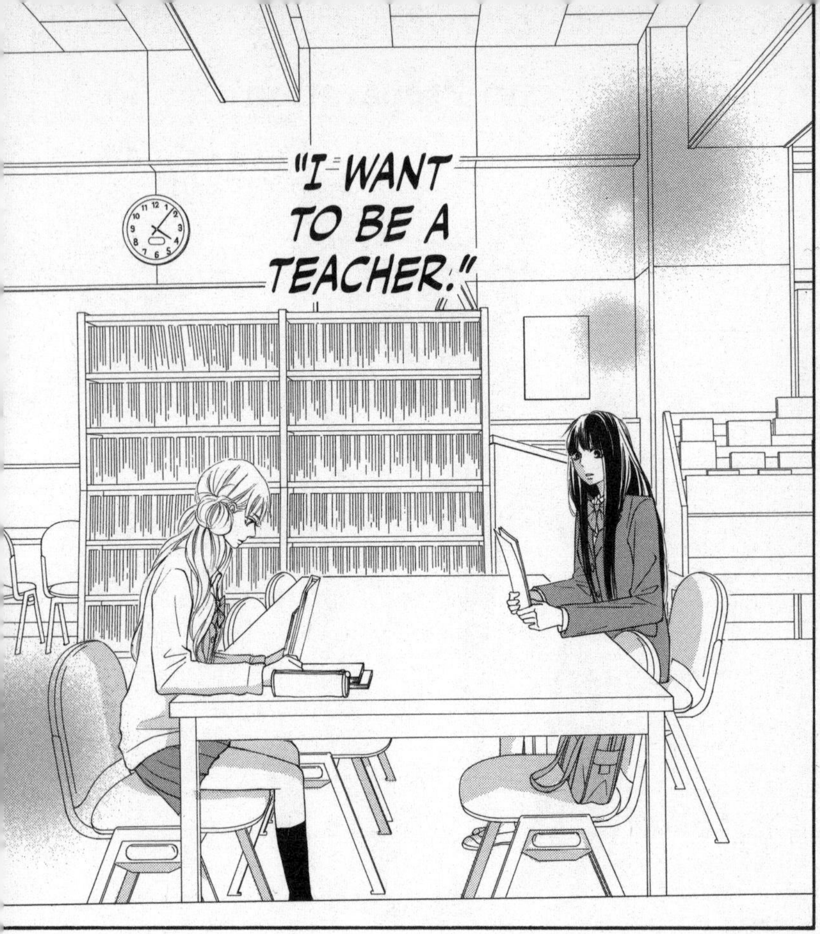
"I WANT TO BE A TEACHER."
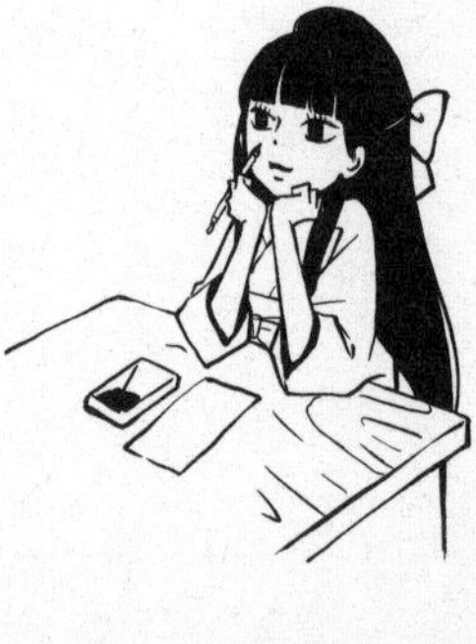

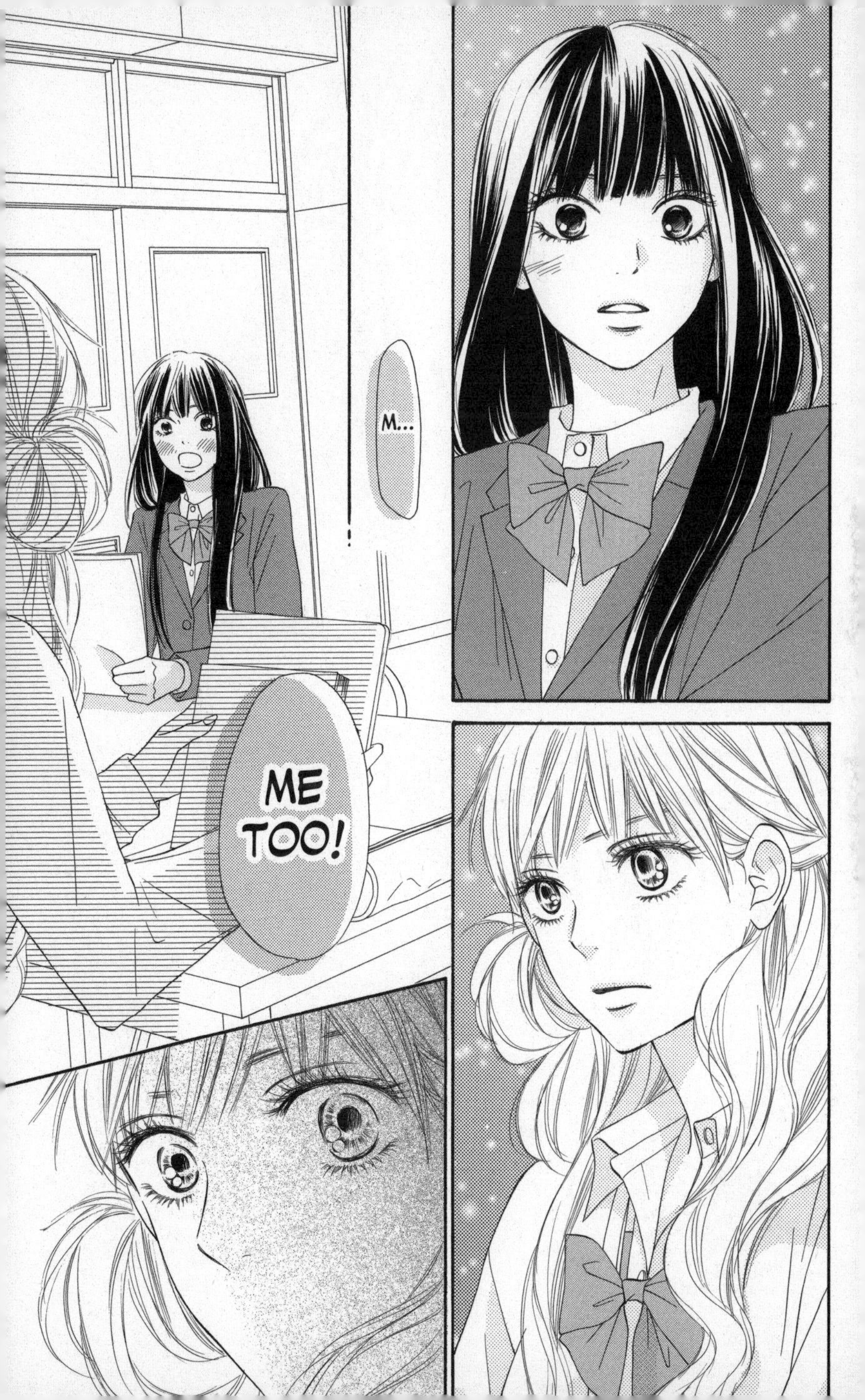
M...
ME TOO!

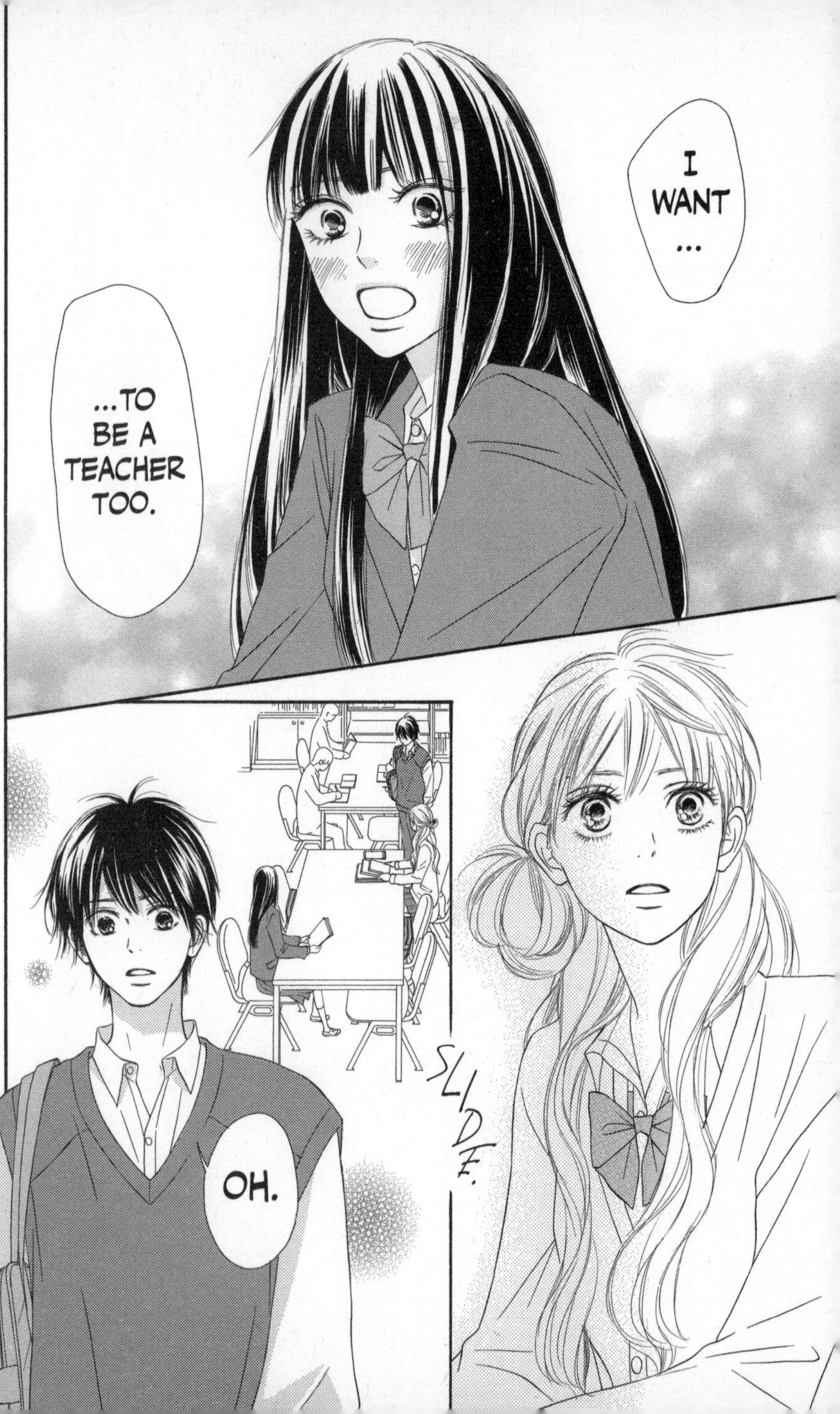
I WANT ...
...TO BE A TEACHER TOO.
SLIDE.
OH.

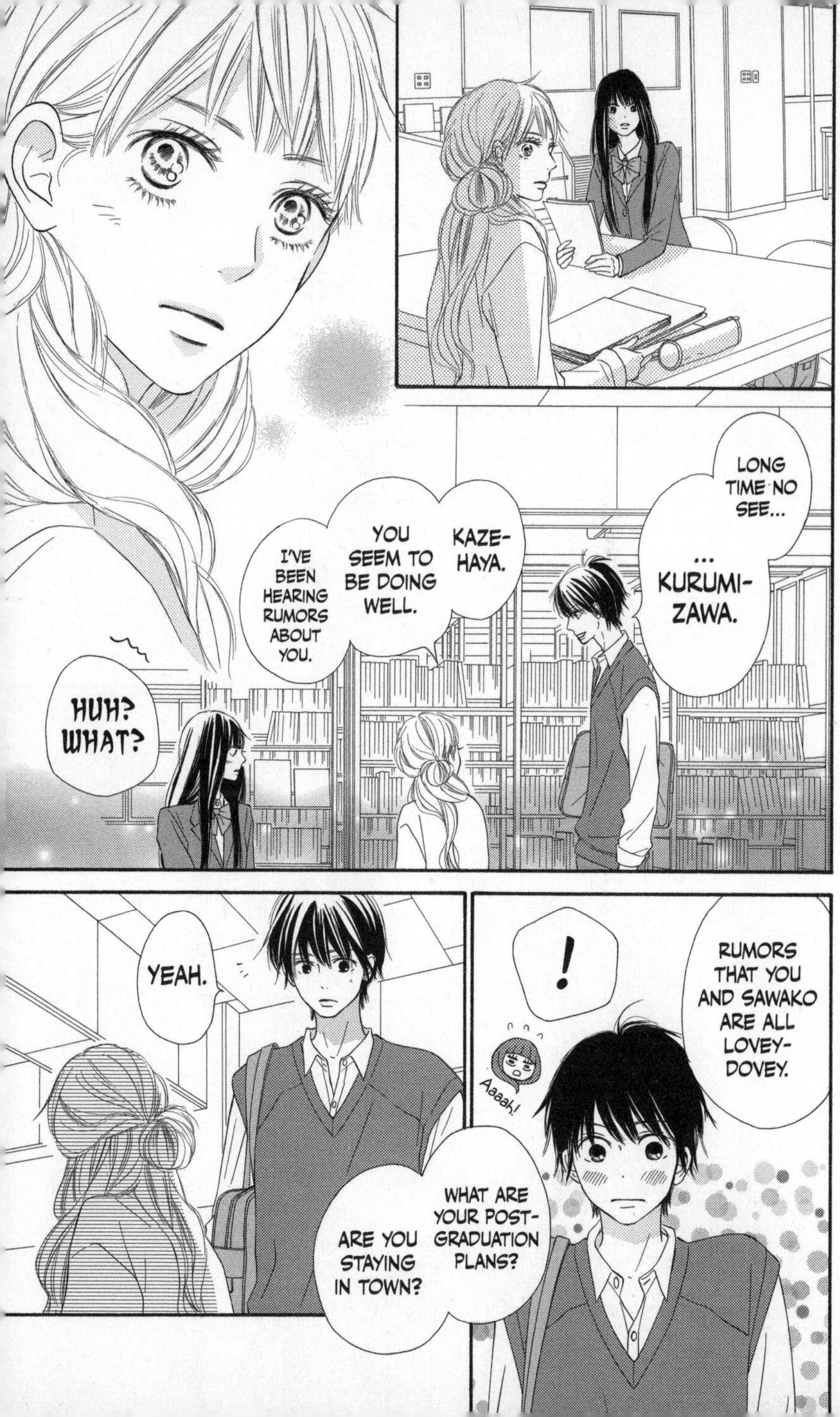
LONG TIME NO SEE...
... KURUMI-ZAWA.
KAZE-HAYA.
YOU SEEM TO BE DOING WELL.
I'VE BEEN HEARING RUMORS ABOUT YOU.
HUH? WHAT?
RUMORS THAT YOU AND SAWAKO ARE ALL LOVEY-DOVEY.
!
Aaaah!
YEAH.
WHAT ARE YOUR POST-GRADUATION PLANS?
ARE YOU STAYING IN TOWN?

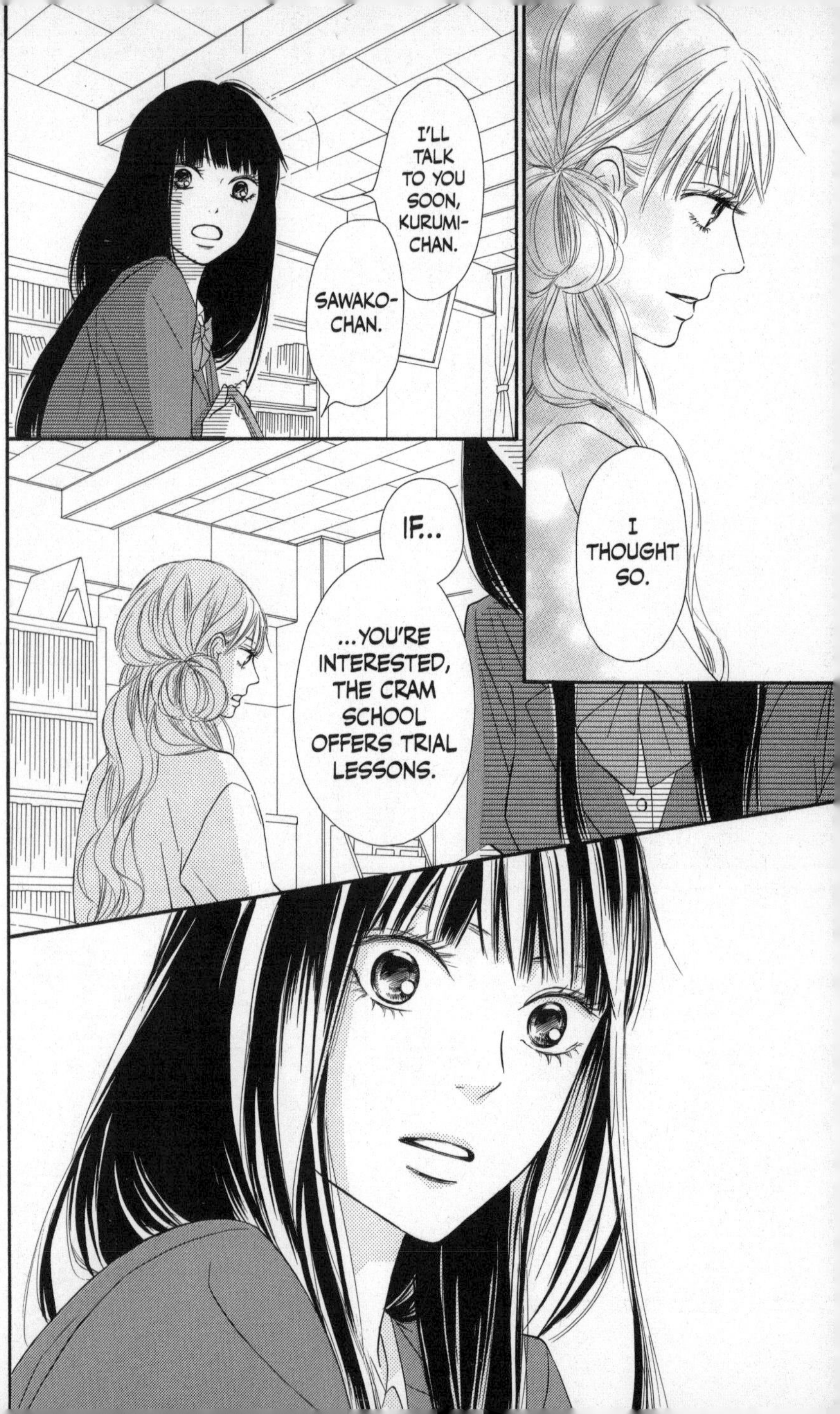
I THOUGHT SO.
I'LL TALK TO YOU SOON, KURUMI-CHAN.
SAWAKO-CHAN.
IF...
...YOU'RE INTERESTED, THE CRAM SCHOOL OFFERS TRIAL LESSONS.

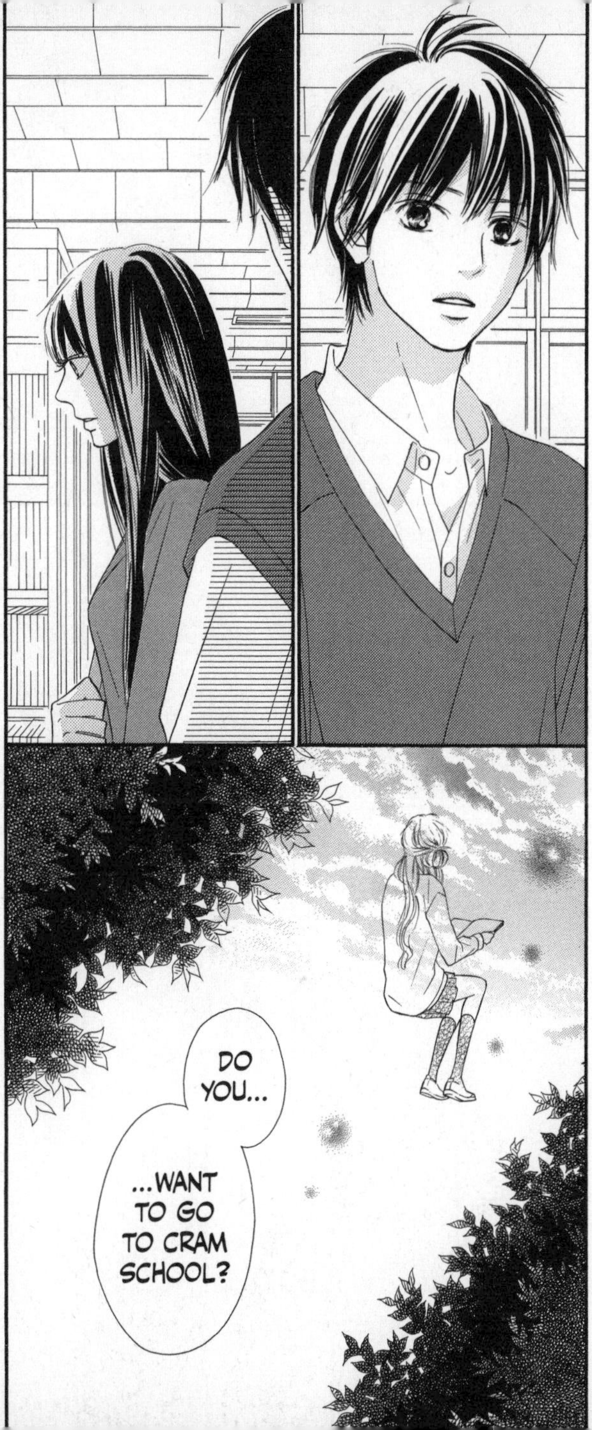
DO YOU...
...WANT TO GO TO CRAM SCHOOL?
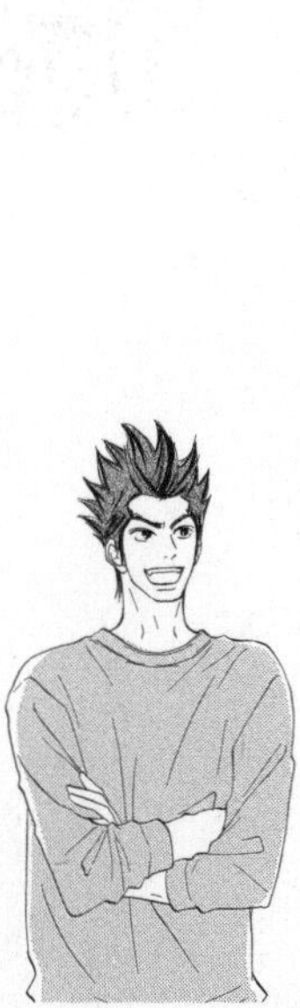

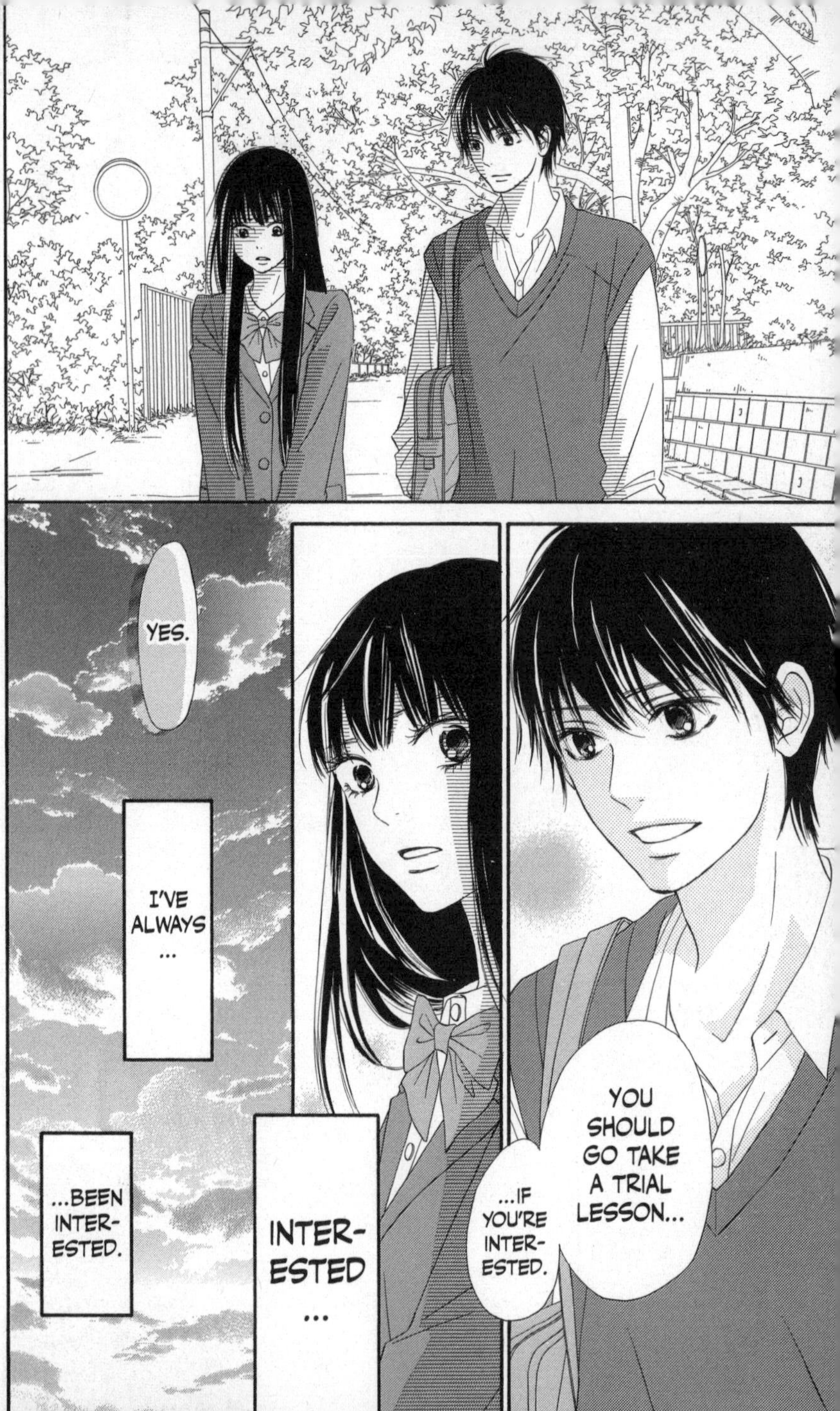
YOU SHOULD GO TAKE A TRIAL LESSON...
...IF YOU'RE INTER-ESTED.
INTER-ESTED...
YES.
I'VE ALWAYS...
...BEEN INTER-ESTED.

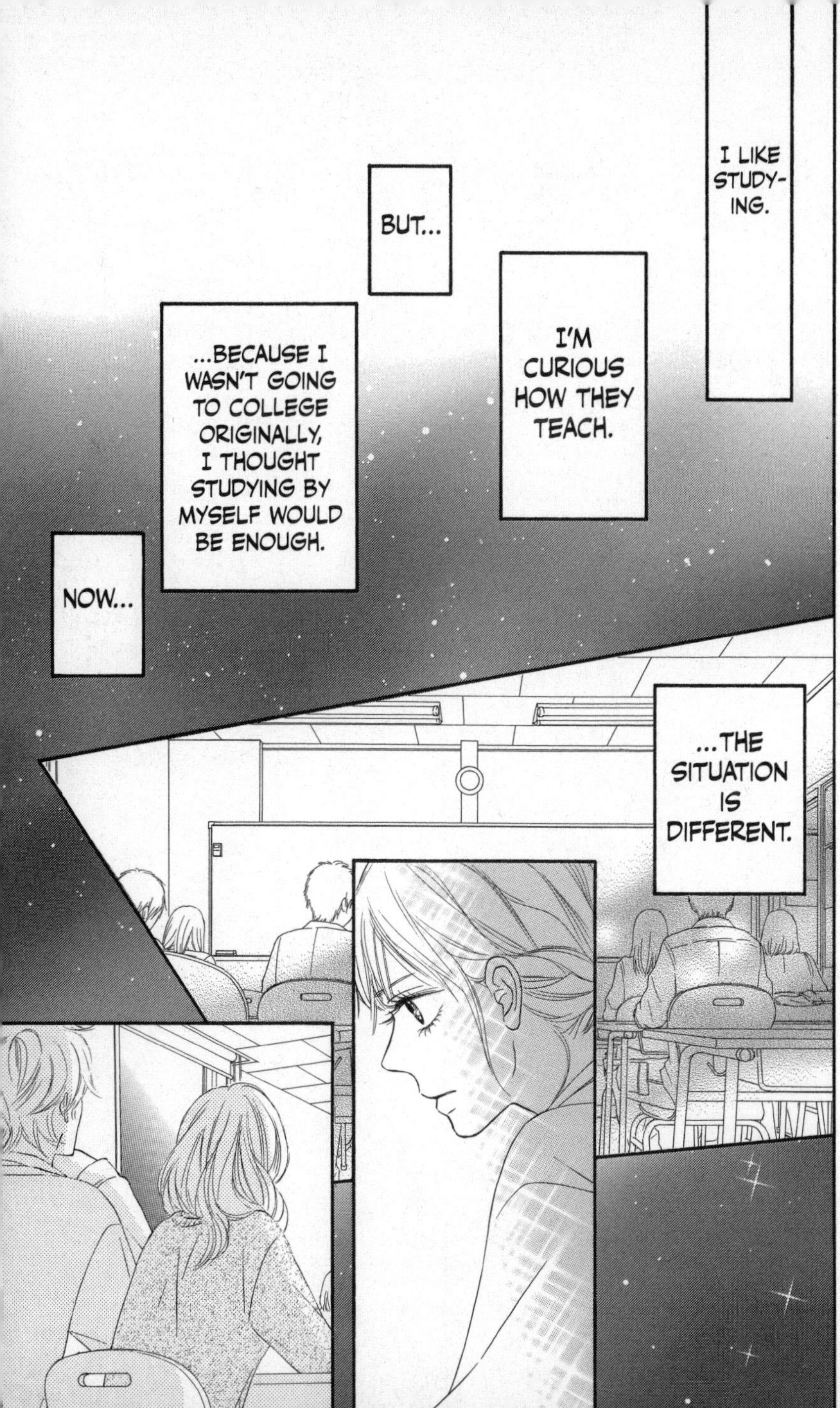
I LIKE STUDYING.
I'M CURIOUS HOW THEY TEACH.
BUT...
...BECAUSE I WASN'T GOING TO COLLEGE ORIGINALLY, I THOUGHT STUDYING BY MYSELF WOULD BE ENOUGH.
NOW...
...THE SITUATION IS DIFFERENT.

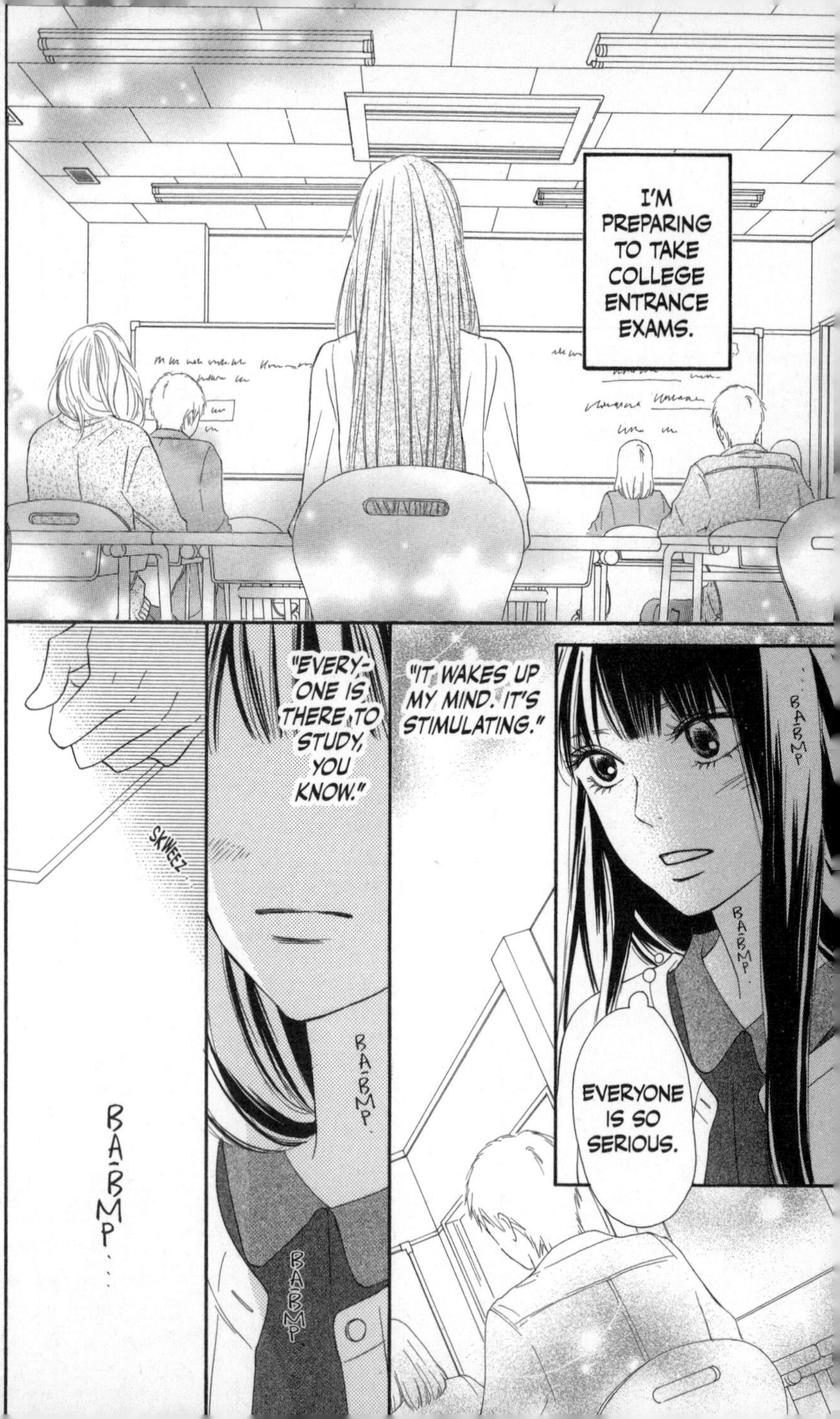

I'M PREPARING TO TAKE COLLEGE ENTRANCE EXAMS.
...BA-BMP
BA-BMP
EVERYONE IS SO SERIOUS.
"IT WAKES UP MY MIND. IT'S STIMULATING."
"EVERY-ONE IS THERE TO STUDY, YOU KNOW."
BA-BMP.
BA-BMP
SKWEEZ
BA-BMP...

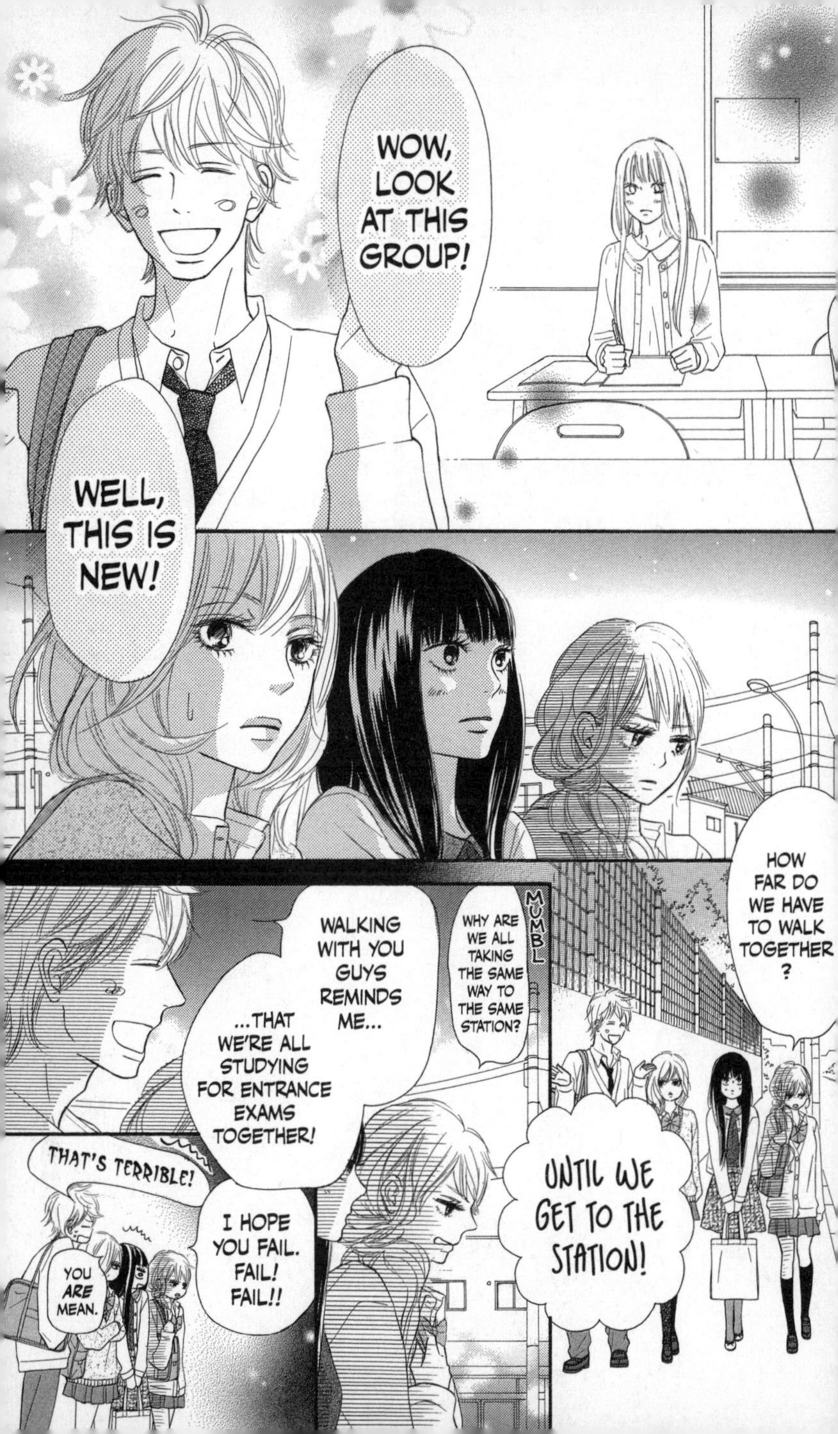
WOW, LOOK AT THIS GROUP!
WELL, THIS IS NEW!
HOW FAR DO WE HAVE TO WALK TOGETHER?
MUMBL
WHY ARE WE ALL TAKING THE SAME WAY TO THE SAME STATION?
WALKING WITH YOU GUYS REMINDS ME...
...THAT WE'RE ALL STUDYING FOR ENTRANCE EXAMS TOGETHER!
UNTIL WE GET TO THE STATION!
I HOPE YOU FAIL. FAIL! FAIL!!
THAT'S TERRIBLE!
YOU ARE MEAN.

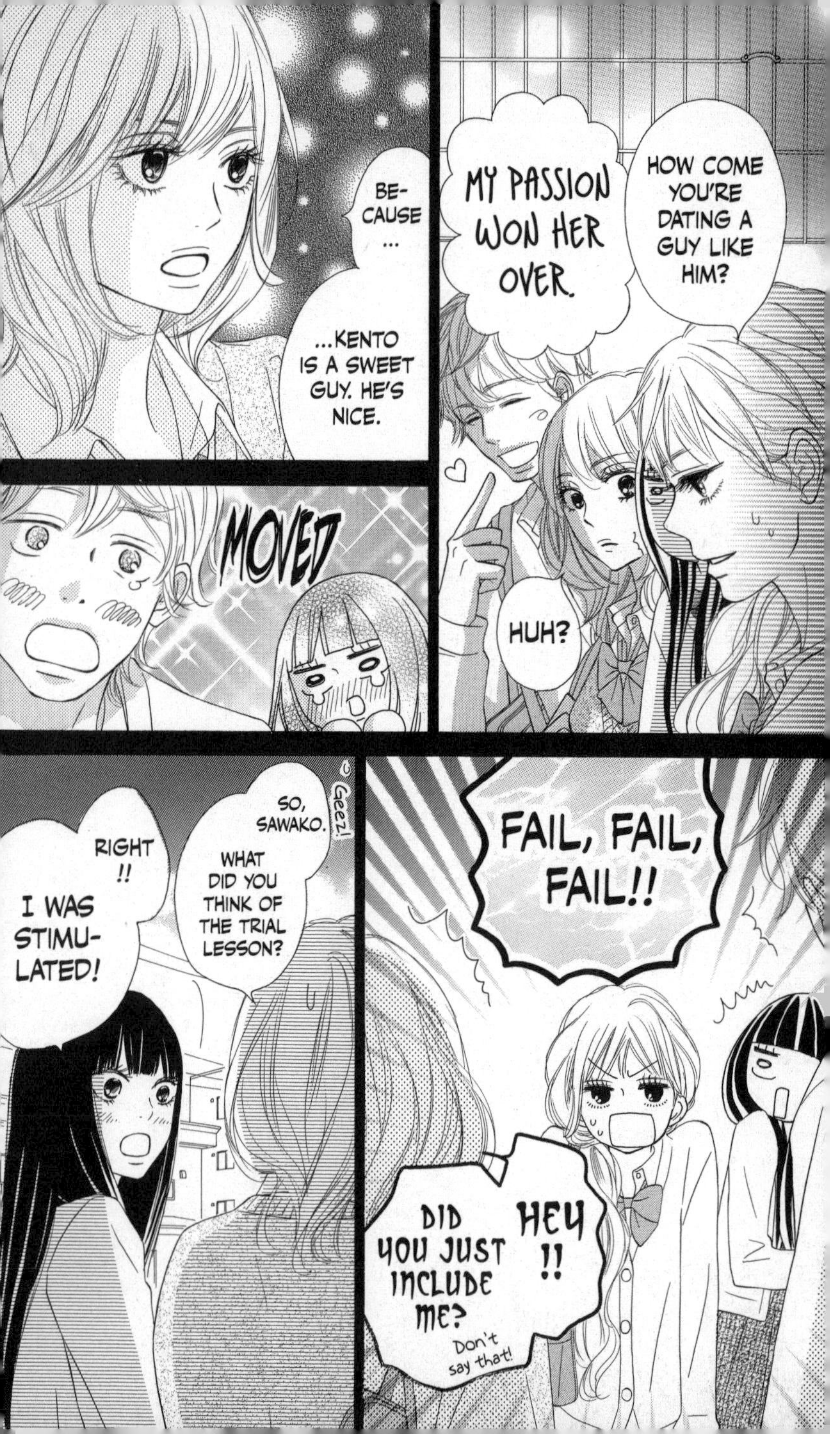
HOW COME YOU'RE DATING A GUY LIKE HIM?
MY PASSION WON HER OVER.
HUH?
BE-CAUSE ...
...KENTO IS A SWEET GUY. HE'S NICE.
MOVED
FAIL, FAIL, FAIL!!
HEY !!
DID YOU JUST INCLUDE ME?
Don't say that!
Geez!
SO, SAWAKO.
WHAT DID YOU THINK OF THE TRIAL LESSON?
RIGHT !!
I WAS STIMU-LATED!

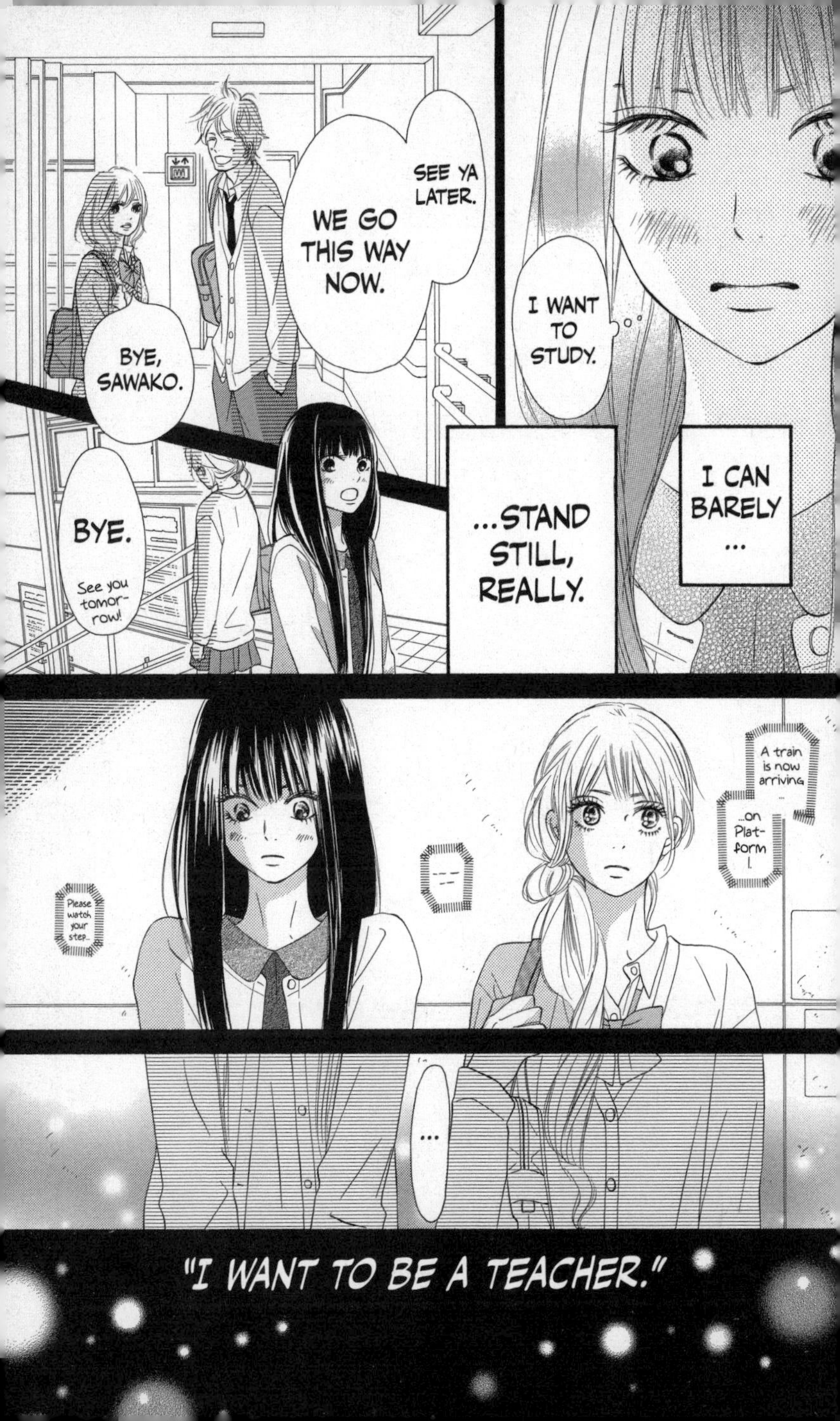
I WANT TO STUDY.
I CAN BARELY...
...STAND STILL, REALLY.
SEE YA LATER.
WE GO THIS WAY NOW.
BYE, SAWAKO.
BYE.
See you tomorrow!
A train is now arriving...
...on Platform 1.
Please watch your step...
...
"I WANT TO BE A TEACHER."

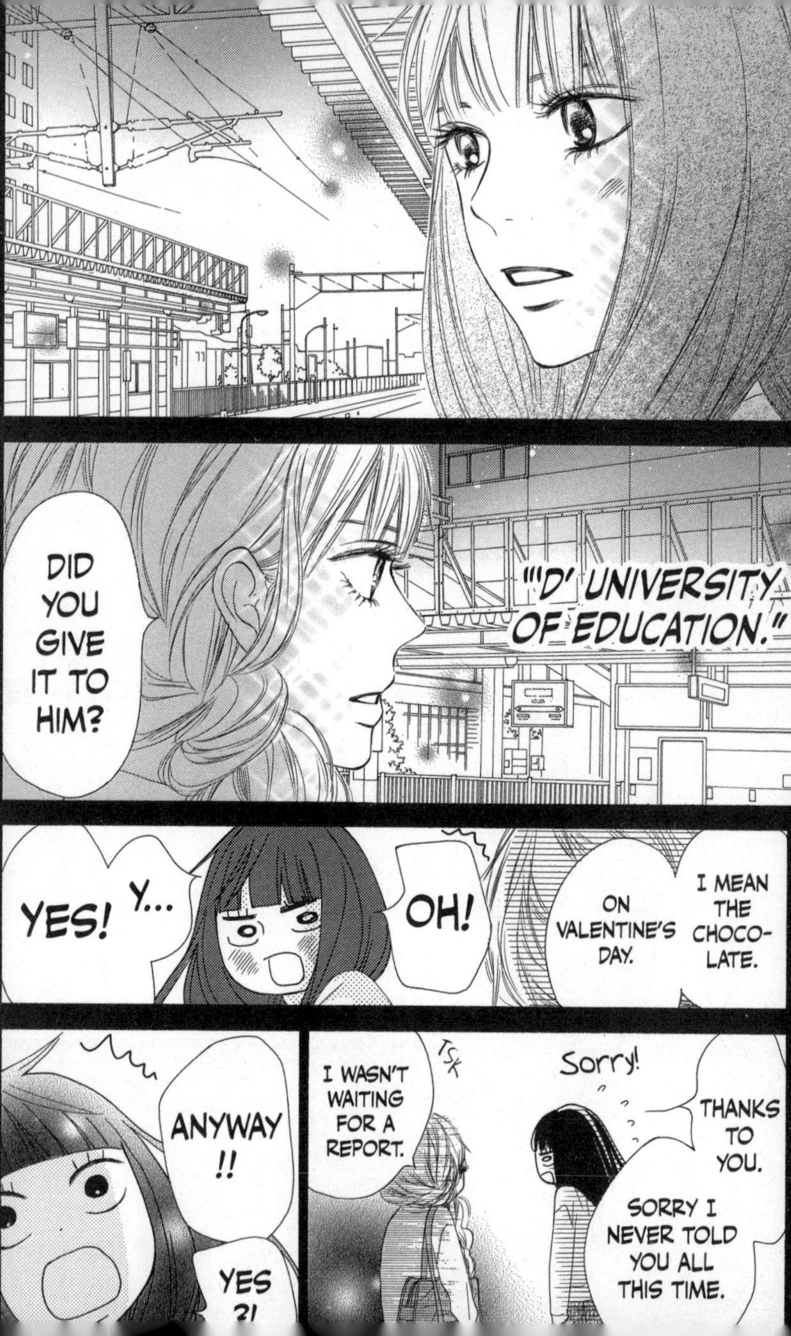
"'D' UNIVERSITY OF EDUCATION."
DID YOU GIVE IT TO HIM?
I MEAN THE CHOCOLATE.
ON VALENTINE'S DAY.
OH!
Y...
YES!
THANKS TO YOU.
Sorry!
SORRY I NEVER TOLD YOU ALL THIS TIME.
TSK
I WASN'T WAITING FOR A REPORT.
ANYWAY !!
YES

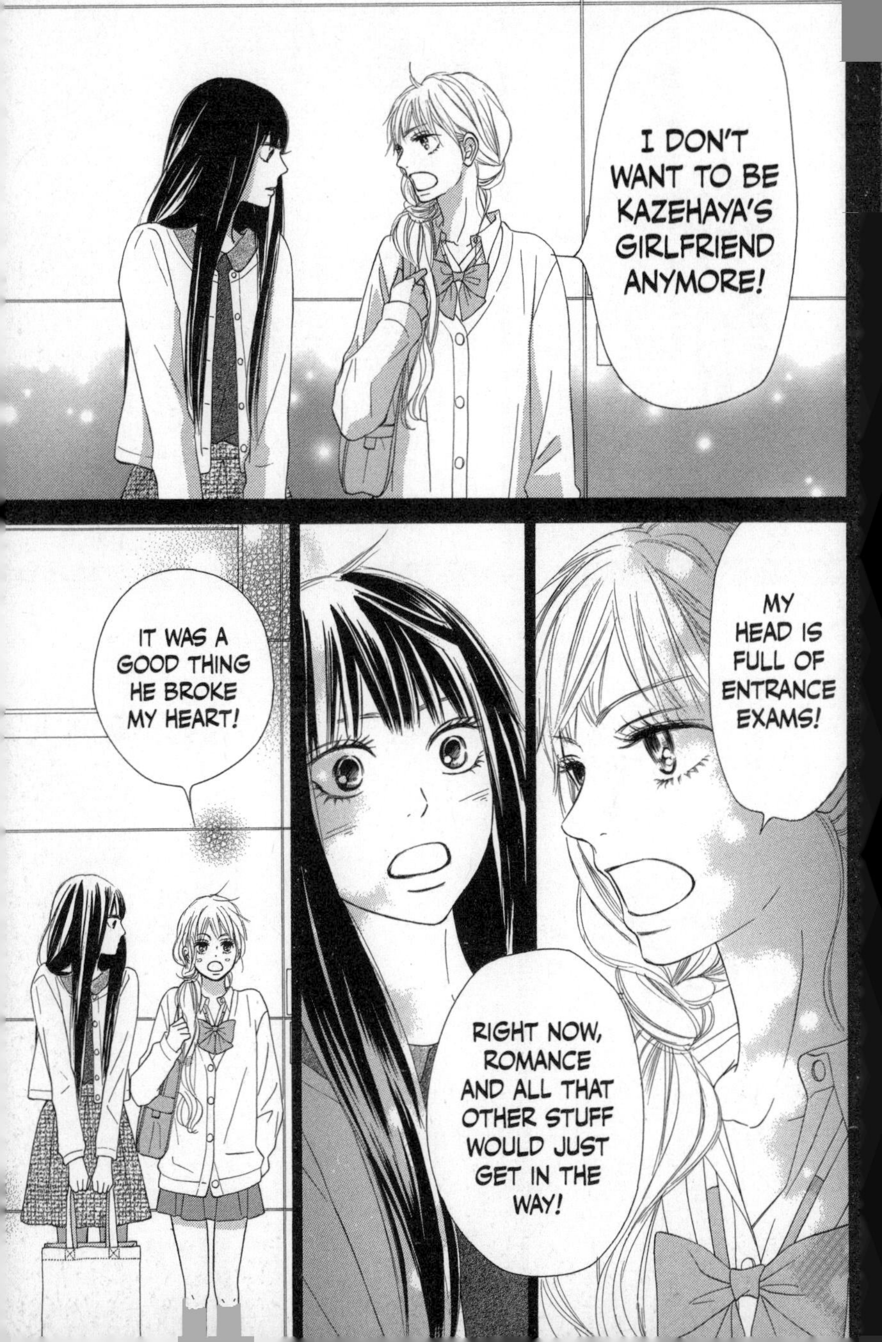
I DON'T WANT TO BE KAZEHAYA'S GIRLFRIEND ANYMORE!
MY HEAD IS FULL OF ENTRANCE EXAMS!
RIGHT NOW, ROMANCE AND ALL THAT OTHER STUFF WOULD JUST GET IN THE WAY!
IT WAS A GOOD THING HE BROKE MY HEART!

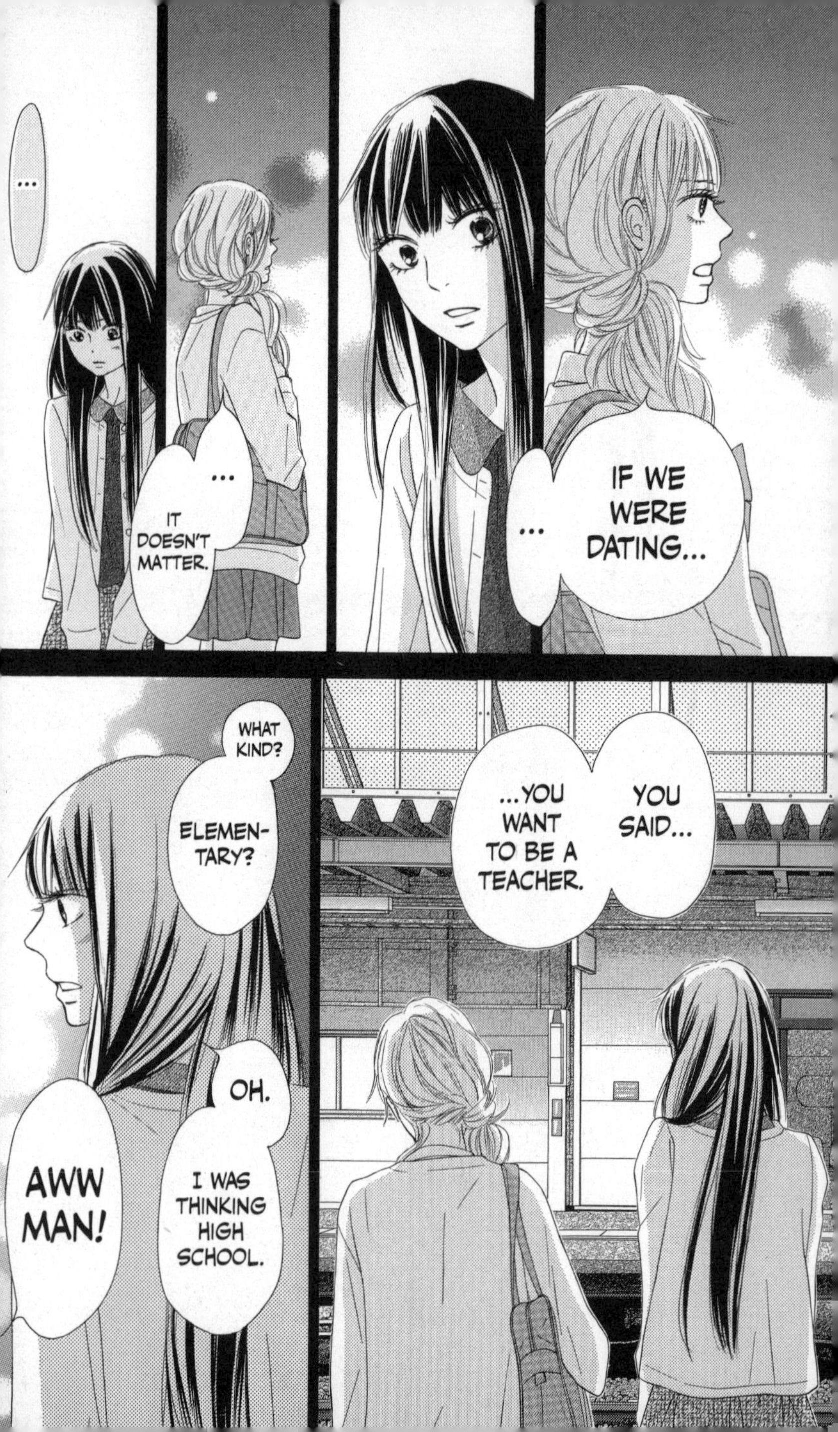
IF WE WERE DATING...
...
...
IT DOESN'T MATTER.
...
YOU SAID...
...YOU WANT TO BE A TEACHER.
WHAT KIND?
ELEMENTARY?
OH.
I WAS THINKING HIGH SCHOOL.
AWW MAN!

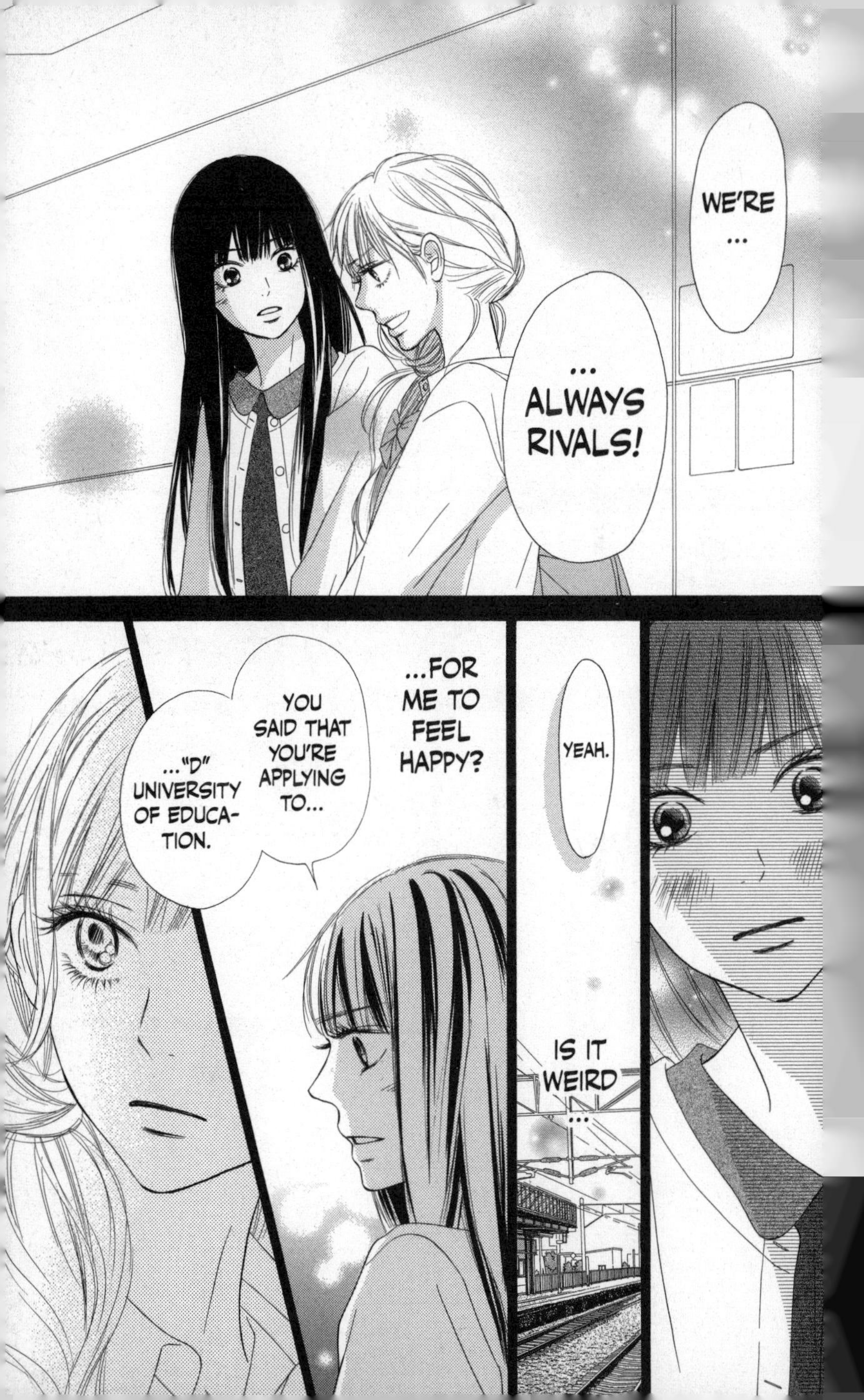
WE'RE ...
... ALWAYS RIVALS!
YEAH.
IS IT WEIRD ...
...FOR ME TO FEEL HAPPY?
YOU SAID THAT YOU'RE APPLYING TO...
..."D" UNIVERSITY OF EDUCA-TION.

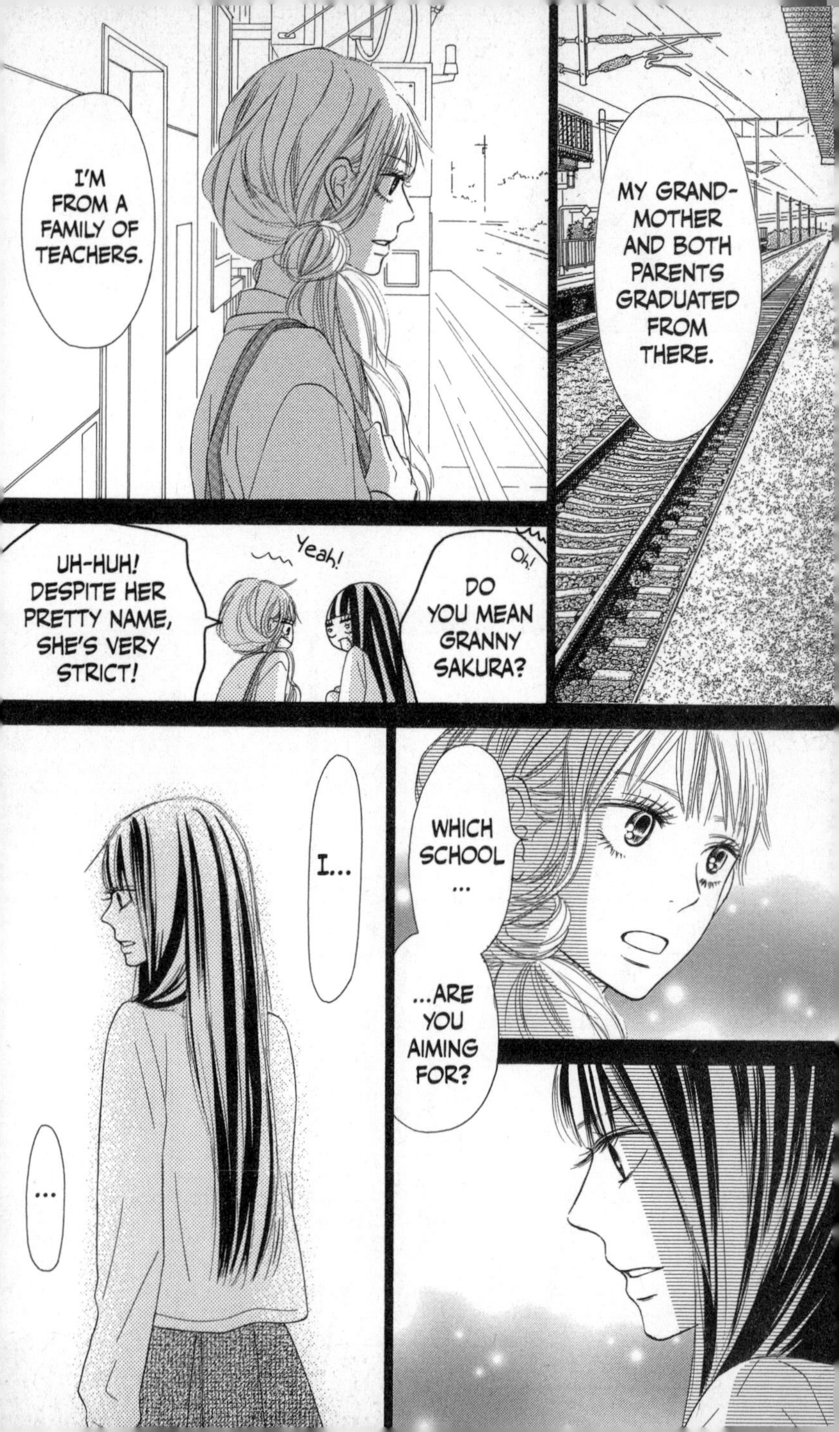
MY GRAND-MOTHER AND BOTH PARENTS GRADUATED FROM THERE.
I'M FROM A FAMILY OF TEACHERS.
Oh!
DO YOU MEAN GRANNY SAKURA?
Yeah!
UH-HUH! DESPITE HER PRETTY NAME, SHE'S VERY STRICT!
WHICH SCHOOL ...
...ARE YOU AIMING FOR?
I...
...

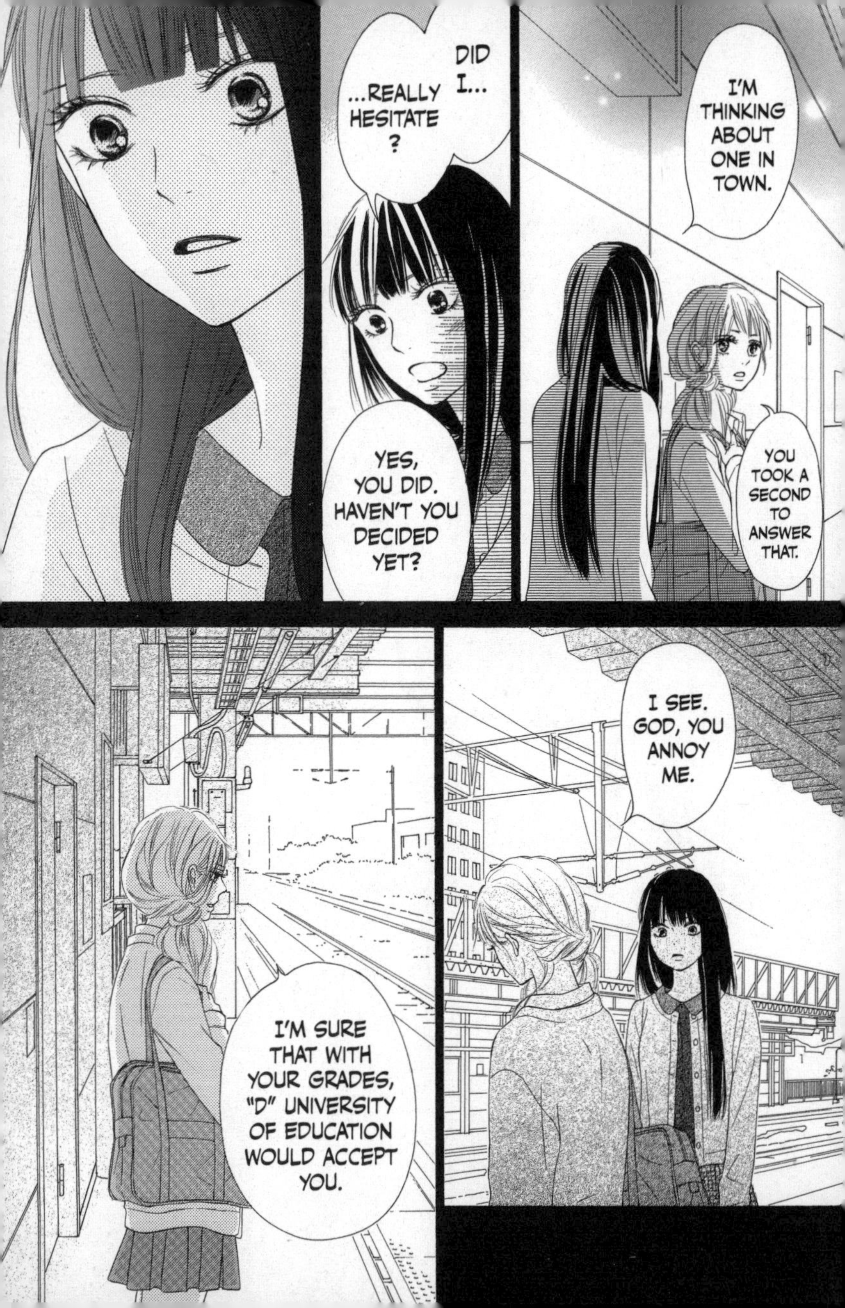
I'M THINKING ABOUT ONE IN TOWN.
YOU TOOK A SECOND TO ANSWER THAT.
DID I...
...REALLY HESITATE?
YES, YOU DID. HAVEN'T YOU DECIDED YET?
I SEE. GOD, YOU ANNOY ME.
I'M SURE THAT WITH YOUR GRADES, "D" UNIVERSITY OF EDUCATION WOULD ACCEPT YOU.

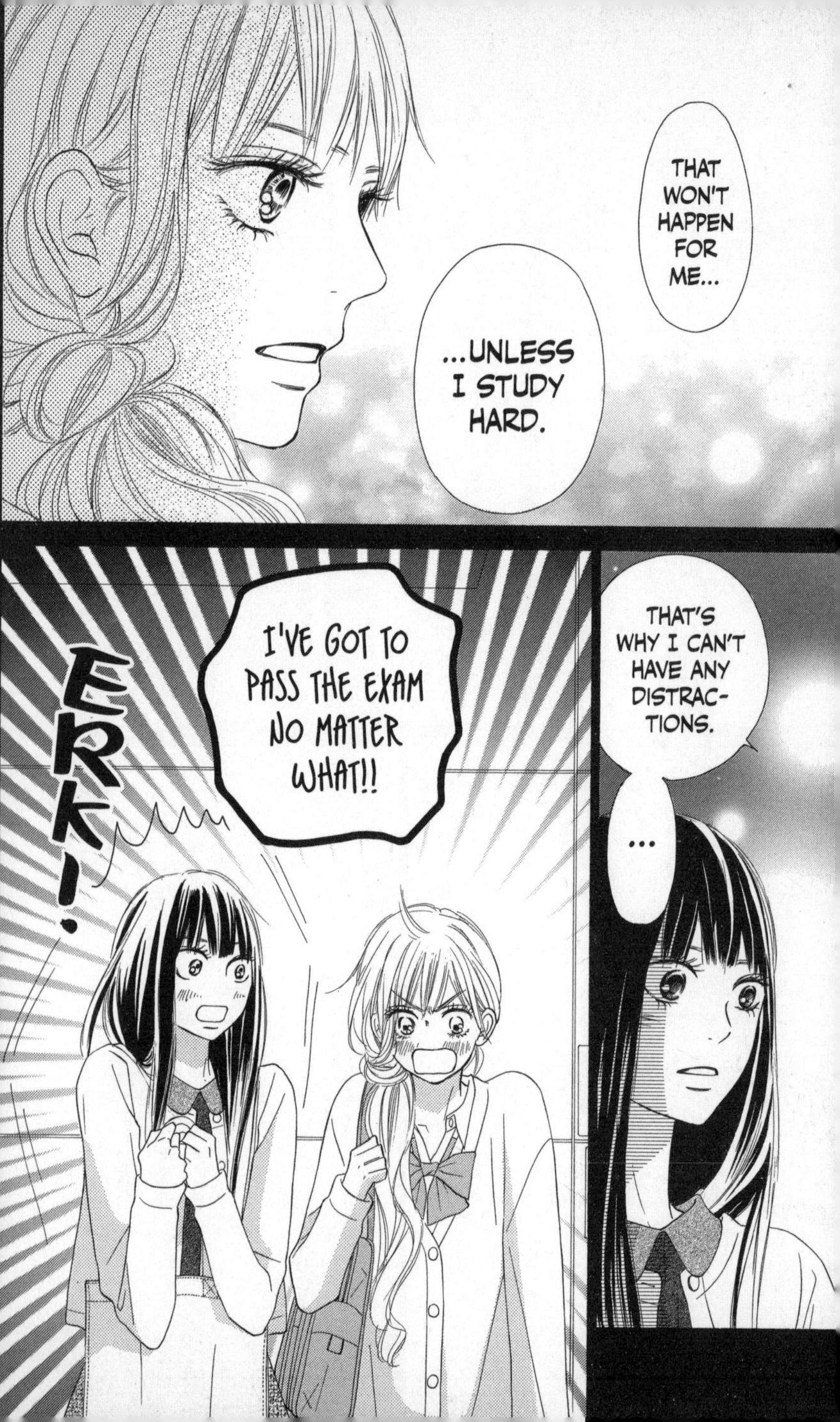
THAT WON'T HAPPEN FOR ME...
...UNLESS I STUDY HARD.
THAT'S WHY I CAN'T HAVE ANY DISTRAC- TIONS.
...
I'VE GOT TO PASS THE EXAM NO MATTER WHAT!!
ERK!

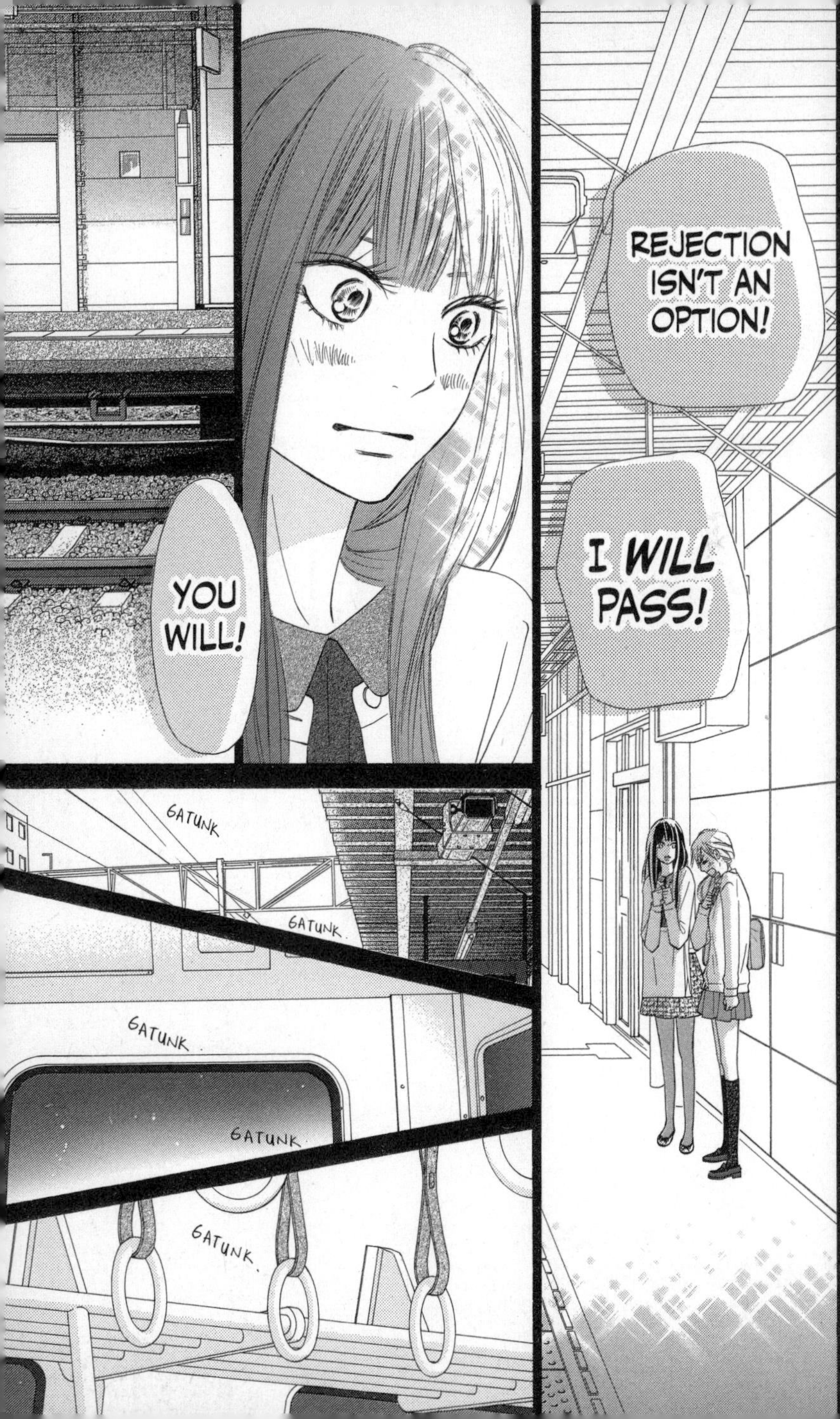
REJECTION ISN'T AN OPTION!
I WILL PASS!
YOU WILL!
GATUNK
GATUNK
GATUNK
GATUNK
GATUNK

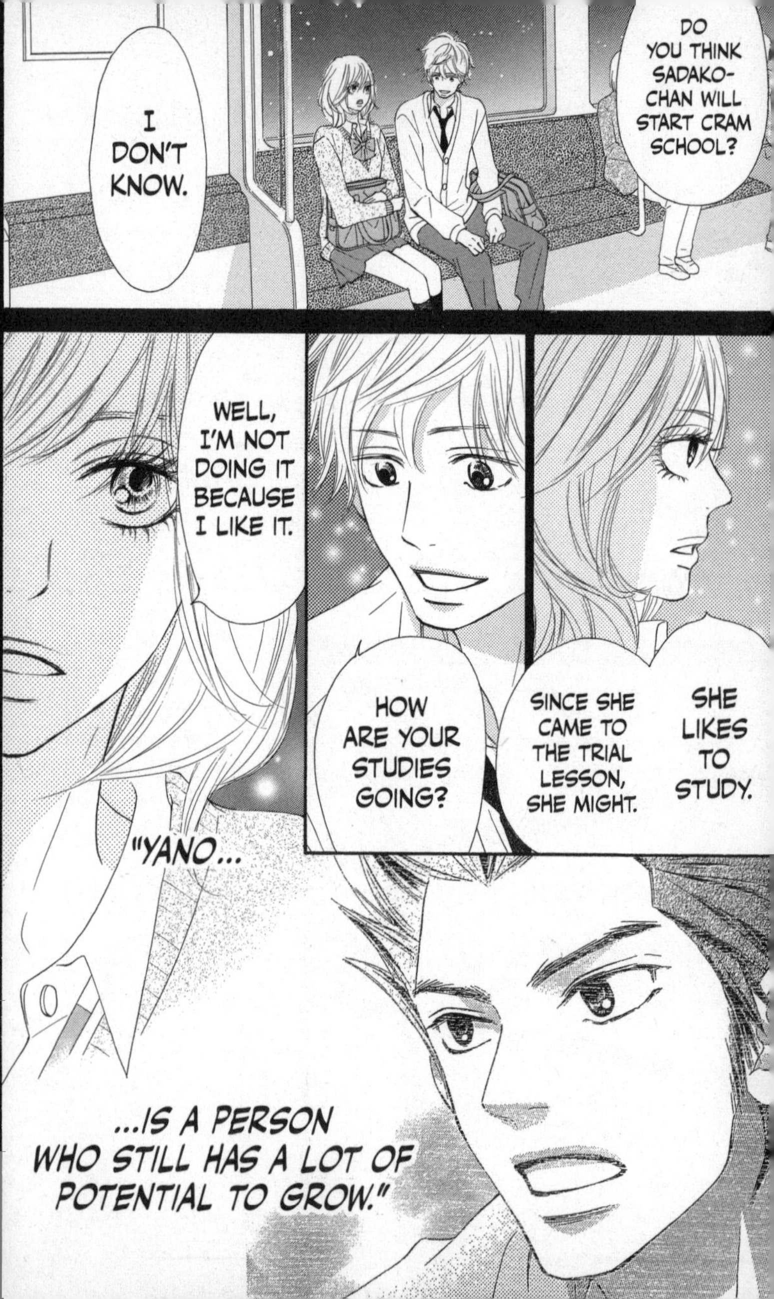
DO YOU THINK SADAKO-CHAN WILL START CRAM SCHOOL?
I DON'T KNOW.
SHE LIKES TO STUDY.
SINCE SHE CAME TO THE TRIAL LESSON, SHE MIGHT.
HOW ARE YOUR STUDIES GOING?
WELL, I'M NOT DOING IT BECAUSE I LIKE IT.
"YANO...
...IS A PERSON WHO STILL HAS A LOT OF POTENTIAL TO GROW."

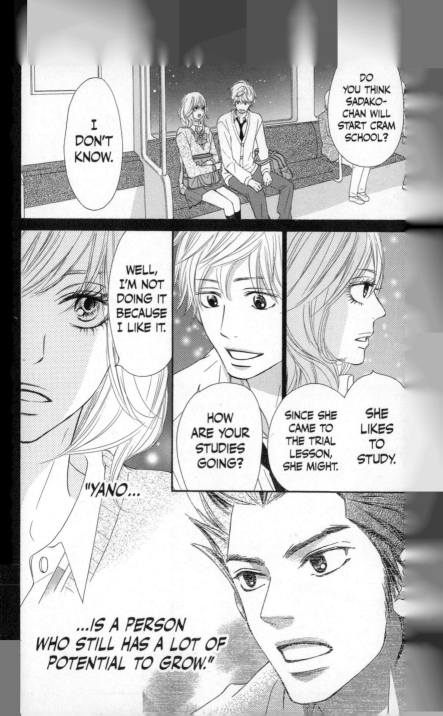

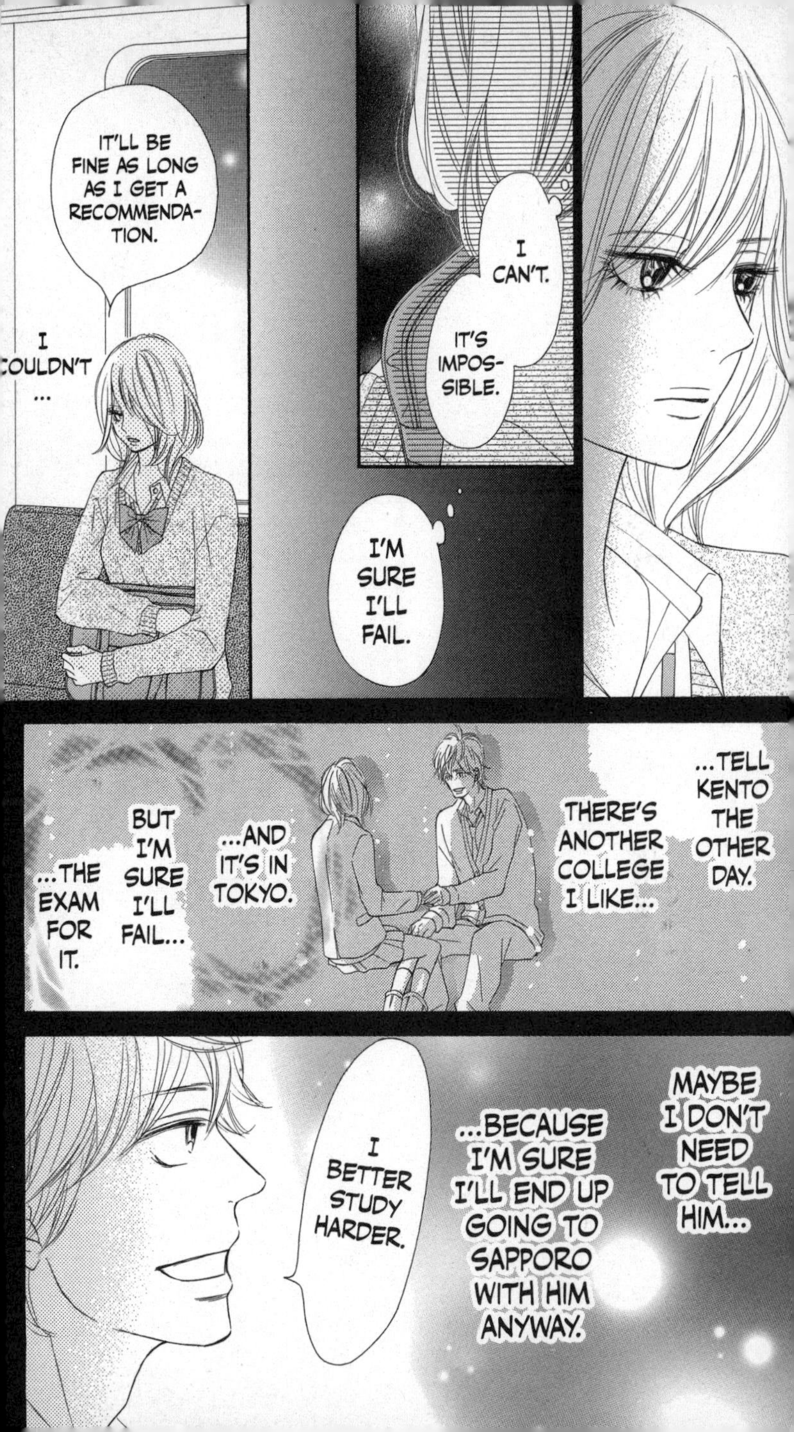
I CAN'T.
IT'S IMPOSSIBLE.
I'M SURE I'LL FAIL.
IT'LL BE FINE AS LONG AS I GET A RECOMMENDATION.
I COULDN'T ...
...TELL KENTO THE OTHER DAY.
THERE'S ANOTHER COLLEGE I LIKE...
...AND IT'S IN TOKYO.
BUT I'M SURE I'LL FAIL...
...THE EXAM FOR IT.
MAYBE I DON'T NEED TO TELL HIM...
...BECAUSE I'M SURE I'LL END UP GOING TO SAPPORO WITH HIM ANYWAY.
I BETTER STUDY HARDER.

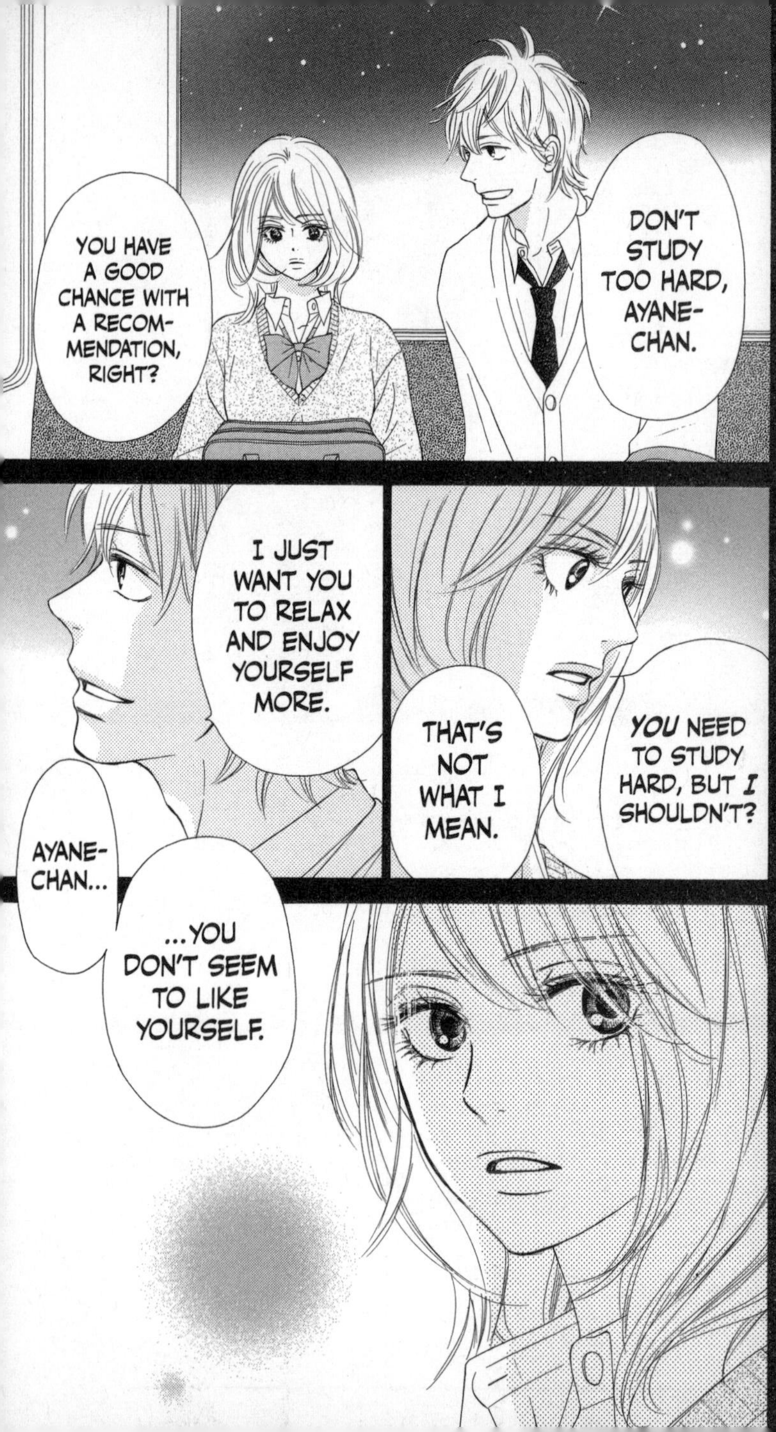
DON'T STUDY TOO HARD, AYANE-CHAN.
YOU HAVE A GOOD CHANCE WITH A RECOM-MENDATION, RIGHT?
YOU NEED TO STUDY HARD, BUT *I* SHOULDN'T?
THAT'S NOT WHAT I MEAN.
I JUST WANT YOU TO RELAX AND ENJOY YOURSELF MORE.
AYANE-CHAN...
...YOU DON'T SEEM TO LIKE YOURSELF.

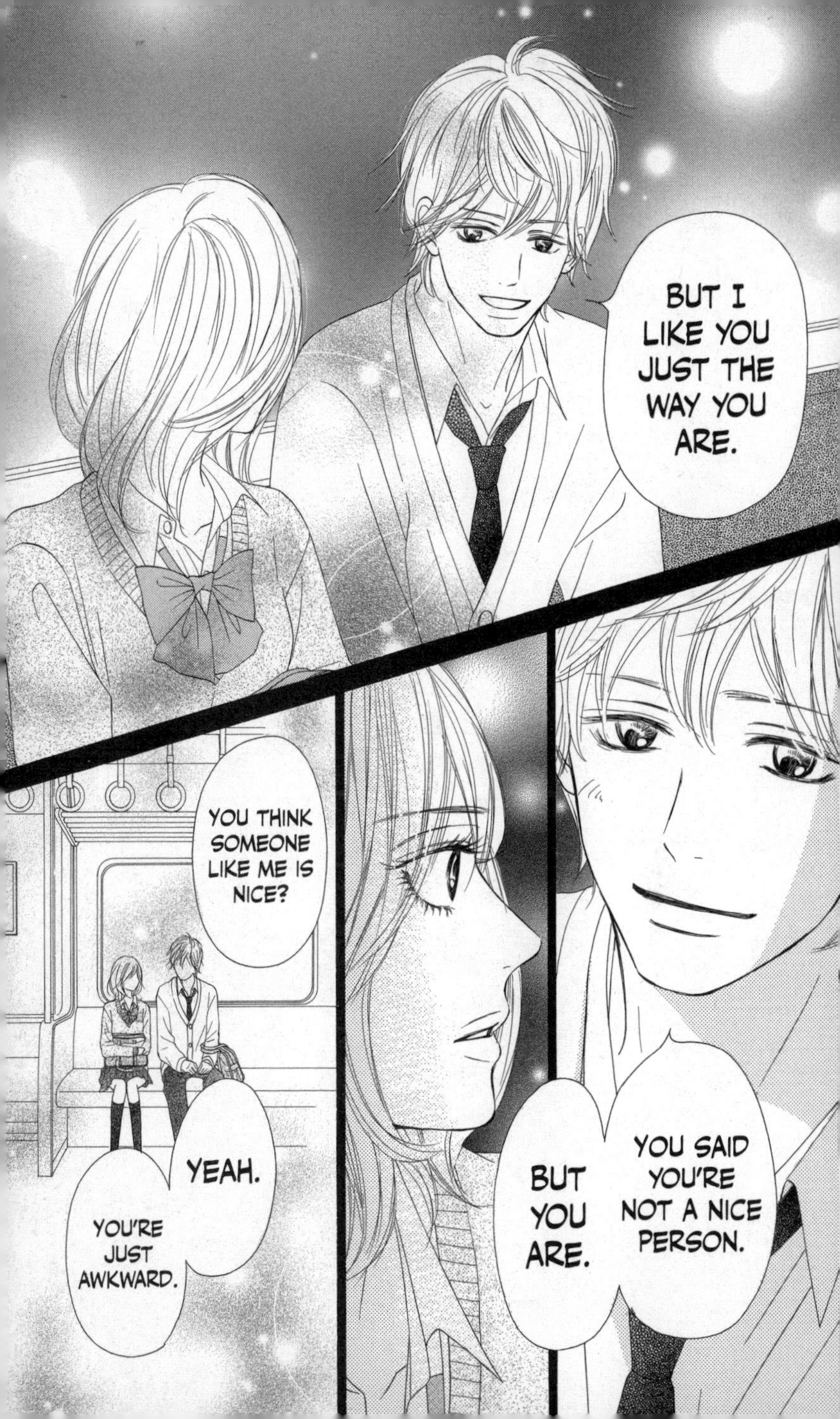
BUT I LIKE YOU JUST THE WAY YOU ARE.
YOU SAID YOU'RE NOT A NICE PERSON.
BUT YOU ARE.
YOU THINK SOMEONE LIKE ME IS NICE?
YEAH.
YOU'RE JUST AWKWARD.

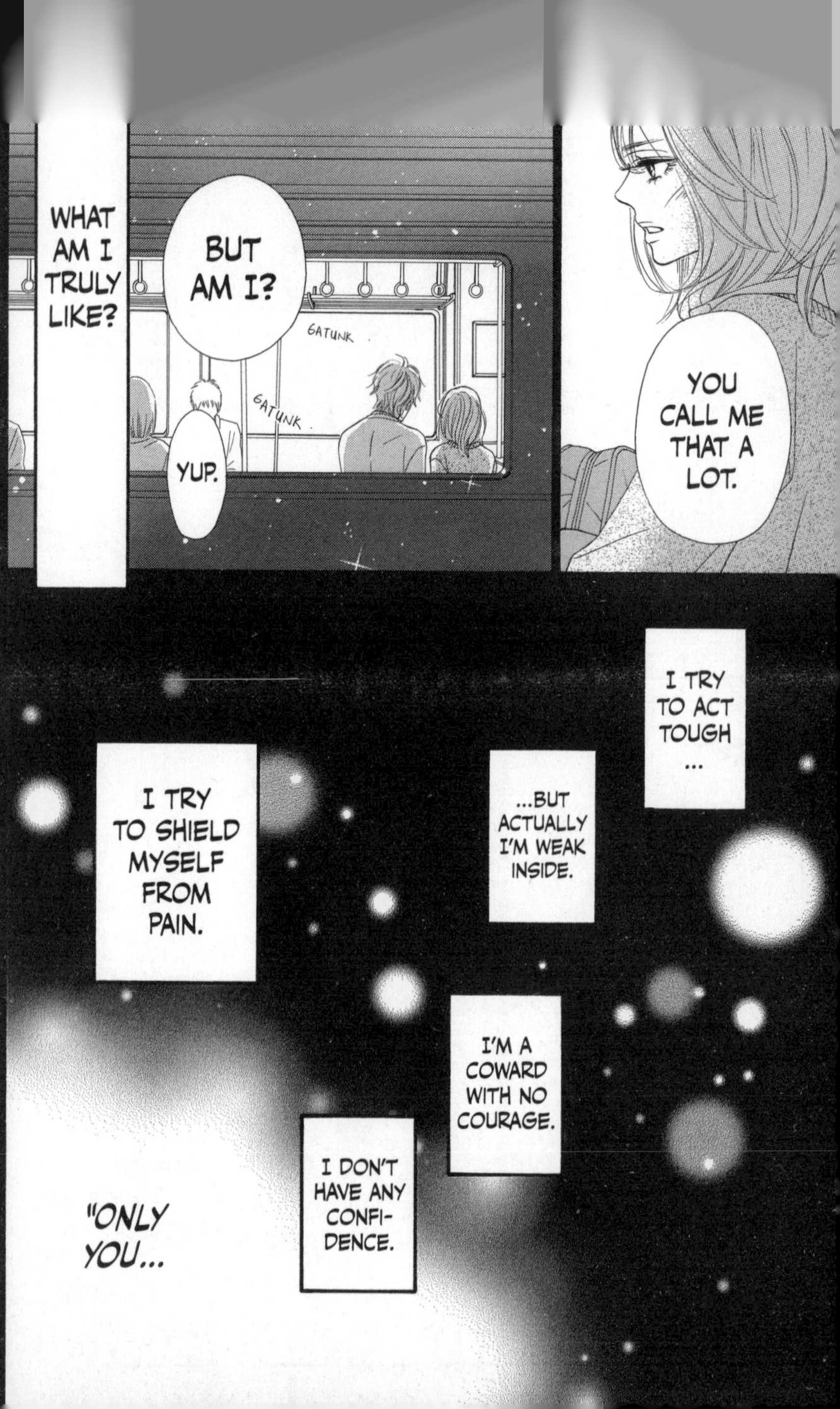
YOU CALL ME THAT A LOT.
BUT AM I?
GATUNK
GATUNK
YUP.
WHAT AM I TRULY LIKE?
I TRY TO ACT TOUGH...
...BUT ACTUALLY I'M WEAK INSIDE.
I TRY TO SHIELD MYSELF FROM PAIN.
I'M A COWARD WITH NO COURAGE.
I DON'T HAVE ANY CONFI-DENCE.
"ONLY YOU...

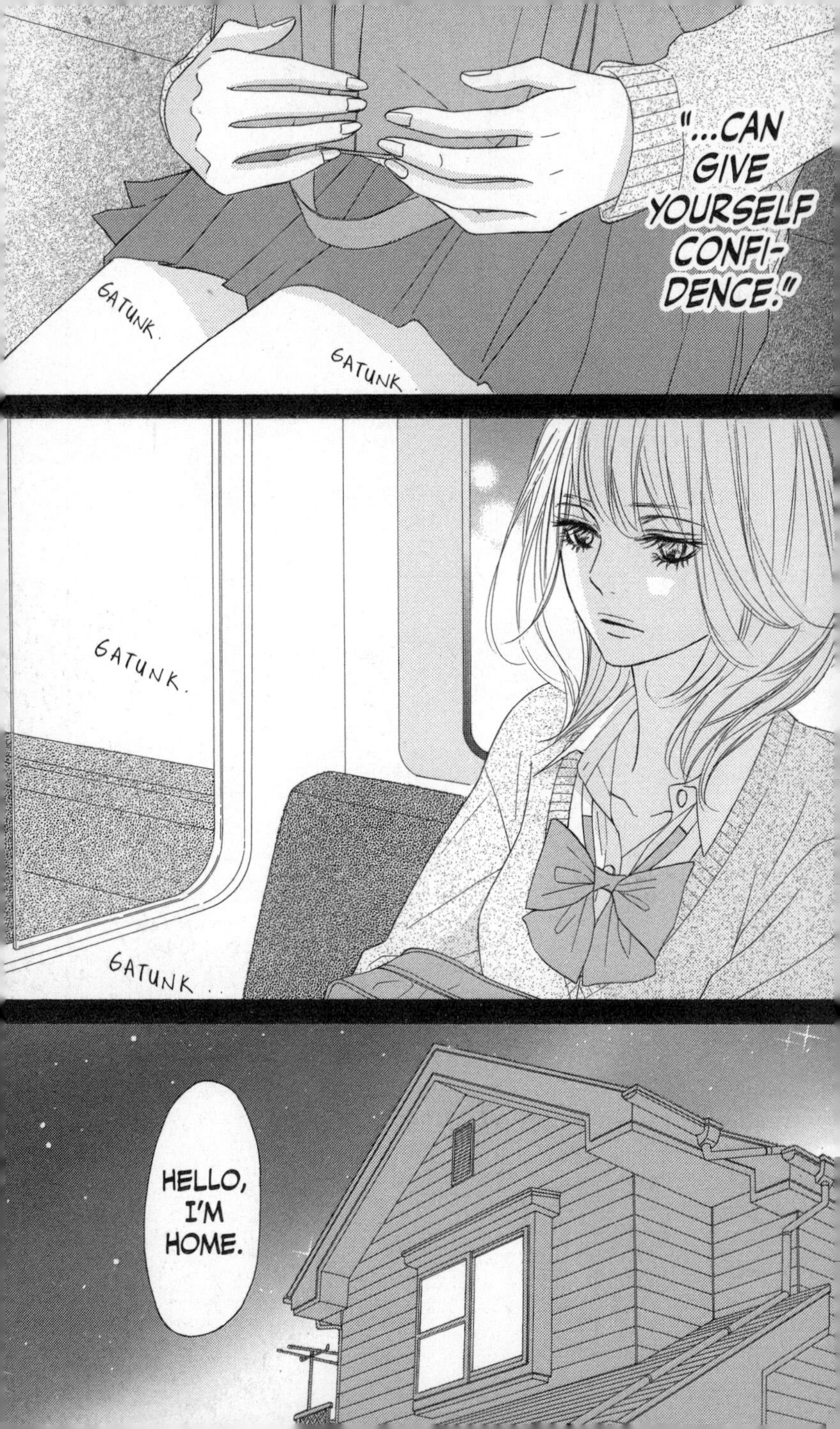
"...CAN GIVE YOURSELF CONFI- DENCE."
GATUNK.
GATUNK
GATUNK.
GATUNK...
HELLO, I'M HOME.

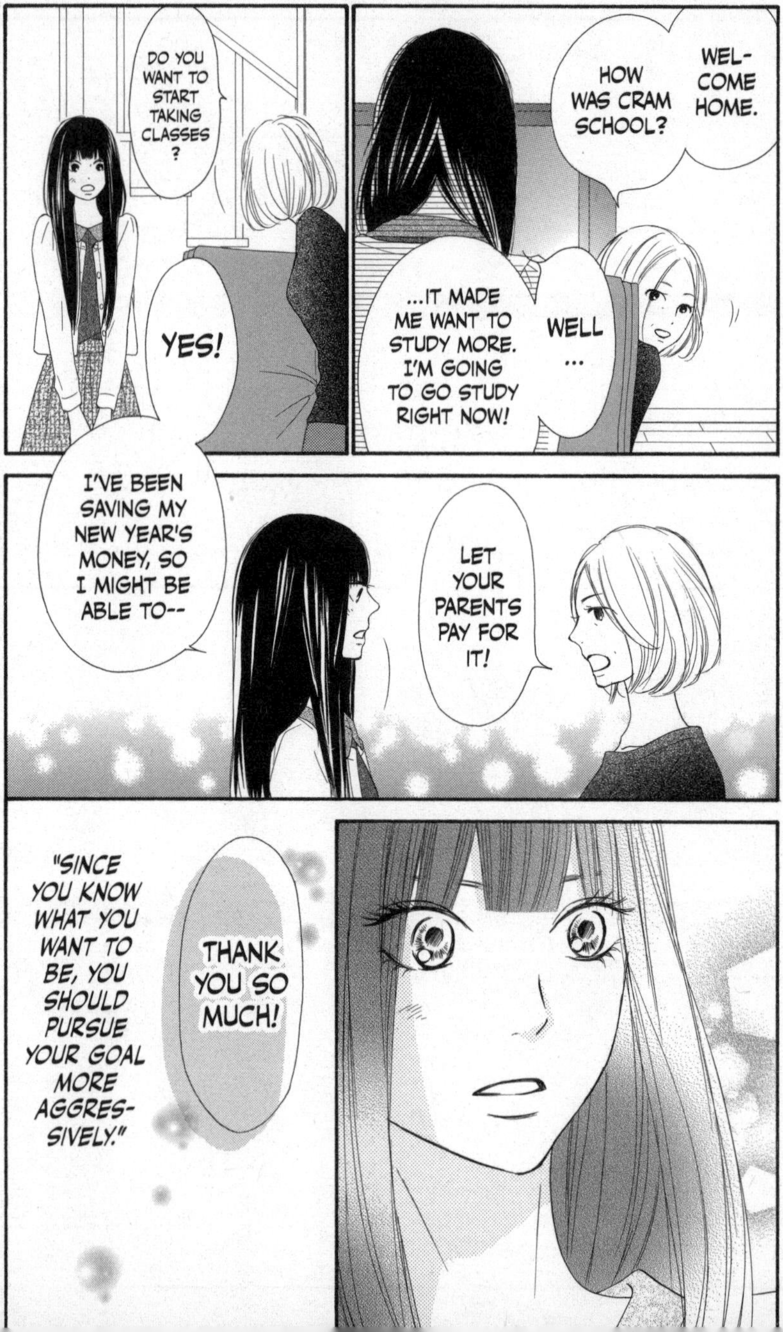
WEL-COME HOME.
HOW WAS CRAM SCHOOL?
WELL ...
...IT MADE ME WANT TO STUDY MORE. I'M GOING TO GO STUDY RIGHT NOW!
DO YOU WANT TO START TAKING CLASSES?
YES!
I'VE BEEN SAVING MY NEW YEAR'S MONEY, SO I MIGHT BE ABLE TO--
LET YOUR PARENTS PAY FOR IT!
THANK YOU SO MUCH!
"SINCE YOU KNOW WHAT YOU WANT TO BE, YOU SHOULD PURSUE YOUR GOAL MORE AGGRES-SIVELY."

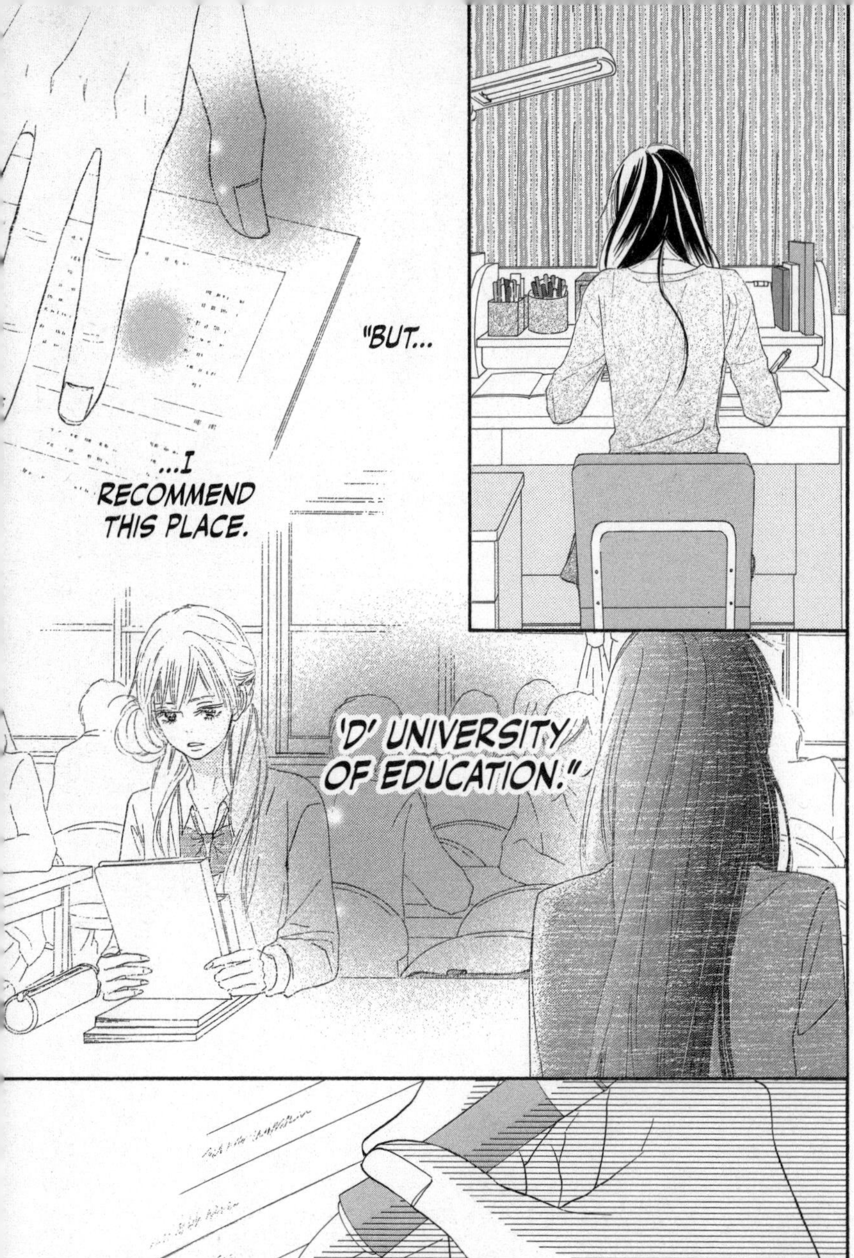
"BUT...
...I RECOMMEND THIS PLACE.
'D' UNIVERSITY OF EDUCATION."

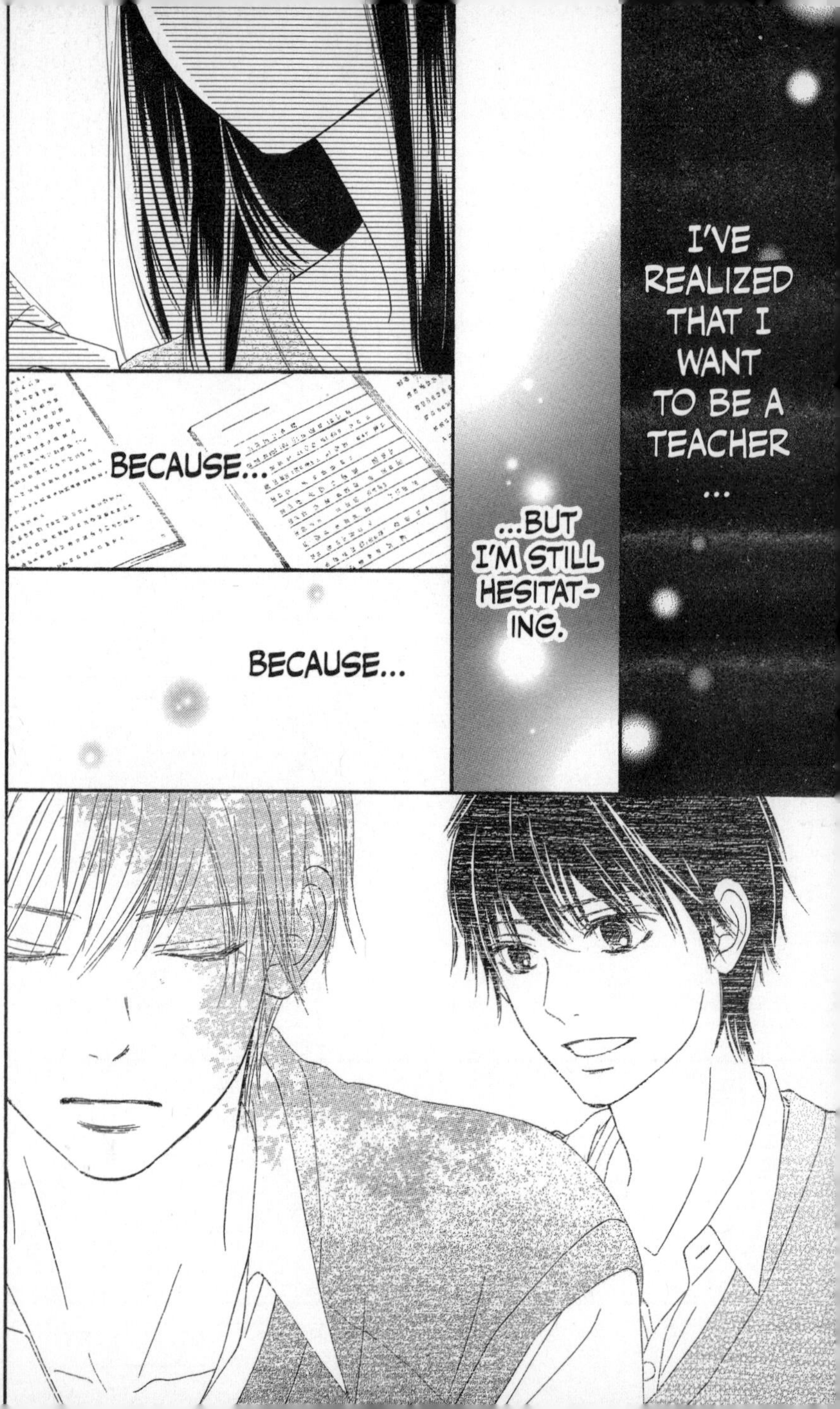
I'VE REALIZED THAT I WANT TO BE A TEACHER...
...BUT I'M STILL HESITATING.
BECAUSE...
BECAUSE...

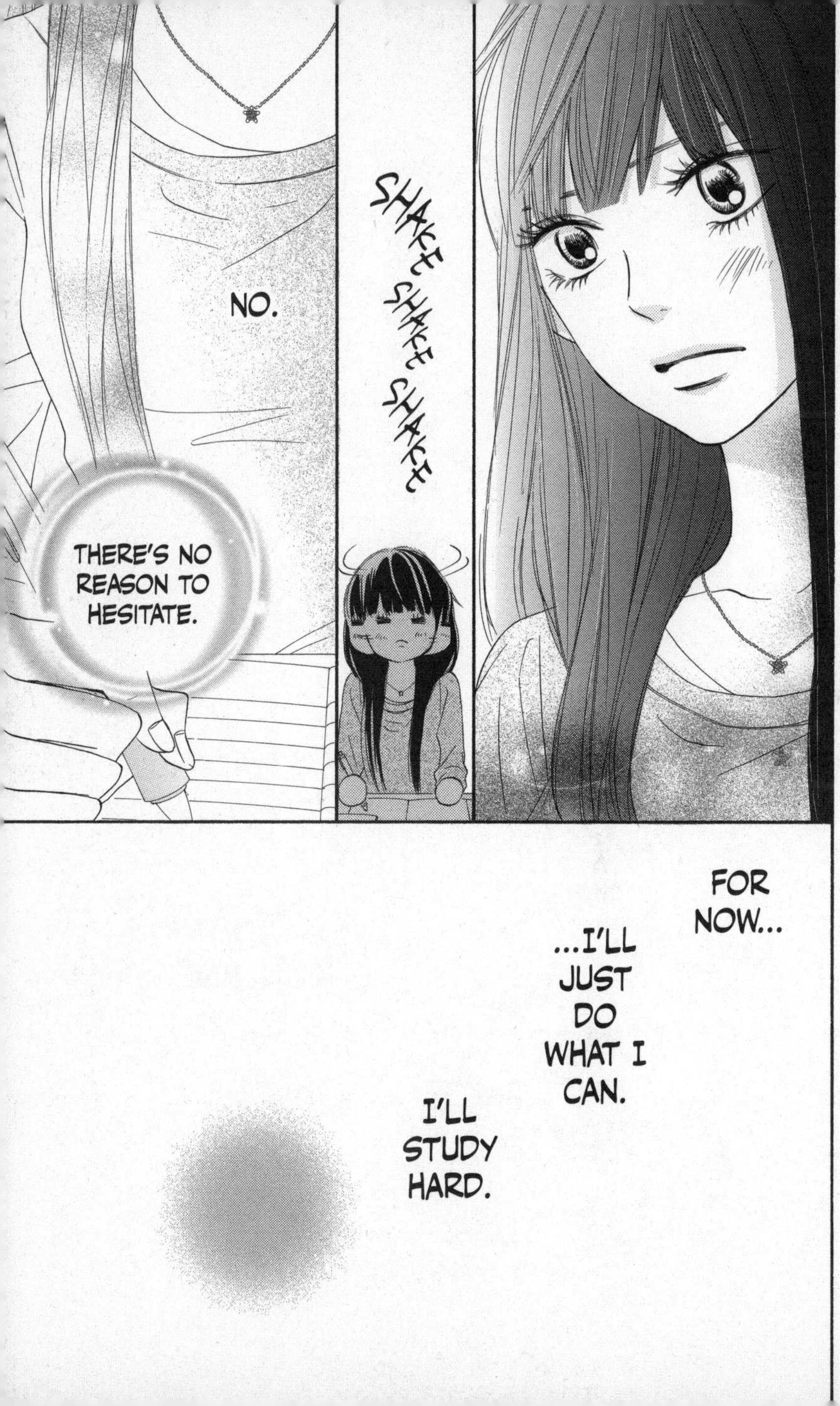
SHAKE SHAKE SHAKE
NO.
THERE'S NO REASON TO HESITATE.
FOR NOW...
...I'LL JUST DO WHAT I CAN.
I'LL STUDY HARD.

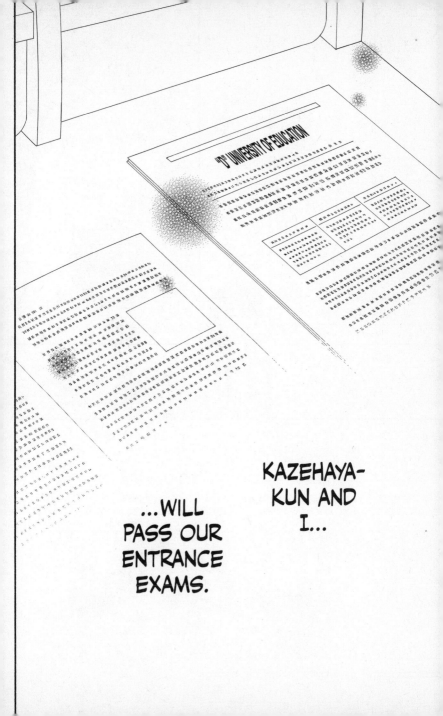

"U" UNIVERSITY OF EDUCATION

KAZEHAYA-KUN AND I...

...WILL PASS OUR ENTRANCE EXAMS.

Episode 87: Desired Path

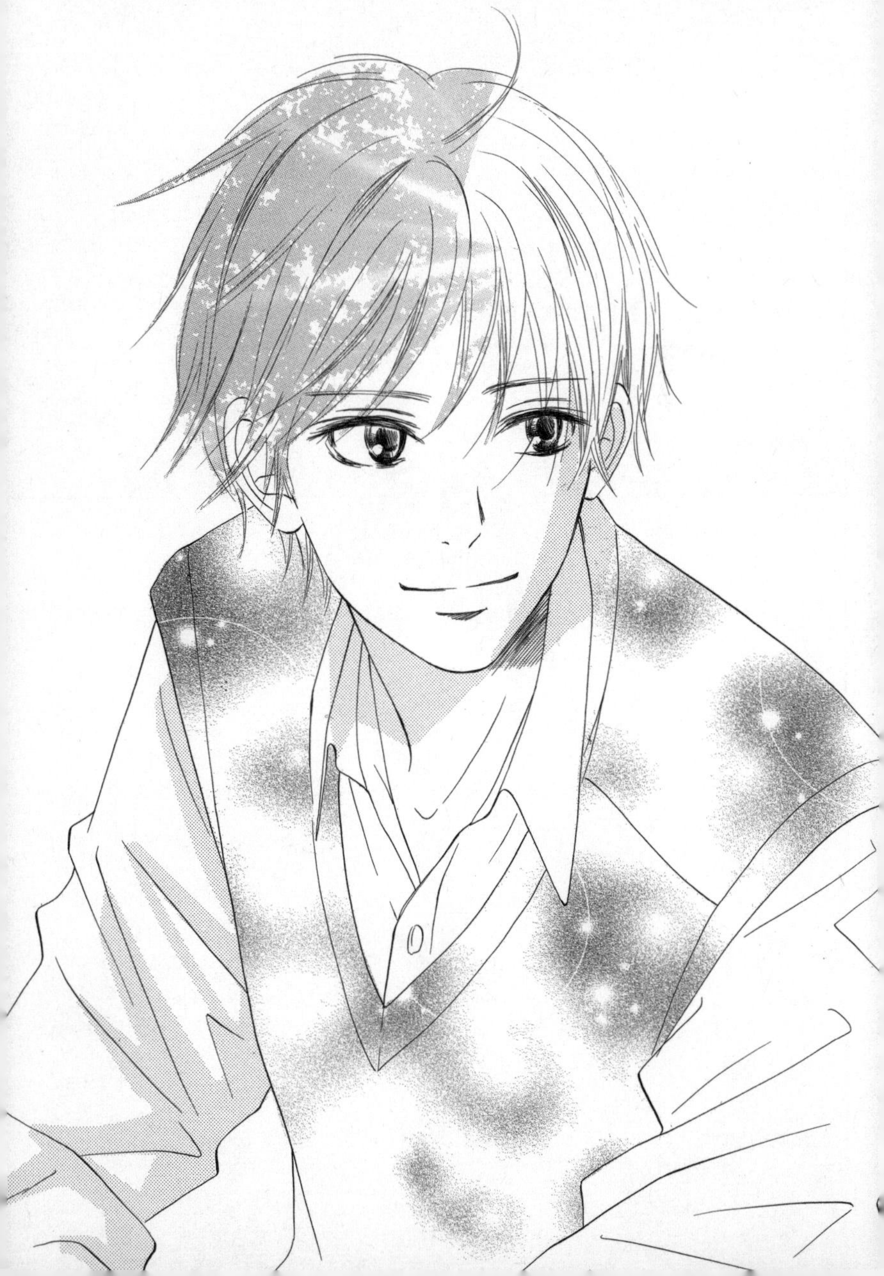

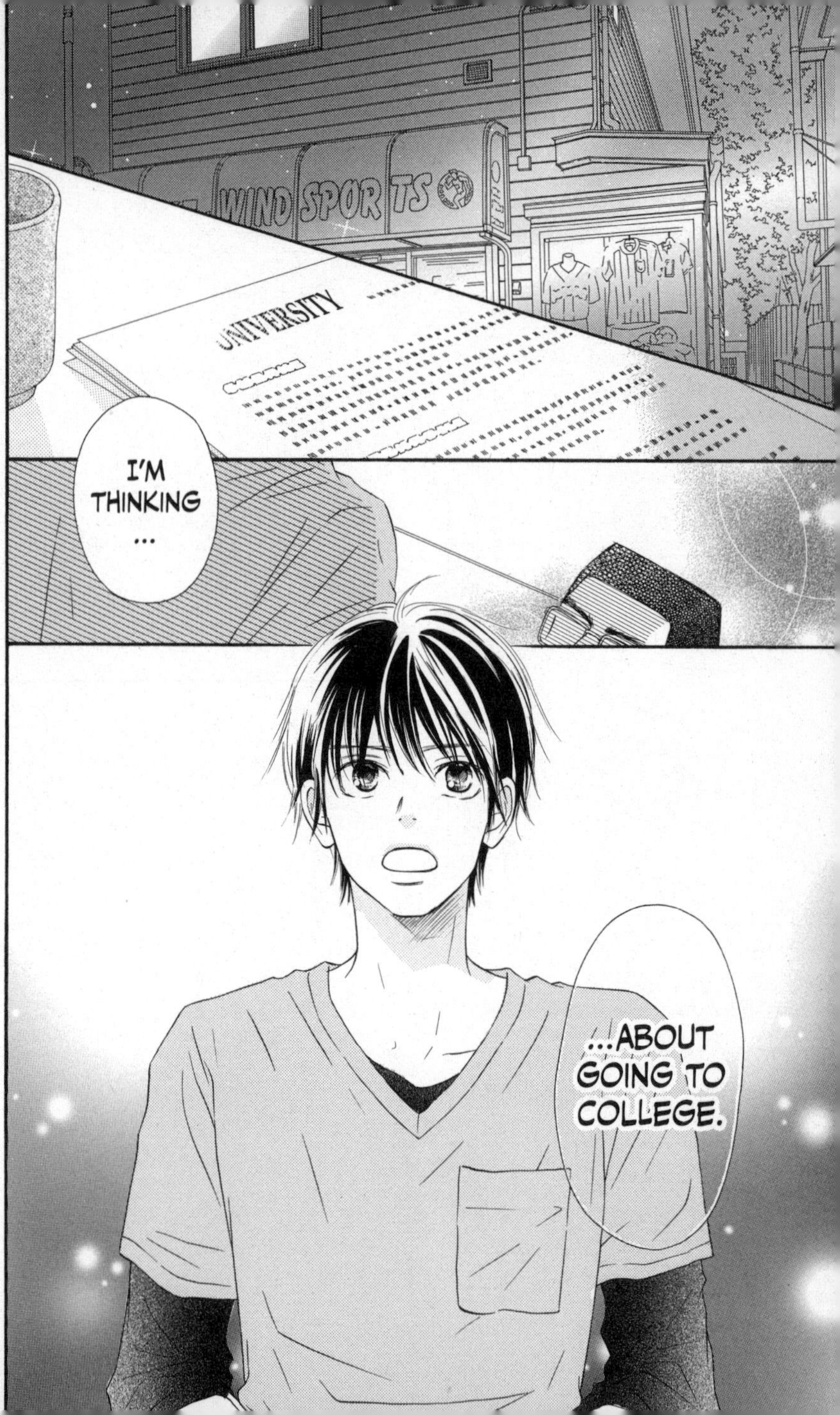
WIND SPORTS
UNIVERSITY
I'M THINKING ...
...ABOUT GOING TO COLLEGE.

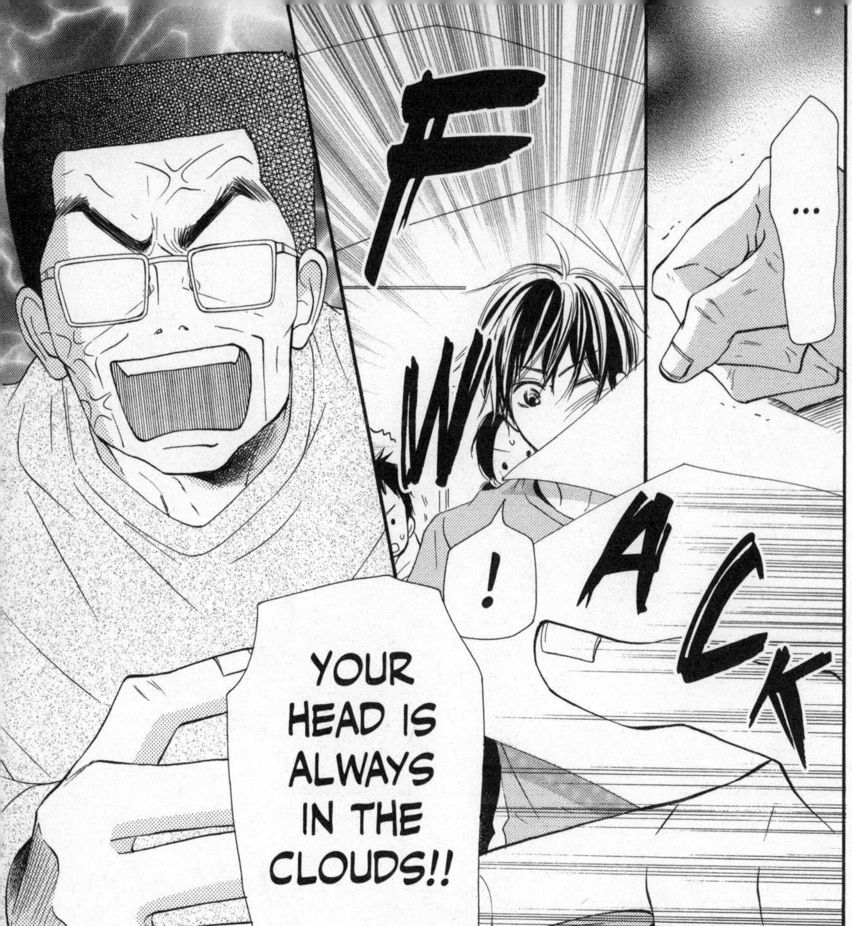
...
FWACK
!
YOUR HEAD IS ALWAYS IN THE CLOUDS!!

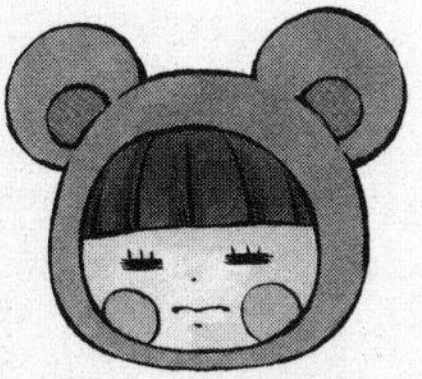

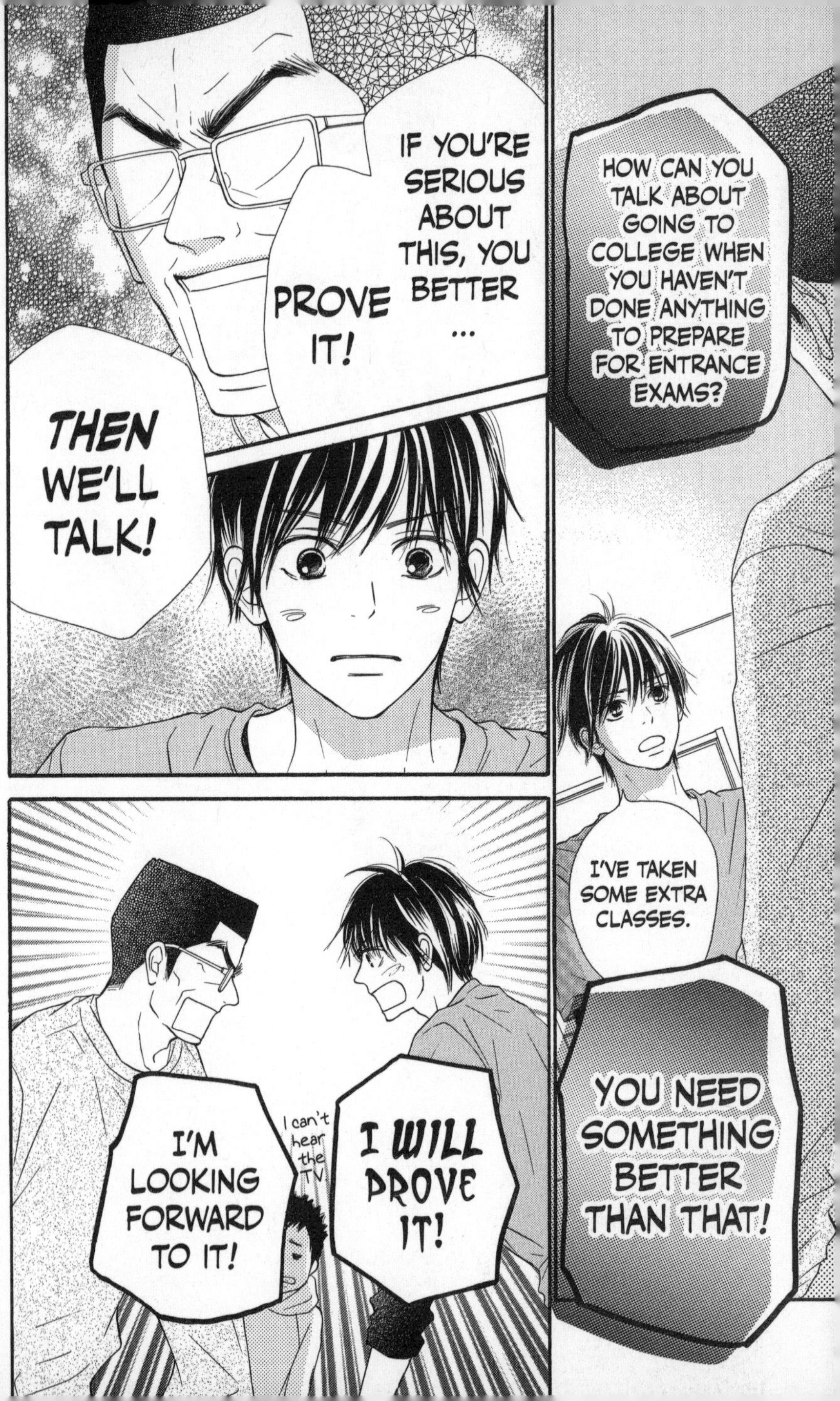
HOW CAN YOU TALK ABOUT GOING TO COLLEGE WHEN YOU HAVEN'T DONE ANYTHING TO PREPARE FOR ENTRANCE EXAMS?
I'VE TAKEN SOME EXTRA CLASSES.
YOU NEED SOMETHING BETTER THAN THAT!
IF YOU'RE SERIOUS ABOUT THIS, YOU BETTER ...
PROVE IT!
THEN WE'LL TALK!
I *WILL* PROVE IT!
I can't hear the TV
I'M LOOKING FORWARD TO IT!

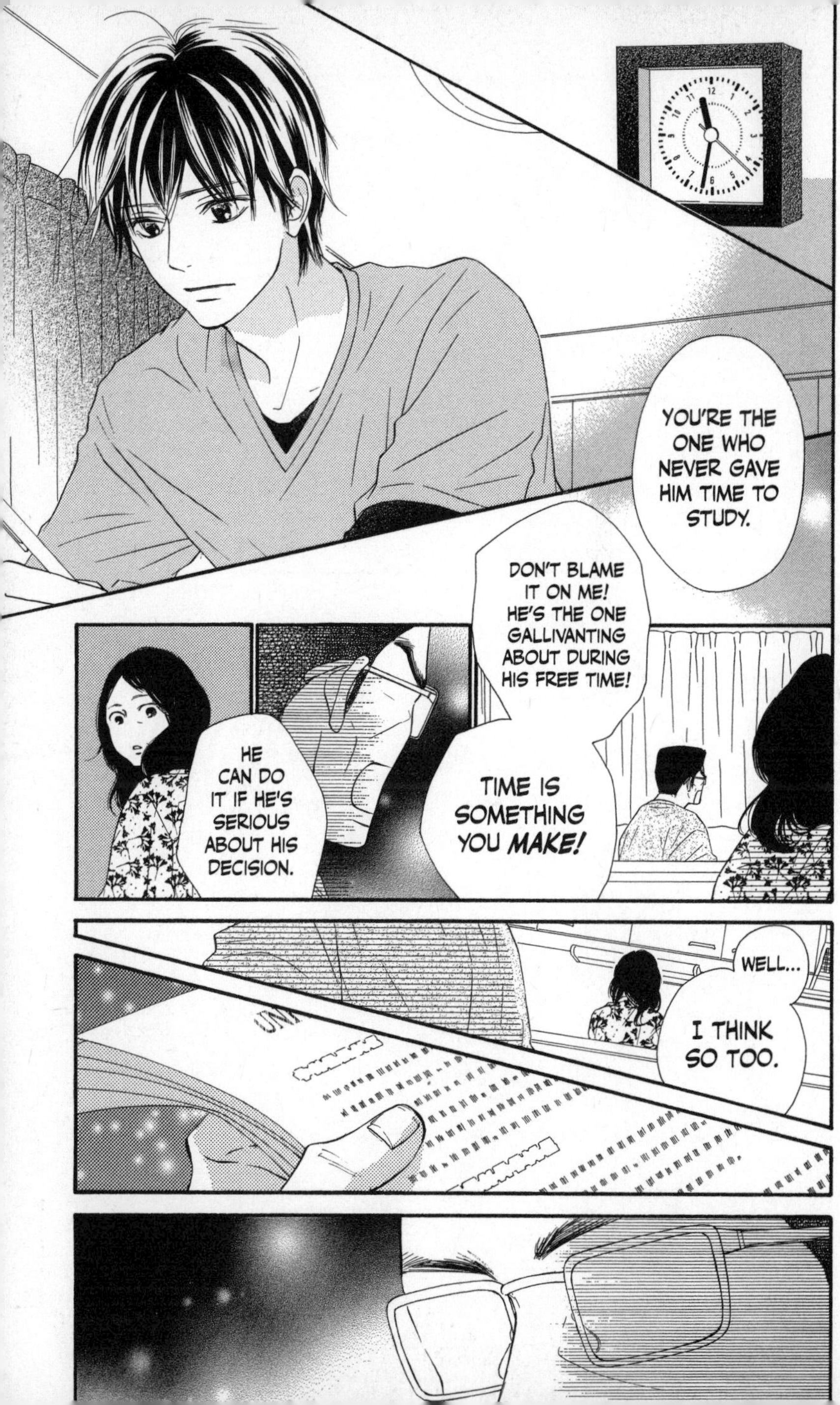
YOU'RE THE ONE WHO NEVER GAVE HIM TIME TO STUDY.
DON'T BLAME IT ON ME! HE'S THE ONE GALLIVANTING ABOUT DURING HIS FREE TIME!
TIME IS SOMETHING YOU *MAKE!*
HE CAN DO IT IF HE'S SERIOUS ABOUT HIS DECISION.
WELL...
I THINK SO TOO.

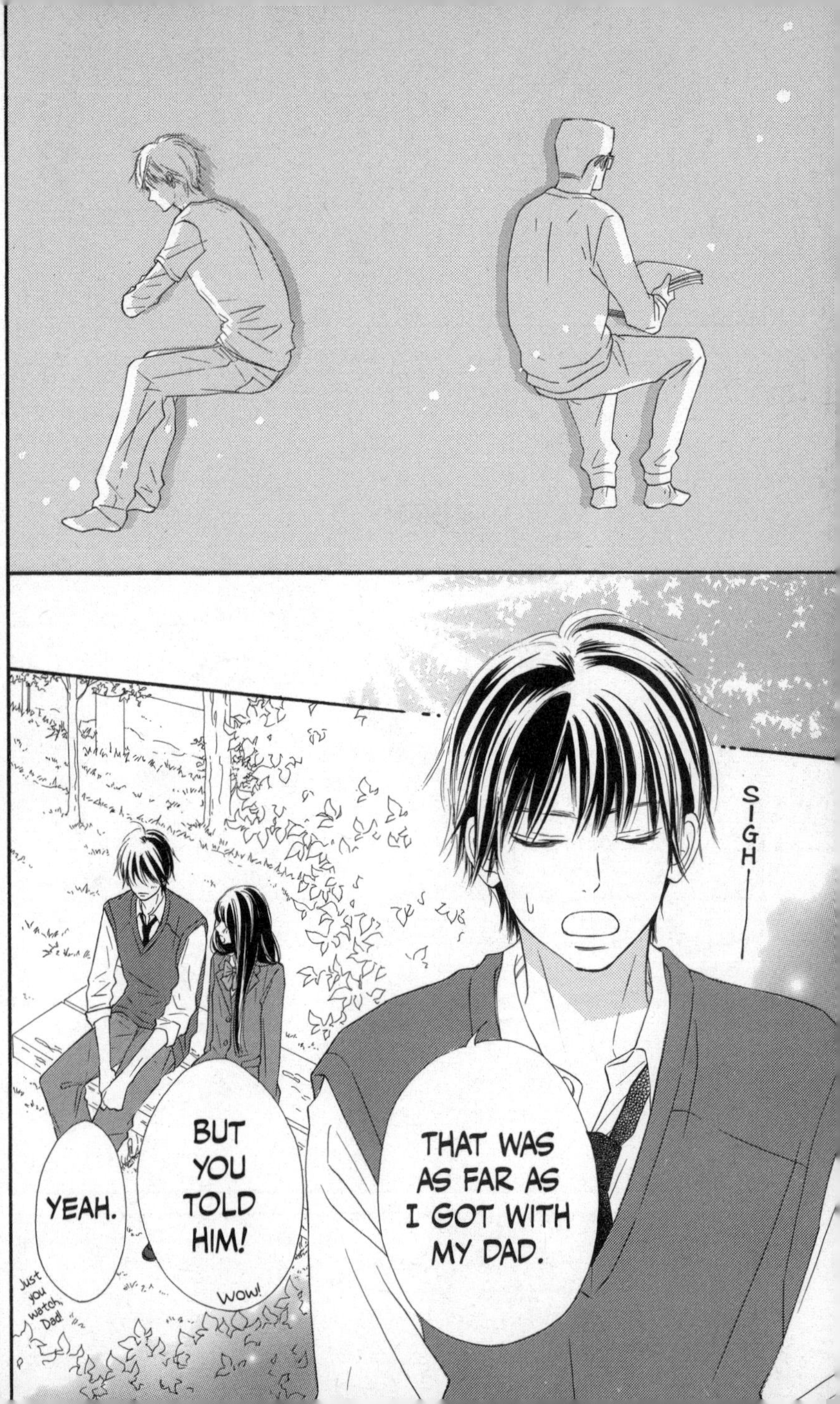
SIGH
THAT WAS AS FAR AS I GOT WITH MY DAD.
BUT YOU TOLD HIM!
WOW!
YEAH.
Just you watch, Dad!

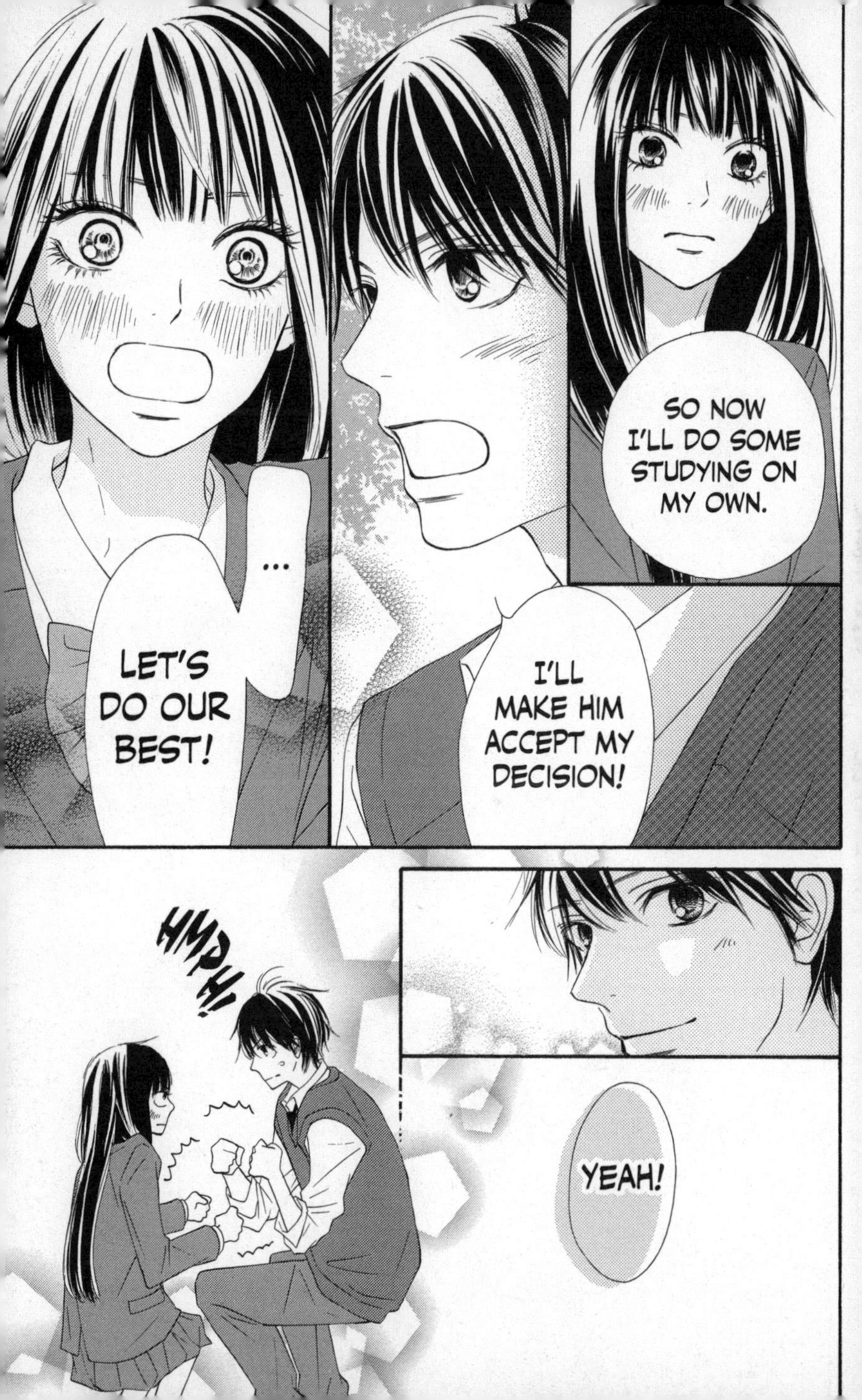
SO NOW I'LL DO SOME STUDYING ON MY OWN.
I'LL MAKE HIM ACCEPT MY DECISION!
...
LET'S DO OUR BEST!
YEAH!
HMPH!

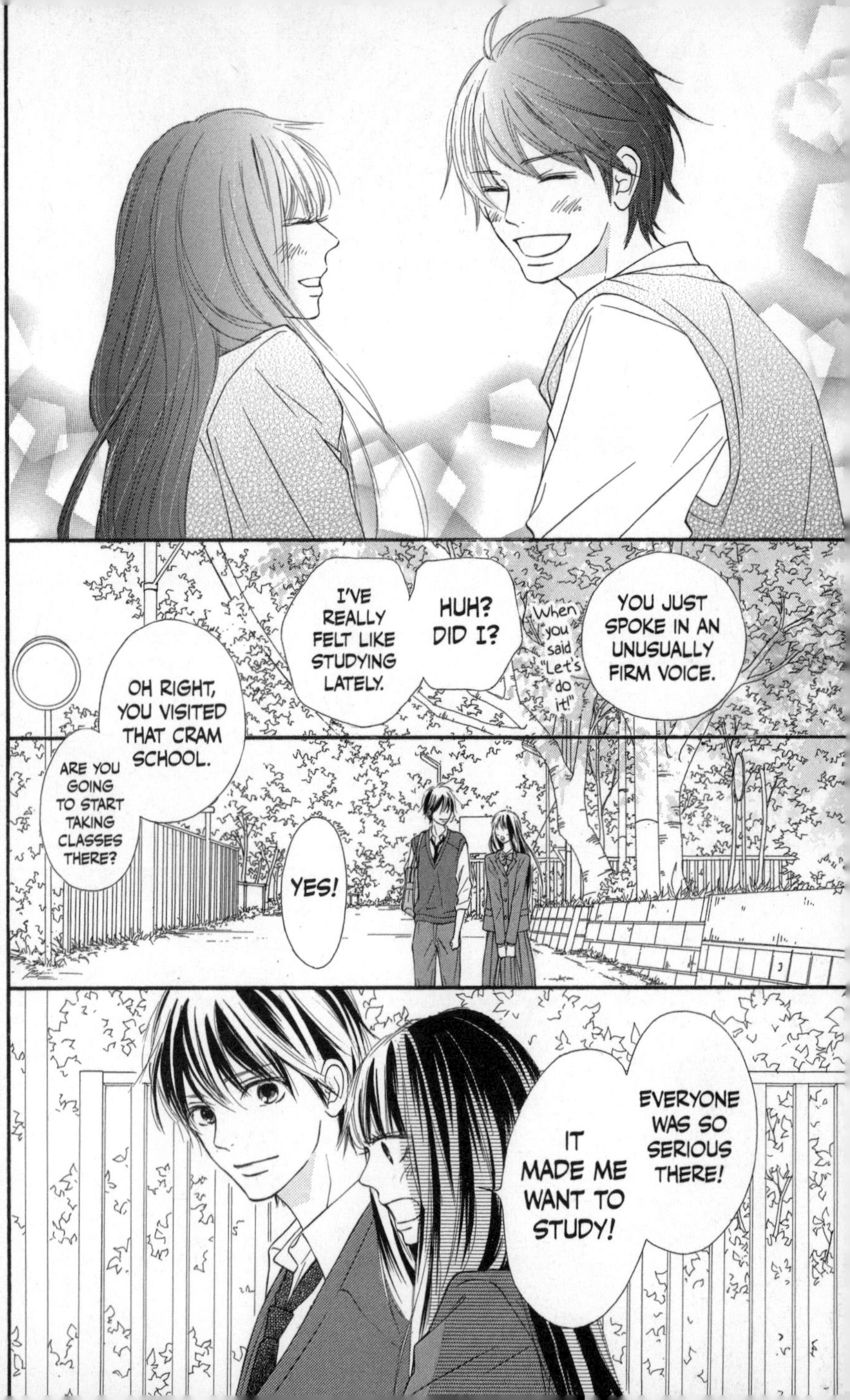
YOU JUST SPOKE IN AN UNUSUALLY FIRM VOICE.
When you said "Let's do it!"
HUH? DID I?
I'VE REALLY FELT LIKE STUDYING LATELY.
OH RIGHT, YOU VISITED THAT CRAM SCHOOL.
ARE YOU GOING TO START TAKING CLASSES THERE?
YES!
EVERYONE WAS SO SERIOUS THERE!
IT MADE ME WANT TO STUDY!

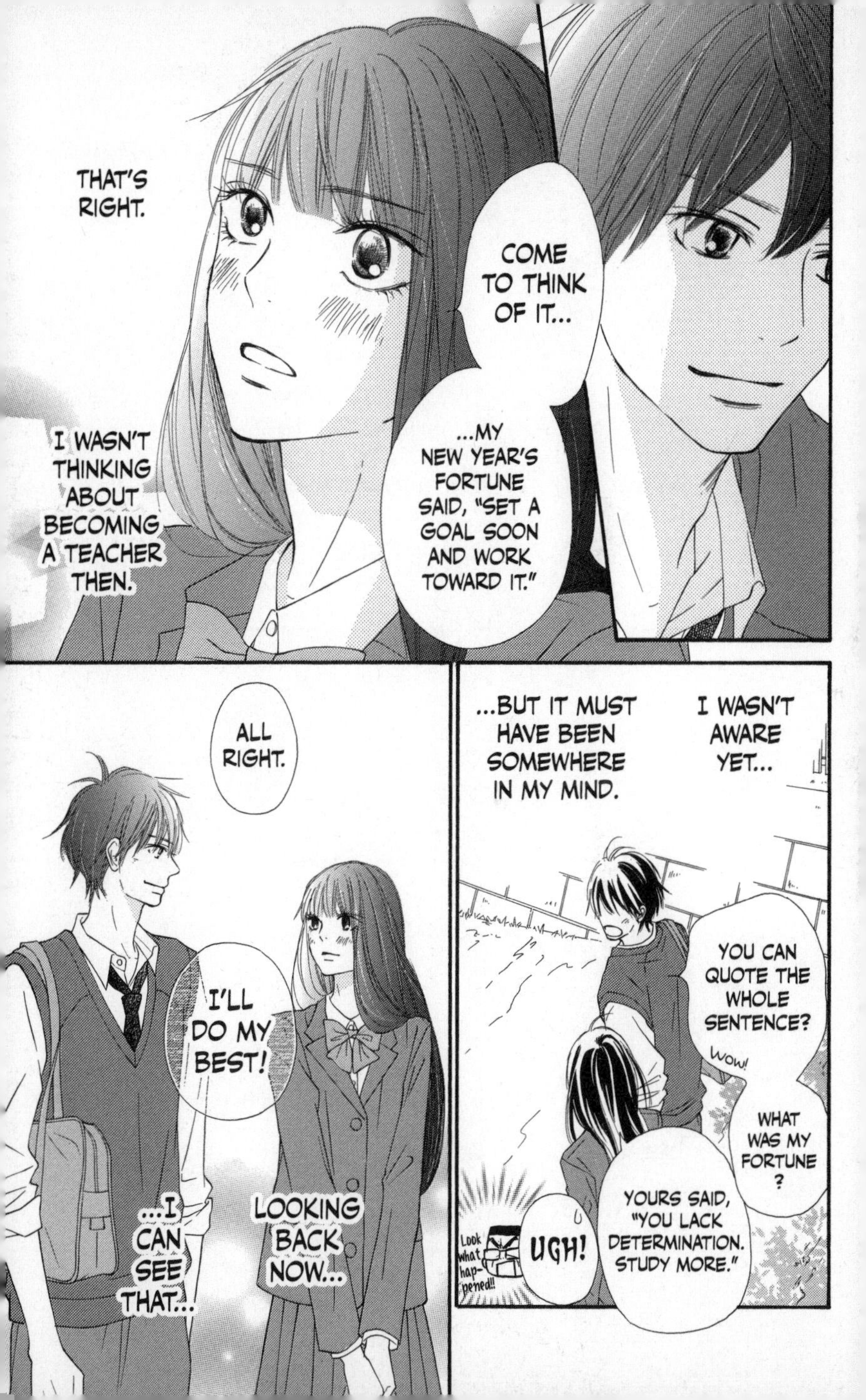
COME TO THINK OF IT...
...MY NEW YEAR'S FORTUNE SAID, "SET A GOAL SOON AND WORK TOWARD IT."
THAT'S RIGHT.
I WASN'T THINKING ABOUT BECOMING A TEACHER THEN.
I WASN'T AWARE YET...
...BUT IT MUST HAVE BEEN SOMEWHERE IN MY MIND.
YOU CAN QUOTE THE WHOLE SENTENCE?
WOW!
WHAT WAS MY FORTUNE?
YOURS SAID, "YOU LACK DETERMINATION. STUDY MORE."
UGH!
Look what hap-pened!!
ALL RIGHT.
I'LL DO MY BEST!
LOOKING BACK NOW...
...I CAN SEE THAT...

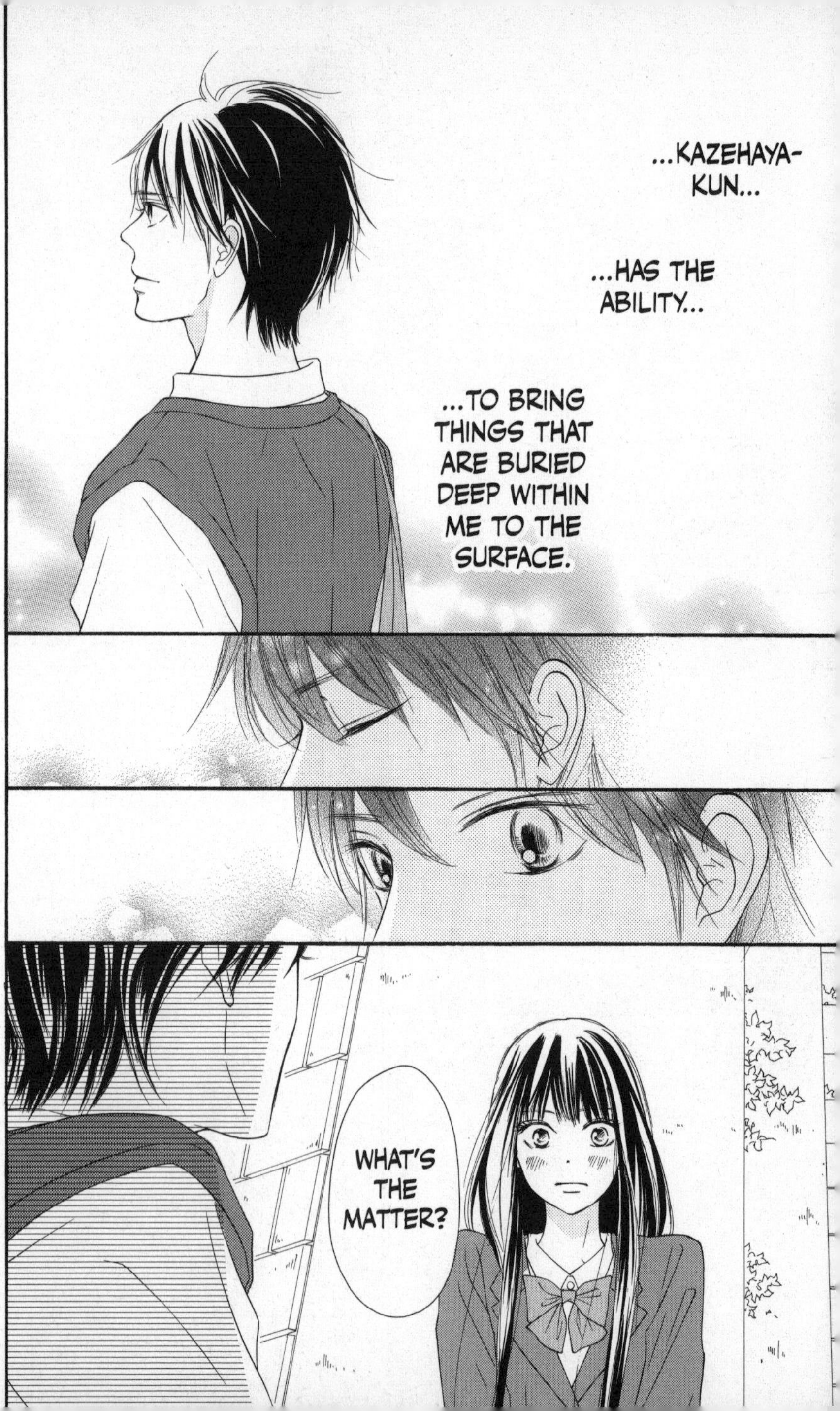
...KAZEHAYA-KUN...
...HAS THE ABILITY...
...TO BRING THINGS THAT ARE BURIED DEEP WITHIN ME TO THE SURFACE.
WHAT'S THE MATTER?

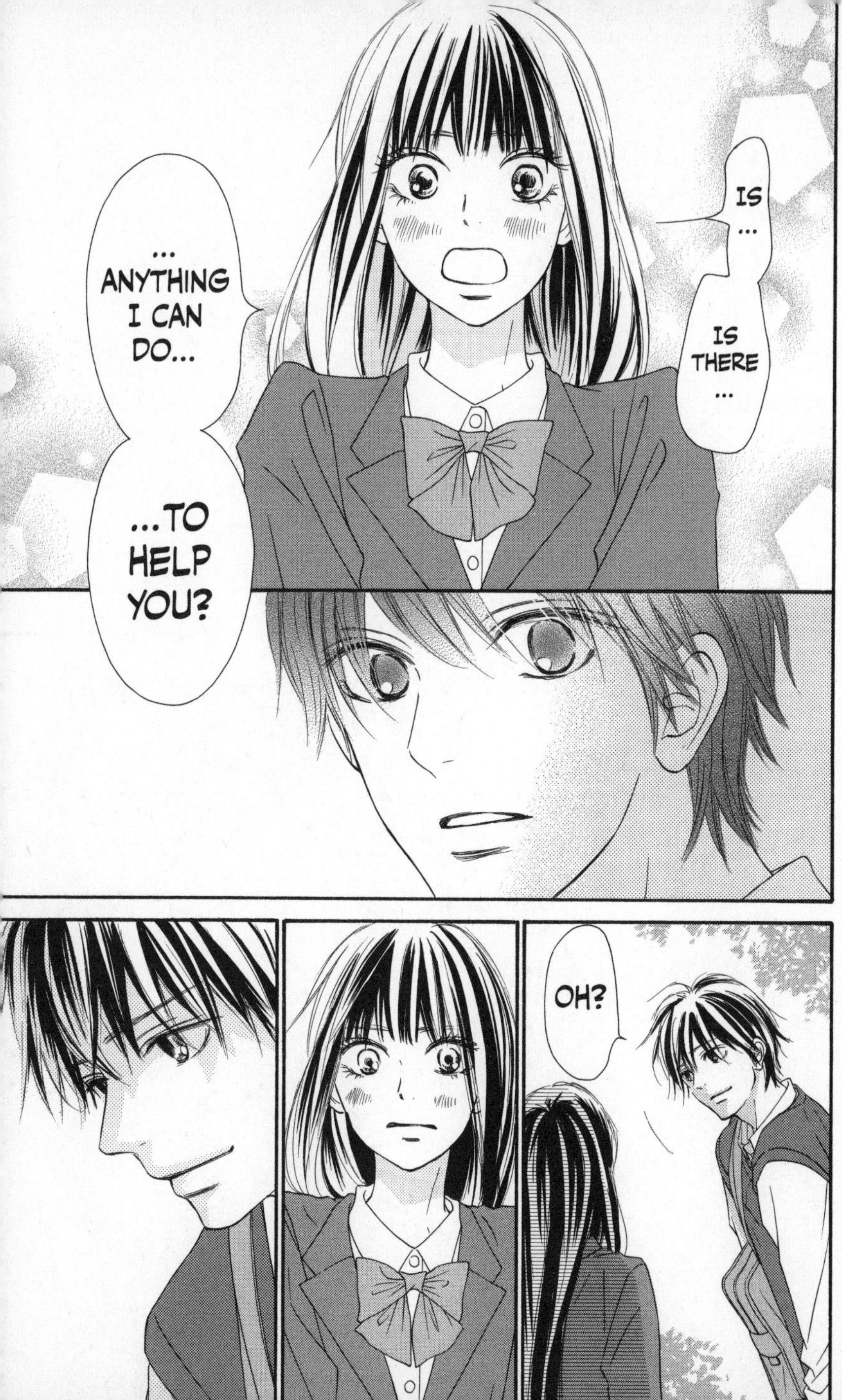
IS ...
IS THERE ...
... ANYTHING I CAN DO...
...TO HELP YOU?
OH?

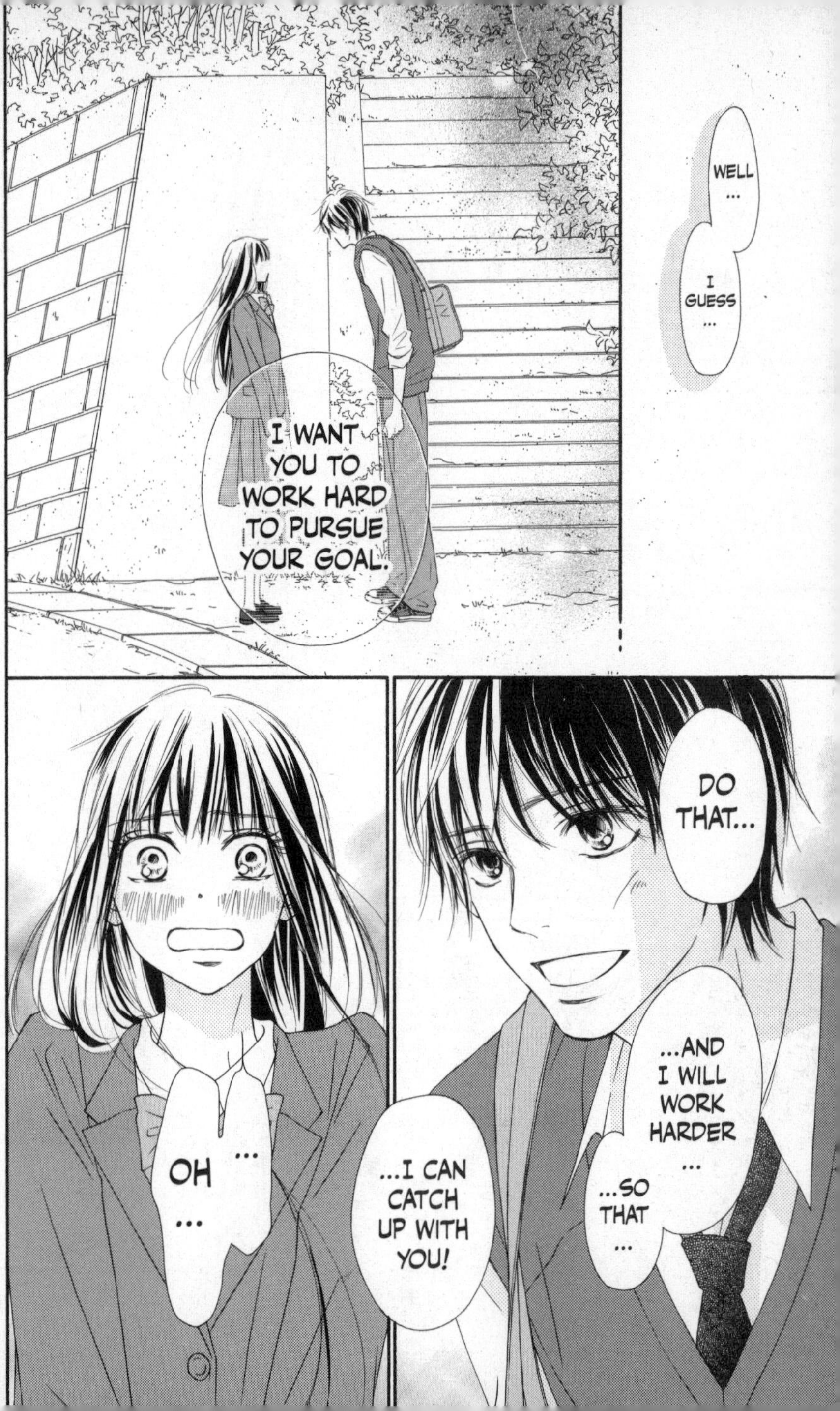
WELL... I GUESS...
I WANT YOU TO WORK HARD TO PURSUE YOUR GOAL.
DO THAT...
...AND I WILL WORK HARDER...
...SO THAT...
...I CAN CATCH UP WITH YOU!
OH... ...

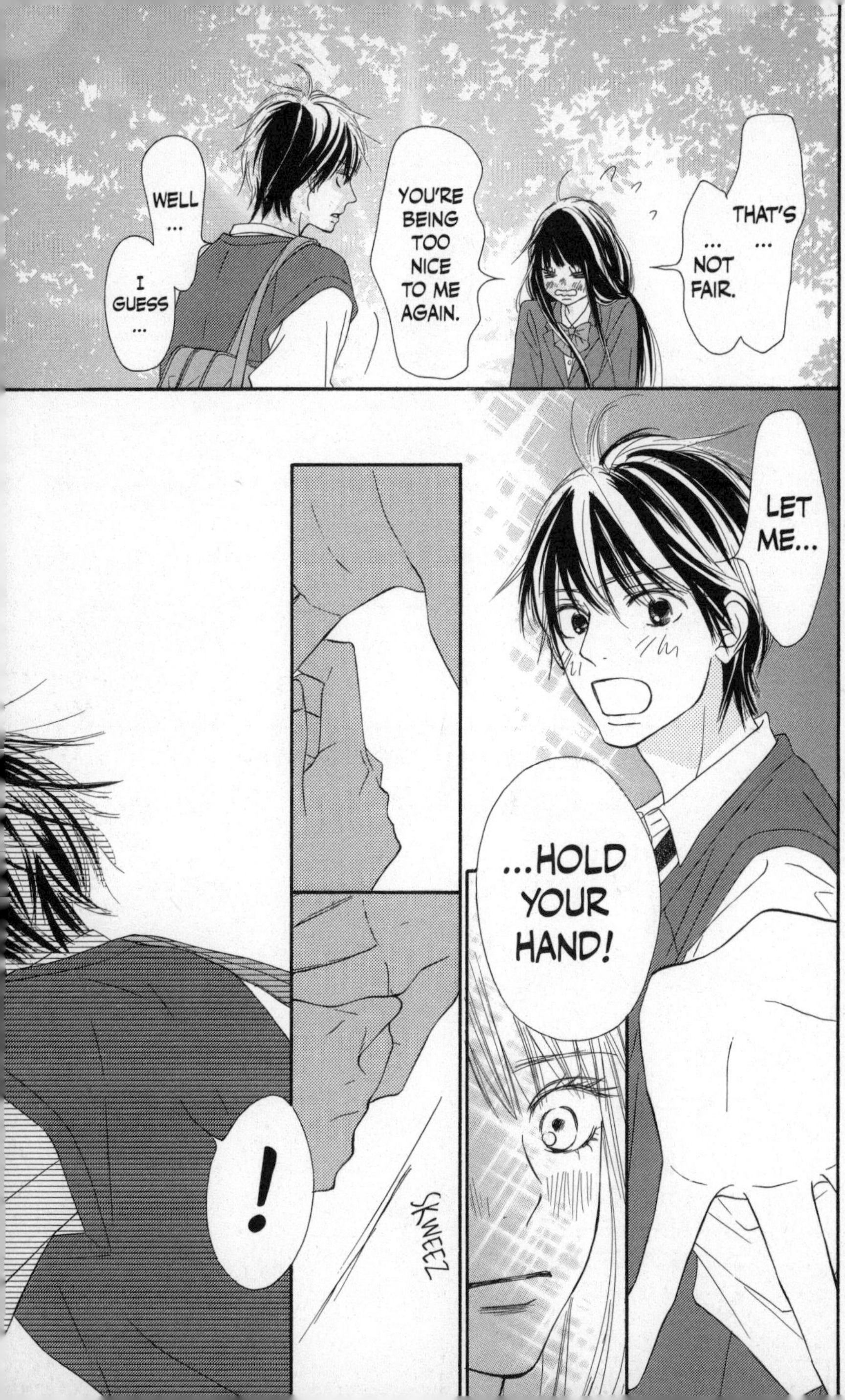
THAT'S ... ... NOT FAIR.
YOU'RE BEING TOO NICE TO ME AGAIN.
WELL ... I GUESS ...
LET ME...
...HOLD YOUR HAND!
SKWEEZ
!

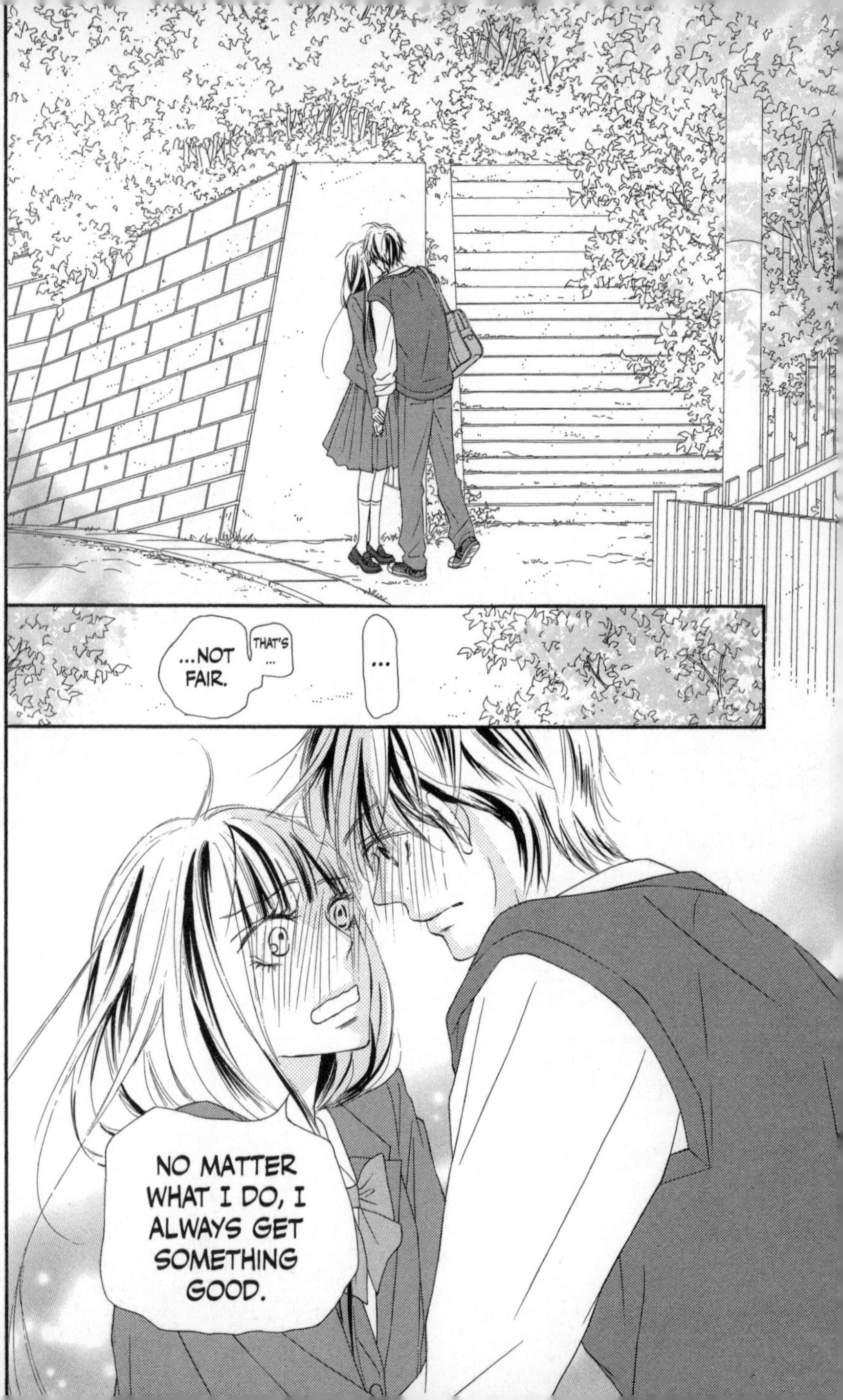
...
THAT'S ...
...NOT FAIR.
NO MATTER WHAT I DO, I ALWAYS GET SOMETHING GOOD.

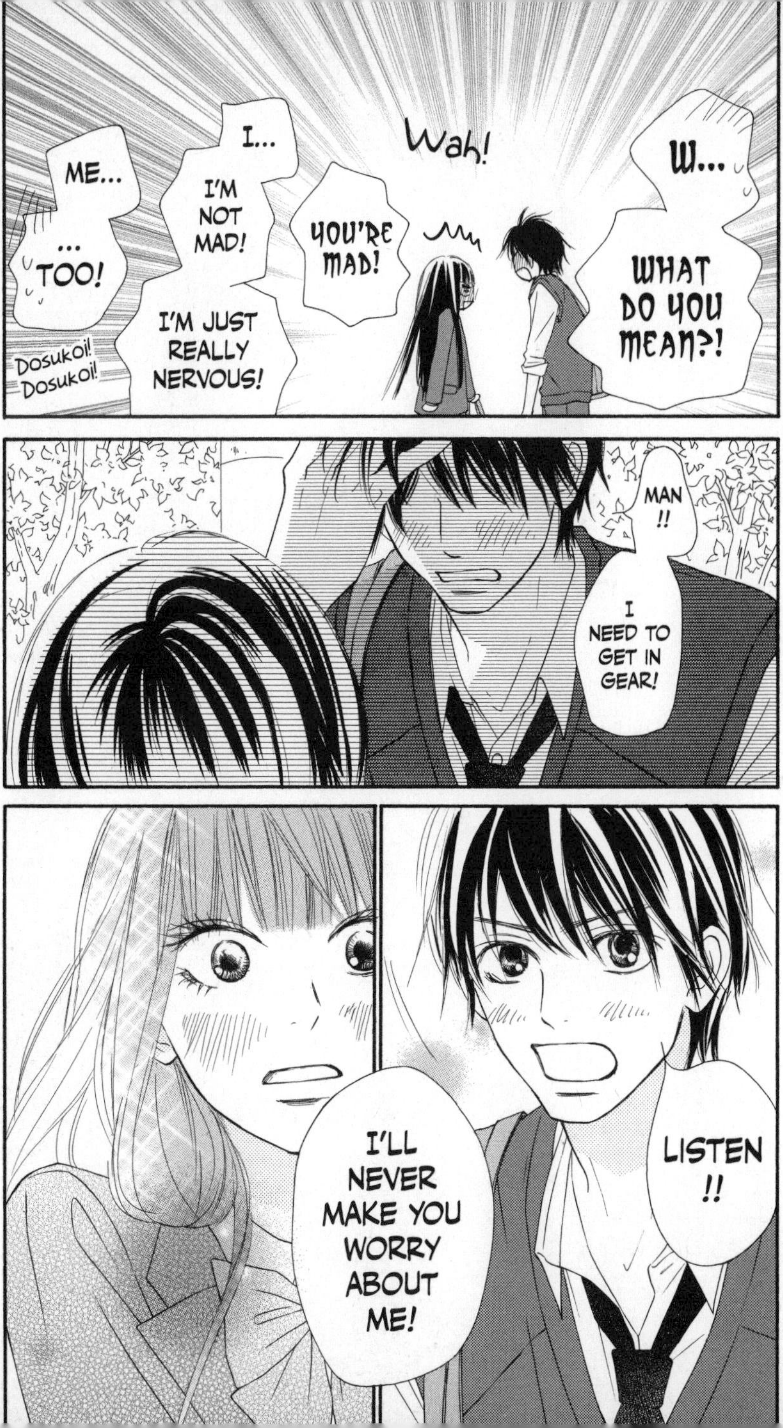
W...
WHAT DO YOU MEAN?!
Wah!
YOU'RE MAD!
I...
I'M NOT MAD!
I'M JUST REALLY NERVOUS!
ME...
...TOO!
Dosukoi! Dosukoi!
MAN!!
I NEED TO GET IN GEAR!
LISTEN!!
I'LL NEVER MAKE YOU WORRY ABOUT ME!

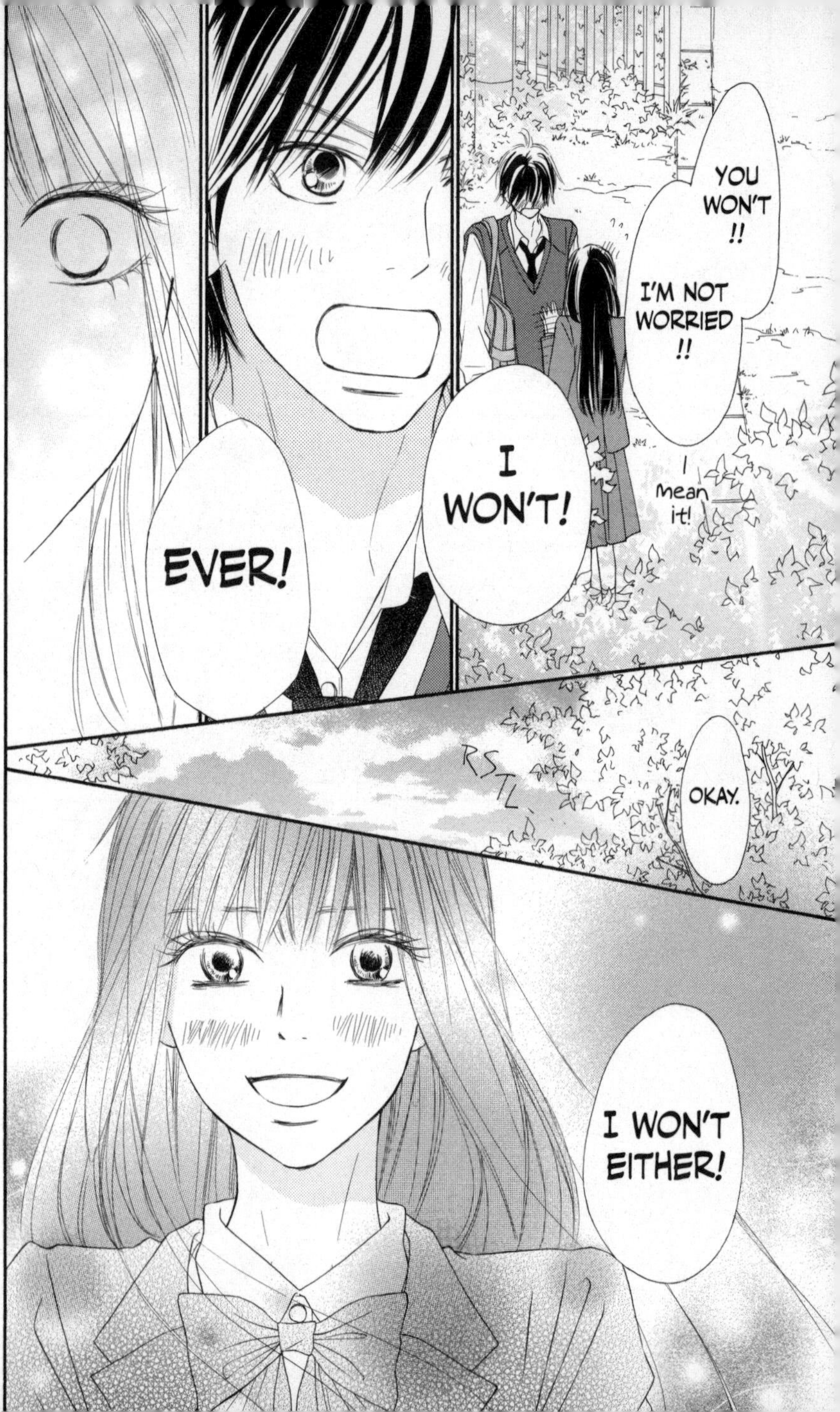
YOU WON'T !!
I'M NOT WORRIED !!
I mean it!
I WON'T!
EVER!
RSTL
OKAY.
I WON'T EITHER!

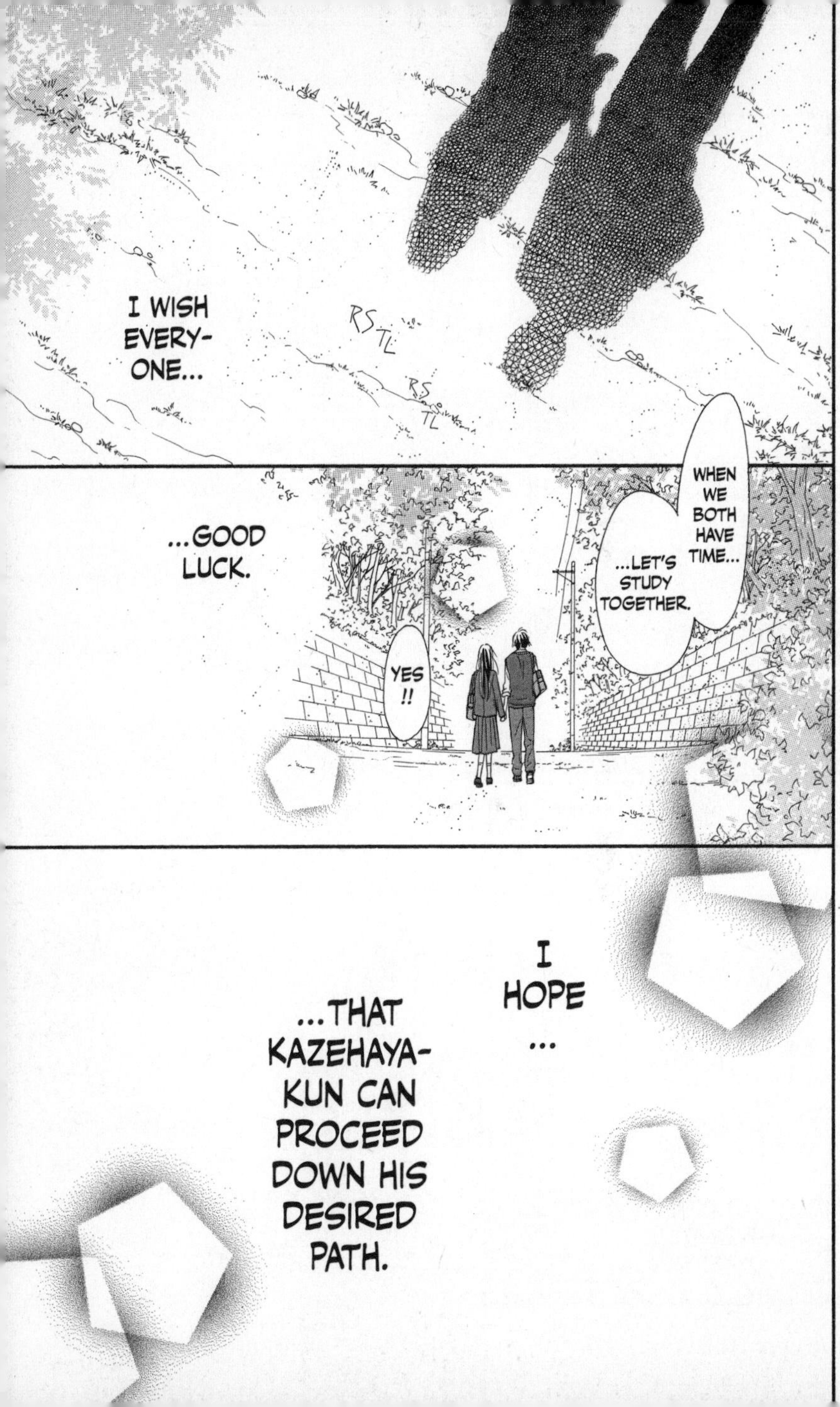
RSTL
RSTL
I WISH EVERY-ONE...
WHEN WE BOTH HAVE TIME...
...LET'S STUDY TOGETHER.
YES!!
...GOOD LUCK.
I HOPE...
...THAT KAZEHAYA-KUN CAN PROCEED DOWN HIS DESIRED PATH.

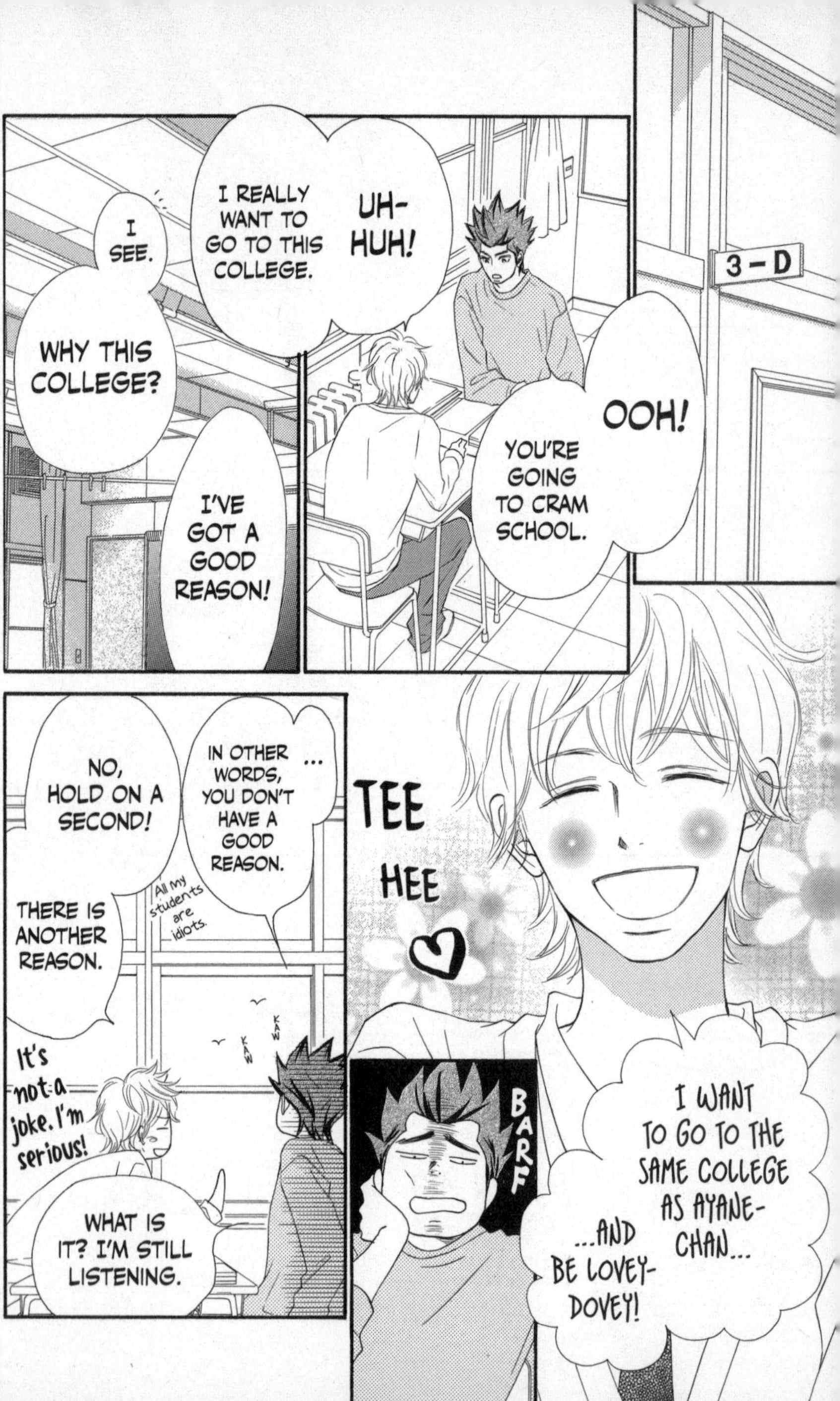

3-D
OOH!
YOU'RE GOING TO CRAM SCHOOL.
UH-HUH!
I REALLY WANT TO GO TO THIS COLLEGE.
I SEE.
WHY THIS COLLEGE?
I'VE GOT A GOOD REASON!
...
IN OTHER WORDS, YOU DON'T HAVE A GOOD REASON.
NO, HOLD ON A SECOND!
THERE IS ANOTHER REASON.
All my students are idiots.
KAW
KAW
It's not a joke. I'm serious!
WHAT IS IT? I'M STILL LISTENING.
TEE HEE
I WANT TO GO TO THE SAME COLLEGE AS AYANE-CHAN...
...AND BE LOVEY-DOVEY!
BARF

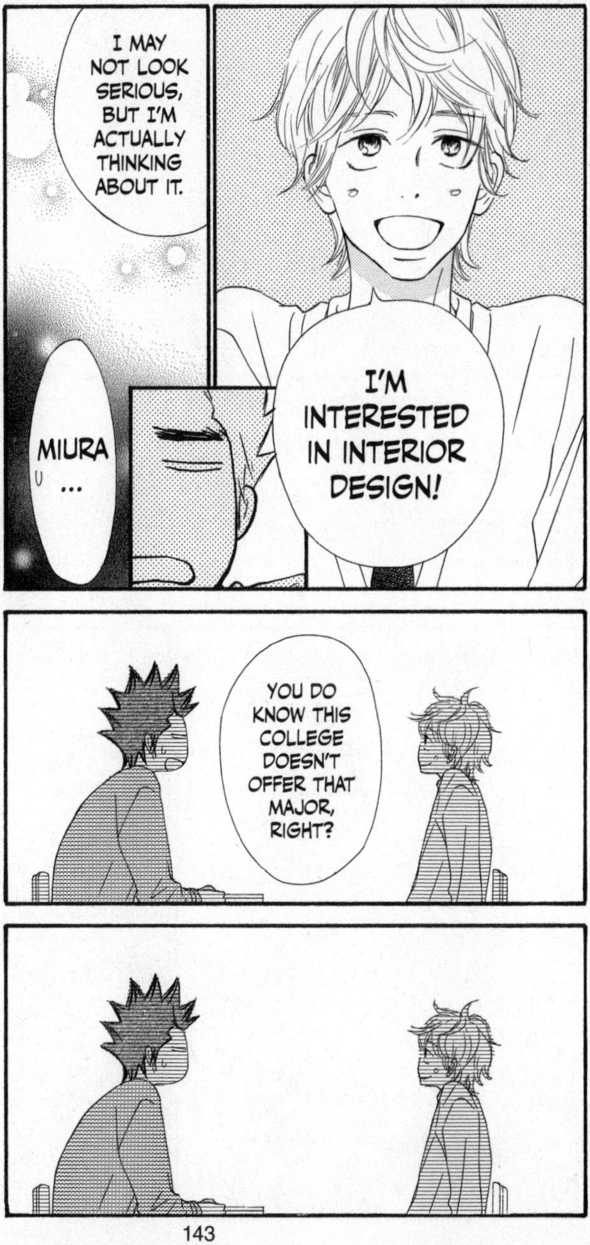
I'M INTERESTED IN INTERIOR DESIGN!
I MAY NOT LOOK SERIOUS, BUT I'M ACTUALLY THINKING ABOUT IT.
MIURA ...
YOU DO KNOW THIS COLLEGE DOESN'T OFFER THAT MAJOR, RIGHT?
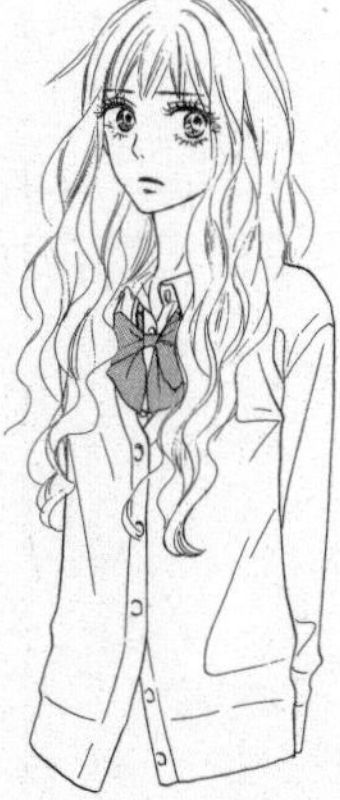

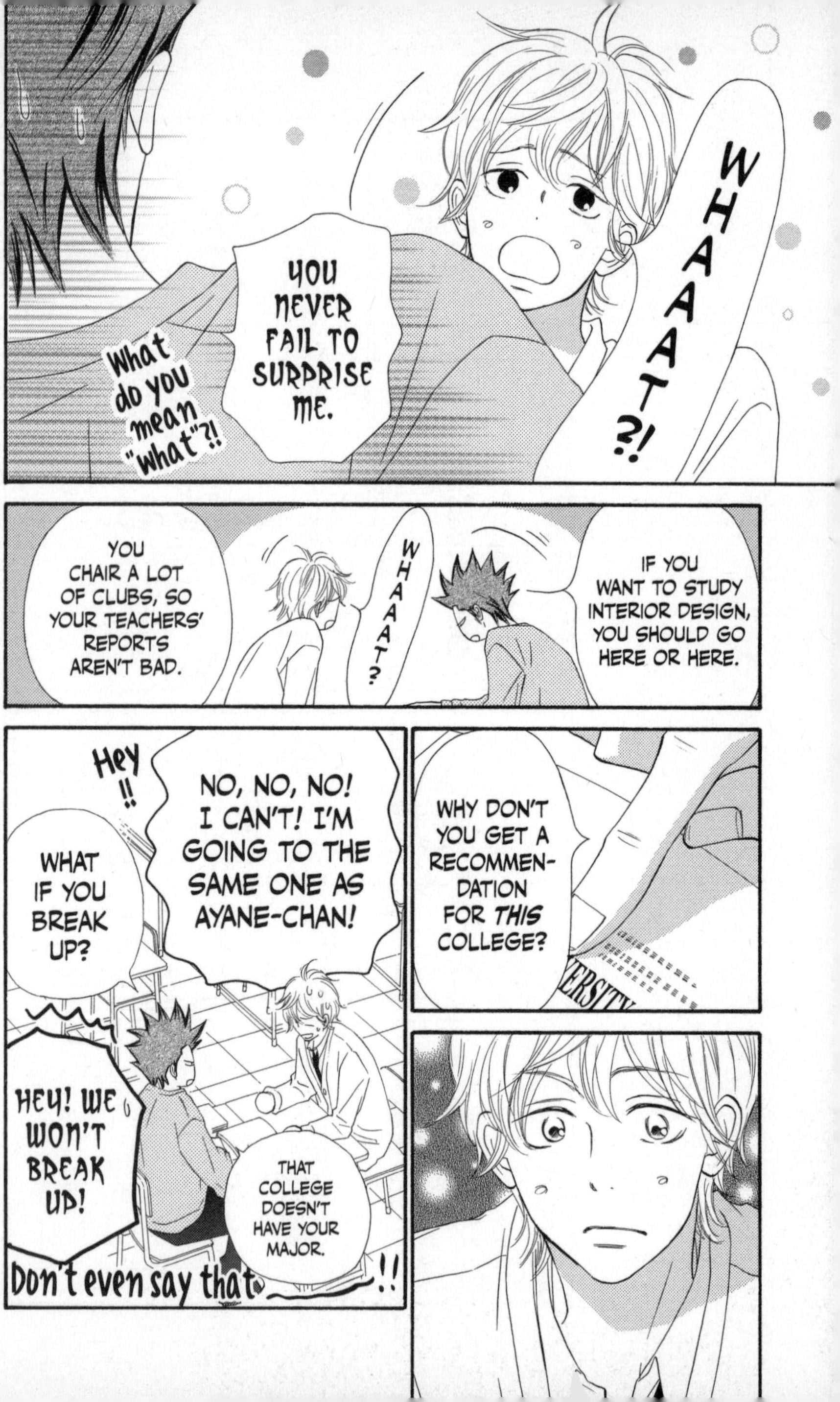
WHAAAT?!
YOU NEVER FAIL TO SURPRISE ME.
What do you mean "what"?!
IF YOU WANT TO STUDY INTERIOR DESIGN, YOU SHOULD GO HERE OR HERE.
WHAAAT?
YOU CHAIR A LOT OF CLUBS, SO YOUR TEACHERS' REPORTS AREN'T BAD.
WHY DON'T YOU GET A RECOMMEN-DATION FOR *THIS* COLLEGE?
NO, NO, NO! I CAN'T! I'M GOING TO THE SAME ONE AS AYANE-CHAN!
Hey!!
WHAT IF YOU BREAK UP?
HEY! WE WON'T BREAK UP!
Don't even say that!!
THAT COLLEGE DOESN'T HAVE YOUR MAJOR.

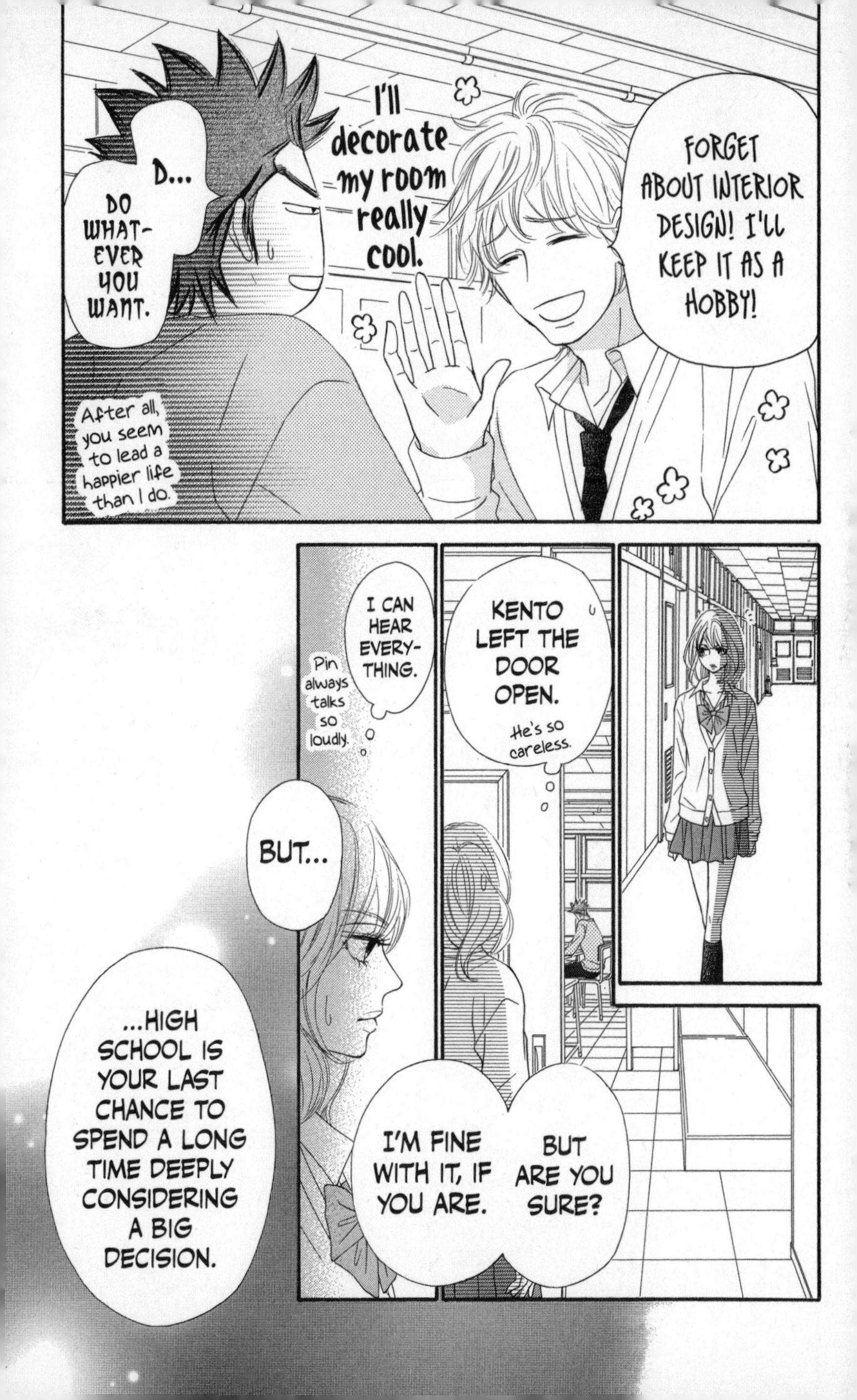
FORGET ABOUT INTERIOR DESIGN! I'LL KEEP IT AS A HOBBY!
I'll decorate my room really cool.
D...
DO WHATEVER YOU WANT.
After all, you seem to lead a happier life than I do.
KENTO LEFT THE DOOR OPEN.
He's so careless.
I CAN HEAR EVERYTHING.
Pin always talks so loudly.
BUT...
BUT ARE YOU SURE?
I'M FINE WITH IT, IF YOU ARE.
...HIGH SCHOOL IS YOUR LAST CHANCE TO SPEND A LONG TIME DEEPLY CONSIDERING A BIG DECISION.

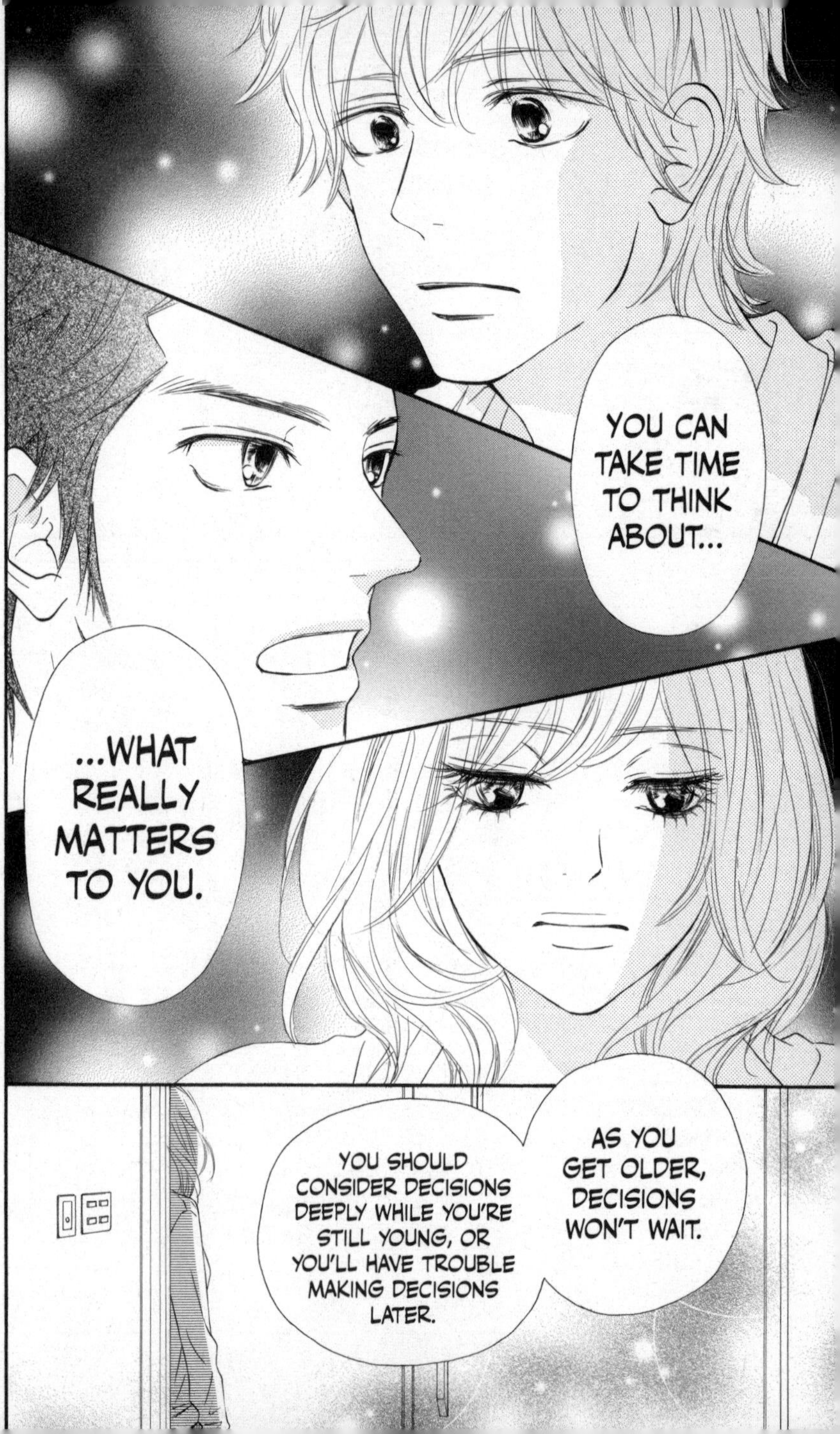
YOU CAN TAKE TIME TO THINK ABOUT...
...WHAT REALLY MATTERS TO YOU.
AS YOU GET OLDER, DECISIONS WON'T WAIT.
YOU SHOULD CONSIDER DECISIONS DEEPLY WHILE YOU'RE STILL YOUNG, OR YOU'LL HAVE TROUBLE MAKING DECISIONS LATER.

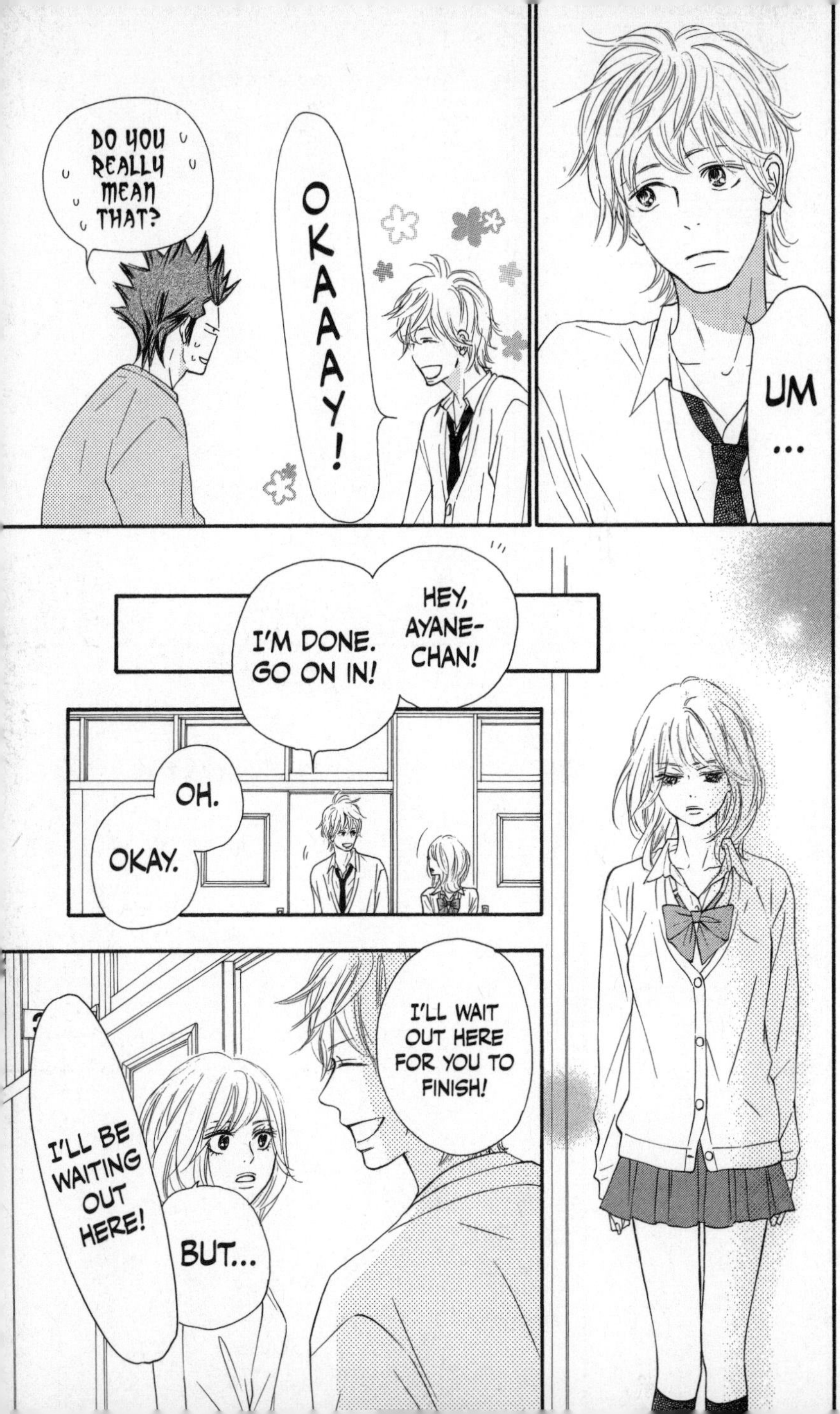
UM...
OKAAAY!
DO YOU REALLY MEAN THAT?
HEY, AYANE-CHAN!
I'M DONE. GO ON IN!
OH.
OKAY.
I'LL WAIT OUT HERE FOR YOU TO FINISH!
I'LL BE WAITING OUT HERE!
BUT...

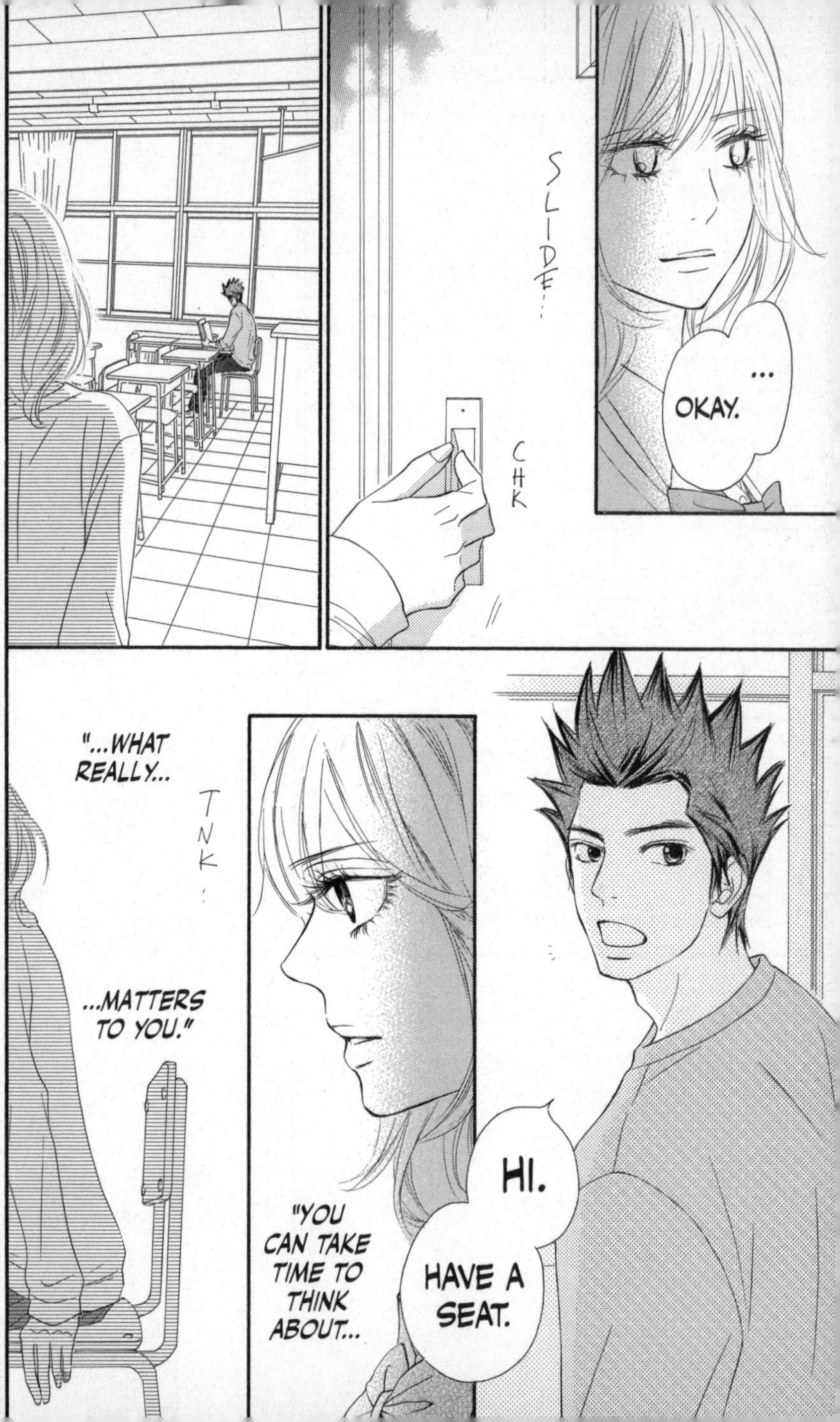

... OKAY.
SLIDE
CHK
HI.
HAVE A SEAT.
"YOU CAN TAKE TIME TO THINK ABOUT...
"...WHAT REALLY...
TNK
...MATTERS TO YOU."

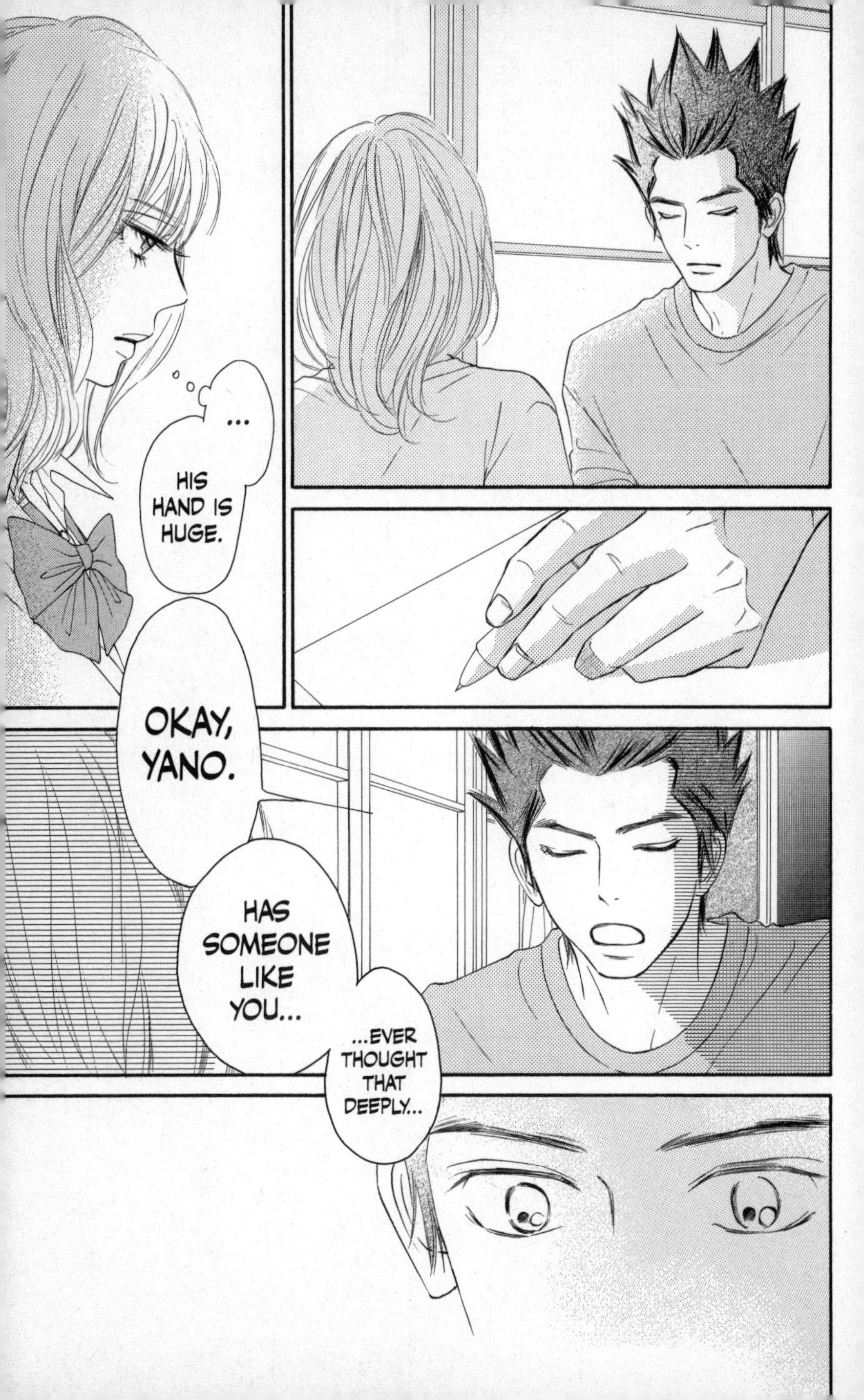
...
HIS HAND IS HUGE.
OKAY, YANO.
HAS SOMEONE LIKE YOU...
...EVER THOUGHT THAT DEEPLY...

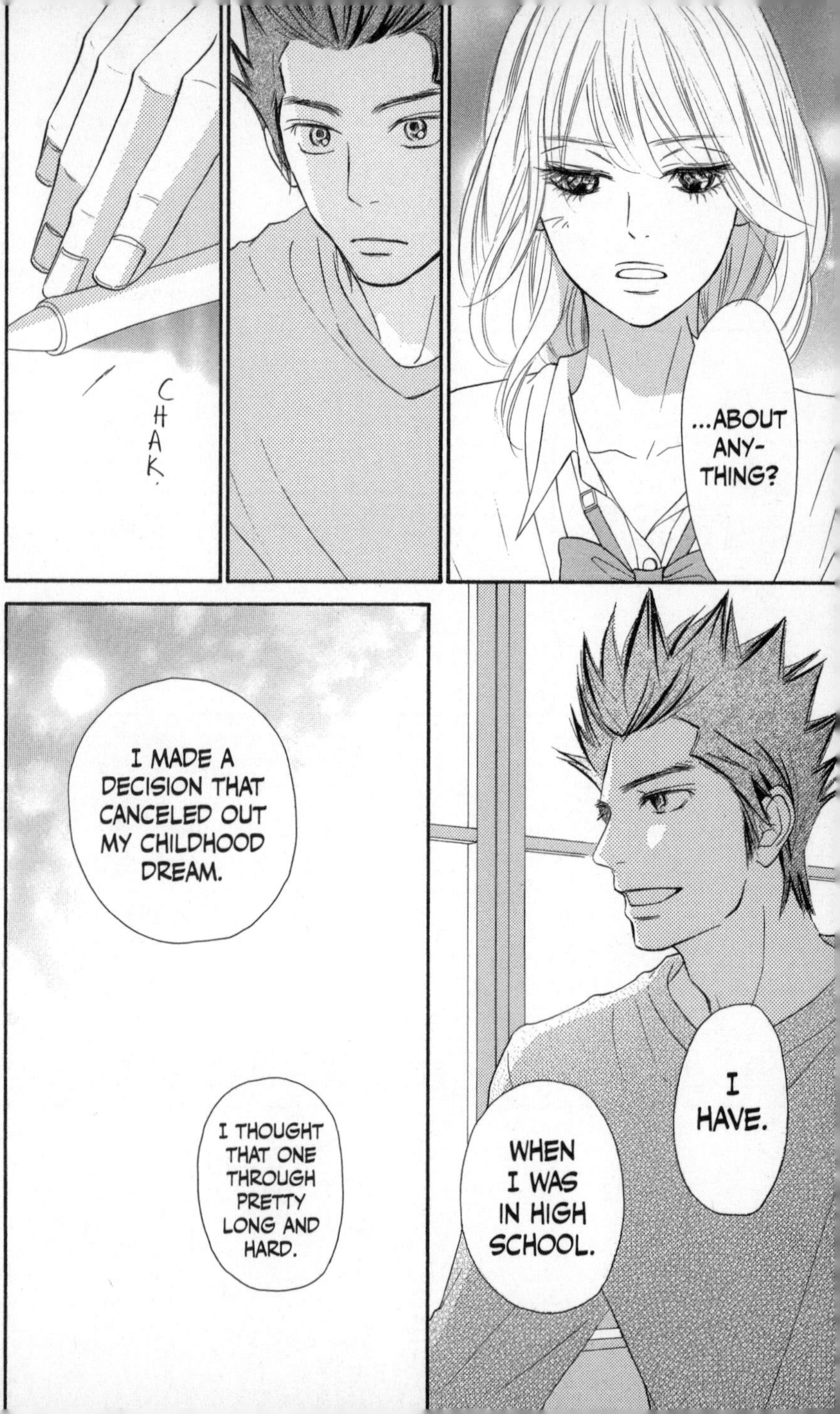
...ABOUT ANY-THING?
CHAK.
I HAVE.
WHEN I WAS IN HIGH SCHOOL.
I MADE A DECISION THAT CANCELED OUT MY CHILDHOOD DREAM.
I THOUGHT THAT ONE THROUGH PRETTY LONG AND HARD.

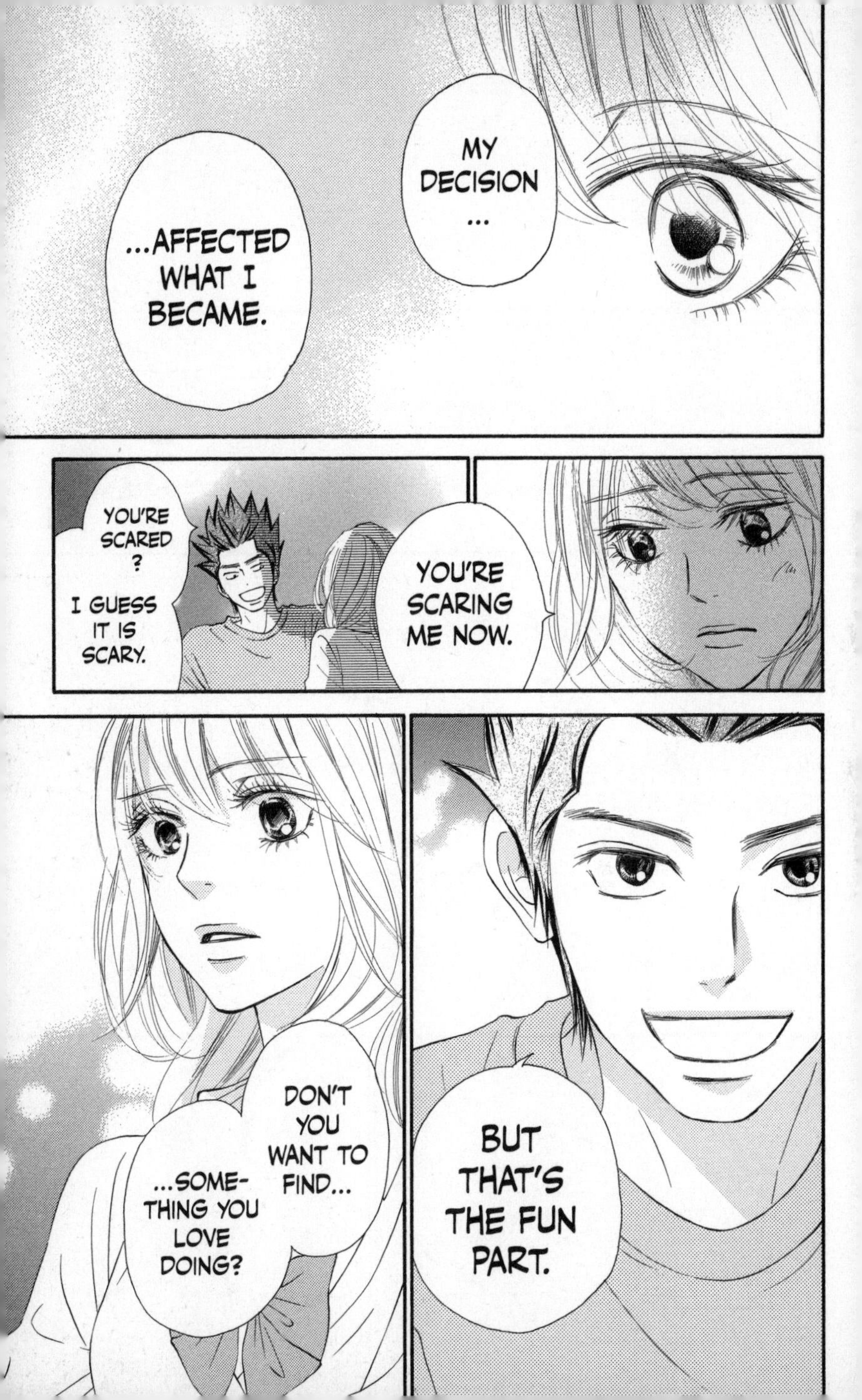
MY DECISION ...
...AFFECTED WHAT I BECAME.
YOU'RE SCARING ME NOW.
YOU'RE SCARED? I GUESS IT IS SCARY.
BUT THAT'S THE FUN PART.
DON'T YOU WANT TO FIND...
...SOME-THING YOU LOVE DOING?

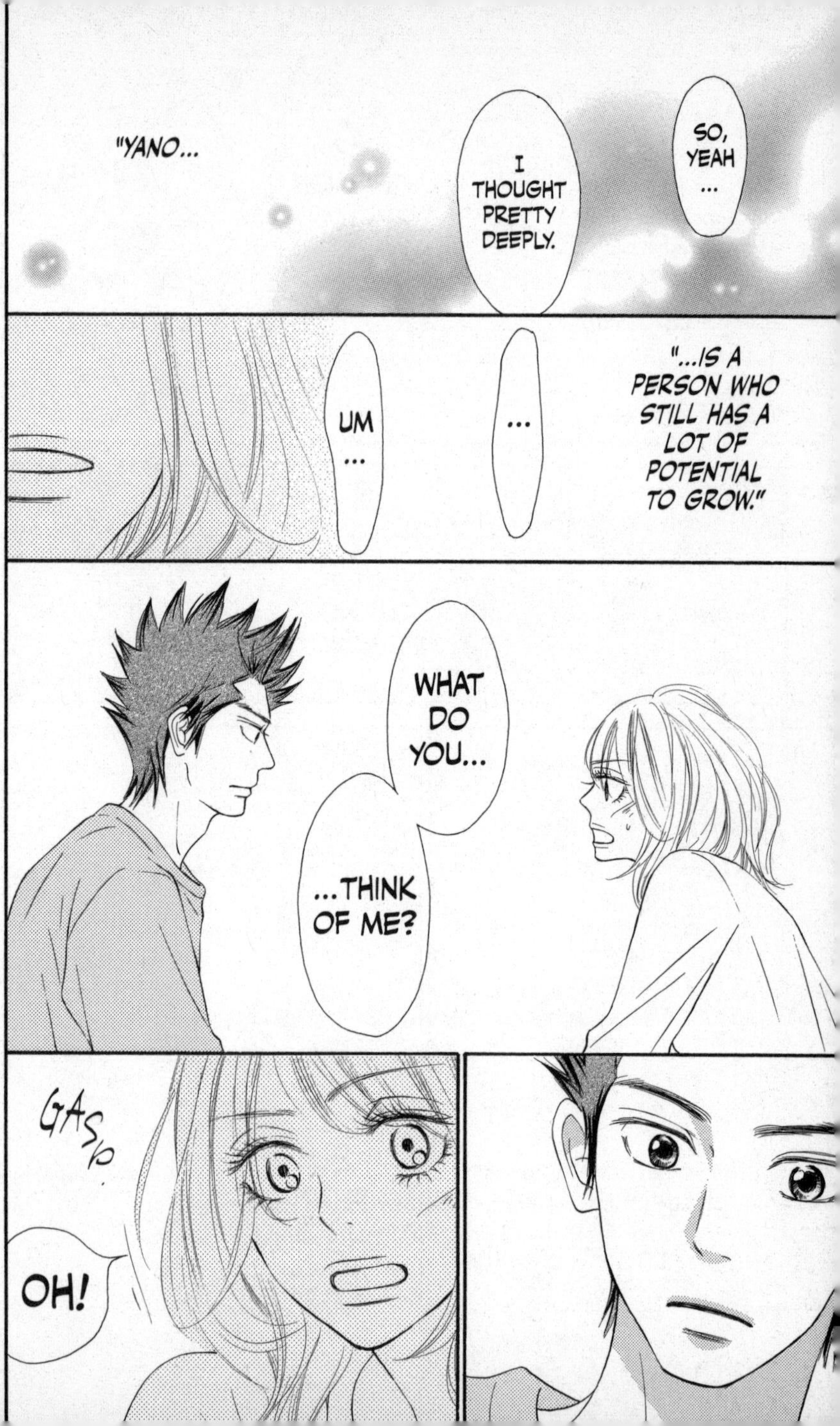
SO, YEAH ...
I THOUGHT PRETTY DEEPLY.
"YANO...
"...IS A PERSON WHO STILL HAS A LOT OF POTENTIAL TO GROW."
...
UM ...
WHAT DO YOU...
...THINK OF ME?
GASP
OH!

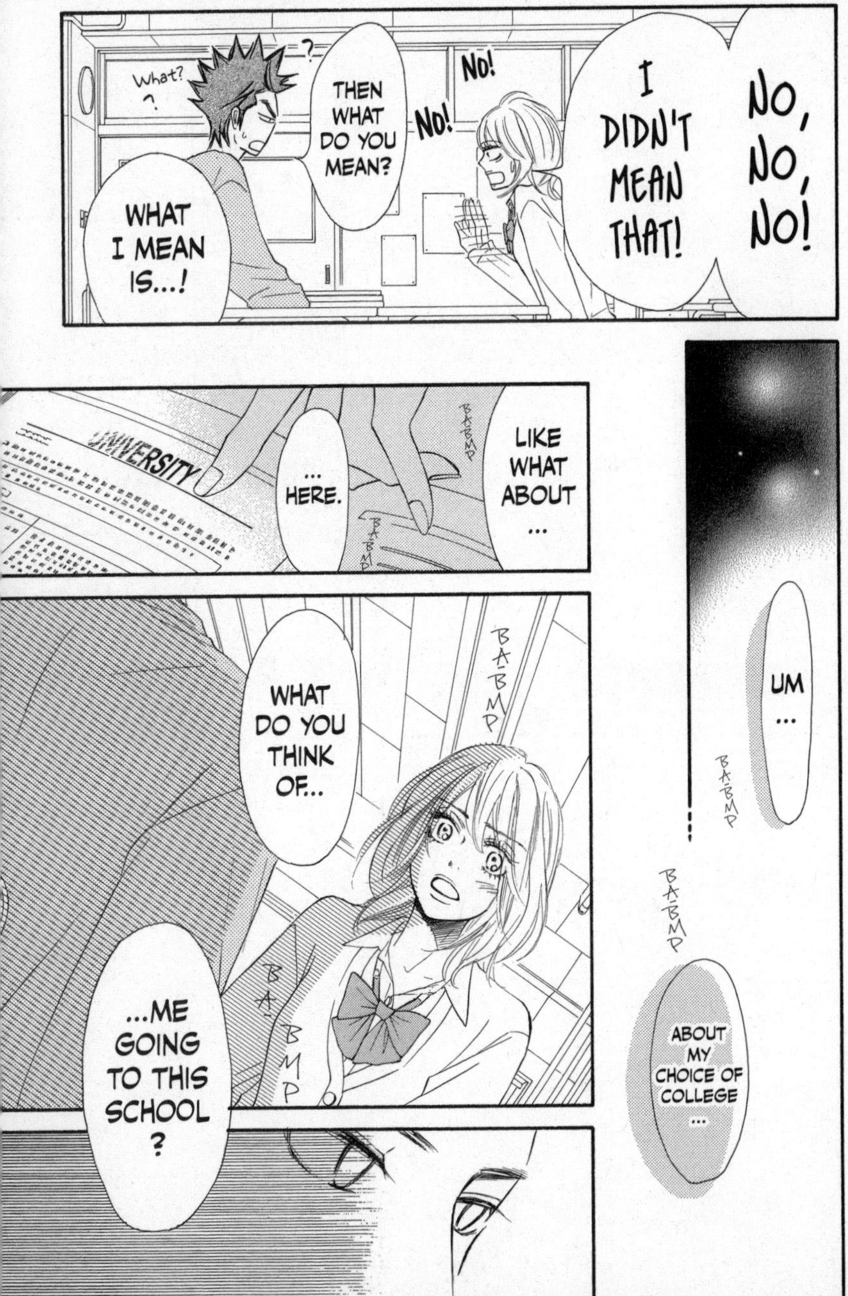
NO, NO, NO!
I DIDN'T MEAN THAT!
No!
No!
THEN WHAT DO YOU MEAN?
?
What?
WHAT I MEAN IS...!
UM...
BA-BMP
BA-BMP
ABOUT MY CHOICE OF COLLEGE...
LIKE WHAT ABOUT...
BA-BMP
...HERE.
BA-BMP
UNIVERSITY
BA-BMP
WHAT DO YOU THINK OF...
BA-BMP
...ME GOING TO THIS SCHOOL?

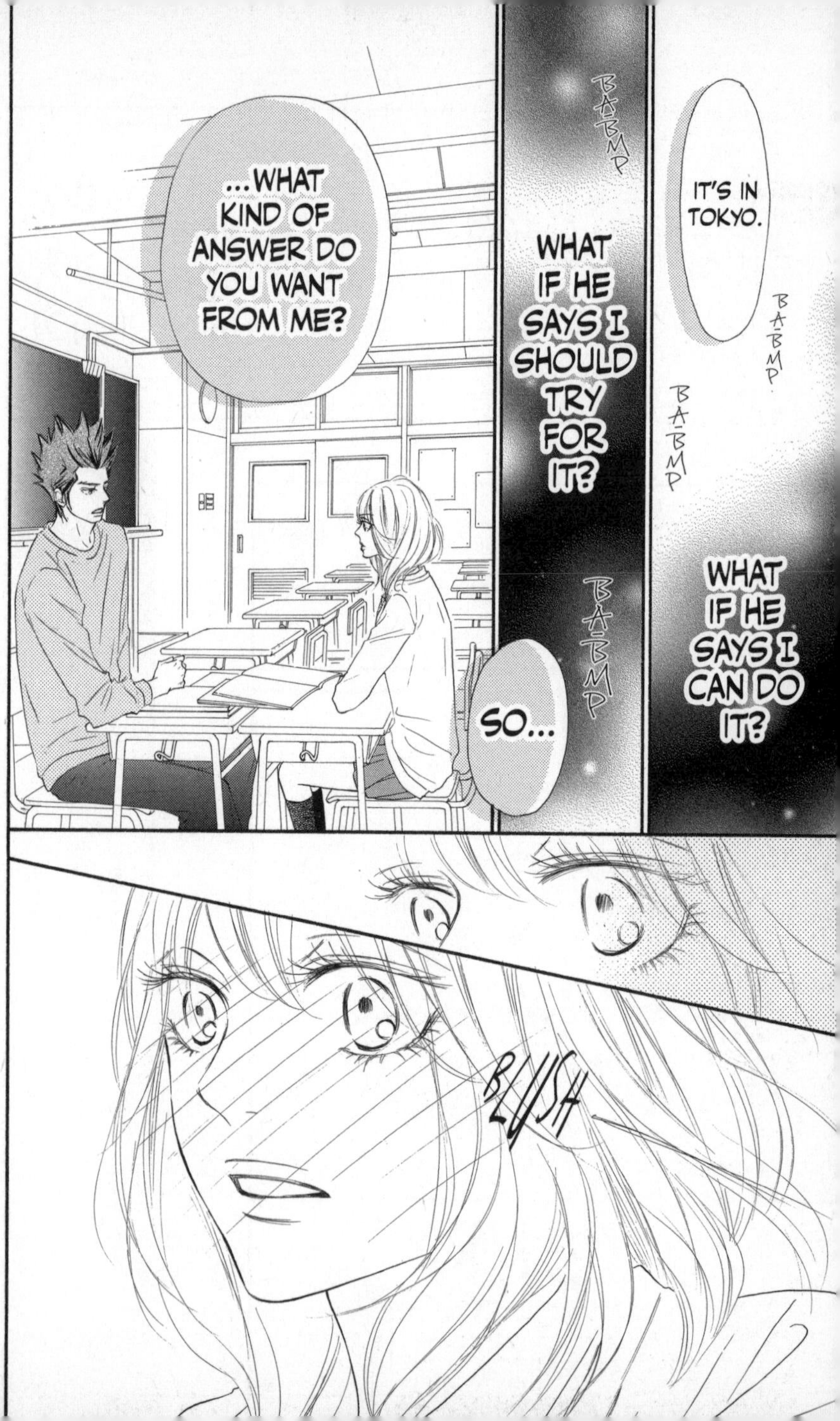
IT'S IN TOKYO.
BA-BMP
BA-BMP
WHAT IF HE SAYS I CAN DO IT?
BA-BMP
WHAT IF HE SAYS I SHOULD TRY FOR IT?
BA-BMP
SO...
...WHAT KIND OF ANSWER DO YOU WANT FROM ME?
BLUSH

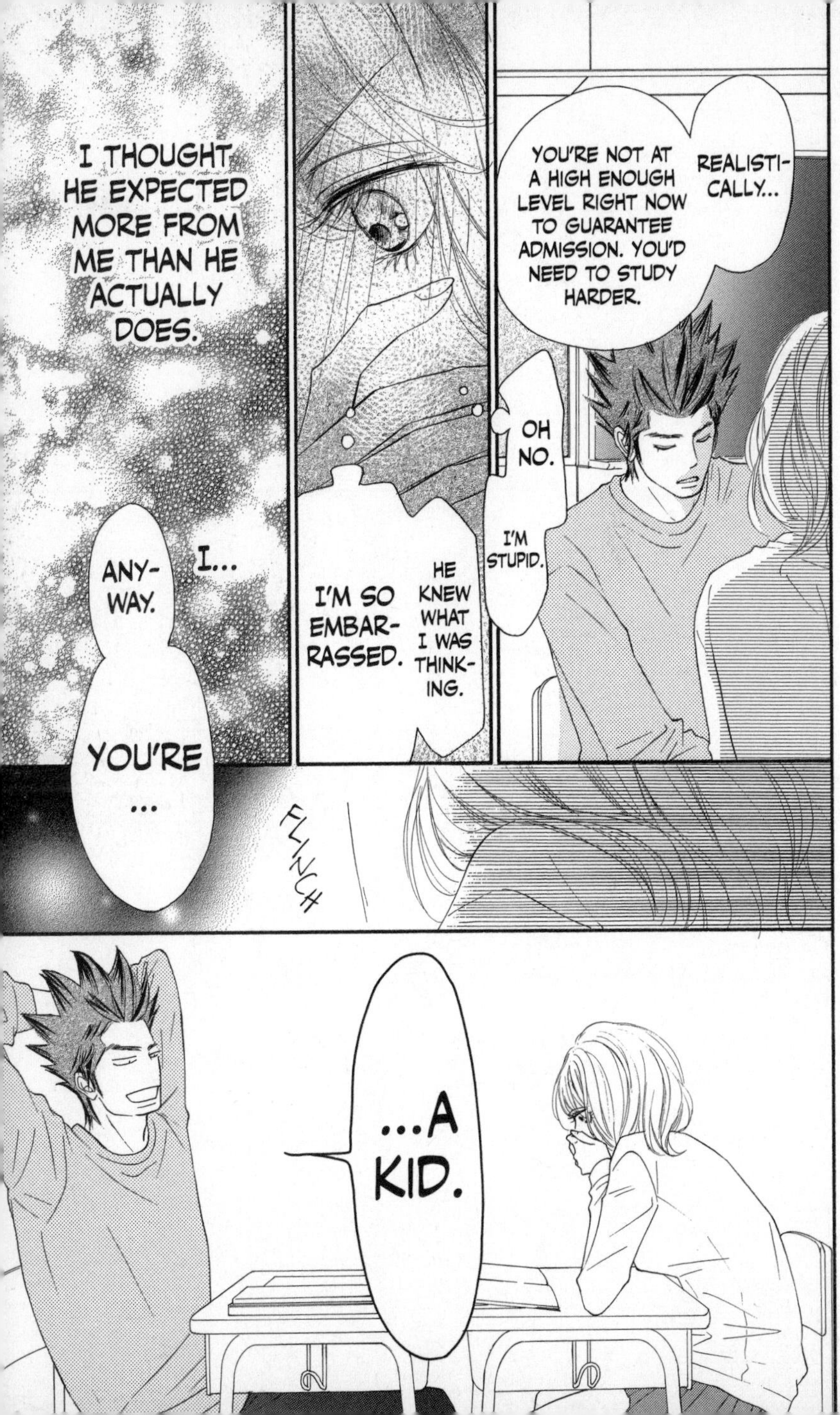
REALISTICALLY...
YOU'RE NOT AT A HIGH ENOUGH LEVEL RIGHT NOW TO GUARANTEE ADMISSION. YOU'D NEED TO STUDY HARDER.
OH NO.
I'M STUPID.
HE KNEW WHAT I WAS THINKING.
I'M SO EMBARRASSED.
I THOUGHT HE EXPECTED MORE FROM ME THAN HE ACTUALLY DOES.
I...
ANYWAY.
FLINCH
YOU'RE ...
...A KID.

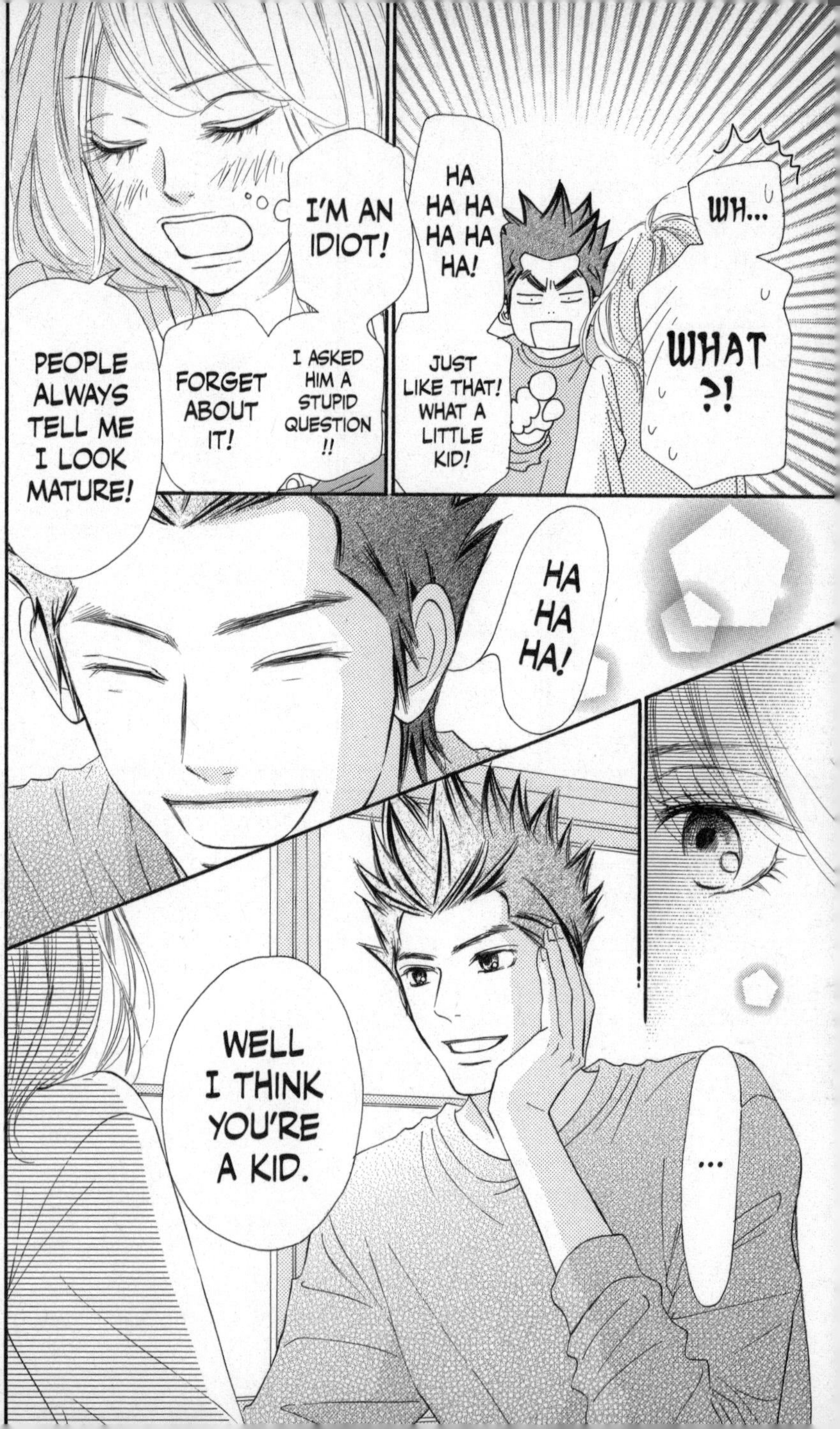
WH...
HA HA HA HA HA HA!
WHAT ?!
JUST LIKE THAT! WHAT A LITTLE KID!
I'M AN IDIOT!
I ASKED HIM A STUPID QUESTION !!
FORGET ABOUT IT!
PEOPLE ALWAYS TELL ME I LOOK MATURE!
HA HA HA!
WELL I THINK YOU'RE A KID.
...

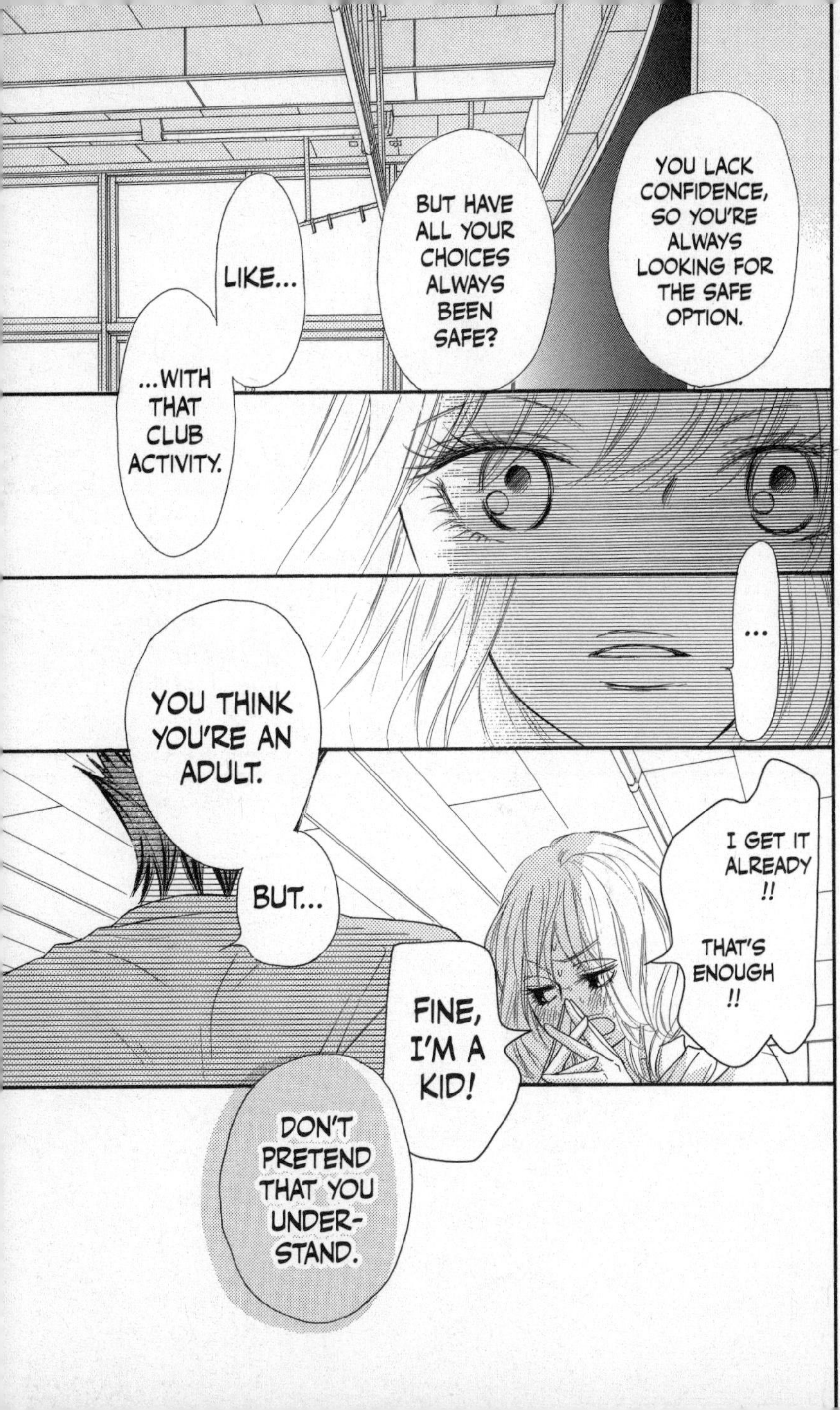
YOU LACK CONFIDENCE, SO YOU'RE ALWAYS LOOKING FOR THE SAFE OPTION.
BUT HAVE ALL YOUR CHOICES ALWAYS BEEN SAFE?
LIKE...
...WITH THAT CLUB ACTIVITY.
...
YOU THINK YOU'RE AN ADULT.
BUT...
I GET IT ALREADY!!
THAT'S ENOUGH!!
FINE, I'M A KID!
DON'T PRETEND THAT YOU UNDER-STAND.

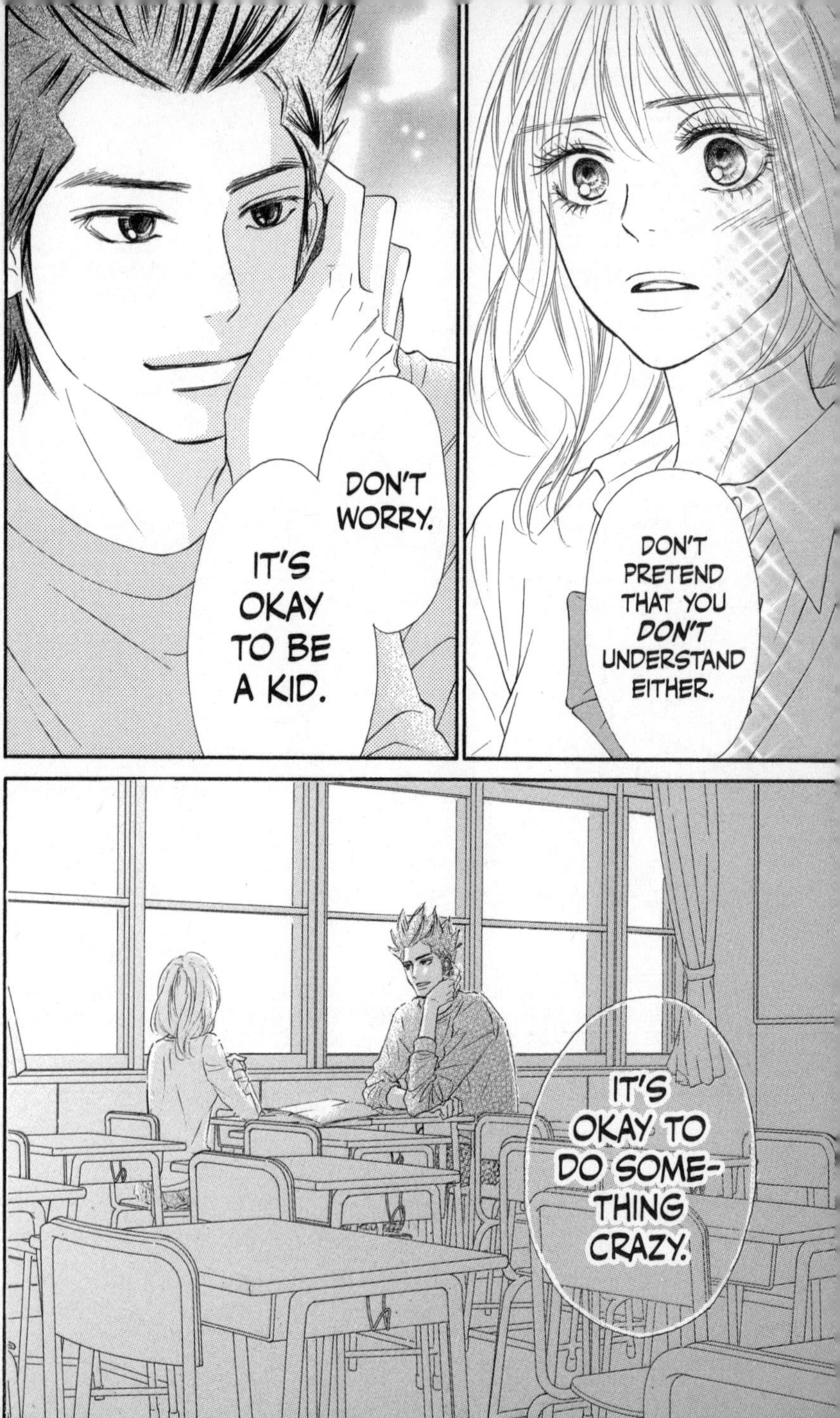
DON'T PRETEND THAT YOU *DON'T* UNDERSTAND EITHER.
DON'T WORRY.
IT'S OKAY TO BE A KID.
IT'S OKAY TO DO SOME-THING CRAZY.

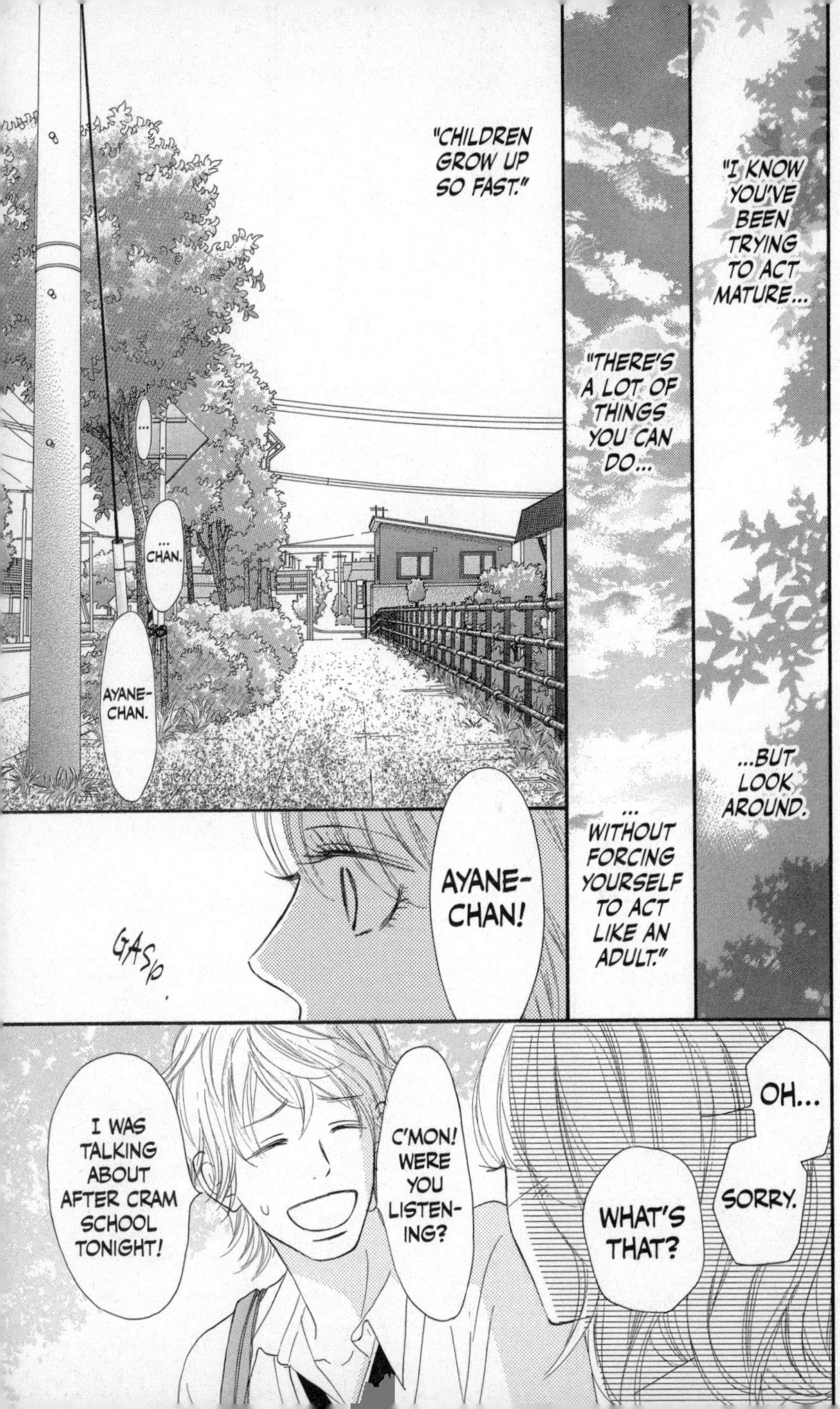
"I KNOW YOU'VE BEEN TRYING TO ACT MATURE...
...BUT LOOK AROUND.
"THERE'S A LOT OF THINGS YOU CAN DO...
...WITHOUT FORCING YOURSELF TO ACT LIKE AN ADULT."
"CHILDREN GROW UP SO FAST."
...
...CHAN.
AYANE-CHAN.
AYANE-CHAN!
GASP
OH...
SORRY.
WHAT'S THAT?
C'MON! WERE YOU LISTEN-ING?
I WAS TALKING ABOUT AFTER CRAM SCHOOL TONIGHT!

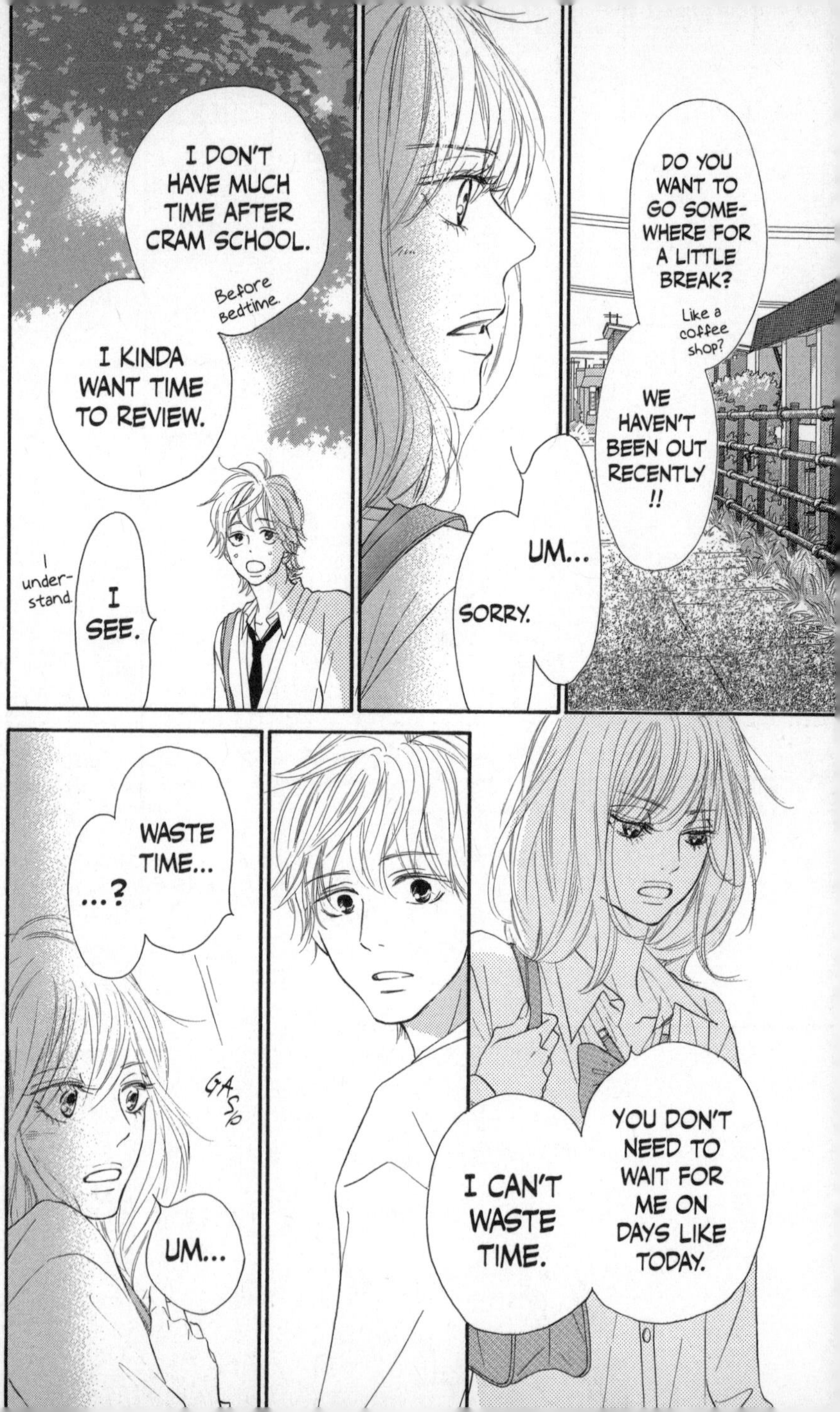
DO YOU WANT TO GO SOME-WHERE FOR A LITTLE BREAK?
Like a coffee shop?
WE HAVEN'T BEEN OUT RECENTLY !!
UM...
SORRY.
I DON'T HAVE MUCH TIME AFTER CRAM SCHOOL.
Before bedtime.
I KINDA WANT TIME TO REVIEW.
I SEE.
I under-stand.
YOU DON'T NEED TO WAIT FOR ME ON DAYS LIKE TODAY.
I CAN'T WASTE TIME.
WASTE TIME...
...?
GASP
UM...

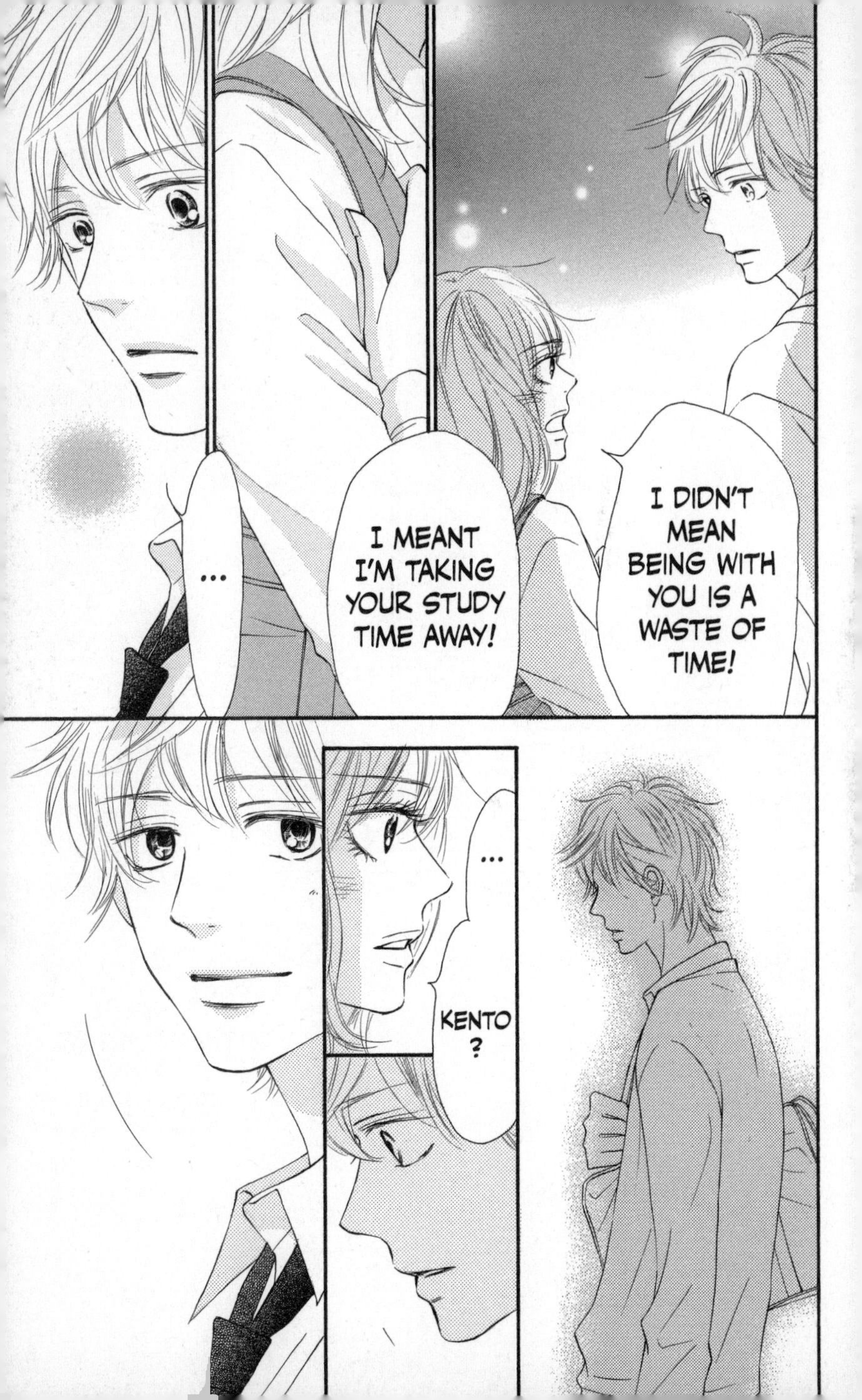
I DIDN'T MEAN BEING WITH YOU IS A WASTE OF TIME!
I MEANT I'M TAKING YOUR STUDY TIME AWAY!
...
...
KENTO?

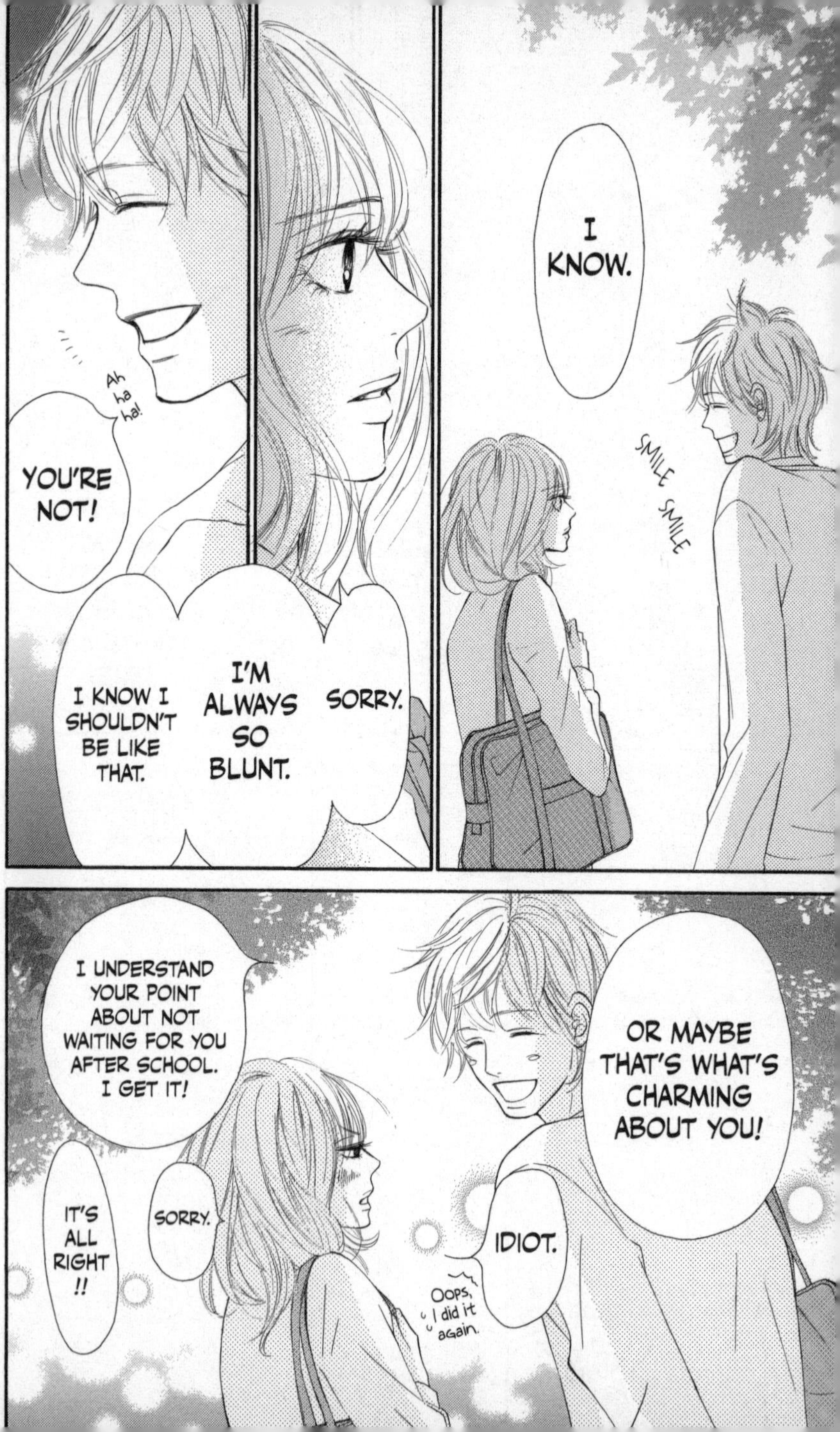
I KNOW.
SMILE SMILE
SORRY.
I'M ALWAYS SO BLUNT.
I KNOW I SHOULDN'T BE LIKE THAT.
Ah ha ha!
YOU'RE NOT!
OR MAYBE THAT'S WHAT'S CHARMING ABOUT YOU!
IDIOT.
Oops, I did it again.
SORRY.
IT'S ALL RIGHT!!
I UNDERSTAND YOUR POINT ABOUT NOT WAITING FOR YOU AFTER SCHOOL. I GET IT!

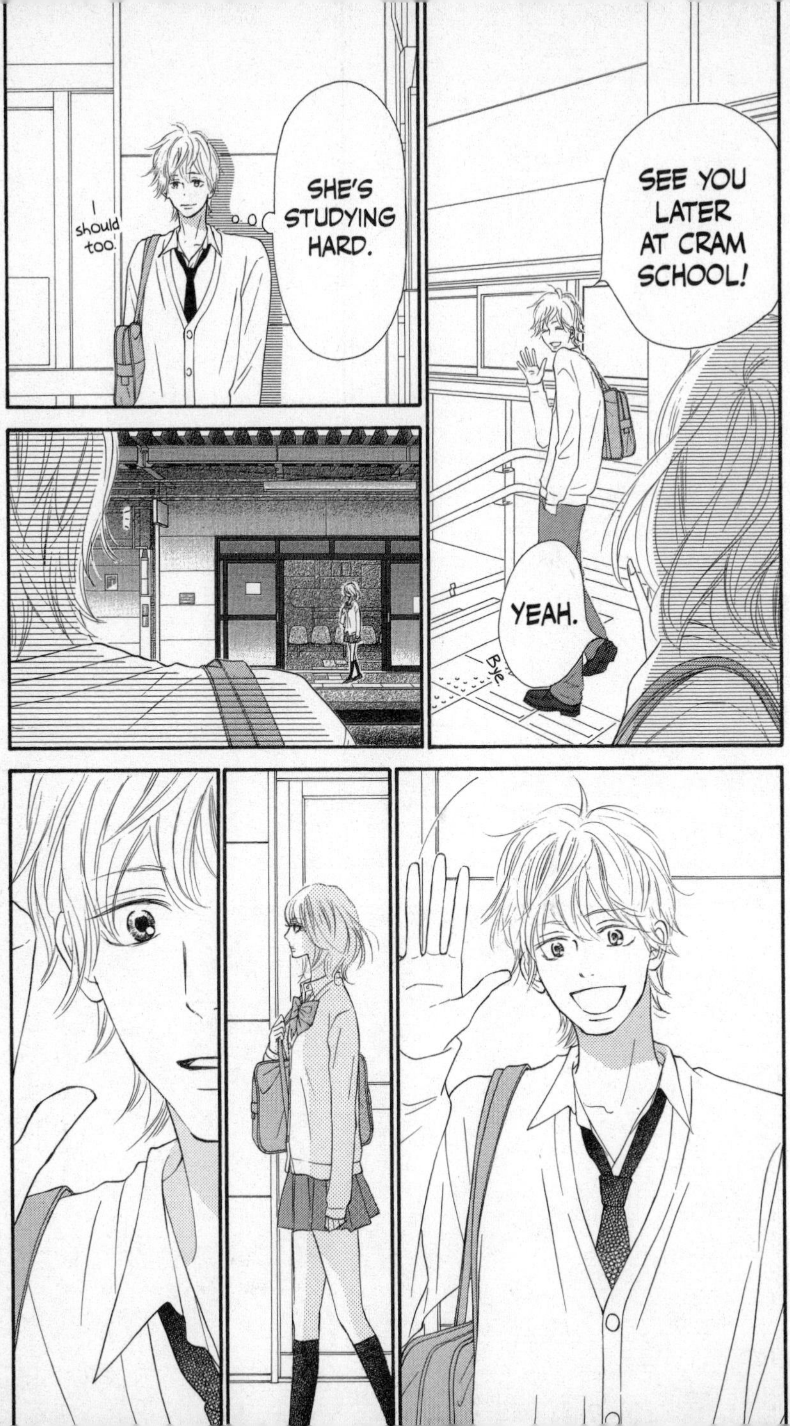
SEE YOU LATER AT CRAM SCHOOL!
YEAH.
Bye.
SHE'S STUDYING HARD.
I should too.

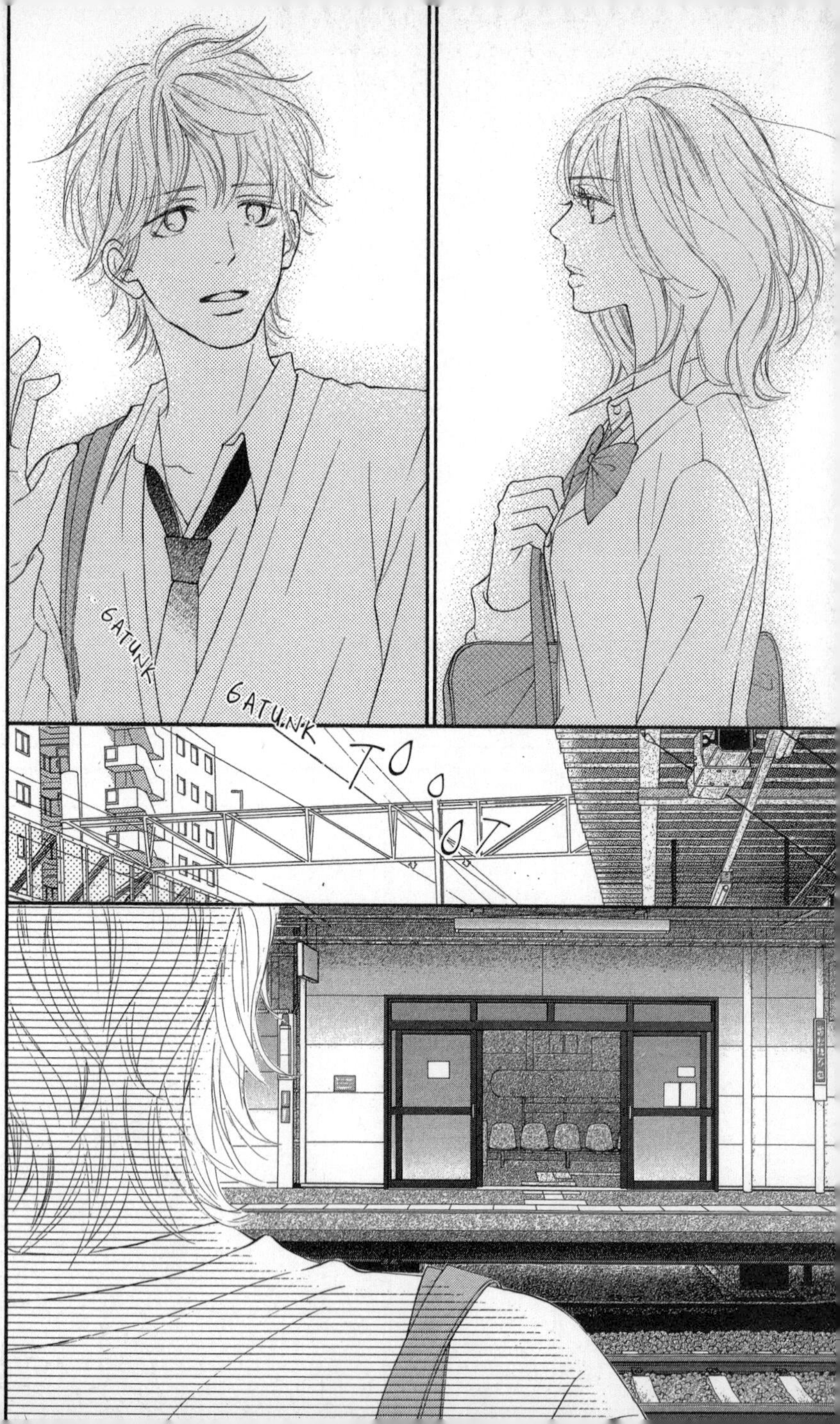
GATUNK
GATUNK
TOOOT

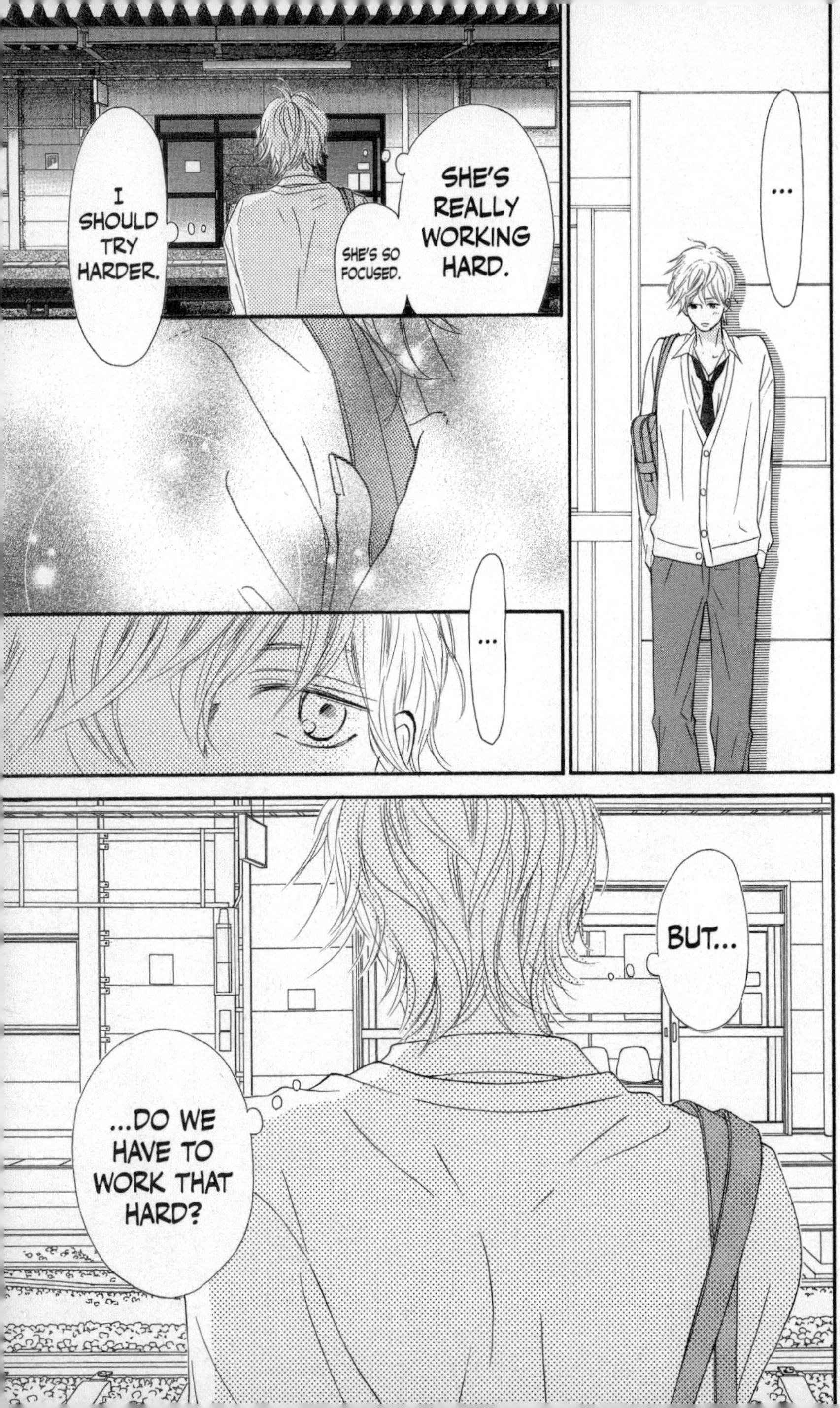
...
SHE'S REALLY WORKING HARD.
SHE'S SO FOCUSED.
I SHOULD TRY HARDER.
...
BUT...
...DO WE HAVE TO WORK THAT HARD?

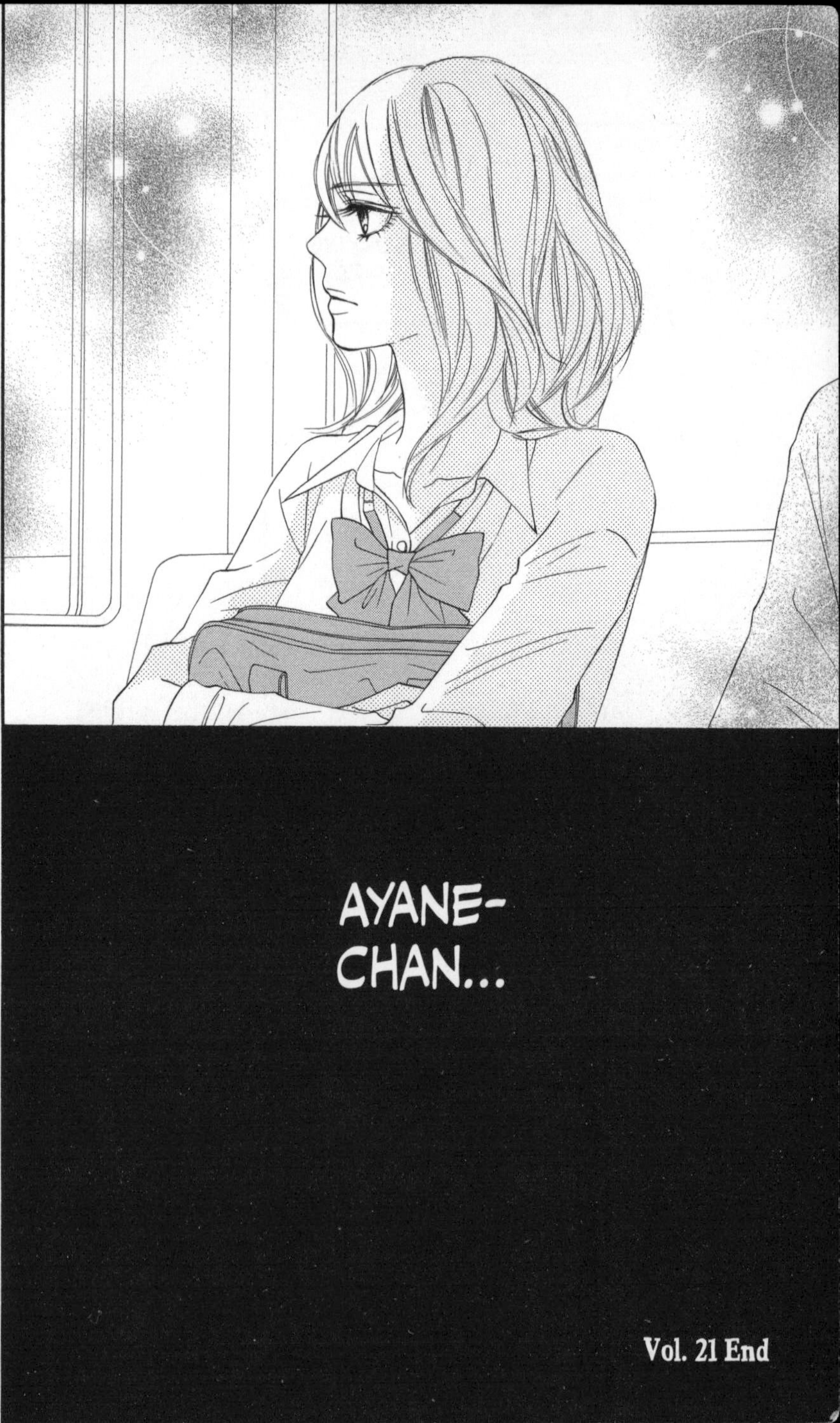
AYANE-CHAN...
Vol. 21 End

From me (the editor) to you (the reader).

Here are some Japanese culture explanations that will help you better understand the references in the *Kimi ni Todoke* world.

Honorifics:
When saying someone's name in Japanese, a suffix is often attached to indicate how familiar the speaker is with the person. Some are more polite and respectful, while others are endearing. Calling someone by just their first name is the most informal.
-kun is used for young men or boys, usually someone you are familiar with.
-chan is used for young women, girls or young children and can be used as a term of endearment.
-san is used for someone you respect or are not close to, or to be polite.

Page 8, White Day:
A holiday where boys return gifts for those they received on Valentine's Day.

Page 8, Fujitoya:
Based on a sweets shop in Sapporo.

Page 8, Nakamurado:
A real company based in Kyoto.

Page 8, *daifuku*:
A Japanese sweet made of sweet rice flour and often a sweet red bean filling.

Page 9, sound of rice crackers:
The sound of eating rice crackers (*senbei*) noisily is considered a good one in Japan, so Ryu is being serious and not sarcastic.

Page 83, "D" University:
"D" is being used to avoid having to name an actual university.

Page 120, New Year's money:
Around New Year's, children often receive money from parents or relatives. This is called *otoshidama*.

Page 139, *dosukoi*:
An exclamation in sumo.

I've been feeling my age... Staying healthy is the most important thing! Take care of yourself!

--Karuho Shiina

Karuho Shiina was born and raised in Hokkaido, Japan. Though *Kimi ni Todoke* is only her second series following many one-shot stories, it has already racked up accolades from various "Best Manga of the Year" lists. Winner of the 2008 Kodansha Manga Award for the shojo category, *Kimi ni Todoke* also placed fifth in the first-ever Manga Taisho (Cartoon Grand Prize) contest in 2008. In Japan, an animated TV series debuted in October 2009, and a live-action film was released in 2010.

Kimi ni Todoke
VOL. 21

Shojo Beat Edition

STORY AND ART BY
KARUHO SHIINA

Translation/Ari Yasuda, HC Language Solutions, Inc.
Touch-up Art & Lettering/Vanessa Satone
Design/Nozomi Akashi
Editor/Hope Donovan

KIMI NI TODOKE © 2005 by Karuho Shiina
All rights reserved. First published in Japan in 2005 by SHUEISHA Inc.,
Tokyo. English translation rights arranged by SHUEISHA Inc.

The stories, characters and incidents mentioned
in this publication are entirely fictional.

Printed in the U.S.A.

Published by VIZ Media, LLC
P.O. Box 77010
San Francisco, CA 94107

10 9 8 7 6 5 4 3 2 1
First printing, June 2015

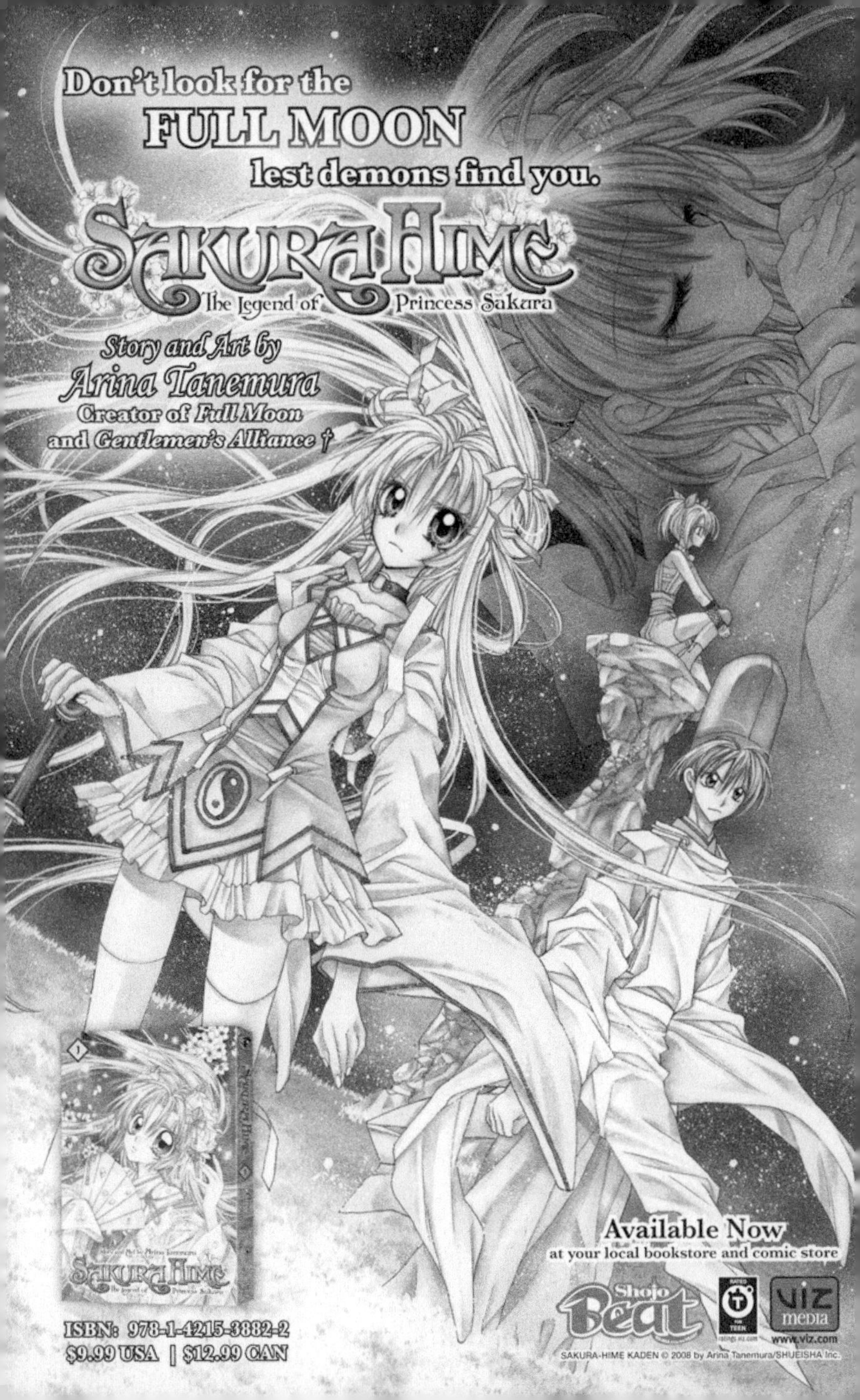
Don't look for the
FULL MOON
lest demons find you.
SAKURA HIME
The Legend of Princess Sakura
Story and Art by
Arina Tanemura
Creator of Full Moon
and Gentlemen's Alliance †
ISBN: 978-1-4215-3882-2
$9.99 USA | $12.99 CAN
Available Now
at your local bookstore and comic store
Shojo Beat
VIZ media
www.viz.com
SAKURA-HIME KADEN © 2008 by Arina Tanemura/SHUEISHA Inc.

Is this girl a devil in disguise...
or a misunderstood angel?

A Devil and Her Love Song

Story and Art by Miyoshi Tomori

Meet Maria Kawai—she's gorgeous and whip-smart, a girl who seems to have it all. But when she unleashes her sharp tongue, it's no wonder some consider her to be the very devil! Maria's difficult ways even get her kicked out of an elite school, but this particular fall may actually turn out to be her saving grace...

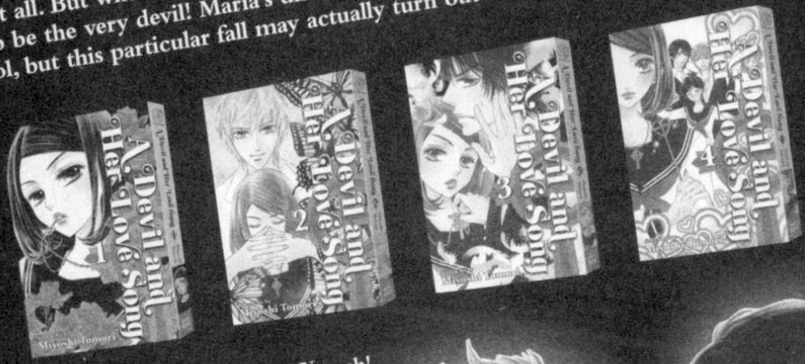

A Devil and Her Love Song 1
Miyoshi Tomori
A Devil and Her Love Song 2
Miyoshi Tomori
A Devil and Her Love Song 3
Miyoshi Tomori
A Devil and Her Love Song 4

Only **$9.99 US / $12.99 CAN** each!

Vol. 1 ISBN: 978-1-4215-4164-8
Vol. 2 ISBN: 978-1-4215-4165-5
Vol. 3 ISBN: 978-1-4215-4166-2
Vol. 4 ISBN: 978-1-4215-4167-9

Check your local manga retailer for availability!

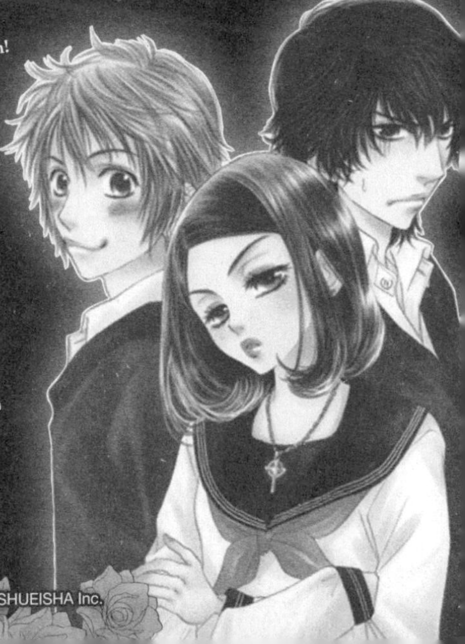

RATED T FOR TEEN ratings.viz.com

Shojo Beat

VIZ MEDIA
www.viz.com

Surprise!

You may be reading the wrong way!

It's true: In keeping with the original Japanese comic format, this book reads from right to left—so action, sound effects, and word balloons are completely reversed. This preserves the orientation of the original artwork—plus, it's fun! Check out the diagram shown here to get the hang of things, and then turn to the other side of the book to get started!

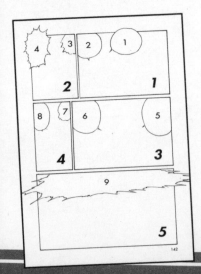